Django 3 By Example

Third Edition

Build powerful and reliable Python web applications from scratch

Antonio Melé

BIRMINGHAM - MUMBAI

Django 3 By Example
Third Edition

Commissioning Editor: Pavan Ramchandani
Producer: Ben Renow-Clarke
Acquisition Editor – Peer Reviews: Suresh Jain
Content Development Editor: Joanne Lovell
Technical Editor: Saby D'silva
Project Editor: Kishor Rit
Proofreader: Safis Editing
Indexer: Pratik Shirodkar
Presentation Designer: Sandip Tadge

First published: November 2015
Second edition: May 2018
Third edition: March 2020

Production reference: 2140420

Published by Packt Publishing Ltd.
Livery Place
35 Livery Street
Birmingham B3 2PB, UK.

ISBN 978-1-83898-195-2

www.packt.com

This book is dedicated to my parents, Antonio and Lola,
who have always supported me in all my ventures.

packt.com

Subscribe to our online digital library for full access to over 7,000 books and videos, as well as industry leading tools to help you plan your personal development and advance your career. For more information, please visit our website.

Why subscribe?

- Spend less time learning and more time coding with practical eBooks and videos from over 4,000 industry professionals

- Learn better with Skill Plans built especially for you

- Get a free eBook or video every month

- Fully searchable for easy access to vital information

- Copy and paste, print, and bookmark content

Did you know that Packt offers eBook versions of every book published, with PDF and ePub files available? You can upgrade to the eBook version at www.Packt.com and, as a print book customer, you are entitled to a discount on the eBook copy. Get in touch with us at customercare@packtpub.com for more details.

At www.Packt.com, you can also read a collection of free technical articles, sign up for a range of free newsletters, and receive exclusive discounts and offers on Packt books and eBooks.

Contributors

About the author

Antonio Melé is the chief technology officer (CTO) at Nucoro, a London-based fintech company that provides a leading technology platform to build digital wealth management solutions. Antonio has been developing Django projects since 2006 for clients across several industries. In 2009, he founded Zenx IT, a development company specializing in building digital products. He has worked as a CTO and technology consultant for multiple technology-based start-ups and he has managed development teams building projects for large digital businesses. Antonio holds an M.Sc. in computer science from Universidad Pontificia Comillas. His father inspired his passion for computers and programming. You can find out more about Antonio on his website `https://antoniomele.es/`.

About the reviewers

Jake Kronika, a senior software engineer with nearly 25 years' experience, has been working with Python since 2005, and Django since 2007. Evolving alongside the web development space, his skill set encompasses HTML5, CSS3, and JavaScript (ECMAScript 6) on the frontend, plus Python, Django, Node.js, PHP, Ruby on Rails, and much more besides on the server side.

Currently a software architect and development team lead, Jake collaborates with skilled designers, business stakeholders, and developers around the world to plan and implement robust web applications. In his spare time, he also provides full-spectrum web services as sole proprietor of Gridline Design and Development, works on home improvement projects, and spends valued time with his wife and two children.

Jake coauthored *Django 2 Web Development Cookbook, Third Edition*, published in October 2018, and *Django 3 Web Development Cookbook, Fourth Edition*, published in March 2020. In addition, he has acted as a technical reviewer for several other Packt titles, including:

- *Web Development with Django Cookbook – Second Edition* (2016)
- *Developing Responsive Web Applications with AJAX and jQuery* (2014)
- *jQuery Tools UI Library* (2012)
- *jQuery UI 1.8: The User Interface Library for jQuery* (2011)
- *Django JavaScript Integration: AJAX and jQuery* (2011)

"I would like to thank my wife, Veronica, for all that she does to support me. Without her, I would be a fraction of the person I am, and would have accomplished only a small percentage of what I've been able to.

Also, I would like to acknowledge my manager, Ravi, for his ongoing support and advice. His guidance has been critical at several points of advancement in my career."

David Stanek has been developing software professionally for over 22 years. He currently enjoys building distributed systems with Kubernetes and cloud technologies. Python has been his language of choice for over 19 years, but he also enjoys writing in Go and other specialized languages. In recent years, he has been involved with various cloud-related projects and enjoys the challenges of running applications at scale. For him, there's nothing better than writing a web service in Python, deploying it on infrastructure orchestrated with Terraform, and automating its business processes with Ansible.

David spends much of his free work time working on open source projects and sharpening his technical skills. He enjoys teaching, reading technical books, and listening to a variety of podcasts and audio books. When he's not working, he enjoys spending time with his beautiful wife, four wonderful children, and miniature dachshund.

You can find out more about David on his website (`http://dstanek.com/`).

Table of Contents

Preface

Django is a powerful Python web framework that encourages rapid development and clean, pragmatic design, while offering a relatively shallow learning curve. This makes it attractive to both novice and expert programmers.

This book will guide you through the entire process of developing professional web applications with Django. The book not only covers the most relevant aspects of the framework, but it will also teach you how to integrate other popular technologies into your Django projects.

The book will walk you through the creation of real-world applications, solving common problems, and implementing best practices, using a step-by-step approach that is easy to follow.

After reading this book, you will have a good understanding of how Django works and how to build practical, advanced web applications.

Who this book is for

This book is intended for developers with Python knowledge who wish to learn Django in a pragmatic way. Perhaps you are completely new to Django, or you already know a little but you want to get the most out of it. This book will help you to master the most relevant areas of the framework by building practical projects from scratch. You need to have familiarity with programming concepts in order to read this book. Some previous knowledge of HTML and JavaScript is assumed.

What this book covers

Chapter 1, Building a Blog Application, will introduce you to the framework through a blog application. You will create the basic blog models, views, templates, and URLs to display blog posts. You will learn how to build QuerySets with the Django **object-relational mapper (ORM)**, and you will configure the Django administration site.

Chapter 2, Enhancing Your Blog with Advanced Features, will teach you how to handle forms and ModelForms, send emails with Django, and integrate third-party applications. You will implement a comment system for your blog posts and allow your users to share posts via email. The chapter will also guide you through the process of creating a tagging system.

Chapter 3, Extending Your Blog Application, explores how to create custom template tags and filters. The chapter will also show you how to use the sitemap framework and create an RSS feed for your posts. You will complete your blog application by building a search engine with PostgreSQL's full-text search capabilities.

Chapter 4, Building a Social Website, explains how to build a social website. You will use the Django authentication framework to create user account views. You will also learn how to create a custom user profile model and build social authentication into your project using major social networks.

Chapter 5, Sharing Content on Your Website, will teach you how to transform your social application into an image bookmarking website. You will define many-to-many relationships for models, and you will create an AJAX bookmarklet in JavaScript and integrate it into your project. The chapter will show you how to generate image thumbnails and create custom decorators for your views.

Chapter 6, Tracking User Actions, will show you how to build a follower system for users. You will complete your image bookmarking website by creating a user activity stream application. You will learn how to optimize QuerySets, and you will work with signals. Finally, you will integrate Redis into your project to count image views.

Chapter 7, Building an Online Shop, explores how to create an online shop. You will build catalog models, and you will create a shopping cart using Django sessions. You will build a context processor for the shopping cart, and you will learn how to implement sending asynchronous notifications to users using Celery.

Chapter 8, Managing Payments and Orders, explains how to integrate a payment gateway into your shop. You will also customize the administration site to export orders to CSV files, and you will generate PDF invoices dynamically.

Chapter 9, Extending Your Shop, will teach you how to create a coupon system to apply discounts to orders. The chapter will also show you how to add internationalization to your project and how to translate models. Finally, you will build a product recommendation engine using Redis.

Chapter 10, Building an E-Learning Platform, will guide you through creating an e-learning platform. You will add fixtures to your project, use model inheritance, create custom model fields, use class-based views, and manage groups and permissions. You will also create a content management system and handle formsets.

Chapter 11, Rendering and Caching Content, will show you how to create a student registration system and manage student enrollment on courses. You will render diverse course contents and learn how to use the cache framework.

Chapter 12, Building an API, explores building a RESTful API for your project using Django REST framework.

Chapter 13, Building a Chat Server, explains how to use Django Channels to create a real-time chat server for students. You will learn how to implement functionalities that rely on asynchronous communication through WebSockets.

Chapter 14, Going Live, will show you how to set up a production environment using uWSGI, NGINX, and Daphne. You will learn how to secure the environment through HTTPS. The chapter also explains how to build a custom middleware and create custom management commands.

Get the most out of this book

The reader should:

- Possess a good working knowledge of Python
- Be comfortable with HTML and JavaScript
- Have gone through parts 1 to 3 of the tutorial in the official Django documentation at `https://docs.djangoproject.com/en/3.0/intro/tutorial01/`

Download the example code files

You can download the example code files for this book from your account at `www.packt.com/`. If you purchased this book elsewhere, you can visit `www.packtpub.com/support` and register to have the files emailed directly to you.

You can download the code files by following these steps:

1. Log in or register at http://www.packt.com
2. Select the **Support** tab
3. Click on **Code Downloads**
4. Enter the name of the book in the **Search** box and follow the on-screen instructions

Once the file is downloaded, please make sure that you unzip or extract the folder using the latest version of:

- WinRAR/7-Zip for Windows
- Zipeg/iZip/UnRarX for Mac
- 7-Zip/PeaZip for Linux

The code bundle for the book is also hosted on GitHub at https://github.com/PacktPublishing/Django-3-by-Example. In case there's an update to the code, it will be updated on the existing GitHub repository.

We also have other code bundles from our rich catalog of books and videos available at https://github.com/PacktPublishing/. Check them out!

Download the color images

We also provide a PDF file that has color images of the screenshots/diagrams used in this book. You can download it here: https://static.packt-cdn.com/downloads/9781838981952_ColorImages.pdf.

Conventions used

There are a number of text conventions used throughout this book.

CodeInText: Indicates code words in the text, database table names, folder names, filenames, file extensions, pathnames, dummy URLs, user input, and Twitter handles. For example: "Edit the models.py file of the shop application."

A block of code is set as follows:

```
from django.contrib import admin
from .models import Post

admin.site.register(Post)
```

When we wish to draw your attention to a particular part of a code block, the relevant lines or items are set in bold:

```
INSTALLED_APPS = [
    'django.contrib.admin',
    'django.contrib.auth',
    'django.contrib.contenttypes',
    'django.contrib.sessions',
    'django.contrib.messages',
    'django.contrib.staticfiles',
    'blog.apps.BlogConfig',
]
```

Any command-line input or output is written as follows:

```
python manage.py runserver
```

Bold: Indicates a new term, an important word, or words that you see on the screen. For example: "Fill in the form and click on the Save button."

 Warnings or important notes appear like this.

 Tips and tricks appear like this.

Get in touch

Feedback from our readers is always welcome.

General feedback: If you have questions about any aspect of this book, mention the book title in the subject of your message and email us at customercare@packtpub.com.

Errata: Although we have taken every care to ensure the accuracy of our content, mistakes do happen. If you have found a mistake in this book, we would be grateful if you could report this to us. Please visit www.packtpub.com/support/errata, select your book, click on the Errata Submission Form link, and enter the details.

Piracy: If you come across any illegal copies of our works in any form on the Internet, we would be grateful if you could provide us with the location address or website name. Please contact us at copyright@packt.com with a link to the material.

If you are interested in becoming an author: If there is a topic that you have expertise in and you are interested in either writing or contributing to a book, please visit authors.packtpub.com.

Reviews

Please leave a review. Once you have read and used this book, why not leave a review on the site that you purchased it from? Potential readers can then see and use your unbiased opinion to make a purchase decision, we at Packt can understand what you think about our product, and our author can see your feedback on their book. Thank you!

For more information about Packt, please visit packt.com.

1
Building a Blog Application

Django is a powerful Python web framework with a relatively shallow learning curve. You can easily build simple web applications in a short time. Django is also a robust and scalable framework that can be used to create large-scale web applications with complex requirements and integrations. This makes Django attractive for both beginners and expert programmers.

In this book, you will learn how to build complete Django projects that are ready for production use. If you haven't installed Django yet, you will discover how to do so in the first part of this chapter.

This chapter covers how to create a simple blog application using Django. The chapter's purpose is to help you to get a general idea of how the framework works, an understanding of how the different components interact with each other, and the skills to easily create Django projects with basic functionality. You will be guided through the creation of a complete project, but I will go into more detail on this later. The different framework components will be explored in detail throughout this book.

This chapter will cover the following topics:

- Installing Django
- Creating and configuring a Django project
- Creating a Django application
- Designing models and generating model migrations
- Creating an administration site for your models
- Working with QuerySets and managers

- Building views, templates, and URLs
- Adding pagination to list views
- Using Django's class-based views

Installing Django

If you have already installed Django, you can skip this section and jump directly to the *Creating your first project* section. Django comes as a Python package and thus can be installed in any Python environment. If you haven't installed Django yet, the following is a quick guide to installing it for local development.

Django 3 continues the path of providing new features while maintaining the core functionalities of the framework. The 3.0 release includes for the first time **Asynchronous Server Gateway Interface (ASGI)** support, which makes Django fully async-capable. Django 3.0 also includes official support for MariaDB, new exclusion constraints on PostgreSQL, filter expressions enhancements, and enumerations for model field choices, as well as other new features.

Django 3.0 supports Python 3.6, 3.7, and 3.8. In the examples in this book, we will use Python 3.8.2. If you're using Linux or macOS, you probably have Python installed. If you're using Windows, you can download a Python installer at `https://www.python.org/downloads/windows/`.

If you're not sure whether Python is installed on your computer, you can verify this by typing `python` into the shell. If you see something like the following, then Python is installed on your computer:

```
Python 3.8.2 (v3.8.2:7b3ab5921f, Feb 24 2020, 17:52:18)
[Clang 6.0 (clang-600.0.57)] on darwin
Type "help", "copyright", "credits" or "license" for more information.
```

If your installed Python version is lower than 3.6, or if Python is not installed on your computer, download Python 3.8.2 from `https://www.python.org/downloads/` and install it.

Since you will be using Python 3, you don't have to install a database. This Python version comes with a built-in SQLite database. SQLite is a lightweight database that you can use with Django for development. If you plan to deploy your application in a production environment, you should use a full-featured database, such as PostgreSQL, MySQL, or Oracle. You can find more information about how to get your database running with Django at `https://docs.djangoproject.com/en/3.0/topics/install/#database-installation`.

Creating an isolated Python environment

Since version 3.3, Python has come with the venv library, which provides support for creating lightweight virtual environments. Each virtual environment has its own Python binary and can have its own independent set of installed Python packages in its site directories. Using the Python venv module to create isolated Python environments allows you to use different package versions for different projects, which is far more practical than installing Python packages system-wide. Another advantage of using venv is that you won't need any administration privileges to install Python packages.

Create an isolated environment with the following command:

```
python -m venv my_env
```

This will create a my_env/ directory, including your Python environment. Any Python libraries you install while your virtual environment is active will go into the my_env/lib/python3.8/site-packages directory.

Run the following command to activate your virtual environment:

```
source my_env/bin/activate
```

The shell prompt will include the name of the active virtual environment enclosed in parentheses, as follows:

```
(my_env)laptop:~ zenx$
```

You can deactivate your environment at any time with the deactivate command. You can find more information about venv at https://docs.python.org/3/library/venv.html.

Installing Django with pip

The pip package management system is the preferred method for installing Django. Python 3.8 comes with pip preinstalled, but you can find pip installation instructions at https://pip.pypa.io/en/stable/installing/.

Run the following command at the shell prompt to install Django with pip:

```
pip install "Django==3.0.*"
```

Django will be installed in the Python site-packages/ directory of your virtual environment.

Now check whether Django has been successfully installed. Run `python` on a terminal, import Django, and check its version, as follows:

```
>>> import django
>>> django.get_version()
'3.0.4'
```

If you get an output like `3.0.X`, Django has been successfully installed on your machine.

 Django can be installed in several other ways. You can find a complete installation guide at `https://docs.djangoproject.com/en/3.0/topics/install/`.

Creating your first project

Our first Django project will be building a complete blog. Django provides a command that allows you to create an initial project file structure. Run the following command from your shell:

```
django-admin startproject mysite
```

This will create a Django project with the name `mysite`.

 Avoid naming projects after built-in Python or Django modules in order to avoid conflicts.

Let's take a look at the project structure generated:

```
mysite/
    manage.py
    mysite/
        __init__.py
        asgi.py
        wsgi.py
        settings.py
        urls.py
```

These files are as follows:

- `manage.py`: This is a command-line utility used to interact with your project. It is a thin wrapper around the `django-admin.py` tool. You don't need to edit this file.
- `mysite/`: This is your project directory, which consists of the following files:
  - `__init__.py`: An empty file that tells Python to treat the `mysite` directory as a Python module.
  - `asgi.py`: This is the configuration to run your project as ASGI, the emerging Python standard for asynchronous web servers and applications.
  - `settings.py`: This indicates settings and configuration for your project and contains initial default settings.
  - `urls.py`: This is the place where your URL patterns live. Each URL defined here is mapped to a view.
  - `wsgi.py`: This is the configuration to run your project as a **Web Server Gateway Interface (WSGI)** application.

The generated `settings.py` file contains the project settings, including a basic configuration to use an SQLite3 database and a list named `INSTALLED_APPS` that contains common Django applications that are added to your project by default. We will go through these applications later in the *Project settings* section.

Django applications contain a `models.py` file where data models are defined. Each data model is mapped to a database table. To complete the project setup, you need to create the tables associated with the models of the applications listed in `INSTALLED_APPS`. Django includes a migration system that manages this.

Open the shell and run the following commands:

```
cd mysite
python manage.py migrate
```

You will note an output that ends with the following lines:

```
Applying contenttypes.0001_initial... OK
Applying auth.0001_initial... OK
Applying admin.0001_initial... OK
Applying admin.0002_logentry_remove_auto_add... OK
Applying admin.0003_logentry_add_action_flag_choices... OK
Applying contenttypes.0002_remove_content_type_name... OK
Applying auth.0002_alter_permission_name_max_length... OK
```

```
Applying auth.0003_alter_user_email_max_length... OK

Applying auth.0004_alter_user_username_opts... OK

Applying auth.0005_alter_user_last_login_null... OK

Applying auth.0006_require_contenttypes_0002... OK

Applying auth.0007_alter_validators_add_error_messages... OK

Applying auth.0008_alter_user_username_max_length... OK

Applying auth.0009_alter_user_last_name_max_length... OK

Applying auth.0010_alter_group_name_max_length... OK

Applying auth.0011_update_proxy_permissions... OK

Applying sessions.0001_initial... OK
```

The preceding lines are the database migrations that are applied by Django.
By applying migrations, the tables for the initial applications are created in the
database. You will learn about the migrate management command in the *Creating
and applying migrations* section of this chapter.

Running the development server

Django comes with a lightweight web server to run your code quickly, without
needing to spend time configuring a production server. When you run the
Django development server, it keeps checking for changes in your code. It reloads
automatically, freeing you from manually reloading it after code changes. However,
it might not notice some actions, such as adding new files to your project, so you
will have to restart the server manually in these cases.

Start the development server by typing the following command from your project's
root folder:

```
python manage.py runserver
```

You should see something like this:

```
Watching for file changes with StatReloader

Performing system checks...


System check identified no issues (0 silenced).


January 01, 2020 - 10:00:00

Django version 3.0, using settings 'mysite.settings'

Starting development server at http://127.0.0.1:8000/

Quit the server with CONTROL-C.
```

Now open `http://127.0.0.1:8000/` in your browser. You should see a page stating that the project is successfully running, as shown in the following screenshot:

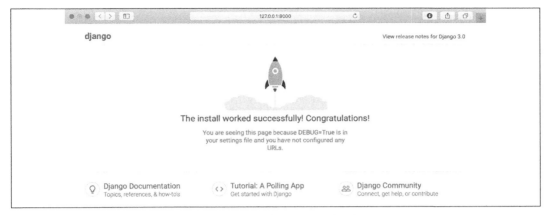

Figure 1.1: The default page of the Django development server

The preceding screenshot indicates that Django is running. If you take a look at your console, you will see the GET request performed by your browser:

```
[01/Jan/2020 17:20:30] "GET / HTTP/1.1" 200 16351
```

Each HTTP request is logged in the console by the development server. Any error that occurs while running the development server will also appear in the console.

You can run the Django development server on a custom host and port or tell Django to load a specific settings file, as follows:

```
python manage.py runserver 127.0.0.1:8001 \--settings=mysite.settings
```

 When you have to deal with multiple environments that require different configurations, you can create a different settings file for each environment.

Remember that this server is only intended for development and is not suitable for production use. In order to deploy Django in a production environment, you should run it as a WSGI application using a web server, such as Apache, Gunicorn, or uWSGI, or as an ASGI application using a server like Uvicorn or Daphne. You can find more information on how to deploy Django with different web servers at `https://docs.djangoproject.com/en/3.0/howto/deployment/wsgi/`.

Chapter 14, Going Live, explains how to set up a production environment for your Django projects.

Project settings

Let's open the settings.py file and take a look at the configuration of the project. There are several settings that Django includes in this file, but these are only part of all the Django settings available. You can see all the settings and their default values at https://docs.djangoproject.com/en/3.0/ref/settings/.

The following settings are worth looking at:

- DEBUG is a Boolean that turns the debug mode of the project on and off. If it is set to True, Django will display detailed error pages when an uncaught exception is thrown by your application. When you move to a production environment, remember that you have to set it to False. Never deploy a site into production with DEBUG turned on because you will expose sensitive project-related data.

- ALLOWED_HOSTS is not applied while debug mode is on or when the tests are run. Once you move your site to production and set DEBUG to False, you will have to add your domain/host to this setting in order to allow it to serve your Django site.

- INSTALLED_APPS is a setting you will have to edit for all projects. This setting tells Django which applications are active for this site. By default, Django includes the following applications:
  - django.contrib.admin: An administration site
  - django.contrib.auth: An authentication framework
  - django.contrib.contenttypes: A framework for handling content types
  - django.contrib.sessions: A session framework
  - django.contrib.messages: A messaging framework
  - django.contrib.staticfiles: A framework for managing static files

- MIDDLEWARE is a list that contains middleware to be executed.

- ROOT_URLCONF indicates the Python module where the root URL patterns of your application are defined.

- DATABASES is a dictionary that contains the settings for all the databases to be used in the project. There must always be a default database. The default configuration uses an SQLite3 database.

- LANGUAGE_CODE defines the default language code for this Django site.

- USE_TZ tells Django to activate/deactivate timezone support. Django comes with support for timezone-aware datetime. This setting is set to True when you create a new project using the startproject management command.

Don't worry if you don't understand much about what you're seeing here. You will learn the different Django settings in the following chapters.

Projects and applications

Throughout this book, you will encounter the terms **project** and **application** over and over. In Django, a project is considered a Django installation with some settings. An application is a group of models, views, templates, and URLs. Applications interact with the framework to provide some specific functionalities and may be reused in various projects. You can think of a project as your website, which contains several applications, such as a blog, wiki, or forum, that can also be used by other projects.

The following diagram shows the structure of a Django project:

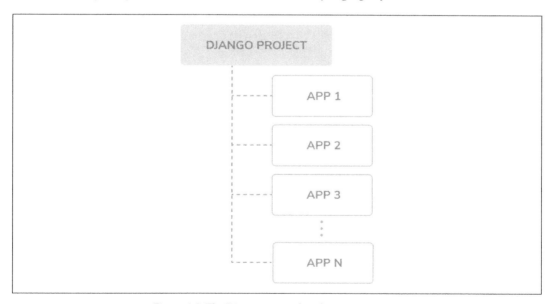

Figure 1.2: The Django project/application structure

Creating an application

Now let's create your first Django application. You will create a blog application from scratch. From the project's root directory, run the following command:

```
python manage.py startapp blog
```

This will create the basic structure of the application, which looks like this:

```
blog/
    __init__.py
    admin.py
    apps.py
    migrations/
        __init__.py
    models.py
    tests.py
    views.py
```

These files are as follows:

- `admin.py`: This is where you register models to include them in the Django administration site—using this site is optional.

- `apps.py`: This includes the main configuration of the `blog` application.

- `migrations`: This directory will contain database migrations of your application. Migrations allow Django to track your model changes and synchronize the database accordingly.

- `models.py`: This includes the data models of your application; all Django applications need to have a `models.py` file, but this file can be left empty.

- `tests.py`: This is where you can add tests for your application.

- `views.py`: The logic of your application goes here; each view receives an HTTP request, processes it, and returns a response.

Designing the blog data schema

You will start designing your blog data schema by defining the data models for your blog. A model is a Python class that subclasses `django.db.models.Model` in which each attribute represents a database field. Django will create a table for each model defined in the `models.py` file. When you create a model, Django will provide you with a practical API to query objects in the database easily.

First, you need to define a `Post` model. Add the following lines to the `models.py` file of the `blog` application:

```python
from django.db import models
from django.utils import timezone
from django.contrib.auth.models import User

class Post(models.Model):
    STATUS_CHOICES = (
        ('draft', 'Draft'),
        ('published', 'Published'),
    )
    title = models.CharField(max_length=250)
    slug = models.SlugField(max_length=250,
                            unique_for_date='publish')
    author = models.ForeignKey(User,
                               on_delete=models.CASCADE,
                               related_name='blog_posts')
    body = models.TextField()
    publish = models.DateTimeField(default=timezone.now)
    created = models.DateTimeField(auto_now_add=True)
    updated = models.DateTimeField(auto_now=True)
    status = models.CharField(max_length=10,
                              choices=STATUS_CHOICES,
                              default='draft')

    class Meta:
        ordering = ('-publish',)

    def __str__(self):
        return self.title
```

This is your data model for blog posts. Let's take a look at the fields you just defined for this model:

- `title`: This is the field for the post title. This field is `CharField`, which translates into a VARCHAR column in the SQL database.

- `slug`: This is a field intended to be used in URLs. A slug is a short label that contains only letters, numbers, underscores, or hyphens. You will use the `slug` field to build beautiful, SEO-friendly URLs for your blog posts. You have added the `unique_for_date` parameter to this field so that you can build URLs for posts using their `publish` date and `slug`. Django will prevent multiple posts from having the same slug for a given date.

- author: This field defines a many-to-one relationship, meaning that each post is written by a user, and a user can write any number of posts. For this field, Django will create a foreign key in the database using the primary key of the related model. In this case, you are relying on the User model of the Django authentication system. The on_delete parameter specifies the behavior to adopt when the referenced object is deleted. This is not specific to Django; it is an SQL standard. Using CASCADE, you specify that when the referenced user is deleted, the database will also delete all related blog posts. You can take a look at all the possible options at https://docs.djangoproject.com/en/3.0/ref/models/fields/#django.db.models.ForeignKey.on_delete. You specify the name of the reverse relationship, from User to Post, with the related_name attribute. This will allow you to access related objects easily. You will learn more about this later.

- body: This is the body of the post. This field is a text field that translates into a TEXT column in the SQL database.

- publish: This datetime indicates when the post was published. You use Django's timezone now method as the default value. This returns the current datetime in a timezone-aware format. You can think of it as a timezone-aware version of the standard Python datetime.now method.

- created: This datetime indicates when the post was created. Since you are using auto_now_add here, the date will be saved automatically when creating an object.

- updated: This datetime indicates the last time the post was updated. Since you are using auto_now here, the date will be updated automatically when saving an object.

- status: This field shows the status of a post. You use a choices parameter, so the value of this field can only be set to one of the given choices.

Django comes with different types of fields that you can use to define your models. You can find all field types at https://docs.djangoproject.com/en/3.0/ref/models/fields/.

The Meta class inside the model contains metadata. You tell Django to sort results by the publish field in descending order by default when you query the database. You specify the descending order using the negative prefix. By doing this, posts published recently will appear first.

The __str__() method is the default human-readable representation of the object. Django will use it in many places, such as the administration site.

If you are coming from using Python 2.x, note that in Python 3, all strings are natively considered Unicode; therefore, we only use the __str__() method and the __unicode__() method is obsolete.

Activating the application

In order for Django to keep track of your application and be able to create database tables for its models, you have to activate it. To do this, edit the settings.py file and add blog.apps.BlogConfig to the INSTALLED_APPS setting. It should look like this:

```
INSTALLED_APPS = [
    'django.contrib.admin',
    'django.contrib.auth',
    'django.contrib.contenttypes',
    'django.contrib.sessions',
    'django.contrib.messages',
    'django.contrib.staticfiles',
    'blog.apps.BlogConfig',
]
```

The BlogConfig class is your application configuration. Now Django knows that your application is active for this project and will be able to load its models.

Creating and applying migrations

Now that you have a data model for your blog posts, you will need a database table for it. Django comes with a migration system that tracks the changes made to models and enables them to propagate into the database. As mentioned, the migrate command applies migrations for all applications listed in INSTALLED_APPS; it synchronizes the database with the current models and existing migrations.

First, you will need to create an initial migration for your Post model. In the root directory of your project, run the following command:

```
python manage.py makemigrations blog
```

You should get the following output:

```
Migrations for 'blog':
    blog/migrations/0001_initial.py
        - Create model Post
```

Django just created the `0001_initial.py` file inside the `migrations` directory of the `blog` application. You can open that file to see how a migration appears. A migration specifies dependencies on other migrations and operations to perform in the database to synchronize it with model changes.

Let's take a look at the SQL code that Django will execute in the database to create the table for your model. The `sqlmigrate` command takes the migration names and returns their SQL without executing it. Run the following command to inspect the SQL output of your first migration:

```
python manage.py sqlmigrate blog 0001
```

The output should look as follows:

```
BEGIN;

--

-- Create model Post

--

CREATE TABLE "blog_post" ("id" integer NOT NULL PRIMARY KEY
AUTOINCREMENT, "title" varchar(250) NOT NULL, "slug" varchar(250) NOT
NULL, "body" text NOT NULL, "publish" datetime NOT NULL, "created"
datetime NOT NULL, "updated" datetime NOT NULL, "status" varchar(10)
NOT NULL, "author_id" integer NOT NULL REFERENCES "auth_user" ("id")
DEFERRABLE INITIALLY DEFERRED);

CREATE INDEX "blog_post_slug_b95473f2" ON "blog_post" ("slug");

CREATE INDEX "blog_post_author_id_dd7a8485" ON "blog_post" ("author_id");

COMMIT;
```

The exact output depends on the database you are using. The preceding output is generated for SQLite. As you can see in the output, Django generates the table names by combining the application name and the lowercase name of the model (`blog_post`), but you can also specify a custom database name for your model in the `Meta` class of the model using the `db_table` attribute.

Django creates a primary key automatically for each model, but you can also override this by specifying `primary_key=True` in one of your model fields. The default primary key is an `id` column, which consists of an integer that is incremented automatically. This column corresponds to the `id` field that is automatically added to your models.

Let's sync your database with the new model. Run the following command to apply existing migrations:

```
python manage.py migrate
```

You will get an output that ends with the following line:

```
Applying blog.0001_initial... OK
```

You just applied migrations for the applications listed in INSTALLED_APPS, including your blog application. After applying the migrations, the database reflects the current status of your models.

If you edit the models.py file in order to add, remove, or change the fields of existing models, or if you add new models, you will have to create a new migration using the makemigrations command. The migration will allow Django to keep track of model changes. Then, you will have to apply it with the migrate command to keep the database in sync with your models.

Creating an administration site for models

Now that you have defined the Post model, you will create a simple administration site to manage your blog posts. Django comes with a built-in administration interface that is very useful for editing content. The Django site is built dynamically by reading your model metadata and providing a production-ready interface for editing content. You can use it out of the box, configuring how you want your models to be displayed in it.

The django.contrib.admin application is already included in the INSTALLED_APPS setting, so you don't need to add it.

Creating a superuser

First, you will need to create a user to manage the administration site. Run the following command:

```
python manage.py createsuperuser
```

You will see the following output; enter your desired username, email, and password, as follows:

```
Username (leave blank to use 'admin'): admin
Email address: admin@admin.com
Password: ********
Password (again): ********
Superuser created successfully.
```

The Django administration site

Now start the development server with the python manage.py runserver command and open http://127.0.0.1:8000/admin/ in your browser. You should see the administration login page, as shown in the following screenshot:

Figure 1.3: The Django administration site login screen

Log in using the credentials of the user you created in the preceding step. You will see the administration site index page, as shown in the following screenshot:

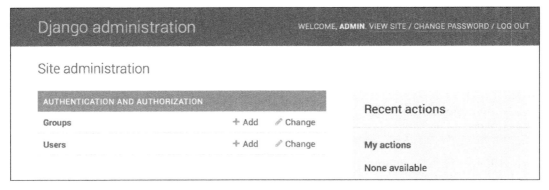

Figure 1.4: The Django administration site index page

The `Group` and `User` models that you can see in the preceding screenshot are part of the Django authentication framework located in `django.contrib.auth`. If you click on **Users**, you will see the user you created previously.

Adding models to the administration site

Let's add your blog models to the administration site. Edit the `admin.py` file of the `blog` application and make it look like this:

```
from django.contrib import admin
from .models import Post

admin.site.register(Post)
```

Now reload the administration site in your browser. You should see your `Post` model on the site, as follows:

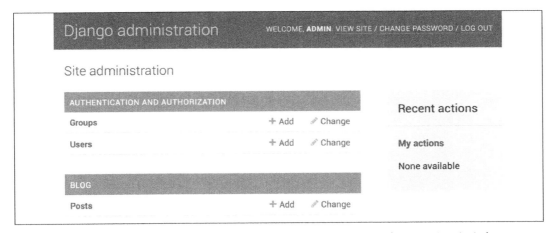

Figure 1.5: The Post model of the blog application included in the Django administration site index page

That was easy, right? When you register a model in the Django administration site, you get a user-friendly interface generated by introspecting your models that allows you to list, edit, create, and delete objects in a simple way.

Click on the **Add** link beside **Posts** to add a new post. You will note the form that Django has generated dynamically for your model, as shown in the following screenshot:

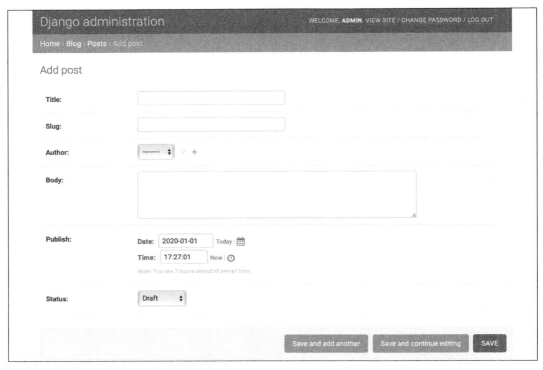

Figure 1.6: The Django administration site edit form for the Post model

Django uses different form widgets for each type of field. Even complex fields, such as the `DateTimeField`, are displayed with an easy interface, such as a JavaScript date picker.

Fill in the form and click on the **SAVE** button. You should be redirected to the post list page with a success message and the post you just created, as shown in the following screenshot:

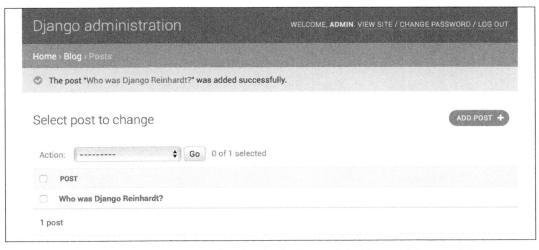

Figure 1.7: The Django administration site list view for the Post model with an added successfully message

Customizing the way that models are displayed

Now, we will take a look at how to customize the administration site. Edit the `admin.py` file of your `blog` application and change it, as follows:

```
from django.contrib import admin
from .models import Post

@admin.register(Post)
class PostAdmin(admin.ModelAdmin):
    list_display = ('title', 'slug', 'author', 'publish', 'status')
```

You are telling the Django administration site that your model is registered in the site using a custom class that inherits from `ModelAdmin`. In this class, you can include information about how to display the model in the site and how to interact with it.

The `list_display` attribute allows you to set the fields of your model that you want to display on the administration object list page. The `@admin.register()` decorator performs the same function as the `admin.site.register()` function that you replaced, registering the `ModelAdmin` class that it decorates.

Let's customize the `admin` model with some more options, using the following code:

```
@admin.register(Post)
class PostAdmin(admin.ModelAdmin):
    list_display = ('title', 'slug', 'author', 'publish', 'status')
    list_filter = ('status', 'created', 'publish', 'author')
    search_fields = ('title', 'body')
    prepopulated_fields = {'slug': ('title',)}
    raw_id_fields = ('author',)
    date_hierarchy = 'publish'
    ordering = ('status', 'publish')
```

Return to your browser and reload the post list page. Now, it will look like this:

Figure 1.8: The Django administration site custom list view for the Post model

You can see that the fields displayed on the post list page are the ones you specified in the `list_display` attribute. The list page now includes a right sidebar that allows you to filter the results by the fields included in the `list_filter` attribute.

A search bar has appeared on the page. This is because you have defined a list of searchable fields using the `search_fields` attribute. Just below the search bar, there are navigation links to navigate through a date hierarchy; this has been defined by the `date_hierarchy` attribute. You can also see that the posts are ordered by **STATUS** and **PUBLISH** columns by default. You have specified the default sorting criteria using the `ordering` attribute.

Next, click on the **ADD POST** link. You will also note some changes here. As you type the title of a new post, the `slug` field is filled in automatically. You have told Django to prepopulate the `slug` field with the input of the `title` field using the `prepopulated_fields` attribute.

Also, the `author` field is now displayed with a lookup widget that can scale much better than a drop-down select input when you have thousands of users. This is achieved with the `raw_id_fields` attribute and it looks like this:

Figure 1.9: The widget to select related objects for the author field of the Post model

With a few lines of code, you have customized the way your model is displayed on the administration site. There are plenty of ways to customize and extend the Django administration site; you will learn more about this later in this book.

Working with QuerySets and managers

Now that you have a fully functional administration site to manage your blog's content, it's time to learn how to retrieve information from the database and interact with it. Django comes with a powerful database abstraction API that lets you create, retrieve, update, and delete objects easily. The Django **object-relational mapper (ORM)** is compatible with MySQL, PostgreSQL, SQLite, Oracle, and MariaDB. Remember that you can define the database of your project in the DATABASES setting of your project's `settings.py` file. Django can work with multiple databases at a time, and you can program database routers to create custom routing schemes.

Once you have created your data models, Django gives you a free API to interact with them. You can find the data model reference of the official documentation at `https://docs.djangoproject.com/en/3.0/ref/models/`.

The Django ORM is based on QuerySets. A QuerySet is a collection of database queries to retrieve objects from your database. You can apply filters to QuerySets to narrow down the query results based on given parameters.

Creating objects

Open the terminal and run the following command to open the Python shell:

```
python manage.py shell
```

Then, type the following lines:

```
>>> from django.contrib.auth.models import User
>>> from blog.models import Post
>>> user = User.objects.get(username='admin')
>>> post = Post(title='Another post',
...             slug='another-post',
...             body='Post body.',
...             author=user)
>>> post.save()
```

Let's analyze what this code does. First, you retrieve the user object with the username admin:

```
user = User.objects.get(username='admin')
```

The get() method allows you to retrieve a single object from the database. Note that this method expects a result that matches the query. If no results are returned by the database, this method will raise a DoesNotExist exception, and if the database returns more than one result, it will raise a MultipleObjectsReturned exception. Both exceptions are attributes of the model class that the query is being performed on.

Then, you create a Post instance with a custom title, slug, and body, and set the user that you previously retrieved as the author of the post:

```
post = Post(title='Another post', slug='another-post', body='Post
body.', author=user)
```

 This object is in memory and is not persisted to the database.

Finally, you save the Post object to the database using the save() method:

```
post.save()
```

The preceding action performs an INSERT SQL statement behind the scenes. You have seen how to create an object in memory first and then persist it to the database, but you can also create the object and persist it into the database in a single operation using the create() method, as follows:

```
Post.objects.create(title='One more post',
                    slug='one-more-post',
                    body='Post body.',
                    author=user)
```

Updating objects

Now, change the title of the post to something different and save the object again:

```
>>> post.title = 'New title'
>>> post.save()
```

This time, the `save()` method performs an UPDATE SQL statement.

 The changes you make to the object are not persisted to the database until you call the `save()` method.

Retrieving objects

You already know how to retrieve a single object from the database using the `get()` method. You accessed this method using `Post.objects.get()`. Each Django model has at least one manager, and the default manager is called `objects`. You get a `QuerySet` object using your model manager. To retrieve all objects from a table, you just use the `all()` method on the default objects manager, like this:

```
>>> all_posts = Post.objects.all()
```

This is how you create a QuerySet that returns all objects in the database. Note that this QuerySet has not been executed yet. Django QuerySets are *lazy*, which means they are only evaluated when they are forced to be. This behavior makes QuerySets very efficient. If you don't set the QuerySet to a variable, but instead write it directly on the Python shell, the SQL statement of the QuerySet is executed because you force it to output results:

```
>>> all_posts
```

Using the filter() method

To filter a QuerySet, you can use the `filter()` method of the manager. For example, you can retrieve all posts published in the year 2020 using the following QuerySet:

```
>>> Post.objects.filter(publish__year=2020)
```

You can also filter by multiple fields. For example, you can retrieve all posts published in 2020 by the author with the username `admin`:

```
>>> Post.objects.filter(publish__year=2020, author__username='admin')
```

This equates to building the same QuerySet chaining multiple filters:

```
>>> Post.objects.filter(publish__year=2020) \
>>>             .filter(author__username='admin')
```

 Queries with field lookup methods are built using two underscores, for example, publish__year, but the same notation is also used for accessing fields of related models, such as author__username.

Using exclude()

You can exclude certain results from your QuerySet using the exclude() method of the manager. For example, you can retrieve all posts published in 2020 whose titles don't start with Why:

```
>>> Post.objects.filter(publish__year=2020) \
>>>             .exclude(title__startswith='Why')
```

Using order_by()

You can order results by different fields using the order_by() method of the manager. For example, you can retrieve all objects ordered by their title, as follows:

```
>>> Post.objects.order_by('title')
```

Ascending order is implied. You can indicate descending order with a negative sign prefix, like this:

```
>>> Post.objects.order_by('-title')
```

Deleting objects

If you want to delete an object, you can do it from the object instance using the delete() method:

```
>>> post = Post.objects.get(id=1)
>>> post.delete()
```

 Note that deleting objects will also delete any dependent relationships for ForeignKey objects defined with on_delete set to CASCADE.

When QuerySets are evaluated

Creating a QuerySet doesn't involve any database activity until it is evaluated. QuerySets usually return another unevaluated QuerySet. You can concatenate as many filters as you like to a QuerySet, and you will not hit the database until the QuerySet is evaluated. When a QuerySet is evaluated, it translates into an SQL query to the database.

QuerySets are only evaluated in the following cases:

- The first time you iterate over them
- When you slice them, for instance, `Post.objects.all()[:3]`
- When you pickle or cache them
- When you call `repr()` or `len()` on them
- When you explicitly call `list()` on them
- When you test them in a statement, such as `bool()`, `or`, `and`, or `if`

Creating model managers

As I previously mentioned, `objects` is the default manager of every model that retrieves all objects in the database. However, you can also define custom managers for your models. You will create a custom manager to retrieve all posts with the `published` status.

There are two ways to add or customize managers for your models: you can add extra manager methods to an existing manager, or create a new manager by modifying the initial QuerySet that the manager returns. The first method provides you with a QuerySet API such as `Post.objects.my_manager()`, and the latter provides you with `Post.my_manager.all()`. The manager will allow you to retrieve posts using `Post.published.all()`.

Edit the `models.py` file of your `blog` application to add the custom manager:

```
class PublishedManager(models.Manager):
    def get_queryset(self):
        return super(PublishedManager,
                     self).get_queryset()\
                        .filter(status='published')


class Post(models.Model):
    # ...
    objects = models.Manager() # The default manager.
    published = PublishedManager() # Our custom manager.
```

The first manager declared in a model becomes the default manager. You can use the `Meta` attribute `default_manager_name` to specify a different default manager. If no manager is defined in the model, Django automatically creates the `objects` default manager for it. If you declare any managers for your model but you want to keep the `objects` manager as well, you have to add it explicitly to your model. In the preceding code, you add the default `objects` manager and the `published` custom manager to the `Post` model.

The `get_queryset()` method of a manager returns the QuerySet that will be executed. You override this method to include your custom filter in the final QuerySet.

You have now defined your custom manager and added it to the `Post` model; you can use it to perform queries. Let's test it.

Start the development server again with the following command:

```
python manage.py shell
```

Now, you can import the `Post` model and retrieve all published posts whose title starts with `Who`, executing the following QuerySet:

```
>>> from blog.models import Post
>>> Post.published.filter(title__startswith='Who')
```

To obtain results for this QuerySet, make sure that you set the `published` field to `True` in the `Post` object whose `title` starts with `Who`.

Building list and detail views

Now that you have knowledge of how to use the ORM, you are ready to build the views of the `blog` application. A Django view is just a Python function that receives a web request and returns a web response. All the logic to return the desired response goes inside the view.

First, you will create your application views, then you will define a URL pattern for each view, and finally, you will create HTML templates to render the data generated by the views. Each view will render a template, passing variables to it, and will return an HTTP response with the rendered output.

Creating list and detail views

Let's start by creating a view to display the list of posts. Edit the `views.py` file of your `blog` application and make it look like this:

```
from django.shortcuts import render, get_object_or_404
from .models import Post

def post_list(request):
    posts = Post.published.all()
    return render(request,
                  'blog/post/list.html',
                  {'posts': posts})
```

You just created your first Django view. The post_list view takes the request object as the only parameter. This parameter is required by all views. In this view, you retrieve all the posts with the published status using the published manager that you created previously.

Finally, you use the render() shortcut provided by Django to render the list of posts with the given template. This function takes the request object, the template path, and the context variables to render the given template. It returns an HttpResponse object with the rendered text (normally HTML code). The render() shortcut takes the request context into account, so any variable set by the template context processors is accessible by the given template. Template context processors are just callables that set variables into the context. You will learn how to use them in *Chapter 3, Extending Your Blog Application.*

Let's create a second view to display a single post. Add the following function to the views.py file:

```
def post_detail(request, year, month, day, post):
    post = get_object_or_404(Post, slug=post,
                                   status='published',
                                   publish__year=year,
                                   publish__month=month,
                                   publish__day=day)
    return render(request,
                  'blog/post/detail.html',
                  {'post': post})
```

This is the post detail view. This view takes the year, month, day, and post arguments to retrieve a published post with the given slug and date. Note that when you created the Post model, you added the unique_for_date parameter to the slug field. This ensures that there will be only one post with a slug for a given date, and thus, you can retrieve single posts using the date and slug. In the detail view, you use the get_object_or_404() shortcut to retrieve the desired post. This function retrieves the object that matches the given parameters or an HTTP 404 (not found) exception if no object is found. Finally, you use the render() shortcut to render the retrieved post using a template.

Adding URL patterns for your views

URL patterns allow you to map URLs to views. A URL pattern is composed of a string pattern, a view, and, optionally, a name that allows you to name the URL project-wide. Django runs through each URL pattern and stops at the first one that matches the requested URL. Then, Django imports the view of the matching URL pattern and executes it, passing an instance of the `HttpRequest` class and the keyword or positional arguments.

Create a `urls.py` file in the directory of the `blog` application and add the following lines to it:

```
from django.urls import path
from . import views

app_name = 'blog'

urlpatterns = [
    # post views
    path('', views.post_list, name='post_list'),
    path('<int:year>/<int:month>/<int:day>/<slug:post>/',
        views.post_detail,
        name='post_detail'),
]
```

In the preceding code, you define an application namespace with the `app_name` variable. This allows you to organize URLs by application and use the name when referring to them. You define two different patterns using the `path()` function. The first URL pattern doesn't take any arguments and is mapped to the `post_list` view. The second pattern takes the following four arguments and is mapped to the `post_detail` view:

- `year`: Requires an integer
- `month`: Requires an integer
- `day`: Requires an integer
- `post`: Can be composed of words and hyphens

You use angle brackets to capture the values from the URL. Any value specified in the URL pattern as `<parameter>` is captured as a string. You use path converters, such as `<int:year>`, to specifically match and return an integer and `<slug:post>` to specifically match a slug. You can see all path converters provided by Django at https://docs.djangoproject.com/en/3.0/topics/http/urls/#path-converters.

If using `path()` and converters isn't sufficient for you, you can use `re_path()` instead to define complex URL patterns with Python regular expressions. You can learn more about defining URL patterns with regular expressions at `https://docs.djangoproject.com/en/3.0/ref/urls/#django.urls.re_path`. If you haven't worked with regular expressions before, you might want to take a look at the *Regular Expression HOWTO* located at `https://docs.python.org/3/howto/regex.html` first.

 Creating a `urls.py` file for each application is the best way to make your applications reusable by other projects.

Next, you have to include the URL patterns of the `blog` application in the main URL patterns of the project.

Edit the `urls.py` file located in the `mysite` directory of your project and make it look like the following:

```
from django.urls import path, include
from django.contrib import admin

urlpatterns = [
    path('admin/', admin.site.urls),
    path('blog/', include('blog.urls', namespace='blog')),
]
```

The new URL pattern defined with `include` refers to the URL patterns defined in the `blog` application so that they are included under the `blog/` path. You include these patterns under the namespace `blog`. Namespaces have to be unique across your entire project. Later, you will refer to your blog URLs easily by using the namespace followed by a colon and the URL name, for example, `blog:post_list` and `blog:post_detail`. You can learn more about URL namespaces at `https://docs.djangoproject.com/en/3.0/topics/http/urls/#url-namespaces`.

Canonical URLs for models

A canonical URL is the preferred URL for a resource. You may have different pages in your site where you display posts, but there is a single URL that you use as the main URL for a blog post. The convention in Django is to add a `get_absolute_url()` method to the model that returns the canonical URL for the object.

You can use the `post_detail` URL that you have defined in the preceding section to build the canonical URL for `Post` objects. For this method, you will use the `reverse()` method, which allows you to build URLs by their name and pass optional parameters. You can learn more about the URLs utility functions at `https://docs.djangoproject.com/en/3.0/ref/urlresolvers/`.

Edit the `models.py` file of the `blog` application and add the following code:

```
from django.urls import reverse

class Post(models.Model):
    # ...
    def get_absolute_url(self):
        return reverse('blog:post_detail',
                       args=[self.publish.year,
                             self.publish.month,
                             self.publish.day, self.slug])
```

You will use the `get_absolute_url()` method in your templates to link to specific posts.

Creating templates for your views

You have created views and URL patterns for the `blog` application. URL patterns map URLs to views, and views decide which data gets returned to the user. Templates define how the data is displayed; they are usually written in HTML in combination with the Django template language. You can find more information about the Django template language at `https://docs.djangoproject.com/en/3.0/ref/templates/language/`.

Let's add templates to your application to display posts in a user-friendly manner.

Create the following directories and files inside your `blog` application directory:

```
templates/
    blog/
        base.html
        post/
            list.html
            detail.html
```

The preceding structure will be the file structure for your templates. The `base.html` file will include the main HTML structure of the website and divide the content into the main content area and a sidebar. The `list.html` and `detail.html` files will inherit from the `base.html` file to render the blog post list and detail views, respectively.

Django has a powerful template language that allows you to specify how data is displayed. It is based on *template tags*, *template variables*, and *template filters*:

- Template tags control the rendering of the template and look like `{% tag %}`
- Template variables get replaced with values when the template is rendered and look like `{{ variable }}`
- Template filters allow you to modify variables for display and look like `{{ variable|filter }}`.

You can see all built-in template tags and filters at `https://docs.djangoproject.com/en/3.0/ref/templates/builtins/`.

Edit the `base.html` file and add the following code:

```
{% load static %}
<!DOCTYPE html>
<html>
<head>
  <title>{% block title %}{% endblock %}</title>
  <link href="{% static "css/blog.css" %}" rel="stylesheet">
</head>
<body>
  <div id="content">
    {% block content %}
    {% endblock %}
  </div>
  <div id="sidebar">
    <h2>My blog</h2>
    <p>This is my blog.</p>
  </div>
</body>
</html>
```

`{% load static %}` tells Django to load the `static` template tags that are provided by the `django.contrib.staticfiles` application, which is contained in the `INSTALLED_APPS` setting. After loading them, you are able to use the `{% static %}` template tag throughout this template. With this template tag, you can include the static files, such as the `blog.css` file, which you will find in the code of this example under the `static/` directory of the `blog` application. Copy the `static/` directory from the code that comes along with this chapter into the same location as your project to apply the CSS styles to the templates. You can find the directory's contents at `https://github.com/PacktPublishing/Django-3-by-Example/tree/master/Chapter01/mysite/blog/static`.

You can see that there are two {% block %} tags. These tell Django that you want to define a block in that area. Templates that inherit from this template can fill in the blocks with content. You have defined a block called title and a block called content.

Let's edit the post/list.html file and make it look like the following:

```
{% extends "blog/base.html" %}

{% block title %}My Blog{% endblock %}

{% block content %}
  <h1>My Blog</h1>
  {% for post in posts %}
    <h2>
      <a href="{{ post.get_absolute_url }}">
        {{ post.title }}
      </a>
    </h2>
    <p class="date">
      Published {{ post.publish }} by {{ post.author }}
    </p>
    {{ post.body|truncatewords:30|linebreaks }}
  {% endfor %}
{% endblock %}
```

With the {% extends %} template tag, you tell Django to inherit from the blog/base.html template. Then, you fill the title and content blocks of the base template with content. You iterate through the posts and display their title, date, author, and body, including a link in the title to the canonical URL of the post.

In the body of the post, you apply two template filters: truncatewords truncates the value to the number of words specified, and linebreaks converts the output into HTML line breaks. You can concatenate as many template filters as you wish; each one will be applied to the output generated by the preceding one.

Open the shell and execute the python manage.py runserver command to start the development server. Open http://127.0.0.1:8000/blog/ in your browser; you will see everything running. Note that you need to have some posts with the Published status to show them here. You should see something like this:

Figure 1.10: The page for the post list view

Next, edit the post/detail.html file:

```
{% extends "blog/base.html" %}

{% block title %}{{ post.title }}{% endblock %}

{% block content %}
  <h1>{{ post.title }}</h1>
  <p class="date">
    Published {{ post.publish }} by {{ post.author }}
  </p>
  {{ post.body|linebreaks }}
{% endblock %}
```

Next, you can return to your browser and click on one of the post titles to take a look at the detail view of the post. You should see something like this:

Figure 1.11: The page for the post's detail view

Take a look at the URL—it should be `/blog/2020/1/1/who-was-django-reinhardt/`. You have designed SEO-friendly URLs for your blog posts.

Adding pagination

When you start adding content to your blog, you might easily reach the point where tens or hundreds of posts are stored in your database. Instead of displaying all the posts on a single page, you may want to split the list of posts across several pages. This can be achieved through pagination. You can define the number of posts you want to be displayed per page and retrieve the posts that correspond to the page requested by the user. Django has a built-in pagination class that allows you to manage paginated data easily.

Edit the `views.py` file of the `blog` application to import the Django paginator classes and modify the `post_list` view, as follows:

```python
from django.core.paginator import Paginator, EmptyPage,\
                                  PageNotAnInteger

def post_list(request):
    object_list = Post.published.all()
    paginator = Paginator(object_list, 3) # 3 posts in each page
    page = request.GET.get('page')
    try:
        posts = paginator.page(page)
    except PageNotAnInteger:
        # If page is not an integer deliver the first page
        posts = paginator.page(1)
    except EmptyPage:
        # If page is out of range deliver last page of results
        posts = paginator.page(paginator.num_pages)
    return render(request,
                  'blog/post/list.html',
                  {'page': page,
                   'posts': posts})
```

This is how pagination works:

1. You instantiate the `Paginator` class with the number of objects that you want to display on each page.

2. You get the `page` GET parameter, which indicates the current page number.

3. You obtain the objects for the desired page by calling the `page()` method of `Paginator`.

4. If the `page` parameter is not an integer, you retrieve the first page of results. If this parameter is a number higher than the last page of results, you retrieve the last page.

5. You pass the page number and retrieved objects to the template.

Now you have to create a template to display the paginator so that it can be included in any template that uses pagination. In the `templates/` folder of the `blog` application, create a new file and name it `pagination.html`. Add the following HTML code to the file:

```
<div class="pagination">
  <span class="step-links">
    {% if page.has_previous %}
      <a href="?page={{ page.previous_page_number }}">Previous</a>
    {% endif %}
    <span class="current">
      Page {{ page.number }} of {{ page.paginator.num_pages }}.
    </span>
    {% if page.has_next %}
      <a href="?page={{ page.next_page_number }}">Next</a>
    {% endif %}
  </span>
</div>
```

The pagination template expects a `Page` object in order to render the previous and next links, and to display the current page and total pages of results. Let's return to the `blog/post/list.html` template and include the `pagination.html` template at the bottom of the `{% content %}` block, as follows:

```
{% block content %}
  ...
  {% include "pagination.html" with page=posts %}
{% endblock %}
```

Since the `Page` object you are passing to the template is called `posts`, you include the pagination template in the post list template, passing the parameters to render it correctly. You can follow this method to reuse your pagination template in the paginated views of different models.

Now open `http://127.0.0.1:8000/blog/` in your browser. You should see the pagination at the bottom of the post list and should be able to navigate through pages:

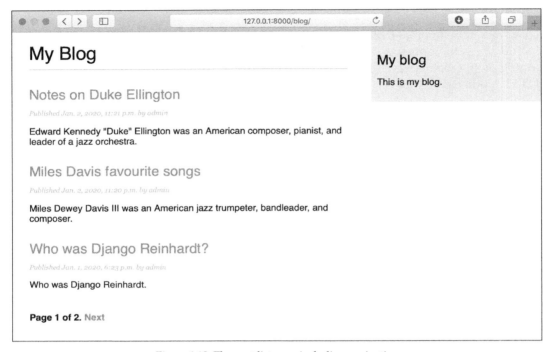

Figure 1.12: The post list page including pagination

Using class-based views

Class-based views are an alternative way to implement views as Python objects instead of functions. Since a view is a callable that takes a web request and returns a web response, you can also define your views as class methods. Django provides base view classes for this. All of them inherit from the View class, which handles HTTP method dispatching and other common functionalities.

Class-based views offer advantages over function-based views for some use cases. They have the following features:

- Organizing code related to HTTP methods, such as GET, POST, or PUT, in separate methods, instead of using conditional branching
- Using multiple inheritance to create reusable view classes (also known as *mixins*)

You can take a look at an introduction to class-based views at `https://docs.djangoproject.com/en/3.0/topics/class-based-views/intro/`.

You will change your `post_list` view into a class-based view to use the generic `ListView` offered by Django. This base view allows you to list objects of any kind.

Edit the `views.py` file of your `blog` application and add the following code:

```python
from django.views.generic import ListView


class PostListView(ListView):
    queryset = Post.published.all()
    context_object_name = 'posts'
    paginate_by = 3
    template_name = 'blog/post/list.html'
```

This class-based view is analogous to the previous `post_list` view. In the preceding code, you are telling `ListView` to do the following things:

- Use a specific QuerySet instead of retrieving all objects. Instead of defining a `queryset` attribute, you could have specified `model = Post` and Django would have built the generic `Post.objects.all()` QuerySet for you.
- Use the context variable `posts` for the query results. The default variable is `object_list` if you don't specify any `context_object_name`.
- Paginate the result, displaying three objects per page.
- Use a custom template to render the page. If you don't set a default template, `ListView` will use `blog/post_list.html`.

Now open the `urls.py` file of your `blog` application, comment the preceding `post_list` URL pattern, and add a new URL pattern using the `PostListView` class, as follows:

```python
urlpatterns = [
    # post views
    # path('', views.post_list, name='post_list'),
    path('', views.PostListView.as_view(), name='post_list'),
    path('<int:year>/<int:month>/<int:day>/<slug:post>/',
        views.post_detail,
        name='post_detail'),
]
```

In order to keep pagination working, you have to use the right page object that is passed to the template. Django's `ListView` generic view passes the selected page in a variable called `page_obj`, so you have to edit your `post/list.html` template accordingly to include the paginator using the right variable, as follows:

```
{% include "pagination.html" with page=page_obj %}
```

Open `http://127.0.0.1:8000/blog/` in your browser and verify that everything works the same way as with the previous `post_list` view. This is a simple example of a class-based view that uses a generic class provided by Django. You will learn more about class-based views in *Chapter 10, Building an E-Learning Platform*, and successive chapters.

Summary

In this chapter, you learned the basics of the Django web framework by creating a simple blog application. You designed the data models and applied migrations to your project. You also created the views, templates, and URLs for your blog, including object pagination.

In the next chapter, you will discover how to enhance your blog application with a comment system and tagging functionality, and how to allow your users to share posts by email.

2

Enhancing Your Blog with Advanced Features

In the preceding chapter, you created a basic blog application. Next, you will turn your application into a fully functional blog with the advanced functionalities that many blogs feature nowadays. You will implement the following features in your blog:

- **Sharing posts via email**: When readers like an article, they might want to share it with somebody else. You will implement the functionality to share posts via email.

- **Adding comments to a post**: Many people want to allow their audience to comment on posts and create discussions. You will let your readers add comments to your blog posts.

- **Tagging posts**: Tags allow you to categorize content in a non-hierarchical manner, using simple keywords. You will implement a tagging system, which is a very popular feature for blogs.

- **Recommending similar posts**: Once you have a classification method in place, such as a tagging system, you can use it to provide content recommendations to your readers. You will build a system that recommends other posts that share tags with a certain blog post.

These functionalities will turn your application into a fully featured blog.

In this chapter, we will cover the following topics:

- Sending emails with Django
- Creating forms and handling them in views
- Creating forms from models
- Integrating third-party applications
- Building complex QuerySets

Sharing posts by email

First, let's allow users to share posts by sending them via email. Take a minute to think about how you could use *views*, *URLs*, and *templates* to create this functionality using what you learned in the preceding chapter. In order to allow your users to share posts via email, you will need to do the following things:

- Create a form for users to fill in their name, their email, the email recipient, and optional comments
- Create a view in the `views.py` file that handles the posted data and sends the email
- Add a URL pattern for the new view in the `urls.py` file of the blog application
- Create a template to display the form

Creating forms with Django

Let's start by building the form to share posts. Django has a built-in forms framework that allows you to create forms in an easy manner. The forms framework makes it simple to define the fields of your form, specify how they have to be displayed, and indicate how they have to validate input data. The Django forms framework offers a flexible way to render forms and handle data.

Django comes with two base classes to build forms:

- `Form`: Allows you to build standard forms
- `ModelForm`: Allows you to build forms tied to model instances

First, create a `forms.py` file inside the directory of your `blog` application and make it look like this:

```
from django import forms
```

```
class EmailPostForm(forms.Form):
    name = forms.CharField(max_length=25)
    email = forms.EmailField()
    to = forms.EmailField()
    comments = forms.CharField(required=False,
                               widget=forms.Textarea)
```

This is your first Django form. Take a look at the code. You have created a form by inheriting the base `Form` class. You use different field types for Django to validate fields accordingly.

 Forms can reside anywhere in your Django project. The convention is to place them inside a `forms.py` file for each application.

The `name` field is `CharField`. This type of field is rendered as an `<input type="text">` HTML element. Each field type has a default widget that determines how the field is rendered in HTML. The default widget can be overridden with the `widget` attribute. In the `comments` field, you use a `Textarea` widget to display it as a `<textarea>` HTML element instead of the default `<input>` element.

Field validation also depends on the field type. For example, the `email` and `to` fields are `EmailField` fields. Both fields require a valid email address; the field validation will otherwise raise a `forms.ValidationError` exception and the form will not validate. Other parameters are also taken into account for form validation: you define a maximum length of 25 characters for the `name` field and make the `comments` field optional with `required=False`. All of this is also taken into account for field validation. The field types used in this form are only a part of Django form fields. For a list of all form fields available, you can visit `https://docs.djangoproject.com/en/3.0/ref/forms/fields/`.

Handling forms in views

You need to create a new view that handles the form and sends an email when it's successfully submitted. Edit the `views.py` file of your `blog` application and add the following code to it:

```
from .forms import EmailPostForm

def post_share(request, post_id):
    # Retrieve post by id
    post = get_object_or_404(Post, id=post_id, status='published')
```

```
if request.method == 'POST':
    # Form was submitted
    form = EmailPostForm(request.POST)
    if form.is_valid():
        # Form fields passed validation
        cd = form.cleaned_data
        # ... send email
else:
    form = EmailPostForm()
return render(request, 'blog/post/share.html', {'post': post,
                                                 'form': form})
```

This view works as follows:

- You define the `post_share` view that takes the `request` object and the `post_id` variable as parameters.

- You use the `get_object_or_404()` shortcut to retrieve the post by ID and make sure that the retrieved post has a `published` status.

- You use the same view for both displaying the initial form and processing the submitted data. You differentiate whether the form was submitted or not based on the `request` method and submit the form using POST. You assume that if you get a GET request, an empty form has to be displayed, and if you get a POST request, the form is submitted and needs to be processed. Therefore, you use `request.method == 'POST'` to distinguish between the two scenarios.

The following is the process to display and handle the form:

1. When the view is loaded initially with a GET request, you create a new `form` instance that will be used to display the empty form in the template:

   ```
   form = EmailPostForm()
   ```

2. The user fills in the form and submits it via POST. Then, you create a form instance using the submitted data that is contained in `request.POST`:

   ```
   if request.method == 'POST':
       # Form was submitted
       form = EmailPostForm(request.POST)
   ```

3. After this, you validate the submitted data using the form's `is_valid()` method. This method validates the data introduced in the form and returns `True` if all fields contain valid data. If any field contains invalid data, then `is_valid()` returns `False`. You can see a list of validation errors by accessing `form.errors`.

4. If the form is not valid, you render the form in the template again with the submitted data. You will display validation errors in the template.

5. If the form is valid, you retrieve the validated data by accessing `form.cleaned_data`. This attribute is a dictionary of form fields and their values.

 If your form data does not validate, `cleaned_data` will contain only the valid fields.

Now, let's explore how to send emails using Django to put everything together.

Sending emails with Django

Sending emails with Django is pretty straightforward. First, you need to have a local **Simple Mail Transfer Protocol** (**SMTP**) server, or you need to define the configuration of an external SMTP server by adding the following settings to the `settings.py` file of your project:

- `EMAIL_HOST`: The SMTP server host; the default is `localhost`
- `EMAIL_PORT`: The SMTP port; the default is `25`
- `EMAIL_HOST_USER`: The username for the SMTP server
- `EMAIL_HOST_PASSWORD`: The password for the SMTP server
- `EMAIL_USE_TLS`: Whether to use a **Transport Layer Security** (**TLS**) secure connection
- `EMAIL_USE_SSL`: Whether to use an implicit TLS secure connection

If you can't use an SMTP server, you can tell Django to write emails to the console by adding the following setting to the `settings.py` file:

```
EMAIL_BACKEND = 'django.core.mail.backends.console.EmailBackend'
```

By using this setting, Django will output all emails to the shell. This is very useful for testing your application without an SMTP server.

If you want to send emails but you don't have a local SMTP server, you can probably use the SMTP server of your email service provider. The following sample configuration is valid for sending emails via Gmail servers using a Google account:

```
EMAIL_HOST = 'smtp.gmail.com'
EMAIL_HOST_USER = 'your_account@gmail.com'
EMAIL_HOST_PASSWORD = 'your_password'
```

```
EMAIL_PORT = 587
EMAIL_USE_TLS = True
```

Run the `python manage.py shell` command to open the Python shell and send an email, as follows:

```
>>> from django.core.mail import send_mail
>>> send_mail('Django mail', 'This e-mail was sent with Django.', 'your_
account@gmail.com', ['your_account@gmail.com'], fail_silently=False)
```

The `send_mail()` function takes the subject, message, sender, and list of recipients as required arguments. By setting the optional argument `fail_silently=False`, you are telling it to raise an exception if the email couldn't be sent correctly. If the output you see is `1`, then your email was successfully sent.

If you are sending emails using Gmail with the preceding configuration, you will have to enable access for less secure applications at `https://myaccount.google.com/lesssecureapps`, as follows:

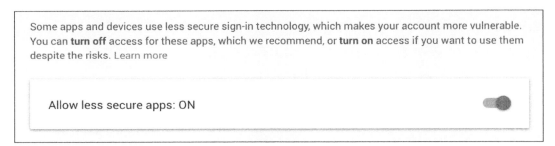

Figure 2.1: The Google less secure application access screen

In some cases, you may also have to disable Gmail captcha at `https://accounts.google.com/displayunlockcaptcha` in order to send emails with Django.

Edit the `post_share` view in the `views.py` file of the `blog` application, as follows:

```
from django.core.mail import send_mail

def post_share(request, post_id):
    # Retrieve post by id
    post = get_object_or_404(Post, id=post_id, status='published')
    sent = False

    if request.method == 'POST':
        # Form was submitted
        form = EmailPostForm(request.POST)
        if form.is_valid():
```

```
        # Form fields passed validation
        cd = form.cleaned_data
        post_url = request.build_absolute_uri(
            post.get_absolute_url())
        subject = f"{cd['name']} recommends you read " \
                  f"{post.title}"
        message = f"Read {post.title} at {post_url}\n\n" \
                  f"{cd['name']}\'s comments: {cd['comments']}"
        send_mail(subject, message, 'admin@myblog.com',
                  [cd['to']])
        sent = True
    else:
        form = EmailPostForm()
    return render(request, 'blog/post/share.html', {'post': post,
                                                     'form': form,
                                                     'sent': sent})
```

Replace admin@myblog.com with your real email account if you are using an SMTP server instead of the console EmailBackend.

In the code above you declare a sent variable and set it to True when the post was sent. You will use that variable later in the template to display a success message when the form is successfully submitted.

Since you have to include a link to the post in the email, you retrieve the absolute path of the post using its get_absolute_url() method. You use this path as an input for request.build_absolute_uri() to build a complete URL, including the HTTP schema and hostname. You build the subject and the message body of the email using the cleaned data of the validated form and, finally, send the email to the email address contained in the to field of the form.

Now that your view is complete, remember to add a new URL pattern for it. Open the urls.py file of your blog application and add the post_share URL pattern, as follows:

```
urlpatterns = [
    # ...
    path('<int:post_id>/share/',
         views.post_share, name='post_share'),
]
```

Rendering forms in templates

After creating the form, programming the view, and adding the URL pattern, you are only missing the template for this view. Create a new file in the blog/templates/blog/post/ directory and name it share.html. Add the following code to it:

```
{% extends "blog/base.html" %}
```

```
{% block title %}Share a post{% endblock %}

{% block content %}
  {% if sent %}
    <h1>E-mail successfully sent</h1>
    <p>
      "{{ post.title }}" was successfully sent to {{ form.cleaned_
data.to }}.
    </p>
  {% else %}
    <h1>Share "{{ post.title }}" by e-mail</h1>
    <form method="post">
      {{ form.as_p }}
      {% csrf_token %}
      <input type="submit" value="Send e-mail">
    </form>
  {% endif %}
{% endblock %}
```

This is the template to display the form or a success message when it's sent. As you will notice, you create the HTML form element, indicating that it has to be submitted by the POST method:

```
<form method="post">
```

Then, you include the actual form instance. You tell Django to render its fields in HTML paragraph <p> elements with the as_p method. You can also render the form as an unordered list with as_ul or as an HTML table with as_table. If you want to render each field, you can iterate through the fields, instead of using {{ form.as_p }} as in the following example:

```
{% for field in form %}
  <div>
    {{ field.errors }}
    {{ field.label_tag }} {{ field }}
  </div>
{% endfor %}
```

The {% csrf_token %} template tag introduces a hidden field with an autogenerated token to avoid **cross-site request forgery (CSRF)** attacks. These attacks consist of a malicious website or program performing an unwanted action for a user on your site. You can find more information about this at https://owasp.org/www-community/attacks/csrf.

The preceding tag generates a hidden field that looks like this:

```
<input type='hidden' name='csrfmiddlewaretoken' value='26JjKo2lcEtYkGo
V9z4XmJIEHLXN5LDR' />
```

 By default, Django checks for the CSRF token in all POST requests. Remember to include the csrf_token tag in all forms that are submitted via POST.

Edit the `blog/post/detail.html` template and add the following link to the share post URL after the `{{ post.body|linebreaks }}` variable:

```
<p>
  <a href="{% url "blog:post_share" post.id %}">
    Share this post
  </a>
</p>
```

Remember that you are building the URL dynamically using the `{% url %}` template tag provided by Django. You are using the namespace called `blog` and the URL named `post_share`, and you are passing the post ID as a parameter to build the absolute URL.

Now, start the development server with the `python manage.py runserver` command and open `http://127.0.0.1:8000/blog/` in your browser. Click on any post title to view its detail page. Under the post body, you should see the link that you just added, as shown in the following screenshot:

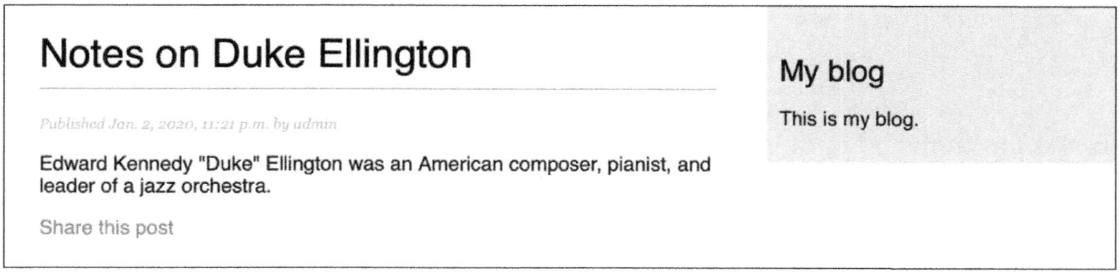

Notes on Duke Ellington

Published Jan. 2, 2020, 11:21 p.m. by admin

Edward Kennedy "Duke" Ellington was an American composer, pianist, and leader of a jazz orchestra.

Share this post

My blog

This is my blog.

Figure 2.2: The post detail page, including a link to share the post

Click on **Share this post**, and you should see the page, including the form to share this post by email, as follows:

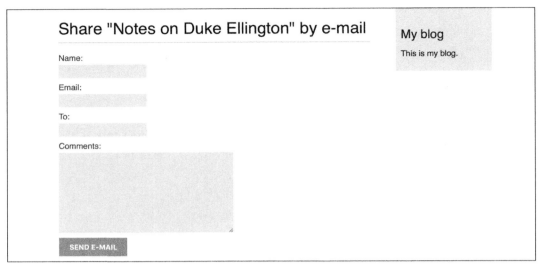

Figure 2.3: The page to share a post via email

CSS styles for the form are included in the example code in the `static/css/blog.css` file. When you click on the **SEND E-MAIL** button, the form is submitted and validated. If all fields contain valid data, you get a success message, as follows:

Figure 2.4: A success message for a post shared via email

If you input invalid data, the form is rendered again, including all validation errors:

Share "Notes on Duke Ellington" by e-mail

Name:

Antonio

- Enter a valid email address.

Email:

invalid

- This field is required.

To:

Comments:

SEND E-MAIL

My blog

This is my blog.

Figure 2.5: The share post form displaying invalid data errors

Note that some modern browsers will prevent you from submitting a form with empty or erroneous fields. This is because of form validation done by the browser based on field types and restrictions per field. In this case, the form won't be submitted and the browser will display an error message for the fields that are wrong.

Your form for sharing posts by email is now complete. Let's now create a comment system for your blog.

Creating a comment system

You will build a comment system wherein users will be able to comment on posts. To build the comment system, you need to do the following:

1. Create a model to save comments
2. Create a form to submit comments and validate the input data
3. Add a view that processes the form and saves a new comment to the database
4. Edit the post detail template to display the list of comments and the form to add a new comment

Building a model

First, let's build a model to store comments. Open the `models.py` file of your `blog` application and add the following code:

```
class Comment(models.Model):
    post = models.ForeignKey(Post,
                             on_delete=models.CASCADE,
                             related_name='comments')
    name = models.CharField(max_length=80)
    email = models.EmailField()
    body = models.TextField()
    created = models.DateTimeField(auto_now_add=True)
    updated = models.DateTimeField(auto_now=True)
    active = models.BooleanField(default=True)

    class Meta:
        ordering = ('created',)

    def __str__(self):
        return f'Comment by {self.name} on {self.post}'
```

This is your `Comment` model. It contains a `ForeignKey` to associate a comment with a single post. This many-to-one relationship is defined in the `Comment` model because each comment will be made on one post, and each post may have multiple comments.

The `related_name` attribute allows you to name the attribute that you use for the relationship from the related object back to this one. After defining this, you can retrieve the post of a comment object using `comment.post` and retrieve all comments of a post using `post.comments.all()`. If you don't define the `related_name` attribute, Django will use the name of the model in lowercase, followed by `_set` (that is, `comment_set`) to name the relationship of the related object to the object of the model, where this relationship has been defined.

You can learn more about many-to-one relationships at `https://docs.djangoproject.com/en/3.0/topics/db/examples/many_to_one/`.

You have included an `active` Boolean field that you will use to manually deactivate inappropriate comments. You use the `created` field to sort comments in a chronological order by default.

The new `Comment` model that you just created is not yet synchronized into the database. Run the following command to generate a new migration that reflects the creation of the new model:

```
python manage.py makemigrations blog
```

You should see the following output:

```
Migrations for 'blog':
  blog/migrations/0002_comment.py
    - Create model Comment
```

Django has generated a `0002_comment.py` file inside the `migrations/` directory of the `blog` application. Now, you need to create the related database schema and apply the changes to the database. Run the following command to apply existing migrations:

```
python manage.py migrate
```

You will get an output that includes the following line:

```
Applying blog.0002_comment... OK
```

The migration that you just created has been applied; now a `blog_comment` table exists in the database.

Next, you can add your new model to the administration site in order to manage comments through a simple interface. Open the `admin.py` file of the `blog` application, import the `Comment` model, and add the following `ModelAdmin` class:

```
from .models import Post, Comment


@admin.register(Comment)
class CommentAdmin(admin.ModelAdmin):
    list_display = ('name', 'email', 'post', 'created', 'active')
    list_filter = ('active', 'created', 'updated')
    search_fields = ('name', 'email', 'body')
```

Start the development server with the `python manage.py runserver` command and open `http://127.0.0.1:8000/admin/` in your browser. You should see the new model included in the **BLOG** section, as shown in the following screenshot:

Figure 2.6: Blog application models on the Django administration index page

The model is now registered in the administration site, and you can manage `Comment` instances using a simple interface.

Creating forms from models

You still need to build a form to let your users comment on blog posts. Remember that Django has two base classes to build forms: `Form` and `ModelForm`. You used the first one previously to let your users share posts by email. In the present case, you will need to use `ModelForm` because you have to build a form dynamically from your `Comment` model. Edit the `forms.py` file of your `blog` application and add the following lines:

```
from .models import Comment

class CommentForm(forms.ModelForm):
    class Meta:
        model = Comment
        fields = ('name', 'email', 'body')
```

To create a form from a model, you just need to indicate which model to use to build the form in the `Meta` class of the form. Django introspects the model and builds the form dynamically for you.

Each model field type has a corresponding default form field type. The way that you define your model fields is taken into account for form validation. By default, Django builds a form field for each field contained in the model. However, you can explicitly tell the framework which fields you want to include in your form using a `fields` list, or define which fields you want to exclude using an `exclude` list of fields. For your `CommentForm` form, you will just use the `name`, `email`, and `body` fields, because those are the only fields that your users will be able to fill in.

Handling ModelForms in views

You will use the post detail view to instantiate the form and process it, in order to keep it simple. Edit the `views.py` file, add imports for the `Comment` model and the `CommentForm` form, and modify the `post_detail` view to make it look like the following:

```python
from .models import Post, Comment
from .forms import EmailPostForm, CommentForm

def post_detail(request, year, month, day, post):
    post = get_object_or_404(Post, slug=post,
                                   status='published',
                                   publish__year=year,
                                   publish__month=month,
                                   publish__day=day)

    # List of active comments for this post
    comments = post.comments.filter(active=True)

    new_comment = None

    if request.method == 'POST':
        # A comment was posted
        comment_form = CommentForm(data=request.POST)
        if comment_form.is_valid():
            # Create Comment object but don't save to database yet
            new_comment = comment_form.save(commit=False)
            # Assign the current post to the comment
            new_comment.post = post
            # Save the comment to the database
            new_comment.save()
    else:
        comment_form = CommentForm()
    return render(request,
                  'blog/post/detail.html',
                  {'post': post,
                   'comments': comments,
                   'new_comment': new_comment,
                   'comment_form': comment_form})
```

Let's review what you have added to your view. You used the `post_detail` view to display the post and its comments. You added a QuerySet to retrieve all active comments for this post, as follows:

```python
comments = post.comments.filter(active=True)
```

You build this QuerySet, starting from the `post` object. Instead of building a QuerySet for the `Comment` model directly, you leverage the `post` object to retrieve the related `Comment` objects. You use the manager for the related objects that you defined as `comments` using the `related_name` attribute of the relationship in the `Comment` model. You use the same view to let your users add a new comment. You initialize the `new_comment` variable by setting it to `None`. You will use this variable when a new comment is created.

You build a form instance with `comment_form = CommentForm()` if the view is called by a `GET` request. If the request is done via `POST`, you instantiate the form using the submitted data and validate it using the `is_valid()` method. If the form is invalid, you render the template with the validation errors. If the form is valid, you take the following actions:

1. You create a new `Comment` object by calling the form's `save()` method and assign it to the `new_comment` variable, as follows:

   ```
   new_comment = comment_form.save(commit=False)
   ```

   The `save()` method creates an instance of the model that the form is linked to and saves it to the database. If you call it using `commit=False`, you create the model instance, but don't save it to the database yet. This comes in handy when you want to modify the object before finally saving it, which is what you will do next.

    The `save()` method is available for `ModelForm` but not for `Form` instances, since they are not linked to any model.

2. You assign the current post to the comment you just created:

   ```
   new_comment.post = post
   ```

   By doing this, you specify that the new comment belongs to this post.

3. Finally, you save the new comment to the database by calling its `save()` method:

   ```
   new_comment.save()
   ```

Your view is now ready to display and process new comments.

Adding comments to the post detail template

You have created the functionality to manage comments for a post. Now you need to adapt your `post/detail.html` template to do the following things:

- Display the total number of comments for a post

- Display the list of comments
- Display a form for users to add a new comment

First, you will add the total comments. Open the `post/detail.html` template and append the following code to the `content` block:

```
{% with comments.count as total_comments %}
  <h2>
    {{ total_comments }} comment{{ total_comments|pluralize }}
  </h2>
{% endwith %}
```

You are using the Django ORM in the template, executing the QuerySet `comments.count()`. Note that the Django template language doesn't use parentheses for calling methods. The `{% with %}` tag allows you to assign a value to a new variable that will be available to be used until the `{% endwith %}` tag.

The `{% with %}` template tag is useful for avoiding hitting the database or accessing expensive methods multiple times.

You use the `pluralize` template filter to display a plural suffix for the word "comment," depending on the `total_comments` value. Template filters take the value of the variable they are applied to as their input and return a computed value. We will discuss template filters in *Chapter 3, Extending Your Blog Application.*

The `pluralize` template filter returns a string with the letter "s" if the value is different from 1. The preceding text will be rendered as *0 comments, 1 comment,* or *N comments.* Django includes plenty of template tags and filters that can help you to display information in the way that you want.

Now, let's include the list of comments. Append the following lines to the `post/detail.html` template below the preceding code:

```
{% for comment in comments %}
  <div class="comment">
    <p class="info">
      Comment {{ forloop.counter }} by {{ comment.name }}
      {{ comment.created }}
    </p>
    {{ comment.body|linebreaks }}
  </div>
{% empty %}
  <p>There are no comments yet.</p>
{% endfor %}
```

You use the {% for %} template tag to loop through comments. You display a default message if the comments list is empty, informing your users that there are no comments on this post yet. You enumerate comments with the {{ forloop.counter }} variable, which contains the loop counter in each iteration. Then, you display the name of the user who posted the comment, the date, and the body of the comment.

Finally, you need to render the form or display a success message instead when it is successfully submitted. Add the following lines just below the preceding code:

```
{% if new_comment %}
  <h2>Your comment has been added.</h2>
{% else %}
  <h2>Add a new comment</h2>
  <form method="post">
    {{ comment_form.as_p }}
    {% csrf_token %}
    <p><input type="submit" value="Add comment"></p>
  </form>
{% endif %}
```

The code is pretty straightforward: if the new_comment object exists, you display a success message because the comment was successfully created. Otherwise, you render the form with a paragraph, <p>, element for each field and include the CSRF token required for POST requests.

Open http://127.0.0.1:8000/blog/ in your browser and click on a post title to take a look at its detail page. You will see something like the following screenshot:

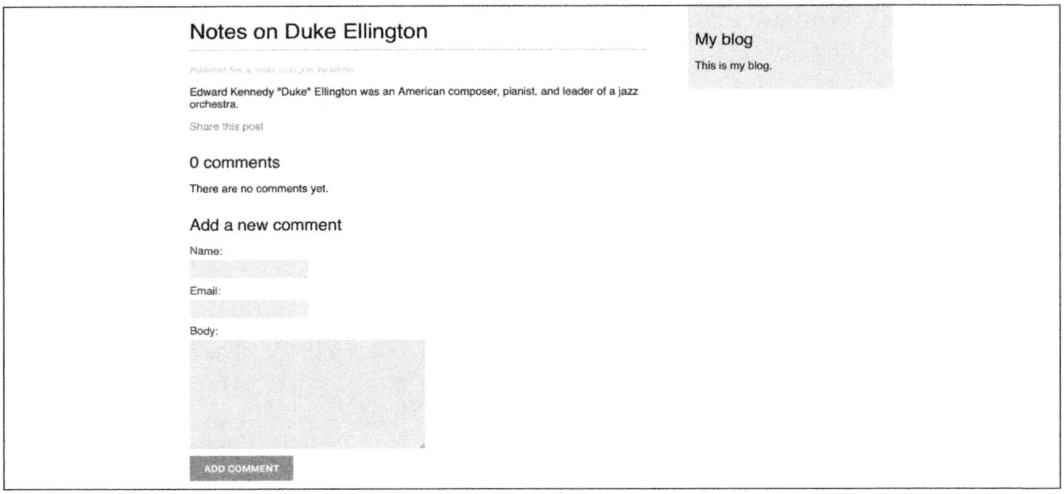

Figure 2.7: The post detail page, including the form to add a comment

Add a couple of comments using the form. They should appear under your post in chronological order, as follows:

Figure 2.8: The comment list on the post detail page

Open `http://127.0.0.1:8000/admin/blog/comment/` in your browser. You will see the administration page with the list of comments you created. Click on the name of one of them to edit it, uncheck the **Active** checkbox, and click on the **Save** button. You will be redirected to the list of comments again, and the **ACTIVE** column will display an inactive icon for the comment. It should look like the first comment in the following screenshot:

Figure 2.9: Active/inactive comments on the Django administration site

If you return to the post detail view, you will note that the inactive comment is not displayed anymore; neither is it counted for the total number of comments. Thanks to the `active` field, you can deactivate inappropriate comments and avoid showing them on your posts.

Adding the tagging functionality

After implementing your comment system, you need to create a way to tag your posts. You will do this by integrating a third-party Django tagging application into your project. django-taggit is a reusable application that primarily offers you a Tag model and a manager to easily add tags to any model. You can take a look at its source code at https://github.com/jazzband/django-taggit.

First, you need to install django-taggit via pip by running the following command:

```
pip install django_taggit==1.2.0
```

Then, open the settings.py file of the mysite project and add taggit to your INSTALLED_APPS setting, as follows:

```
INSTALLED_APPS = [
    # ...
    'blog.apps.BlogConfig',
    'taggit',
]
```

Open the models.py file of your blog application and add the TaggableManager manager provided by django-taggit to the Post model using the following code:

```
from taggit.managers import TaggableManager

class Post(models.Model):
    # ...
    tags = TaggableManager()
```

The tags manager will allow you to add, retrieve, and remove tags from Post objects.

Run the following command to create a migration for your model changes:

```
python manage.py makemigrations blog
```

You should get the following output:

```
Migrations for 'blog':
  blog/migrations/0003_post_tags.py
    - Add field tags to post
```

Now, run the following command to create the required database tables for `django-taggit` models and to synchronize your model changes:

```
python manage.py migrate
```

You will see an output indicating that migrations have been applied, as follows:

```
Applying taggit.0001_initial... OK
Applying taggit.0002_auto_20150616_2121... OK
Applying taggit.0003_taggeditem_add_unique_index... OK
Applying blog.0003_post_tags... OK
```

Your database is now ready to use `django-taggit` models.

Let's explore how to use the `tags` manager. Open the terminal with the `python manage.py shell` command and enter the following code. First, you will retrieve one of your posts (the one with the `1` ID):

```
>>> from blog.models import Post
>>> post = Post.objects.get(id=1)
```

Then, add some tags to it and retrieve its tags to check whether they were successfully added:

```
>>> post.tags.add('music', 'jazz', 'django')
>>> post.tags.all()
<QuerySet [<Tag: jazz>, <Tag: music>, <Tag: django>]>
```

Finally, remove a tag and check the list of tags again:

```
>>> post.tags.remove('django')
>>> post.tags.all()
<QuerySet [<Tag: jazz>, <Tag: music>]>
```

That was easy, right? Run the `python manage.py runserver` command to start the development server again and open `http://127.0.0.1:8000/admin/taggit/tag/` in your browser.

You will see the administration page with the list of `Tag` objects of the `taggit` application:

Figure 2.10: The tag change list view on the Django administration site

Navigate to `http://127.0.0.1:8000/admin/blog/post/` and click on a post to edit it. You will see that posts now include a new **Tags** field, as follows, where you can easily edit tags:

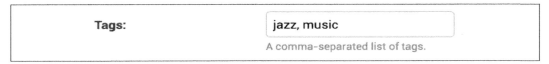

Figure 2.11: The related tags field of a Post object

Now, you need to edit your blog posts to display tags. Open the `blog/post/list.html` template and add the following HTML code below the post title:

```
<p class="tags">Tags: {{ post.tags.all|join:", " }}</p>
```

The `join` template filter works the same as the Python string `join()` method to concatenate elements with the given string. Open `http://127.0.0.1:8000/blog/` in your browser. You should be able to see the list of tags under each post title:

Figure 2.12: The Post list item, including related tags

Next, you will edit the `post_list` view to let users list all posts tagged with a specific tag. Open the `views.py` file of your `blog` application, import the `Tag` model form `django-taggit`, and change the `post_list` view to optionally filter posts by a tag, as follows:

```
from taggit.models import Tag

def post_list(request, tag_slug=None):
    object_list = Post.published.all()
    tag = None

    if tag_slug:
        tag = get_object_or_404(Tag, slug=tag_slug)
        object_list = object_list.filter(tags__in=[tag])

    paginator = Paginator(object_list, 3) # 3 posts in each page
    # ...
```

The `post_list` view now works as follows:

1. It takes an optional `tag_slug` parameter that has a `None` default value. This parameter will be passed in the URL.

2. Inside the view, you build the initial QuerySet, retrieving all published posts, and if there is a given tag slug, you get the `Tag` object with the given slug using the `get_object_or_404()` shortcut.

3. Then, you filter the list of posts by the ones that contain the given tag. Since this is a many-to-many relationship, you have to filter posts by tags contained in a given list, which, in your case, contains only one element. You use the `__in` field lookup. Many-to-many relationships occur when multiple objects of a model are associated with multiple objects of another model. In your application, a post can have multiple tags and a tag can be related to multiple posts. You will learn how to create many-to-many relationships in *Chapter 5*, *Sharing Content on Your Website*. You can discover more about many-to-many relationships at `https://docs.djangoproject.com/en/3.0/topics/db/examples/many_to_many/`.

Remember that QuerySets are lazy. The QuerySets to retrieve posts will only be evaluated when you loop over the post list when rendering the template.

Finally, modify the `render()` function at the bottom of the view to pass the `tag` variable to the template. The view should look like this:

```
def post_list(request, tag_slug=None):
    object_list = Post.published.all()
    tag = None
```

```
if tag_slug:
    tag = get_object_or_404(Tag, slug=tag_slug)
    object_list = object_list.filter(tags__in=[tag])

paginator = Paginator(object_list, 3) # 3 posts in each page
page = request.GET.get('page')
try:
    posts = paginator.page(page)
except PageNotAnInteger:
    # If page is not an integer deliver the first page
    posts = paginator.page(1)
except EmptyPage:
    # If page is out of range deliver last page of results
    posts = paginator.page(paginator.num_pages)
return render(request, 'blog/post/list.html', {'page': page,
                                                'posts': posts,
                                                'tag': tag})
```

Open the `urls.py` file of your `blog` application, comment out the class-based `PostListView` URL pattern, and uncomment the `post_list` view, like this:

```
path('', views.post_list, name='post_list'),
# path('', views.PostListView.as_view(), name='post_list'),
```

Add the following additional URL pattern to list posts by tag:

```
path('tag/<slug:tag_slug>/',
    views.post_list, name='post_list_by_tag'),
```

As you can see, both patterns point to the same view, but you are naming them differently. The first pattern will call the `post_list` view without any optional parameters, whereas the second pattern will call the view with the `tag_slug` parameter. You use a `slug` path converter to match the parameter as a lowercase string with ASCII letters or numbers, plus the hyphen and underscore characters.

Since you are using the `post_list` view, edit the `blog/post/list.html` template and modify the pagination to use the `posts` object:

```
{% include "pagination.html" with page=posts %}
```

Add the following lines above the `{% for %}` loop:

```
{% if tag %}
  <h2>Posts tagged with "{{ tag.name }}"</h2>
{% endif %}
```

If a user is accessing the blog, they will see the list of all posts. If they filter by posts tagged with a specific tag, they will see the tag that they are filtering by.

Now, change the way tags are displayed, as follows:

```
<p class="tags">
  Tags:
  {% for tag in post.tags.all %}
    <a href="{% url "blog:post_list_by_tag" tag.slug %}">
      {{ tag.name }}
    </a>
    {% if not forloop.last %}, {% endif %}
  {% endfor %}
</p>
```

In the code above, you loop through all the tags of a post displaying a custom link to the URL to filter posts by that tag. You build the URL with {% url "blog:post_list_by_tag" tag.slug %}, using the name of the URL and the slug tag as its parameter. You separate the tags by commas.

Open http://127.0.0.1:8000/blog/ in your browser and click on any tag link. You will see the list of posts filtered by that tag, like this:

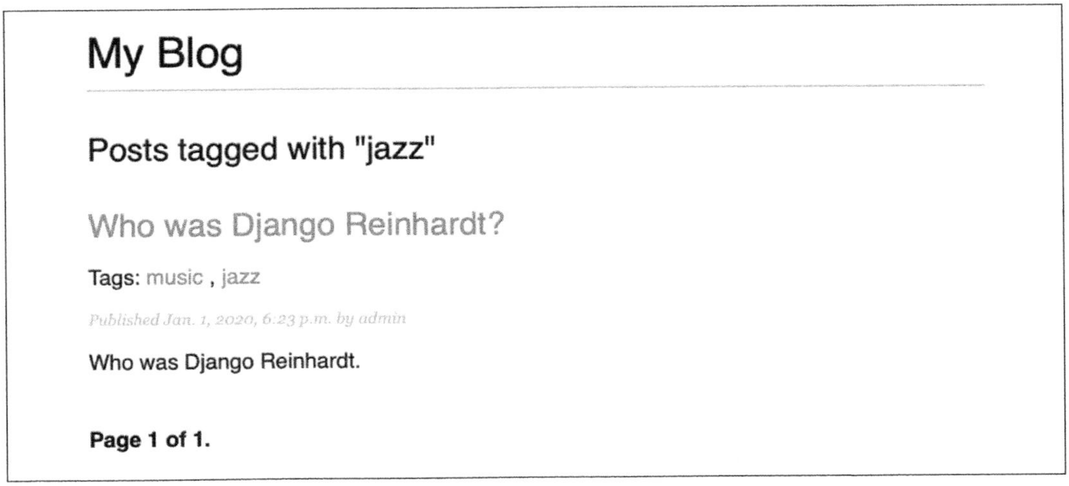

My Blog

Posts tagged with "jazz"

Who was Django Reinhardt?

Tags: music , jazz

Published Jan. 1, 2020, 6:23 p.m. by admin

Who was Django Reinhardt.

Page 1 of 1.

Figure 2.13: A post filtered by the tag "jazz"

Retrieving posts by similarity

Now that you have implemented tagging for your blog posts, you can do many interesting things with tags. Tags allow you to categorize posts in a non-hierarchical manner. Posts about similar topics will have several tags in common. You will build a functionality to display similar posts by the number of tags they share. In this way, when a user reads a post, you can suggest to them that they read other related posts.

In order to retrieve similar posts for a specific post, you need to perform the following steps:

1. Retrieve all tags for the current post

2. Get all posts that are tagged with any of those tags

3. Exclude the current post from that list to avoid recommending the same post

4. Order the results by the number of tags shared with the current post

5. In the case of two or more posts with the same number of tags, recommend the most recent post

6. Limit the query to the number of posts you want to recommend

These steps are translated into a complex QuerySet that you will include in your `post_detail` view.

Open the `views.py` file of your `blog` application and add the following import at the top of it:

```
from django.db.models import Count
```

This is the `Count` aggregation function of the Django ORM. This function will allow you to perform aggregated counts of tags. `django.db.models` includes the following aggregation functions:

- `Avg`: The mean value

- `Max`: The maximum value

- `Min`: The minimum value

- `Count`: The total number of objects

You can learn about aggregation at `https://docs.djangoproject.com/en/3.0/topics/db/aggregation/`.

Add the following lines inside the `post_detail` view before the `render()` function, with the same indentation level:

```
# List of similar posts
post_tags_ids = post.tags.values_list('id', flat=True)
```

```
similar_posts = Post.published.filter(tags__in=post_tags_ids)\
                                 .exclude(id=post.id)
similar_posts = similar_posts.annotate(same_tags=Count('tags'))\
                                 .order_by('-same_tags','-publish')[:4]
```

The preceding code is as follows:

1. You retrieve a Python list of IDs for the tags of the current post. The `values_list()` QuerySet returns tuples with the values for the given fields. You pass `flat=True` to it to get single values such as `[1, 2, 3, ...]` instead of one-tuples such as `[(1,), (2,), (3,) ...]`.

2. You get all posts that contain any of these tags, excluding the current post itself.

3. You use the `Count` aggregation function to generate a calculated field — `same_tags` — that contains the number of tags shared with all the tags queried.

4. You order the result by the number of shared tags (descending order) and by `publish` to display recent posts first for the posts with the same number of shared tags. You slice the result to retrieve only the first four posts.

Add the `similar_posts` object to the context dictionary for the `render()` function, as follows:

```
return render(request,
              'blog/post/detail.html',
              {'post': post,
               'comments': comments,
               'new_comment': new_comment,
               'comment_form': comment_form,
               'similar_posts': similar_posts})
```

Now, edit the `blog/post/detail.html` template and add the following code before the post comment list:

```
<h2>Similar posts</h2>
{% for post in similar_posts %}
  <p>
    <a href="{{ post.get_absolute_url }}">{{ post.title }}</a>
  </p>
{% empty %}
  There are no similar posts yet.
{% endfor %}
```

The post detail page should look like this:

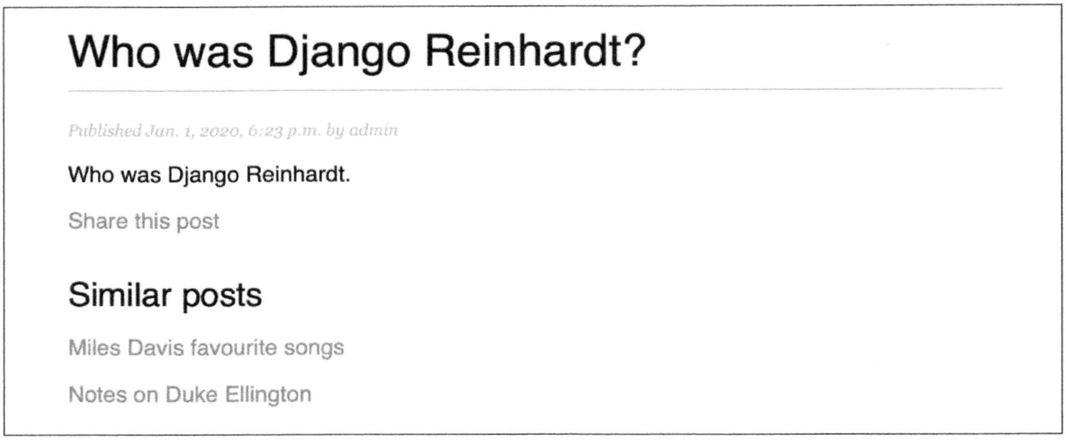

Who was Django Reinhardt?

Published Jan. 1, 2020, 6:23 p.m. by admin

Who was Django Reinhardt.

Share this post

Similar posts

Miles Davis favourite songs

Notes on Duke Ellington

Figure 2.14: The post detail page, including a list of similar posts

You are now able to successfully recommend similar posts to your users. `django-taggit` also includes a `similar_objects()` manager that you can use to retrieve objects by shared tags. You can take a look at all `django-taggit` managers at `https://django-taggit.readthedocs.io/en/latest/api.html`.

You can also add the list of tags to your post detail template in the same way as you did in the `blog/post/list.html` template.

Summary

In this chapter, you learned how to work with Django forms and model forms. You created a system to share your site's content by email and created a comment system for your blog. You added tagging to your blog posts, integrating a reusable application, and built complex QuerySets to retrieve objects by similarity.

In the next chapter, you will learn how to create custom template tags and filters. You will also build a custom sitemap and feed for your blog posts, and implement the full text search functionality for your posts.

3

Extending Your
Blog Application

The previous chapter went through the basics of forms and the creation of
a comment system. You also learned how to send emails with Django, and you
implemented a tagging system by integrating a third-party application with your
project. In this chapter, you will extend your blog application with some other
popular features used on blogging platforms. You will also learn about other
components and functionalities with Django.

The chapter will cover the following points:

- **Creating custom template tags and filters**: You will learn how to build your
  own template tags and template filters to exploit the capabilities of Django
  templates.

- **Adding a sitemap and post feed**: You will learn how to use the sitemaps
  framework and syndication framework that come with Django.

- **Implementing full-text search with PostgreSQL**: Search is a very popular
  feature for blogs. You will learn how to implement an advanced search
  engine for your blog application.

Creating custom template tags and filters

Django offers a variety of built-in template tags, such as {% if %} or {% block %}. You used different template tags in *Chapter 1, Building a Blog Application,* and *Chapter 2, Enhancing Your Blog with Advanced Features.* You can find a complete reference of built-in template tags and filters at https://docs.djangoproject.com/en/3.0/ref/templates/builtins/.

Django also allows you to create your own template tags to perform custom actions. Custom template tags come in very handy when you need to add a functionality to your templates that is not covered by the core set of Django template tags. This could be a tag to perform a QuerySet or any server-side processing that you want to reuse across templates. For example, you could build a template tag to display the list of latest posts published on your blog. You can include this list in the sidebar of the blog for multiple pages, regardless of the view.

Custom template tags

Django provides the following helper functions that allow you to create your own template tags in an easy manner:

- simple_tag: Processes the data and returns a string
- inclusion_tag: Processes the data and returns a rendered template

Template tags must live inside Django applications.

Inside your blog application directory, create a new directory, name it templatetags, and add an empty __init__.py file to it. Create another file in the same folder and name it blog_tags.py. The file structure of the blog application should look like the following:

```
blog/
    __init__.py
    models.py
    ...
    templatetags/
        __init__.py
        blog_tags.py
```

The way you name the file is important. You will use the name of this module to load tags in templates.

Let's start by creating a simple tag to retrieve the total posts published on the blog. Edit the `blog_tags.py` file you just created and add the following code:

```
from django import template
from ..models import Post

register = template.Library()

@register.simple_tag
def total_posts():
    return Post.published.count()
```

You have created a simple template tag that returns the number of posts published so far. Each module that contains template tags needs to define a variable called `register` to be a valid tag library. This variable is an instance of `template.Library`, and it's used to register your own template tags and filters.

In the code above, you define a tag called `total_posts` with a Python function and use the `@register.simple_tag` decorator to register the function as a simple tag. Django will use the function's name as the tag name. If you want to register it using a different name, you can do so by specifying a `name` attribute, such as `@register.simple_tag(name='my_tag')`.

> After adding a new template tags module, you will need to restart the Django development server in order to use the new tags and filters in templates.

Before using custom template tags, you have to make them available for the template using the `{% load %}` tag. As mentioned before, you need to use the name of the Python module containing your template tags and filters.

Open the `blog/templates/base.html` template and add `{% load blog_tags %}` at the top of it to load your template tags module. Then, use the tag you created to display your total posts. Just add `{% total_posts %}` to your template. The template should look like this:

```
{% load blog_tags %}
{% load static %}
<!DOCTYPE html>
<html>
<head>
  <title>{% block title %}{% endblock %}</title>
  <link href="{% static "css/blog.css" %}" rel="stylesheet">
</head>
<body>
```

```
<div id="content">
  {% block content %}
  {% endblock %}
</div>
<div id="sidebar">
  <h2>My blog</h2>
  <p>This is my blog. I've written {% total_posts %} posts so far.</p>
</div>
</body>
</html>
```

You will need to restart the server to keep track of the new files added to the project. Stop the development server with *Ctrl + C* and run it again using the following command:

python manage.py runserver

Open http://127.0.0.1:8000/blog/ in your browser. You should see the total number of posts in the sidebar of the site, as follows:

My blog

This is my blog. I've written 4 posts so far.

Figure 3.1: The total posts published included in the sidebar

The power of custom template tags is that you can process any data and add it to any template regardless of the view executed. You can perform QuerySets or process any data to display results in your templates.

Now, you will create another tag to display the latest posts in the sidebar of your blog. This time, you will use an inclusion tag. Using an inclusion tag, you can render a template with context variables returned by your template tag.

Edit the blog_tags.py file and add the following code:

```
@register.inclusion_tag('blog/post/latest_posts.html')
def show_latest_posts(count=5):
    latest_posts = Post.published.order_by('-publish')[:count]
    return {'latest_posts': latest_posts}
```

In the preceding code, you register the template tag using @register.inclusion_tag and specify the template that will be rendered with the returned values using blog/post/latest_posts.html. Your template tag will accept an optional count parameter that defaults to 5. This parameter you to specify the number of posts that you want to display. You use this variable to limit the results of the query Post.published.order_by('-publish')[:count].

Note that the function returns a dictionary of variables instead of a simple value. Inclusion tags have to return a dictionary of values, which is used as the context to render the specified template. The template tag you just created allows you to specify the optional number of posts to display as {% show_latest_posts 3 %}.

Now, create a new template file under `blog/post/` and name it `latest_posts.html`. Add the following code to it:

```
<ul>
  {% for post in latest_posts %}
    <li>
      <a href="{{ post.get_absolute_url }}">{{ post.title }}</a>
    </li>
  {% endfor %}
</ul>
```

In the preceding code, you display an unordered list of posts using the `latest_posts` variable returned by your template tag. Now, edit the `blog/base.html` template and add the new template tag to display the last three posts. The sidebar code should look like the following:

```
<div id="sidebar">
  <h2>My blog</h2>
  <p>This is my blog. I've written {% total_posts %} posts so far.</p>
  <h3>Latest posts</h3>
  {% show_latest_posts 3 %}
</div>
```

The template tag is called, passing the number of posts to display, and the template is rendered in place with the given context.

Next, return to your browser and refresh the page. The sidebar should now look like this:

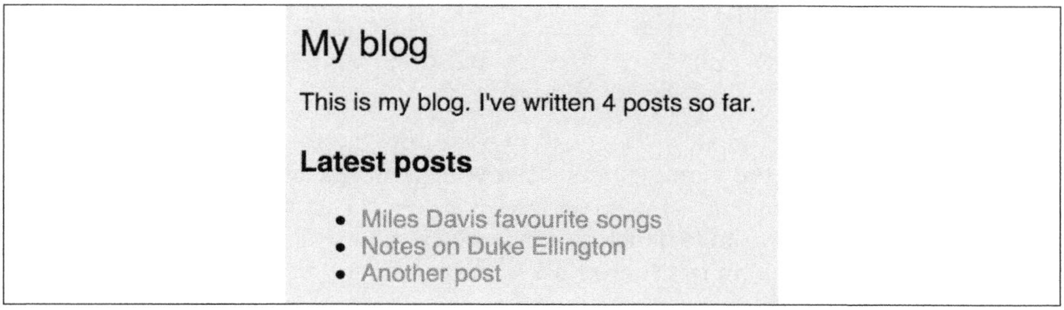

Figure 3.2: The sidebar, including the latest published posts

Finally, you will create a simple template tag that returns a value. You will store the result in a variable that can be reused, rather than directly outputting it. You will create a tag to display the most commented posts.

Edit the `blog_tags.py` file and add the following import and template tag to it:

```
from django.db.models import Count


@register.simple_tag
def get_most_commented_posts(count=5):
    return Post.published.annotate(
            total_comments=Count('comments')
        ).order_by('-total_comments')[:count]
```

In the preceding template tag, you build a QuerySet using the `annotate()` function to aggregate the total number of comments for each post. You use the `Count` aggregation function to store the number of comments in the computed field `total_comments` for each `Post` object. You order the QuerySet by the computed field in descending order. You also provide an optional `count` variable to limit the total number of objects returned.

In addition to `Count`, Django offers the aggregation functions `Avg`, `Max`, `Min`, and `Sum`. You can read more about aggregation functions at `https://docs.djangoproject.com/en/3.0/topics/db/aggregation/`.

Next, edit the `blog/base.html` template and append the following code to the sidebar `<div>` element:

```
<h3>Most commented posts</h3>
{% get_most_commented_posts as most_commented_posts %}
<ul>
  {% for post in most_commented_posts %}
    <li>
      <a href="{{ post.get_absolute_url }}">{{ post.title }}</a>
    </li>
  {% endfor %}
</ul>
```

In the preceding code, you store the result in a custom variable using the `as` argument followed by the variable name. For your template tag, you use `{% get_most_commented_posts as most_commented_posts %}` to store the result of the template tag in a new variable named `most_commented_posts`. Then, you display the returned posts using an unordered list.

Now open your browser and refresh the page to see the final result. It should look like the following:

Figure 3.3: The post list view, including the complete sidebar with the latest and most commented posts

You have now a clear idea about how to build custom template tags. You can read more about them at `https://docs.djangoproject.com/en/3.0/howto/custom-template-tags/`.

Custom template filters

Django has a variety of built-in template filters that allow you to alter variables in templates. These are Python functions that take one or two parameters, the value of the variable that the filter is applied to, and an optional argument. They return a value that can be displayed or treated by another filter. A filter looks like `{{ variable|my_filter }}`. Filters with an argument look like `{{ variable|my_filter:"foo" }}`. For example, you can use the `capfirst` filter to capitalize the first character of the value, like `{{ value|capfirst }}`. If `value` is "django", the output will be "Django". You can apply as many filters as you like to a variable, for example, `{{ variable|filter1|filter2 }}`, and each of them will be applied to the output generated by the preceding filter.

You can find the list of Django's built-in template filters at `https://docs.djangoproject.com/en/3.0/ref/templates/builtins/#built-in-filter-reference`.

You will create a custom filter to enable you to use markdown syntax in your blog posts and then convert the post contents to HTML in the templates. Markdown is a plain-text formatting syntax that is very simple to use, and it's intended to be converted into HTML. You can write posts using simple markdown syntax and get the content automatically converted into HTML code. Learning markdown syntax is much easier than learning HTML. By using markdown, you can get other non-tech savvy contributors to easily write posts for your blog. You can learn the basics of the markdown format at `https://daringfireball.net/projects/markdown/basics`.

First, install the Python `markdown` module via `pip` using the following command:

```
pip install markdown==3.2.1
```

Then, edit the `blog_tags.py` file and include the following code:

```python
from django.utils.safestring import mark_safe
import markdown

@register.filter(name='markdown')
def markdown_format(text):
    return mark_safe(markdown.markdown(text))
```

You register template filters in the same way as template tags. To prevent a name clash between your function name and the `markdown` module, you name your function `markdown_format` and name the filter `markdown` for use in templates, such as `{{ variable|markdown }}`. Django escapes the HTML code generated by filters; characters of HTML entities are replaced with their HTML encoded characters. For example, `<p>` is converted to `&lt;p&gt;` (*less than* symbol, *p* character, *greater than* symbol). You use the `mark_safe` function provided by Django to mark the result as safe HTML to be rendered in the template. By default, Django will not trust any HTML code and will escape it before placing it in the output. The only exceptions are variables that are marked as safe from escaping. This behavior prevents Django from outputting potentially dangerous HTML and allows you to create exceptions for returning safe HTML.

Now, load your template tags module in the post list and detail templates. Add the following line at the top of the `blog/post/list.html` and `blog/post/detail.html` templates after the `{% extends %}` tag:

```
{% load blog_tags %}
```

In the `post/detail.html` template, look for the following line:

```
{{ post.body|linebreaks }}
```

Replace it with the following one:

```
{{ post.body|markdown }}
```

Then, in the `post/list.html` template, find the following line:

```
{{ post.body|truncatewords:30|linebreaks }}
```

Replace it with the following one:

```
{{ post.body|markdown|truncatewords_html:30 }}
```

The `truncatewords_html` filter truncates a string after a certain number of words, avoiding unclosed HTML tags.

Now open `http://127.0.0.1:8000/admin/blog/post/add/` in your browser and add a post with the following body:

```
This is a post formatted with markdown
---------------------------------------

*This is emphasized* and **this is more emphasized**.

Here is a list:

* One
* Two
* Three

And a [link to the Django website](https://www.djangoproject.com/)
```

Open your browser and take a look at how the post is rendered. You should see the following output:

Figure 3.4: The post with markdown content rendered as HTML

As you can see in the preceding screenshot, custom template filters are very useful for customizing formatting. You can find more information about custom filters at https://docs.djangoproject.com/en/3.0/howto/custom-template-tags/#writing-custom-template-filters.

Adding a sitemap to your site

Django comes with a sitemap framework, which allows you to generate sitemaps for your site dynamically. A sitemap is an XML file that tells search engines the pages of your website, their relevance, and how frequently they are updated. Using a sitemap will make your site more visible in search engine rankings: sitemaps help crawlers to index your website's content.

The Django sitemap framework depends on django.contrib.sites, which allows you to associate objects to particular websites that are running with your project. This comes in handy when you want to run multiple sites using a single Django project. To install the sitemap framework, you will need to activate both the sites and the sitemap applications in your project.

Edit the settings.py file of your project and add django.contrib.sites and django.contrib.sitemaps to the INSTALLED_APPS setting. Also, define a new setting for the site ID, as follows:

```
SITE_ID = 1

# Application definition
INSTALLED_APPS = [
    # ...
    'django.contrib.sites',
    'django.contrib.sitemaps',
]
```

Now run the following command to create the tables of the Django site application in the database:

```
python manage.py migrate
```

You should see an output that contains the following lines:

```
Applying sites.0001_initial... OK
Applying sites.0002_alter_domain_unique... OK
```

The sites application is now synced with the database.

Next, create a new file inside your blog application directory and name it sitemaps.py. Open the file and add the following code to it:

```
from django.contrib.sitemaps import Sitemap
```

```
from .models import Post

class PostSitemap(Sitemap):
    changefreq = 'weekly'
    priority = 0.9

    def items(self):
        return Post.published.all()

    def lastmod(self, obj):
        return obj.updated
```

You create a custom sitemap by inheriting the `Sitemap` class of the `sitemaps` module. The `changefreq` and `priority` attributes indicate the change frequency of your post pages and their relevance in your website (the maximum value is 1).

The `items()` method returns the QuerySet of objects to include in this sitemap. By default, Django calls the `get_absolute_url()` method on each object to retrieve its URL. Remember that you created this method in *Chapter 1, Building a Blog Application*, to retrieve the canonical URL for posts. If you want to specify the URL for each object, you can add a `location` method to your sitemap class.

The `lastmod` method receives each object returned by `items()` and returns the last time the object was modified.

Both the `changefreq` and `priority` attributes can be either methods or attributes. You can take a look at the complete sitemap reference in the official Django documentation located at `https://docs.djangoproject.com/en/3.0/ref/contrib/sitemaps/`.

Finally, you just need to add your sitemap URL. Edit the main `urls.py` file of your project and add the sitemap, as follows:

```
from django.urls import path, include
from django.contrib import admin
from django.contrib.sitemaps.views import sitemap
from blog.sitemaps import PostSitemap

sitemaps = {
    'posts': PostSitemap,
}

urlpatterns = [
    path('admin/', admin.site.urls),
    path('blog/', include('blog.urls', namespace='blog')),
    path('sitemap.xml', sitemap, {'sitemaps': sitemaps},
        name='django.contrib.sitemaps.views.sitemap')
]
```

In the preceding code, you include the required imports and define a dictionary of sitemaps. You define a URL pattern that matches `sitemap.xml` and uses the `sitemap` view. The `sitemaps` dictionary is passed to the `sitemap` view.

Now run the development server and open `http://127.0.0.1:8000/sitemap.xml` in your browser. You will see the following XML output:

```
<?xml version="1.0" encoding="utf-8"?>
<urlset xmlns="http://www.sitemaps.org/schemas/sitemap/0.9">
  <url>
    <loc>http://example.com/blog/2020/1/2/markdown-post/</loc>
    <lastmod>2020-01-02</lastmod>
    <changefreq>weekly</changefreq>
    <priority>0.9</priority>
  </url>
  <url>
    <loc>
http://example.com/blog/2020/1/1/who-was-django-reinhardt/
</loc>
    <lastmod>2020-01-02</lastmod>
    <changefreq>weekly</changefreq>
    <priority>0.9</priority>
  </url>
</urlset>
```

The URL for each post has been built calling its `get_absolute_url()` method.

The `lastmod` attribute corresponds to the post `updated` date field, as you specified in your sitemap, and the `changefreq` and `priority` attributes are also taken from the `PostSitemap` class.

You can see that the domain used to build the URLs is `example.com`. This domain comes from a `Site` object stored in the database. This default object was created when you synced the site's framework with your database.

Open `http://127.0.0.1:8000/admin/sites/site/` in your browser. You should see something like this:

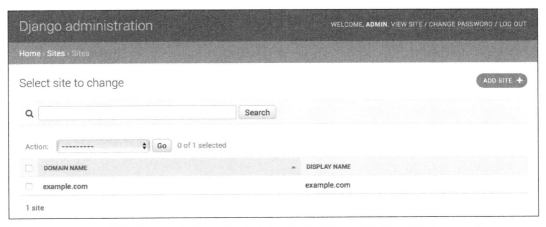

Figure 3.5: The Django administration list view for the Site model of the site's framework

The preceding screenshot contains the list display administration view for the site's framework. Here, you can set the domain or host to be used by the site's framework and the applications that depend on it. In order to generate URLs that exist in your local environment, change the domain name to `localhost:8000`, as shown in the following screenshot, and save it:

Figure 3.6: The Django administration edit view for the Site model of the site's framework

The URLs displayed in your feed will now be built using this hostname. In a production environment, you will have to use your own domain name for the site's framework.

Creating feeds for your blog posts

Django has a built-in syndication feed framework that you can use to dynamically generate RSS or Atom feeds in a similar manner to creating sitemaps using the site's framework. A web feed is a data format (usually XML) that provides users with the most recently updated content. Users will be able to subscribe to your feed using a feed aggregator (software that is used to read feeds and get new content notifications).

Create a new file in your `blog` application directory and name it `feeds.py`. Add the following lines to it:

```python
from django.contrib.syndication.views import Feed
from django.template.defaultfilters import truncatewords
from django.urls import reverse_lazy
from .models import Post


class LatestPostsFeed(Feed):
    title = 'My blog'
    link = reverse_lazy('blog:post_list')
    description = 'New posts of my blog.'

    def items(self):
        return Post.published.all()[:5]

    def item_title(self, item):
        return item.title

    def item_description(self, item):
        return truncatewords(item.body, 30)
```

First, you subclass the `Feed` class of the syndication framework. The `title`, `link`, and `description` attributes correspond to the `<title>`, `<link>`, and `<description>` RSS elements, respectively.

You use `reverse_lazy()` to generate the URL for the `link` attribute. The `reverse()` method allows you to build URLs by their name and pass optional parameters. You used `reverse()` in *Chapter 1, Building a Blog Application*. The `reverse_lazy()` utility function is a lazily evaluated version of `reverse()`. It allows you to use a URL reversal before the project's URL configuration is loaded.

The `items()` method retrieves the objects to be included in the feed. You are retrieving only the last five published posts for this feed. The `item_title()` and `item_description()` methods will receive each object returned by `items()` and return the title and description for each item. You use the `truncatewords` built-in template filter to build the description of the blog post with the first 30 words.

Now edit the `blog/urls.py` file, import the `LatestPostsFeed` you just created, and instantiate the feed in a new URL pattern:

```python
from .feeds import LatestPostsFeed

urlpatterns = [
    # ...
    path('feed/', LatestPostsFeed(), name='post_feed'),
]
```

Navigate to `http://127.0.0.1:8000/blog/feed/` in your browser. You should now see the RSS feed, including the last five blog posts:

```xml
<?xml version="1.0" encoding="utf-8"?>
<rss xmlns:atom="http://www.w3.org/2005/Atom" version="2.0">
  <channel>
    <title>My blog</title>
    <link>http://localhost:8000/blog/</link>
    <description>New posts of my blog.</description>
    <atom:link href="http://localhost:8000/blog/feed/" rel="self"/>
    <language>en-us</language>
    <lastBuildDate>Fri, 2 Jan 2020 09:56:40 +0000</lastBuildDate>
    <item>
      <title>Who was Django Reinhardt?</title>
      <link>http://localhost:8000/blog/2020/1/2/who-was-django-
      reinhardt/</link>
      <description>Who was Django Reinhardt.</description>
      <guid>http://localhost:8000/blog/2020/1/2/who-was-django-
      reinhardt/</guid>
    </item>
    ...
  </channel>
</rss>
```

If you open the same URL in an RSS client, you will be able to see your feed with a user-friendly interface.

The final step is to add a feed subscription link to the blog's sidebar. Open the `blog/base.html` template and add the following line under the number of total posts inside the sidebar `div`:

```html
<p>
  <a href="{% url "blog:post_feed" %}">Subscribe to my RSS feed</a>
</p>
```

Now open `http://127.0.0.1:8000/blog/` in your browser and take a look at the sidebar. The new link should take you to your blog's feed:

My blog

This is my blog. I've written 5 posts so far.

Subscribe to my RSS feed

Figure 3.7: The RSS feed subscription link added to the sidebar

You can read more about the Django syndication feed framework at `https://docs.djangoproject.com/en/3.0/ref/contrib/syndication/`.

Adding full-text search to your blog

Next, you will add search capabilities to your blog. Searching for data in the database with user input is a common task for web applications. The Django ORM allows you to perform simple matching operations using, for example, the `contains` filter (or its case-insensitive version, `icontains`). You can use the following query to find posts that contain the word `framework` in their body:

```
from blog.models import Post
Post.objects.filter(body__contains='framework')
```

However, if you want to perform complex search lookups, retrieving results by similarity, or by weighting terms based on how frequently they appear in the text or by how important different fields are (for example, relevancy of the term appearing in the title versus in the body), you will need to use a full-text search engine. When you consider large blocks of text, building queries with operations on a string of characters is not enough. Full-text search examines the actual words against stored content as it tries to match search criteria.

Django provides a powerful search functionality built on top of PostgreSQL's full-text search features. The `django.contrib.postgres` module provides functionalities offered by PostgreSQL that are not shared by the other databases that Django supports. You can learn about PostgreSQL full-text search at `https://www.postgresql.org/docs/12/static/textsearch.html`.

Although Django is a database-agnostic web framework, it provides a module that supports part of the rich feature set offered by PostgreSQL, which is not offered by other databases that Django supports.

Installing PostgreSQL

You are currently using SQLite for your `blog` project. This is sufficient for development purposes. However, for a production environment, you will need a more powerful database, such as PostgreSQL, MariaDB, MySQL, or Oracle. You will change your database to PostgreSQL to benefit from its full-text search features.

If you are using Linux, install PostgreSQL with the following command:

```
sudo apt-get install postgresql postgresql-contrib
```

If you are using macOS or Windows, download PostgreSQL from https://www.postgresql.org/download/ and install it.

You also need to install the `psycopg2` PostgreSQL adapter for Python. Run the following command in the shell to install it:

```
pip install psycopg2-binary==2.8.4
```

Let's create a user for your PostgreSQL database. Open the shell and run the following commands:

```
su postgres
createuser -dP blog
```

You will be prompted for a password for the new user. Enter the desired password and then create the `blog` database and give ownership to the `blog` user you just created with the following command:

```
createdb -E utf8 -U blog blog
```

Then, edit the `settings.py` file of your project and modify the `DATABASES` setting to make it look as follows:

```
DATABASES = {
    'default': {
        'ENGINE': 'django.db.backends.postgresql',
        'NAME': 'blog',
        'USER': 'blog',
        'PASSWORD': '*****',
    }
```

```
    }
```

Replace the preceding data with the database name and credentials for the user
you created. The new database is empty. Run the following command to apply
all database migrations:

```
python manage.py migrate
```

Finally, create a superuser with the following command:

```
python manage.py createsuperuser
```

You can now run the development server and access the administration site
at http://127.0.0.1:8000/admin/ with the new superuser.

Since you switched the database, there are no posts stored in it. Populate your new
database with a couple of sample blog posts so that you can perform searches against
the database.

Simple search lookups

Edit the settings.py file of your project and add django.contrib.postgres to the
INSTALLED_APPS setting, as follows:

```
INSTALLED_APPS = [
    # ...
    'django.contrib.postgres',
]
```

Now you can search against a single field using the search QuerySet lookup,
like this:

```
from blog.models import Post
Post.objects.filter(body__search='django')
```

This query uses PostgreSQL to create a search vector for the body field and a search
query from the term django. Results are obtained by matching the query with the
vector.

Searching against multiple fields

You might want to search against multiple fields. In this case, you will need to define
a SearchVector object. Let's build a vector that allows you to search against the
title and body fields of the Post model:

```
from django.contrib.postgres.search import SearchVector
from blog.models import Post

Post.objects.annotate(
    search=SearchVector('title', 'body'),
).filter(search='django')
```

Using `annotate` and defining `SearchVector` with both fields, you provide a functionality to match the query against both the title and body of the posts.

 Full-text search is an intensive process. If you are searching for more than a few hundred rows, you should define a functional index that matches the search vector you are using. Django provides a `SearchVectorField` field for your models. You can read more about this at `https://docs.djangoproject.com/en/3.0/ref/contrib/postgres/search/#performance`.

Building a search view

Now, you will create a custom view to allow your users to search posts. First, you will need a search form. Edit the `forms.py` file of the `blog` application and add the following form:

```
class SearchForm(forms.Form):
    query = forms.CharField()
```

You will use the `query` field to let users introduce search terms. Edit the `views.py` file of the `blog` application and add the following code to it:

```
from django.contrib.postgres.search import SearchVector
from .forms import EmailPostForm, CommentForm, SearchForm

def post_search(request):
    form = SearchForm()
    query = None
    results = []
    if 'query' in request.GET:
        form = SearchForm(request.GET)
        if form.is_valid():
            query = form.cleaned_data['query']
            results = Post.published.annotate(
                search=SearchVector('title', 'body'),
            ).filter(search=query)
    return render(request,
```

```
                            'blog/post/search.html',
                            {'form': form,
                             'query': query,
                             'results': results})
```

In the preceding view, first, you instantiate the `SearchForm` form. To check whether the form is submitted, you look for the `query` parameter in the `request.GET` dictionary. You send the form using the GET method instead of POST, so that the resulting URL includes the `query` parameter and is easy to share. When the form is submitted, you instantiate it with the submitted GET data, and verify that the form data is valid. If the form is valid, you search for published posts with a custom `SearchVector` instance built with the `title` and `body` fields.

The search view is ready now. You need to create a template to display the form and the results when the user performs a search. Create a new file inside the `blog/post/` template directory, name it `search.html`, and add the following code to it:

```
{% extends "blog/base.html" %}
{% load blog_tags %}

{% block title %}Search{% endblock %}

{% block content %}
  {% if query %}
    <h1>Posts containing "{{ query }}"</h1>
    <h3>
      {% with results.count as total_results %}
        Found {{ total_results }} result{{ total_results|pluralize }}
      {% endwith %}
    </h3>
    {% for post in results %}
      <h4><a href="{{ post.get_absolute_url }}">{{ post.title }}</a></h4>
      {{ post.body|markdown|truncatewords_html:5 }}
    {% empty %}
      <p>There are no results for your query.</p>
    {% endfor %}
    <p><a href="{% url "blog:post_search" %}">Search again</a></p>
  {% else %}
    <h1>Search for posts</h1>
    <form method="get">
      {{ form.as_p }}
      <input type="submit" value="Search">
    </form>
  {% endif %}
{% endblock %}
```

As in the search view, you can distinguish whether the form has been submitted by the presence of the `query` parameter. Before the query is submitted, you display the form and a submit button. After the post is submitted, you display the query performed, the total number of results, and the list of posts returned.

Finally, edit the `urls.py` file of your `blog` application and add the following URL pattern:

```
path('search/', views.post_search, name='post_search'),
```

Next, open `http://127.0.0.1:8000/blog/search/` in your browser. You should see the following search form:

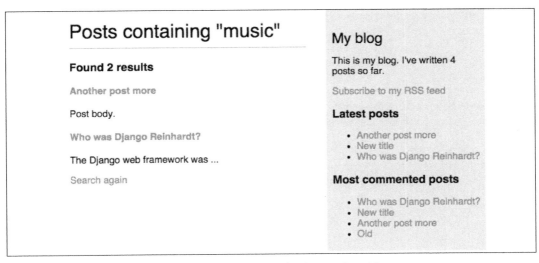

Figure 3.8: The form with the query field to search for posts

Enter a query and click on the **SEARCH** button. You will see the results of the search query, as follows:

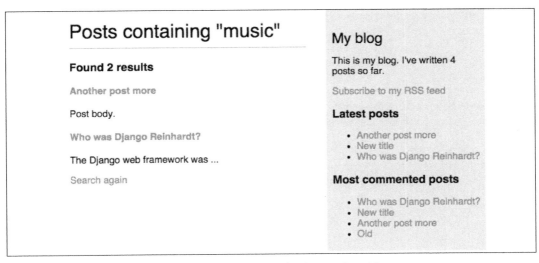

Figure 3.9: Search results for the term "music"

Congratulations! You have created a basic search engine for your blog.

Stemming and ranking results

Stemming is the process of reducing words to their word stem, base, or root form. Stemming is used by search engines to reduce indexed words to their stem, and to be able to match inflected or derived words. For example, "music" and "musician" can be considered similar words by a search engine.

Django provides a `SearchQuery` class to translate terms into a search query object. By default, the terms are passed through stemming algorithms, which helps you to obtain better matches. You also want to order results by relevancy. PostgreSQL provides a ranking function that orders results based on how often the query terms appear and how close together they are.

Edit the `views.py` file of your `blog` application and add the following imports:

```
from django.contrib.postgres.search import SearchVector, SearchQuery,
SearchRank
```

Then, take a look at the following lines:

```
results = Post.published.annotate(
            search=SearchVector('title', 'body'),
        ).filter(search=query)
```

Replace them with the following ones:

```
search_vector = SearchVector('title', 'body')
search_query = SearchQuery(query)
results = Post.published.annotate(
            search=search_vector,
            rank=SearchRank(search_vector, search_query)
        ).filter(search=search_query).order_by('-rank')
```

In the preceding code, you create a `SearchQuery` object, filter results by it, and use `SearchRank` to order the results by relevancy.

You can open `http://127.0.0.1:8000/blog/search/` in your browser and test different searches to test stemming and ranking. The following is an example of ranking by the number of occurrences for the word `django` in the title and body of the posts:

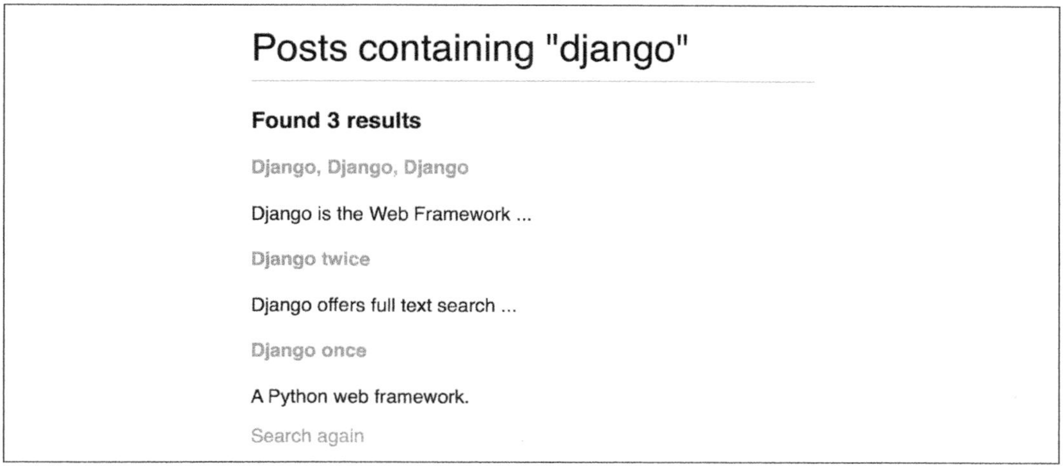

Figure 3.10: Search results for the term "django"

Weighting queries

You can boost specific vectors so that more weight is attributed to them when ordering results by relevancy. For example, you can use this to give more relevance to posts that are matched by title rather than by content.

Edit the previous lines of the `views.py` file of your `blog` application and make them look like this:

```python
search_vector = SearchVector('title', weight='A') + \
                SearchVector('body', weight='B')
search_query = SearchQuery(query)
results = Post.published.annotate(
 rank=SearchRank(search_vector, search_query)
 ).filter(rank__gte=0.3).order_by('-rank')
```

In the preceding code, you apply different weights to the search vectors built using the `title` and `body` fields. The default weights are D, C, B, and A, and they refer to the numbers `0.1`, `0.2`, `0.4`, and `1.0`, respectively. You apply a weight of `1.0` to the `title` search vector and a weight of `0.4` to the `body` vector. Title matches will prevail over body content matches. You filter the results to display only the ones with a rank higher than `0.3`.

Searching with trigram similarity

Another search approach is trigram similarity. A trigram is a group of three consecutive characters. You can measure the similarity of two strings by counting the number of trigrams that they share. This approach turns out to be very effective for measuring the similarity of words in many languages.

In order to use trigrams in PostgreSQL, you will need to install the `pg_trgm` extension first. Execute the following command from the shell to connect to your database:

psql blog

Then, execute the following command to install the `pg_trgm` extension:

CREATE EXTENSION pg_trgm;

Let's edit your view and modify it to search for trigrams. Edit the `views.py` file of your `blog` application and add the following import:

```
from django.contrib.postgres.search import TrigramSimilarity
```

Then, replace the `Post` search query with the following lines:

```
results = Post.published.annotate(
    similarity=TrigramSimilarity('title', query),
).filter(similarity__gt=0.1).order_by('-similarity')
```

Open `http://127.0.0.1:8000/blog/search/` in your browser and test different searches for trigrams. The following example displays a hypothetical typo in the `django` term, showing search results for `yango`:

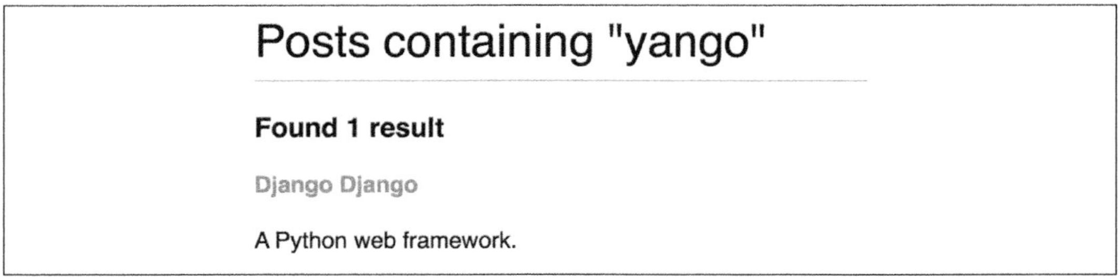

Posts containing "yango"

Found 1 result

Django Django

A Python web framework.

Figure 3.11: Search results for the term "yango"

Now you have a powerful search engine built into your project. You can find more information about full-text search at `https://docs.djangoproject.com/en/3.0/ref/contrib/postgres/search/`.

Other full-text search engines

You may want to use a full-text search engine other than from PostgreSQL. If you want to use Solr or Elasticsearch, you can integrate them into your Django project using Haystack. Haystack is a Django application that works as an abstraction layer for multiple search engines. It offers a simple search API that is very similar to Django QuerySets. You can find more information about Haystack at `https://django-haystack.readthedocs.io/en/master/`.

Summary

In this chapter, you learned how to create custom Django template tags and filters to provide templates with a custom functionality. You also created a sitemap for search engines to crawl your site and an RSS feed for users to subscribe to your blog. You then built a search engine for your blog using the full-text search engine of PostgreSQL.

In the next chapter, you will learn how to build a social website using the Django authentication framework, create custom user profiles, and build social authentication.

Building a Social Website

In the preceding chapter, you learned how to create sitemaps and feeds, and you built a search engine for your blog application. In this chapter, you will discover how to develop a social application, which means that users are able to join an online platform and interact with each other by sharing content. Over the next few chapters, we will focus on building an image sharing platform. Users will be able to bookmark any image on the Internet and share it with others. They will also be able to see activity on the platform from the users they follow and like/unlike the images shared by them.

In this chapter, we will start by creating a functionality for users to log in, log out, edit their password, and reset their password. You will learn how to create a custom profile for your users and you will add social authentication to your site.

This chapter will cover the following topics:

- Using the Django authentication framework
- Creating user registration views
- Extending the user model with a custom profile model
- Adding social authentication with Python Social Auth

Let's start by creating your new project.

Creating a social website project

You are going to create a social application that will allow users to share images that they find on the Internet. You will need to build the following elements for this project:

- An authentication system for users to register, log in, edit their profile, and change or reset their password
- A follow system to allow users to follow each other on the website
- A functionality to display shared images and implement a bookmarklet for users to share images from any website
- An activity stream that allows users to see the content uploaded by the people that they follow

This chapter will address the first point on the list.

Starting your social website project

Open the terminal and use the following commands to create a virtual environment for your project and activate it:

```
mkdir env
python3 -m venv env/bookmarks
source env/bookmarks/bin/activate
```

The shell prompt will display your active virtual environment, as follows:

```
(bookmarks)laptop:~ zenx$
```

Install Django in your virtual environment with the following command:

```
pip install "Django==3.0.*"
```

Run the following command to create a new project:

```
django-admin startproject bookmarks
```

The initial project structure has been created. Use the following commands to get into your project directory and create a new application named `account`:

```
cd bookmarks/
django-admin startapp account
```

Remember that you should add the new application to your project by adding the application's name to the INSTALLED_APPS setting in the settings.py file. Place it in the INSTALLED_APPS list before any of the other installed apps:

```
INSTALLED_APPS = [
    'account.apps.AccountConfig',
    # ...
]
```

You will define Django authentication templates later on. By placing your application first in the INSTALLED_APPS setting, you ensure that your authentication templates will be used by default instead of any other authentication templates contained in other applications. Django looks for templates by order of application appearance in the INSTALLED_APPS setting.

Run the next command to sync the database with the models of the default applications included in the INSTALLED_APPS setting:

```
python manage.py migrate
```

You will see that all initial Django database migrations get applied. Next, you will build an authentication system into your project using the Django authentication framework.

Using the Django authentication framework

Django comes with a built-in authentication framework that can handle user authentication, sessions, permissions, and user groups. The authentication system includes views for common user actions such as log in, log out, password change, and password reset.

The authentication framework is located at django.contrib.auth and is used by other Django contrib packages. Remember that you already used the authentication framework in *Chapter 1, Building a Blog Application*, to create a superuser for your blog application to access the administration site.

When you create a new Django project using the startproject command, the authentication framework is included in the default settings of your project. It consists of the django.contrib.auth application and the following two middleware classes found in the MIDDLEWARE setting of your project:

- AuthenticationMiddleware: Associates users with requests using sessions
- SessionMiddleware: Handles the current session across requests

Middleware are classes with methods that are globally executed during the request or response phase. You will use middleware classes on several occasions throughout this book, and you will learn how to create custom middleware in *Chapter 14, Going Live*.

The authentication framework also includes the following models:

- `User`: A user model with basic fields; the main fields of this model are `username`, `password`, `email`, `first_name`, `last_name`, and `is_active`
- `Group`: A group model to categorize users
- `Permission`: Flags for users or groups to perform certain actions

The framework also includes default authentication views and forms, which you will use later.

Creating a login view

We will start this section by using the Django authentication framework to allow users to log in to your website. Your view should perform the following actions to log in a user:

- Get the username and password that is posted by the user using a login form
- Authenticate the user against the data stored in the database
- Check whether the user is active
- Log the user into the website and start an authenticated session

First, you will create a login form. Create a new `forms.py` file in your `account` application directory and add the following lines to it:

```
from django import forms

class LoginForm(forms.Form):
    username = forms.CharField()
    password = forms.CharField(widget=forms.PasswordInput)
```

This form will be used to authenticate users against the database. Note that you use the `PasswordInput` widget to render the `password` HTML element. This will include `type="password"` in the HTML so that the browser treats it as a password input.

Edit the `views.py` file of your `account` application and add the following code to it:

```
from django.http import HttpResponse
from django.shortcuts import render
from django.contrib.auth import authenticate, login
from .forms import LoginForm
```

```
def user_login(request):
    if request.method == 'POST':
        form = LoginForm(request.POST)
        if form.is_valid():
            cd = form.cleaned_data
            user = authenticate(request,
                                username=cd['username'],
                                password=cd['password'])
            if user is not None:
                if user.is_active:
                    login(request, user)
                    return HttpResponse('Authenticated '\
                                        'successfully')
                else:
                    return HttpResponse('Disabled account')
            else:
                return HttpResponse('Invalid login')
    else:
        form = LoginForm()
    return render(request, 'account/login.html', {'form': form})
```

This is what the basic login view does: when the `user_login` view is called with a GET request, you instantiate a new login form with `form = LoginForm()` to display it in the template. When the user submits the form via POST, you perform the following actions:

- Instantiate the form with the submitted data with `form = LoginForm(request.POST)`.

- Check whether the form is valid with `form.is_valid()`. If it is not valid, you display the form errors in your template (for example, if the user didn't fill in one of the fields).

- If the submitted data is valid, you authenticate the user against the database using the `authenticate()` method. This method takes the `request` object, the `username`, and the `password` parameters and returns the `User` object if the user has been successfully authenticated, or `None` otherwise. If the user has not been authenticated, you return a raw `HttpResponse`, displaying the **Invalid login** message.

- If the user was successfully authenticated, you check whether the user is active by accessing the `is_active` attribute. This is an attribute of Django's user model. If the user is not active, you return an `HttpResponse` that displays the **Disabled account** message.

- If the user is active, you log the user into the website. You set the user in the session by calling the `login()` method and return the **Authenticated successfully** message.

Note the difference between `authenticate` and `login`: `authenticate()` checks user credentials and returns a `User` object if they are correct; `login()` sets the user in the current session.

Now you will need to create a URL pattern for this view. Create a new `urls.py` file in your `account` application directory and add the following code to it:

```python
from django.urls import path
from . import views

urlpatterns = [
    # post views
    path('login/', views.user_login, name='login'),
]
```

Edit the main `urls.py` file located in your `bookmarks` project directory, import `include`, and add the URL patterns of the `account` application, as follows:

```python
from django.urls import path, include
from django.contrib import admin

urlpatterns = [
    path('admin/', admin.site.urls),
    path('account/', include('account.urls')),
]
```

The login view can now be accessed by a URL. It is time to create a template for this view. Since you don't have any templates for this project, you can start by creating a base template that can be extended by the login template. Create the following files and directories inside the `account` application directory:

```
templates/
    account/
        login.html
    base.html
```

Edit the `base.html` template and add the following code to it:

```html
{% load static %}
<!DOCTYPE html>
<html>
<head>
  <title>{% block title %}{% endblock %}</title>
  <link href="{% static "css/base.css" %}" rel="stylesheet">
```

```
    </head>
    <body>
      <div id="header">
        <span class="logo">Bookmarks</span>
      </div>
      <div id="content">
        {% block content %}
        {% endblock %}
      </div>
    </body>
    </html>
```

This will be the base template for the website. As you did in your previous project, include the CSS styles in the main template. You can find these static files in the code that comes along with this chapter. Copy the `static/` directory of the `account` application from the chapter's source code to the same location in your project so that you can use the static files. You can find the directory's contents at `https://github.com/PacktPublishing/Django-3-by-Example/tree/master/Chapter04/bookmarks/account/static`.

The base template defines a `title` block and a `content` block that can be filled with content by the templates that extend from it.

Let's fill in the template for your login form. Open the `account/login.html` template and add the following code to it:

```
{% extends "base.html" %}

{% block title %}Log-in{% endblock %}

{% block content %}
  <h1>Log-in</h1>
  <p>Please, use the following form to log-in:</p>
  <form method="post">
    {{ form.as_p }}
    {% csrf_token %}
    <p><input type="submit" value="Log in"></p>
  </form>
{% endblock %}
```

This template includes the form that is instantiated in the view. Since your form will be submitted via POST, you will include the `{% csrf_token %}` template tag for **cross-site request forgery (CSRF)** protection. You learned about CSRF protection in *Chapter 2, Enhancing Your Blog with Advanced Features*.

There are no users in your database, yet. You will need to create a superuser first in order to be able to access the administration site to manage other users. Open the command line and execute `python manage.py createsuperuser`. Fill in the desired username, email, and password. Then, run the development server using the `python manage.py runserver` command and open `http://127.0.0.1:8000/admin/` in your browser. Access the administration site using the credentials of the user you just created. You will see the Django administration site, including the `User` and `Group` models of the Django authentication framework.

It will look as follows:

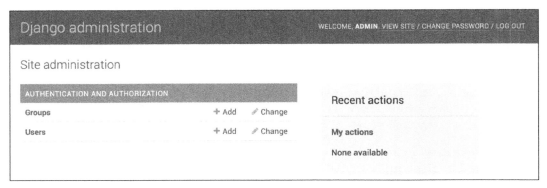

Figure 4.1: The Django administration site index page including Users and Groups

Create a new user using the administration site and open `http://127.0.0.1:8000/account/login/` in your browser. You should see the rendered template, including the login form:

Figure 4.2: The user login page

Now, submit the form, leaving one of the fields empty. In this case, you will see that the form is not valid and displays errors, as follows:

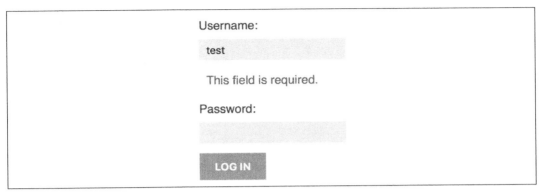

Figure 4.3: The login form with field errors

Note that some modern browsers will prevent you from submitting the form with empty or erroneous fields. This is because of form validation done by the browser based on field types and restrictions per field. In this case, the form won't be submitted and the browser will display an error message for the fields that are wrong.

If you enter a non-existent user or a wrong password, you will get an **Invalid login** message.

If you enter valid credentials, you will get an **Authenticated successfully** message, like this:

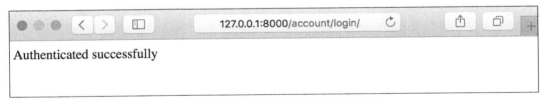

Figure 4.4: The successful authentication plain text response

Using Django authentication views

Django includes several forms and views in the authentication framework that you can use right away. The login view you have created is a good exercise to understand the process of user authentication in Django. However, you can use the default Django authentication views in most cases.

Django provides the following class-based views to deal with authentication. All of them are located in `django.contrib.auth.views`:

- `LoginView`: Handles a login form and logs in a user
- `LogoutView`: Logs out a user

Django provides the following views to handle password changes:

- `PasswordChangeView`: Handles a form to change the user's password
- `PasswordChangeDoneView`: The success view that the user is redirected to after a successful password change

Django also includes the following views to enable users to reset their password:

- `PasswordResetView`: Allows users to reset their password. It generates a one-time-use link with a token and sends it to a user's email account.
- `PasswordResetDoneView`: Tells users that an email—including a link to reset their password—has been sent to them.
- `PasswordResetConfirmView`: Allows users to set a new password.
- `PasswordResetCompleteView`: The success view that the user is redirected to after successfully resetting their password.

The views listed in the preceding lists can save you a lot of time when creating a website with user accounts. The views use default values that you can override, such as the location of the template to be rendered, or the form to be used by the view.

You can get more information about the built-in authentication views at https://docs.djangoproject.com/en/3.0/topics/auth/default/#all-authentication-views.

Login and logout views

Edit the `urls.py` file of your account application, like this:

```
from django.urls import path
from django.contrib.auth import views as auth_views
from . import views

urlpatterns = [
    # previous login view
    # path('login/', views.user_login, name='login'),
    path('login/', auth_views.LoginView.as_view(), name='login'),
    path('logout/', auth_views.LogoutView.as_view(), name='logout'),
]
```

In the preceding code, you comment out the URL pattern for the user_login view that you created previously to use the LoginView view of Django's authentication framework. You also add a URL pattern for the LogoutView view.

Create a new directory inside the templates directory of your account application and name it registration. This is the default path where the Django authentication views expect your authentication templates to be.

The django.contrib.admin module includes some of the authentication templates that are used for the administration site. You have placed the account application at the top of the INSTALLED_APPS setting so that Django uses your templates by default instead of any authentication templates defined in other applications.

Create a new file inside the templates/registration directory, name it login. html, and add the following code to it:

```
{% extends "base.html" %}

{% block title %}Log-in{% endblock %}

{% block content %}
  <h1>Log-in</h1>
  {% if form.errors %}
    <p>
      Your username and password didn't match.
      Please try again.
    </p>
  {% else %}
    <p>Please, use the following form to log-in:</p>
  {% endif %}
  <div class="login-form">
    <form action="{% url 'login' %}" method="post">
      {{ form.as_p }}
      {% csrf_token %}
      <input type="hidden" name="next" value="{{ next }}" />
      <p><input type="submit" value="Log-in"></p>
    </form>
  </div>
{% endblock %}
```

This login template is quite similar to the one you created before. Django uses the AuthenticationForm form located at django.contrib.auth.forms by default. This form tries to authenticate the user and raises a validation error if the login was unsuccessful. In this case, you can look for errors using {% if form.errors %} in the template to check whether the credentials provided are wrong.

Note that you have added a hidden HTML <input> element to submit the value of a variable called next. This variable is first set by the login view when you pass a next parameter in the request (for example, http://127.0.0.1:8000/account/login/?next=/account/).

The next parameter has to be a URL. If this parameter is given, the Django login view will redirect the user to the given URL after a successful login.

Now, create a logged_out.html template inside the registration template directory and make it look like this:

```
{% extends "base.html" %}

{% block title %}Logged out{% endblock %}

{% block content %}
  <h1>Logged out</h1>
  <p>
    You have been successfully logged out.
    You can <a href="{% url "login" %}">log-in again</a>.
  </p>
{% endblock %}
```

This is the template that Django will display after the user logs out.

After adding the URL patterns and the templates for login and logout views, your website is now ready for users to log in using Django authentication views.

Now, you will create a new view to display a dashboard when users log in to their account. Open the views.py file of your account application and add the following code to it:

```
from django.contrib.auth.decorators import login_required

@login_required
def dashboard(request):
    return render(request,
                  'account/dashboard.html',
                  {'section': 'dashboard'})
```

You decorate your view with the login_required decorator of the authentication framework. The login_required decorator checks whether the current user is authenticated. If the user is authenticated, it executes the decorated view; if the user is not authenticated, it redirects the user to the login URL with the originally requested URL as a GET parameter named next.

By doing this, the login view redirects users to the URL that they were trying to access after they successfully log in. Remember that you added a hidden input in the form of your login template for this purpose.

You can also define a `section` variable. You will use this variable to track the site's section that the user is browsing. Multiple views may correspond to the same section. This is a simple way to define the section that each view corresponds to.

Next, you will need to create a template for the dashboard view. Create a new file inside the `templates/account/` directory and name it `dashboard.html`. Make it look like this:

```
{% extends "base.html" %}

{% block title %}Dashboard{% endblock %}

{% block content %}
  <h1>Dashboard</h1>
  <p>Welcome to your dashboard.</p>
{% endblock %}
```

Then, add the following URL pattern for this view in the `urls.py` file of the `account` application:

```
urlpatterns = [
    # ...
    path('', views.dashboard, name='dashboard'),
]
```

Edit the `settings.py` file of your project and add the following code to it:

```
LOGIN_REDIRECT_URL = 'dashboard'
LOGIN_URL = 'login'
LOGOUT_URL = 'logout'
```

The settings defined in the preceding code are as follows:

- `LOGIN_REDIRECT_URL`: Tells Django which URL to redirect the user to after a successful login if no `next` parameter is present in the request
- `LOGIN_URL`: The URL to redirect the user to log in (for example, views using the `login_required` decorator)
- `LOGOUT_URL`: The URL to redirect the user to log out

You are using the names of the URL patterns that you previously defined using the `name` attribute of the `path()` function. Hardcoded URLs instead of URL names can also be used for these settings.

Let's summarize what you have done so far:

- You have added the built-in Django authentication log in and log out views to your project
- You have created custom templates for both views and defined a simple dashboard view to redirect users after they log in
- Finally, you have configured your settings for Django to use these URLs by default

Now, you will add log in and log out links to your base template to put everything together. In order to do this, you have to determine whether the current user is logged in or not in order to display the appropriate link for each case. The current user is set in the HttpRequest object by the authentication middleware. You can access it with request.user. You will find a User object in the request even if the user is not authenticated. A non-authenticated user is set in the request as an instance of AnonymousUser. The best way to check whether the current user is authenticated is by accessing the read-only attribute is_authenticated.

Edit your base.html template and modify the <div> element with a header ID, like this:

```
<div id="header">
  <span class="logo">Bookmarks</span>
  {% if request.user.is_authenticated %}
    <ul class="menu">
      <li {% if section == "dashboard" %}class="selected"{% endif %}>
        <a href="{% url "dashboard" %}">My dashboard</a>
      </li>
      <li {% if section == "images" %}class="selected"{% endif %}>
        <a href="#">Images</a>
      </li>
      <li {% if section == "people" %}class="selected"{% endif %}>
        <a href="#">People</a>
      </li>
    </ul>
  {% endif %}

  <span class="user">
    {% if request.user.is_authenticated %}
      Hello {{ request.user.first_name }},
      <a href="{% url "logout" %}">Logout</a>
    {% else %}
      <a href="{% url "login" %}">Log-in</a>
    {% endif %}
  </span>
</div>
```

As you can see in the preceding code, you only display the site's menu to authenticated users. You also check the current section to add a `selected` class attribute to the corresponding `<li>` item in order to highlight the current section in the menu using CSS. You display the user's first name and a link to log out if the user is authenticated, or a link to log in otherwise.

Now, open `http://127.0.0.1:8000/account/login/` in your browser. You should see the login page. Enter a valid username and password and click on the **Log-in** button. You should see the following output:

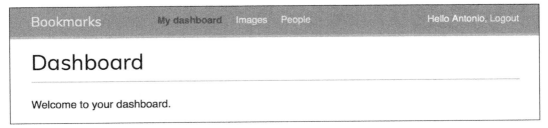

Figure 4.5: The dashboard page

You can see that the **My dashboard** section is highlighted with CSS because it has a `selected` class. Since the user is authenticated, the first name of the user is displayed on the right side of the header. Click on the **Logout** link. You should see the following page:

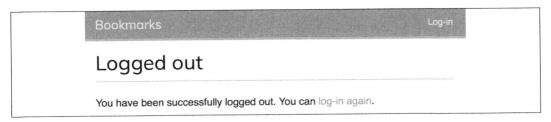

Figure 4.6: The logged out page

In the page from the preceding screenshot, you can see that the user is logged out, and, therefore, the menu of the website is not being displayed anymore. Now, the link on the right side of the header shows **Log-in**.

 If you see the logged out page of the Django administration site instead of your own logged out page, check the `INSTALLED_APPS` setting of your project and make sure that `django.contrib.admin` comes after the `account` application. Both templates are located in the same relative path, and the Django template loader will use the first one it finds.

Changing password views

You also need your users to be able to change their password after they log in to your site. You will integrate Django authentication views for a password change.

Open the `urls.py` file of the `account` application and add the following URL patterns to it:

```
# change password urls
path('password_change/',
     auth_views.PasswordChangeView.as_view(),
     name='password_change'),
path('password_change/done/',
     auth_views.PasswordChangeDoneView.as_view(),
     name='password_change_done'),
```

The `PasswordChangeView` view will handle the form to change the password, and the `PasswordChangeDoneView` view will display a success message after the user has successfully changed their password. Let's create a template for each view.

Add a new file inside the `templates/registration/` directory of your `account` application and name it `password_change_form.html`. Add the following code to it:

```
{% extends "base.html" %}

{% block title %}Change your password{% endblock %}

{% block content %}
  <h1>Change your password</h1>
  <p>Use the form below to change your password.</p>
  <form method="post">
    {{ form.as_p }}
    <p><input type="submit" value="Change"></p>
    {% csrf_token %}
  </form>
{% endblock %}
```

The `password_change_form.html` template includes the form to change the password.

Now create another file in the same directory and name it `password_change_done.html`. Add the following code to it:

```
{% extends "base.html" %}

{% block title %}Password changed{% endblock %}

{% block content %}
  <h1>Password changed</h1>
  <p>Your password has been successfully changed.</p>
{% endblock %}
```

The `password_change_done.html` template only contains the success message to be displayed when the user has successfully changed their password.

Open `http://127.0.0.1:8000/account/password_change/` in your browser. If you are not logged in, the browser will redirect you to the login page. After you are successfully authenticated, you will see the following change password page:

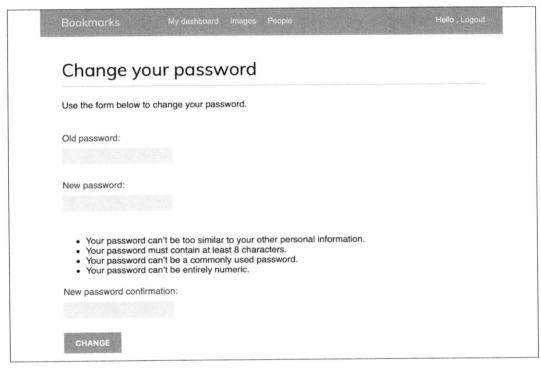

Figure 4.7: The change password form

Fill in the form with your current password and your new password, and click on the **CHANGE** button. You will see the following success page:

Figure 4.8: The successful password change page

Log out and log in again using your new password to verify that everything works as expected.

Resetting password views

Add the following URL patterns for password restoration to the `urls.py` file of the `account` application:

```
# reset password urls
path('password_reset/',
    auth_views.PasswordResetView.as_view(),
    name='password_reset'),
path('password_reset/done/',
    auth_views.PasswordResetDoneView.as_view(),
    name='password_reset_done'),
path('reset/<uidb64>/<token>/',
    auth_views.PasswordResetConfirmView.as_view(),
    name='password_reset_confirm'),
path('reset/done/',
    auth_views.PasswordResetCompleteView.as_view(),
    name='password_reset_complete'),
```

Add a new file in the `templates/registration/` directory of your `account` application and name it `password_reset_form.html`. Add the following code to it:

```
{% extends "base.html" %}

{% block title %}Reset your password{% endblock %}

{% block content %}
  <h1>Forgotten your password?</h1>
  <p>Enter your e-mail address to obtain a new password.</p>
  <form method="post">
    {{ form.as_p }}
    <p><input type="submit" value="Send e-mail"></p>
    {% csrf_token %}
  </form>
{% endblock %}
```

Now create another file in the same directory and name it `password_reset_email. html`. Add the following code to it:

```
Someone asked for password reset for email {{ email }}. Follow the
link below:
{{ protocol }}://{{ domain }}{% url "password_reset_confirm"
uidb64=uid token=token %}
Your username, in case you've forgotten: {{ user.get_username }}
```

The `password_reset_email.html` template will be used to render the email sent to users to reset their password. It includes a reset token that is generated by the view.

Create another file in the same directory and name it `password_reset_done.html`. Add the following code to it:

```
{% extends "base.html" %}

{% block title %}Reset your password{% endblock %}

{% block content %}
  <h1>Reset your password</h1>
  <p>We've emailed you instructions for setting your password.</p>
  <p>If you don't receive an email, please make sure you've entered
the address you registered with.</p>
{% endblock %}
```

Create another template in the same directory and name it `password_reset_confirm.html`. Add the following code to it:

```
{% extends "base.html" %}

{% block title %}Reset your password{% endblock %}

{% block content %}
  <h1>Reset your password</h1>
  {% if validlink %}
    <p>Please enter your new password twice:</p>
    <form method="post">
      {{ form.as_p }}
      {% csrf_token %}
      <p><input type="submit" value="Change my password" /></p>
    </form>
  {% else %}
    <p>The password reset link was invalid, possibly because it has
already been used. Please request a new password reset.</p>
  {% endif %}
{% endblock %}
```

In this template, you check whether the link for resetting the password is valid by checking the `validlink` variable. The view `PasswordResetConfirmView` checks the validity of the token provided in the URL and passes the `validlink` variable to the template. If the link is valid, you display the user password reset form. Users can only set a new password if they have a valid reset password link.

Create another template and name it `password_reset_complete.html`. Enter the following code into it:

```
{% extends "base.html" %}

{% block title %}Password reset{% endblock %}

{% block content %}
  <h1>Password set</h1>
  <p>Your password has been set. You can
<a href="{% url "login" %}">log in now</a></p>
{% endblock %}
```

Finally, edit the `registration/login.html` template of the `account` application, and add the following code after the `<form>` element:

```
<p><a href="{% url "password_reset" %}">Forgotten your password?</a></p>
```

Now, open `http://127.0.0.1:8000/account/login/` in your browser and click on the **Forgotten your password?** link. You should see the following page:

Figure 4.9: The restore password form

At this point, you need to add a **Simple Mail Transfer Protocol (SMTP)** configuration to the `settings.py` file of your project so that Django is able to send emails. You learned how to add email settings to your project in *Chapter 2, Enhancing Your Blog with Advanced Features*. However, during development, you can configure Django to write emails to the standard output instead of sending them through an SMTP server. Django provides an email backend to write emails to the console. Edit the `settings.py` file of your project, and add the following line:

```
EMAIL_BACKEND = 'django.core.mail.backends.console.EmailBackend'
```

The EMAIL_BACKEND setting indicates the class to use to send emails.

Return to your browser, enter the email address of an existing user, and click on the **SEND E-MAIL** button. You should see the following page:

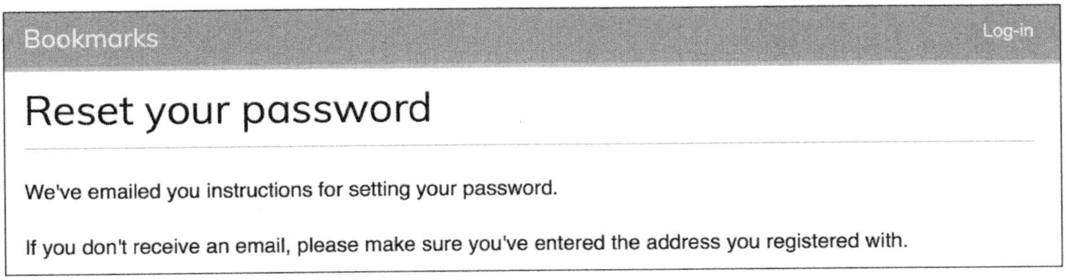

Figure 4.10: The reset password email sent page

Take a look at the console where you are running the development server. You will see the generated email, as follows:

```
Content-Type: text/plain; charset="utf-8"
MIME-Version: 1.0
Content-Transfer-Encoding: 7bit
Subject: Password reset on 127.0.0.1:8000
From: webmaster@localhost
To: user@domain.com
Date: Fri, 3 Jan 2020 14:35:08 -0000
Message-ID: <20150924143508.62996.55653@zenx.local>


Someone asked for password reset for email user@domain.com. Follow the
link below:
http://127.0.0.1:8000/account/reset/MQ/45f-9c3f30caafd523055fcc/
Your username, in case you've forgotten: zenx
```

The email is rendered using the password_reset_email.html template that you created earlier. The URL to reset the password includes a token that was generated dynamically by Django.

Copy the URL and open it in your browser. You should see the following page:

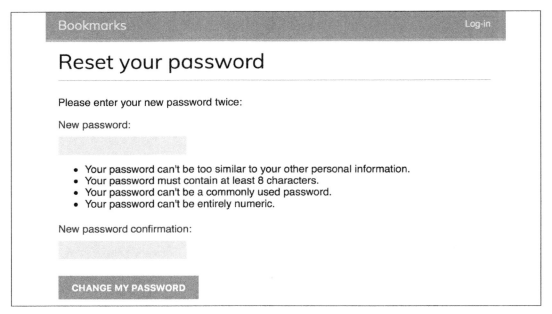

Figure 4.11: The reset password form

The page to set a new password uses the `password_reset_confirm.html` template. Fill in a new password and click on the **CHANGE MY PASSWORD** button. Django creates a new hashed password and saves it in the database. You will see the following success page:

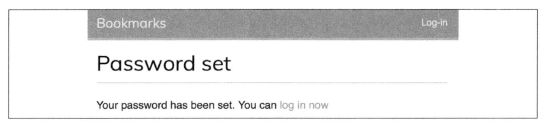

Figure 4.12: The successful password reset page

Now you can log back into your account using your new password.

Each token to set a new password can be used only once. If you open the link you received again, you will get a message stating that the token is invalid.

You have now integrated the views of the Django authentication framework into your project. These views are suitable for most cases. However, you can create your own views if you need a different behavior.

Django also provides the authentication URL patterns that you just created. You can comment out the authentication URL patterns that you added to the `urls.py` file of the `account` application and include `django.contrib.auth.urls` instead, as follows:

```
from django.urls import path, include
# ...

urlpatterns = [
    # ...
    path('', include('django.contrib.auth.urls')),
]
```

You can see the authentication URL patterns included at https://github.com/django/django/blob/stable/3.0.x/django/contrib/auth/urls.py.

User registration and user profiles

Existing users can now log in, log out, change their password, and reset their password. Now, you will need to build a view to allow visitors to create a user account.

User registration

Let's create a simple view to allow user registration on your website. Initially, you have to create a form to let the user enter a username, their real name, and a password.

Edit the `forms.py` file located inside the `account` application directory and add the following code to it:

```
from django.contrib.auth.models import User

class UserRegistrationForm(forms.ModelForm):
    password = forms.CharField(label='Password',
                               widget=forms.PasswordInput)
    password2 = forms.CharField(label='Repeat password',
                                widget=forms.PasswordInput)

    class Meta:
        model = User
        fields = ('username', 'first_name', 'email')

    def clean_password2(self):
```

```
cd = self.cleaned_data
if cd['password'] != cd['password2']:
    raise forms.ValidationError('Passwords don\'t match.')
return cd['password2']
```

You have created a model form for the user model. In your form, you include only the username, first_name, and email fields of the model. These fields will be validated based on their corresponding model fields. For example, if the user chooses a username that already exists, they will get a validation error because username is a field defined with unique=True.

You have added two additional fields—password and password2—for users to set their password and confirm it. You have defined a clean_password2() method to check the second password against the first one and not let the form validate if the passwords don't match. This check is done when you validate the form by calling its is_valid() method. You can provide a clean_<fieldname>() method to any of your form fields in order to clean the value or raise form validation errors for a specific field. Forms also include a general clean() method to validate the entire form, which is useful to validate fields that depend on each other. In this case, you use the field-specific clean_password2() validation instead of overriding the clean() method of the form. This avoids overriding other field-specific checks that the ModelForm gets from the restrictions set in the model (for example, validating that the username is unique).

Django also provides a UserCreationForm form that you can use, which resides in django.contrib.auth.forms and is very similar to the one you have created.

Edit the views.py file of the account application and add the following code to it:

```
from .forms import LoginForm, UserRegistrationForm


def register(request):
    if request.method == 'POST':
        user_form = UserRegistrationForm(request.POST)
        if user_form.is_valid():
            # Create a new user object but avoid saving it yet
            new_user = user_form.save(commit=False)
            # Set the chosen password
            new_user.set_password(
                user_form.cleaned_data['password'])
            # Save the User object
            new_user.save()
            return render(request,
                          'account/register_done.html',
                          {'new_user': new_user})
```

```
    else:
        user_form = UserRegistrationForm()
    return render(request,
                    'account/register.html',
                    {'user_form': user_form})
```

The view for creating user accounts is quite simple. For security reasons, instead of saving the raw password entered by the user, you use the `set_password()` method of the user model that handles hashing.

Now, edit the `urls.py` file of your `account` application and add the following URL pattern:

```
path('register/', views.register, name='register'),
```

Finally, create a new template in the `account/` template directory, name it `register.html`, and make it look as follows:

```
{% extends "base.html" %}

{% block title %}Create an account{% endblock %}

{% block content %}
  <h1>Create an account</h1>
  <p>Please, sign up using the following form:</p>
  <form method="post">
    {{ user_form.as_p }}
    {% csrf_token %}
    <p><input type="submit" value="Create my account"></p>
  </form>
{% endblock %}
```

Add a template file in the same directory and name it `register_done.html`. Add the following code to it:

```
{% extends "base.html" %}

{% block title %}Welcome{% endblock %}

{% block content %}
  <h1>Welcome {{ new_user.first_name }}!</h1>
  <p>Your account has been successfully created. Now you can <a
href="{% url "login" %}">log in</a>.</p>
{% endblock %}
```

Now open `http://127.0.0.1:8000/account/register/` in your browser. You will see the registration page you have created:

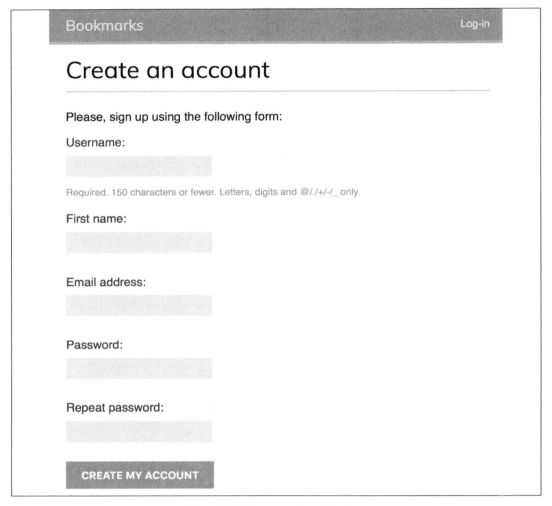

Figure 4.13: The account creation form

Fill in the details for a new user and click on the **CREATE MY ACCOUNT** button. If all fields are valid, the user will be created, and you will get the following success message:

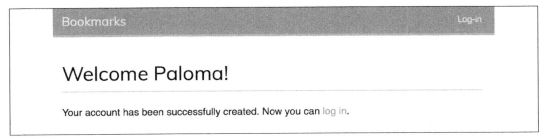

Figure 4.14: The account is successfully created page

Click on the **log in** link and enter your username and password to verify that you can access your account.

You can also add a link to registration in your login template. Edit the `registration/login.html` template and find the following line:

```
<p>Please, use the following form to log-in:</p>
```

Replace it with the following:

```
<p>Please, use the following form to log-in. If you don't have an
account <a href="{% url "register" %}">register here</a></p>
```

You have made the signup page accessible from the login page.

Extending the user model

When you have to deal with user accounts, you will find that the user model of the Django authentication framework is suitable for common cases. However, the user model comes with very basic fields. You may wish to extend it to include additional data. The best way to do this is by creating a profile model that contains all additional fields and a one-to-one relationship with the Django `User` model. A one-to-one relationship is similar to a `ForeignKey` field with the parameter `unique=True`. The reverse side of the relationship is an implicit one-to-one relationship with the related model instead of a manager for multiple elements. From each side of the relationship, you retrieve a single related object.

Edit the `models.py` file of your `account` application and add the following code to it:

```
from django.db import models
from django.conf import settings

class Profile(models.Model):
    user = models.OneToOneField(settings.AUTH_USER_MODEL,
                                on_delete=models.CASCADE)
```

```
date_of_birth = models.DateField(blank=True, null=True)
photo = models.ImageField(upload_to='users/%Y/%m/%d/',
                          blank=True)

def __str__(self):
    return f'Profile for user {self.user.username}'
```

 In order to keep your code generic, use the get_user_model()
method to retrieve the user model and the AUTH_USER_MODEL
setting to refer to it when defining a model's relationship with
the user model, instead of referring to the auth user model
directly. You can read more information about this at https://
docs.djangoproject.com/en/3.0/topics/auth/
customizing/#django.contrib.auth.get_user_model.

The user one-to-one field allows you to associate profiles with users. You use
CASCADE for the on_delete parameter so that its related profile also gets deleted
when a user is deleted. The photo field is an ImageField field. You will need to
install the Pillow library to handle images. Install Pillow by running the following
command in your shell:

pip install Pillow==7.0.0

To enable Django to serve media files uploaded by users with the development
server, add the following settings to the settings.py file of your project:

```
MEDIA_URL = '/media/'
MEDIA_ROOT = os.path.join(BASE_DIR, 'media/')
```

MEDIA_URL is the base URL used to serve the media files uploaded by users, and
MEDIA_ROOT is the local path where they reside. You build the path dynamically
relative to your project path to make your code more generic.

Now, edit the main urls.py file of the bookmarks project and modify the code, as
follows:

```
from django.contrib import admin
from django.urls import path, include
from django.conf import settings
from django.conf.urls.static import static

urlpatterns = [
    path('admin/', admin.site.urls),
    path('account/', include('account.urls')),
]
```

```
if settings.DEBUG:
    urlpatterns += static(settings.MEDIA_URL,
                          document_root=settings.MEDIA_ROOT)
```

In this way, the Django development server will be in charge of serving the media files during development (that is when the DEBUG setting is set to True).

 The static() helper function is suitable for development, but not for production use. Django is very inefficient at serving static files. Never serve your static files with Django in a production environment. You will learn how to serve static files in a production environment in *Chapter 14, Going Live*.

Open the shell and run the following command to create the database migration for the new model:

```
python manage.py makemigrations
```

You will get the following output:

```
Migrations for 'account':
  account/migrations/0001_initial.py
    - Create model Profile
```

Next, sync the database with the following command:

```
python manage.py migrate
```

You will see an output that includes the following line:

```
Applying account.0001_initial... OK
```

Edit the admin.py file of the account application and register the Profile model in the administration site, like this:

```
from django.contrib import admin
from .models import Profile

@admin.register(Profile)
class ProfileAdmin(admin.ModelAdmin):
    list_display = ['user', 'date_of_birth', 'photo']
```

Run the development server using the `python manage.py runserver` command and open `http://127.0.0.1:8000/admin/` in your browser. Now you should be able to see the `Profile` model in the administration site of your project, as follows:

Figure 4.15: The ACCOUNT block of the administration site index page

Next, you will let users edit their profile on the website. Add the following import and model forms to the `forms.py` file of the `account` application:

```
from .models import Profile

class UserEditForm(forms.ModelForm):
    class Meta:
        model = User
        fields = ('first_name', 'last_name', 'email')

class ProfileEditForm(forms.ModelForm):
    class Meta:
        model = Profile
        fields = ('date_of_birth', 'photo')
```

These forms are as follows:

- `UserEditForm`: This will allow users to edit their first name, last name, and email, which are attributes of the built-in Django user model.
- `ProfileEditForm`: This will allow users to edit the profile data that you save in the custom `Profile` model. Users will be able to edit their date of birth and upload a picture for their profile.

Edit the `views.py` file of the `account` application and import the `Profile` model, like this:

```
from .models import Profile
```

Then, add the following lines to the `register` view below `new_user.save()`:

```
# Create the user profile
Profile.objects.create(user=new_user)
```

When users register on your site, you will create an empty profile associated with them. You should create a `Profile` object manually using the administration site for the users that you created before.

Now, you will let users edit their profile. Add the following code to the same file:

```
from .forms import LoginForm, UserRegistrationForm, \
                    UserEditForm, ProfileEditForm


@login_required
def edit(request):
    if request.method == 'POST':
        user_form = UserEditForm(instance=request.user,
                                    data=request.POST)
        profile_form = ProfileEditForm(
                                    instance=request.user.profile,
                                    data=request.POST,
                                    files=request.FILES)
        if user_form.is_valid() and profile_form.is_valid():
            user_form.save()
            profile_form.save()
    else:
        user_form = UserEditForm(instance=request.user)
        profile_form = ProfileEditForm(
                                    instance=request.user.profile)
    return render(request,
                    'account/edit.html',
                    {'user_form': user_form,
                     'profile_form': profile_form})
```

You use the `login_required` decorator because users have to be authenticated to edit their profile. In this case, you are using two model forms: `UserEditForm` to store the data of the built-in user model and `ProfileEditForm` to store the additional profile data in the custom `Profile` model. To validate the submitted data, you execute the `is_valid()` method of both forms. If both forms contain valid data, you save both forms, calling the `save()` method to update the corresponding objects in the database.

Add the following URL pattern to the `urls.py` file of the `account` application:

```
path('edit/', views.edit, name='edit'),
```

Finally, create a template for this view in `templates/account/` and name it `edit.html`. Add the following code to it:

```
{% extends "base.html" %}

{% block title %}Edit your account{% endblock %}
```

```
{% block content %}
  <h1>Edit your account</h1>
  <p>You can edit your account using the following form:</p>
  <form method="post" enctype="multipart/form-data">
    {{ user_form.as_p }}
    {{ profile_form.as_p }}
    {% csrf_token %}
    <p><input type="submit" value="Save changes"></p>
  </form>
{% endblock %}
```

In the preceding code, you include `enctype="multipart/form-data"` in your form to enable file uploads. You use an HTML form to submit both the `user_form` and the `profile_form` forms.

Register a new user from the URL `http://127.0.0.1:8000/account/register/` and open `http://127.0.0.1:8000/account/edit/`. You should see the following page:

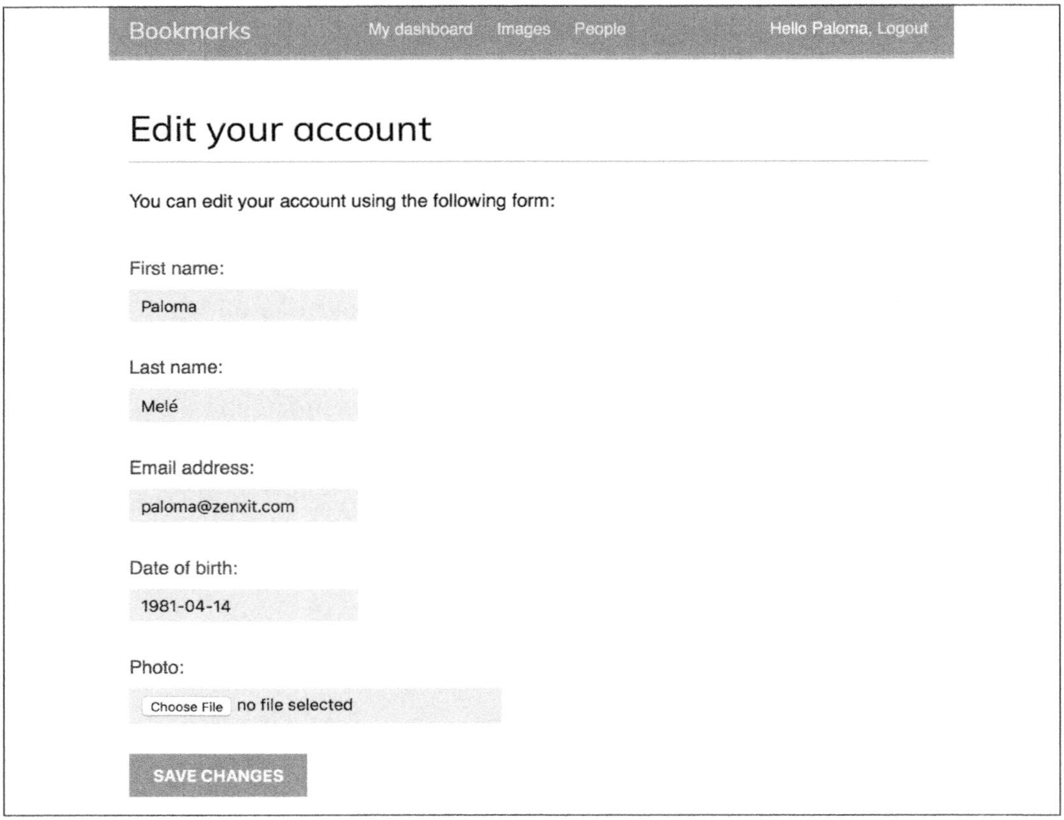

Figure 4.16: The profile edit form

You can also edit the dashboard page and include links to the edit profile and change password pages. Open the `account/dashboard.html` template and find the following line:

```
<p>Welcome to your dashboard.</p>
```

Replace the preceding line with the following one:

```
<p>Welcome to your dashboard. You can <a href="{% url "edit" %}">edit
your profile</a> or <a href="{% url "password_change" %}">change your
password</a>.</p>
```

Users can now access the form to edit their profile from their dashboard. Open `http://127.0.0.1:8000/account/` in your browser and test the new link to edit a user's profile:

Dashboard

Welcome to your dashboard. You can edit your profile or change your password.

Figure 4.17: Dashboard page content, including links to edit a profile and change a password

Using a custom user model

Django also offers a way to substitute the whole user model with your own custom model. Your user class should inherit from Django's `AbstractUser` class, which provides the full implementation of the default user as an abstract model. You can read more about this method at `https://docs.djangoproject.com/en/3.0/topics/auth/customizing/#substituting-a-custom-user-model`.

Using a custom user model will give you more flexibility, but it might also result in more difficult integration with pluggable applications that interact with Django's `auth` user model.

Using the messages framework

When allowing users to interact with your platform, there are many cases where you might want to inform them about the result of their actions. Django has a built-in messages framework that allows you to display one-time notifications to your users.

The messages framework is located at django.contrib.messages and is included in the default INSTALLED_APPS list of the settings.py file when you create new projects using python manage.py startproject. You will note that your settings file contains a middleware named django.contrib.messages.middleware. MessageMiddleware in the MIDDLEWARE settings.

The messages framework provides a simple way to add messages to users. Messages are stored in a cookie by default (falling back to session storage), and they are displayed in the next request from the user. You can use the messages framework in your views by importing the messages module and adding new messages with simple shortcuts, as follows:

```
from django.contrib import messages
messages.error(request, 'Something went wrong')
```

You can create new messages using the add_message() method or any of the following shortcut methods:

- success(): Success messages to be displayed after an action has been successful
- info(): Informational messages
- warning(): Something has not yet failed but may fail imminently
- error(): An action was not successful or something failed
- debug(): Debug messages that will be removed or ignored in a production environment

Let's add messages to your platform. Since the messages framework applies globally to the project, you can display messages for the user in your base template. Open the base.html template of the account application and add the following code between the <div> element with the header ID and the <div> element with the content ID:

```
{% if messages %}
  <ul class="messages">
    {% for message in messages %}
      <li class="{{ message.tags }}">
        {{ message|safe }}
        <a href="#" class="close">x</a>
      </li>
    {% endfor %}
  </ul>
{% endif %}
```

The messages framework includes the context processor `django.contrib.messages.context_processors.messages`, which adds a `messages` variable to the request context. You can find it in the `context_processors` list of the `TEMPLATES` setting of your project. You can use the `messages` variable in your templates to display all existing messages to the user.

 A context processor is a Python function that takes the `request` object as an argument and returns a dictionary that gets added to the request context. You will learn how to create your own context processors in *Chapter 7, Building an Online Shop*.

Let's modify your `edit` view to use the messages framework. Edit the `views.py` file of the `account` application, import `messages`, and make the `edit` view look as follows:

```python
from django.contrib import messages

@login_required
def edit(request):
    if request.method == 'POST':
        # ...
        if user_form.is_valid() and profile_form.is_valid():
            user_form.save()
            profile_form.save()
            messages.success(request, 'Profile updated '\
                                      'successfully')
        else:
            messages.error(request, 'Error updating your profile')
    else:
        user_form = UserEditForm(instance=request.user)
        # ...
```

You add a success message when the user successfully updates their profile. If any of the forms contain invalid data, you add an error message instead.

Open `http://127.0.0.1:8000/account/edit/` in your browser and edit your profile. When the profile is successfully updated, you should see the following message:

Figure 4.18: The successful edit profile message

When data is not valid, for example, if there is an incorrectly formatted date for the **date of birth** field, you should see the following message:

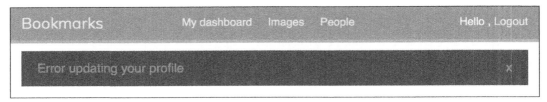

Figure 4.19: The error updating profile message

You can learn more about the messages framework at `https://docs.djangoproject.com/en/3.0/ref/contrib/messages/`.

Building a custom authentication backend

Django allows you to authenticate against different sources. The AUTHENTICATION_ BACKENDS setting includes the list of authentication backends for your project. By default, this setting is set as follows:

```
['django.contrib.auth.backends.ModelBackend']
```

The default `ModelBackend` authenticates users against the database using the user model of `django.contrib.auth`. This will suit most of your projects. However, you can create custom backends to authenticate your user against other sources, such as a **Lightweight Directory Access Protocol (LDAP)** directory or any other system.

You can read more information about customizing authentication at `https://docs.djangoproject.com/en/3.0/topics/auth/customizing/#other-authentication-sources`.

Whenever you use the `authenticate()` function of `django.contrib.auth`, Django tries to authenticate the user against each of the backends defined in `AUTHENTICATION_BACKENDS` one by one, until one of them successfully authenticates the user. Only if all of the backends fail to authenticate will the user not be authenticated into your site.

Django provides a simple way to define your own authentication backends. An authentication backend is a class that provides the following two methods:

- `authenticate()`: It takes the `request` object and user credentials as parameters. It has to return a `user` object that matches those credentials if the credentials are valid, or `None` otherwise. The `request` parameter is an `HttpRequest` object, or `None` if it's not provided to `authenticate()`.
- `get_user()`: This takes a user ID parameter and has to return a `user` object.

Creating a custom authentication backend is as simple as writing a Python class that implements both methods. Let's create an authentication backend to let users authenticate in your site using their email address instead of their username.

Create a new file inside your `account` application directory and name it `authentication.py`. Add the following code to it:

```python
from django.contrib.auth.models import User

class EmailAuthBackend(object):
    """
    Authenticate using an e-mail address.
    """
    def authenticate(self, request, username=None, password=None):
        try:
            user = User.objects.get(email=username)
            if user.check_password(password):
                return user
            return None
        except User.DoesNotExist:
            return None

    def get_user(self, user_id):
        try:
            return User.objects.get(pk=user_id)
        except User.DoesNotExist:
            return None
```

The preceding code is a simple authentication backend. The `authenticate()` method receives a `request` object and the `username` and `password` optional parameters. You could use different parameters, but you use `username` and `password` to make your backend work with the authentication framework views right away. The preceding code works as follows:

- `authenticate()`: You try to retrieve a user with the given email address and check the password using the built-in `check_password()` method of the user model. This method handles the password hashing to compare the given password with the password stored in the database.

- `get_user()`: You get a user through the ID provided in the `user_id` parameter. Django uses the backend that authenticated the user to retrieve the `User` object for the duration of the user session.

Edit the `settings.py` file of your project and add the following setting:

```
AUTHENTICATION_BACKENDS = [
    'django.contrib.auth.backends.ModelBackend',
    'account.authentication.EmailAuthBackend',
]
```

In the preceding setting, you keep the default `ModelBackend` that is used to authenticate with the username and password and include your own email-based authentication backend.

Now open `http://127.0.0.1:8000/account/login/` in your browser. Remember that Django will try to authenticate the user against each of the backends, so now you should be able to log in seamlessly using your username or email account. User credentials will be checked using the `ModelBackend` authentication backend, and if no user is returned, the credentials will be checked using your custom `EmailAuthBackend` backend.

> The order of the backends listed in the `AUTHENTICATION_BACKENDS` setting matters. If the same credentials are valid for multiple backends, Django will stop at the first backend that successfully authenticates the user.

Adding social authentication to your site

You might also want to add social authentication to your site using services such as Facebook, Twitter, or Google. Python Social Auth is a Python module that simplifies the process of adding social authentication to your website. Using this module, you can let your users log in to your website using their accounts from other services.

Social authentication is a widely used feature that makes the authentication process easier for users. You can find the code of this module at `https://github.com/python-social-auth`.

This module comes with authentication backends for different Python frameworks, including Django. To install the Django package via `pip`, open the console and run the following command:

```
pip install social-auth-app-django==3.1.0
```

Then add `social_django` to the `INSTALLED_APPS` setting in the `settings.py` file of your project:

```
INSTALLED_APPS = [
    #...
    'social_django',
]
```

This is the default application to add Python Social Auth to Django projects. Now run the following command to sync Python Social Auth models with your database:

```
python manage.py migrate
```

You should see that the migrations for the default application are applied as follows:

```
Applying social_django.0001_initial... OK
Applying social_django.0002_add_related_name... OK
...
Applying social_django.0008_partial_timestamp... OK
```

Python Social Auth includes backends for multiple services. You can see a list of all backends at `https://python-social-auth.readthedocs.io/en/latest/backends/index.html#supported-backends`.

Let's include authentication backends for Facebook, Twitter, and Google.

You will need to add social login URL patterns to your project. Open the main `urls.py` file of the `bookmarks` project and include the `social_django` URL patterns as follows:

```
urlpatterns = [
    path('admin/', admin.site.urls),
    path('account/', include('account.urls')),
    path('social-auth/',
        include('social_django.urls', namespace='social')),
]
```

Several social services will not allow redirecting users to 127.0.0.1 or localhost after a successful authentication; they expect a domain name. In order to make social authentication work, you will need a domain. To fix this on Linux or macOS, edit your /etc/hosts file and add the following line to it:

```
127.0.0.1 mysite.com
```

This will tell your computer to point the mysite.com hostname to your own machine. If you are using Windows, your hosts file is located at C:\Windows\System32\Drivers\etc\hosts.

To verify that your hostname association worked, start the development server with python manage.py runserver and open http://mysite.com:8000/account/login/ in your browser. You will see the following error:

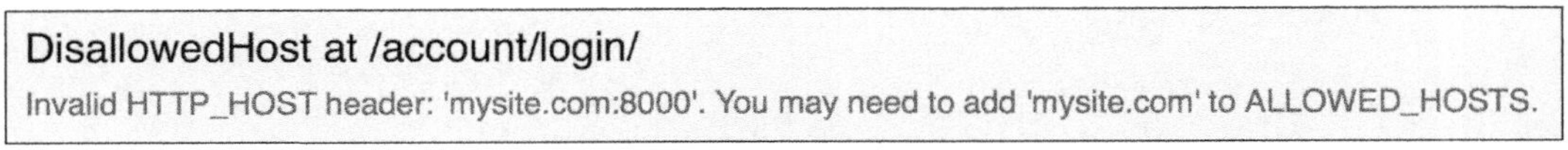

DisallowedHost at /account/login/

Invalid HTTP_HOST header: 'mysite.com:8000'. You may need to add 'mysite.com' to ALLOWED_HOSTS.

Figure 4.20: The invalid host header message

Django controls the hosts that are able to serve your application using the ALLOWED_HOSTS setting. This is a security measure to prevent HTTP host header attacks. Django will only allow the hosts included in this list to serve the application. You can learn more about the ALLOWED_HOSTS setting at https://docs.djangoproject.com/en/3.0/ref/settings/#allowed-hosts.

Edit the settings.py file of your project and edit the ALLOWED_HOSTS setting as follows:

```
ALLOWED_HOSTS = ['mysite.com', 'localhost', '127.0.0.1']
```

Besides the mysite.com host, you explicitly include localhost and 127.0.0.1. This is in order to be able to access the site through localhost, which is the default Django behavior when DEBUG is True and ALLOWED_HOSTS is empty. Now you should be able to open http://mysite.com:8000/account/login/ in your browser.

Running the development server through HTTPS

Some of the social authentication methods you are going to use require an HTTPS connection. The **Transport Layer Security (TLS)** protocol is the standard for serving websites through a secure connection. The TLS predecessor is the **Secure Sockets Layer (SSL)**.

Although SSL is now deprecated, in multiple libraries and online documentation you will find references to both the terms TLS and SSL. The Django development server is not able to serve your site through HTTPS, since that is not its intended use. In order to test the social authentication functionality serving your site through HTTPS, you are going to use the RunServerPlus extension of the package Django Extensions. Django Extensions is a third-party collection of custom extensions for Django. Please note that this is never the method you should use to serve your site in a real environment; this is a development server.

Use the following command to install Django Extensions:

```
pip install django-extensions==2.2.5
```

Now you need to install Werkzeug, which contains a debugger layer required by the RunServerPlus extension. Use the following command to install it:

```
pip install werkzeug==0.16.0
```

Finally, use the following command to install pyOpenSSL, which is required to use the SSL/TLS functionality of RunServerPlus:

```
pip install pyOpenSSL==19.0.0
```

Edit the `settings.py` file of your project and add Django Extensions to the `INSTALLED_APPS` setting, as follows:

```
INSTALLED_APPS = [
    # ...
    'django_extensions',
]
```

Use the management command `runserver_plus` provided by Django Extensions to run the development server, as follows:

```
python manage.py runserver_plus --cert-file cert.crt
```

You provide a file name to the `runserver_plus` command for the SSL/TLS certificate. Django Extensions will generate a key and certificate automatically.

Open `https://mysite.com:8000/account/login/` in your browser. Now you are accessing your site through HTTPS. Your browser might show a security warning because you are using a self-generated certificate. If this is the case, access the advanced information displayed by your browser and accept the self-signed certificate so that your browser trusts the certificate.

You will see that the URL starts with `https://` and a security icon that indicates that the connection is secure.

4.21 The URL with the secured connection icon

You can now serve your site through HTTPS during development in order to test social authentication with Facebook, Twitter, and Google.

Authentication using Facebook

To use Facebook authentication to log in to your site, add the following line to the `AUTHENTICATION_BACKENDS` setting in the `settings.py` file of your project:

```
'social_core.backends.facebook.FacebookOAuth2',
```

You will need a Facebook developer account and you will need to create a new Facebook application. Open `https://developers.facebook.com/apps/` in your browser. After creating a Facebook developer account, you will see a site with the following header:

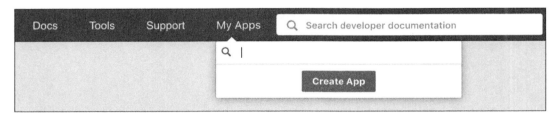

Figure 4.22: The Facebook developer portal menu

Under the menu item **My Apps**, click on the button **Create App**. You will see the following form to create a new application ID:

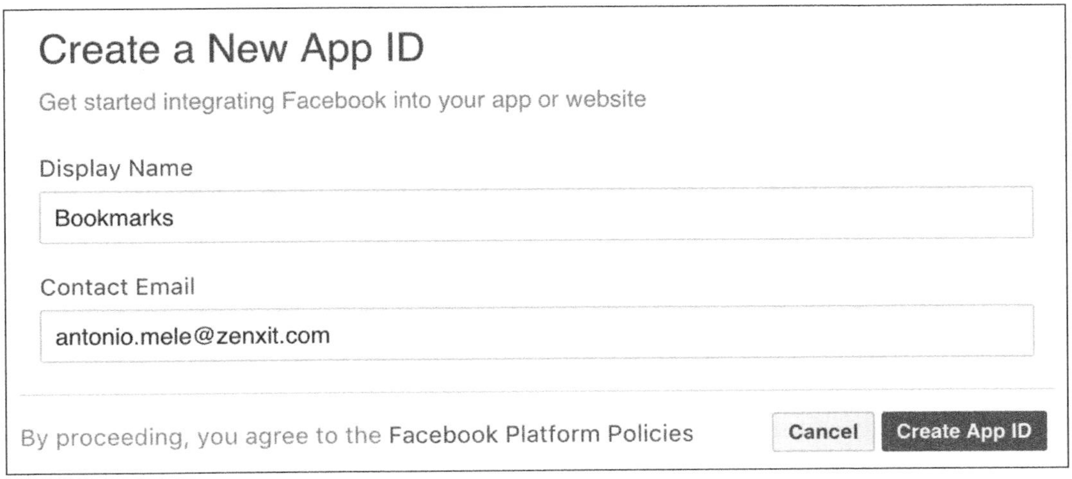

Create a New App ID

Get started integrating Facebook into your app or website

Display Name

Bookmarks

Contact Email

antonio.mele@zenxit.com

By proceeding, you agree to the Facebook Platform Policies   Cancel   **Create App ID**

Figure 4.23: The Facebook create app ID form

Enter `Bookmarks` as the **Display Name**, add a contact email address, and click on **Create App ID**. You will see a dashboard for your new application that displays different features you can set up for it. Look for the following **Facebook Login** box and click on **Set Up**:

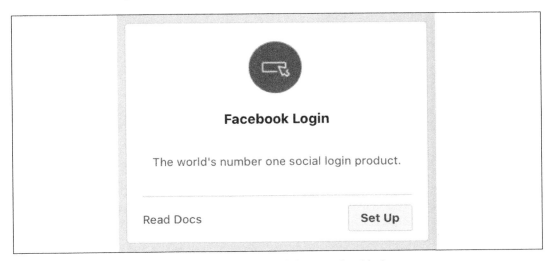

Facebook Login

The world's number one social login product.

Read Docs   Set Up

Figure 4.24: The Facebook login product block

You will be asked to choose the platform, as follows:

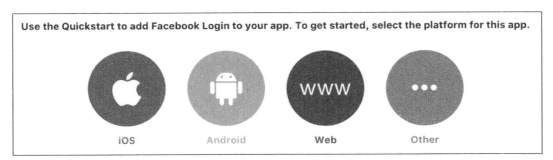

Figure 4.25: Platform selection for Facebook login

Select the **Web** platform. You will see the following form:

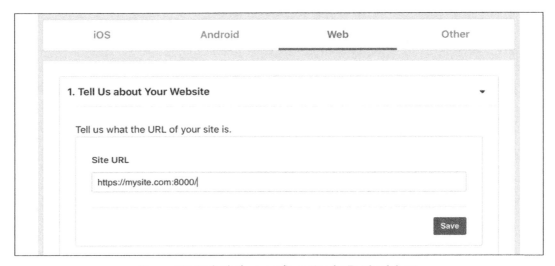

Figure 4.26: Web platform configuration for Facebook login

Enter `http://mysite.com:8000/` as your **Site URL** and click on the **Save** button. You can skip the rest of the quickstart process. In the left-hand menu, click on **Settings** and then on **Basic**. You will see something similar to the following:

Figure 4.27: Application details for the Facebook application

Copy the **App ID** and **App Secret** keys and add them to the `settings.py` file of your project, as follows:

```
SOCIAL_AUTH_FACEBOOK_KEY = 'XXX' # Facebook App ID
SOCIAL_AUTH_FACEBOOK_SECRET = 'XXX' # Facebook App Secret
```

Optionally, you can define a `SOCIAL_AUTH_FACEBOOK_SCOPE` setting with the extra permissions you want to ask Facebook users for:

```
SOCIAL_AUTH_FACEBOOK_SCOPE = ['email']
```

Now, go back to Facebook and click on **Settings**. You will see a form with multiple settings for your application. Add `mysite.com` under **App Domains**, as follows:

Figure 4.28: Allowed domains for the Facebook application

Click on **Save Changes**. Then, in the left-hand menu under **Products**, click on **Facebook Login** and then **Settings**, as shown here:

Figure 4.29: The Facebook login menu

Ensure that only the following settings are active:

- **Client OAuth Login**
- **Web OAuth Login**
- **Enforce HTTPS**
- **Embedded Browser OAuth Login**

Enter `http://mysite.com:8000/social-auth/complete/facebook/` under **Valid OAuth Redirect URIs**. The selection should look like this:

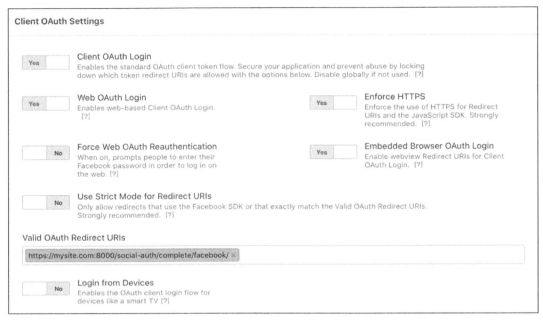

Figure 4.30: Client OAuth settings for Facebook login

Open the `registration/login.html` template of your `account` application and append the following code at the bottom of the `content` block:

```
<div class="social">
  <ul>
    <li class="facebook">
      <a href="{% url "social:begin" "facebook" %}">Sign in with
Facebook</a>
    </li>
  </ul>
</div>
```

Open `https://mysite.com:8000/account/login/` in your browser. Now, the login page will look as follows:

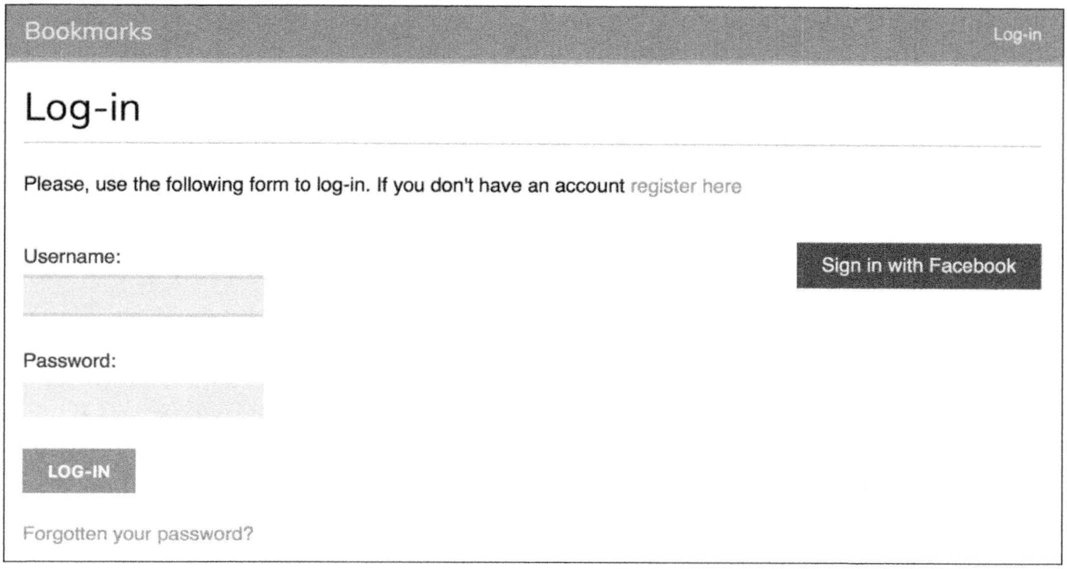

Bookmarks   Log-in

Log-in

Please, use the following form to log-in. If you don't have an account register here

Username:

Sign in with Facebook

Password:

LOG-IN

Forgotten your password?

Figure 4.31: The login page including the button for Facebook authentication

Click on the **Sign in with Facebook** button. You will be redirected to Facebook, and you will see a modal dialog asking for your permission to let the *Bookmarks* application access your public Facebook profile:

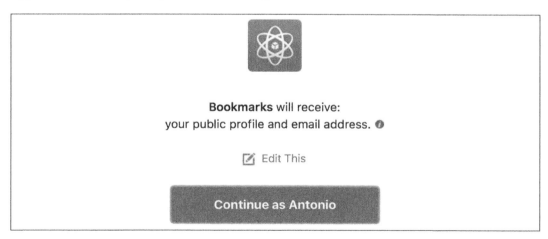

Bookmarks will receive:
your public profile and email address. ❶

✐ Edit This

Continue as Antonio

Figure 4.32: The modal dialog to grant application permissions

Click on the **Continue as** button. You will be logged in and redirected to the dashboard page of your site. Remember that you have set this URL in the `LOGIN_REDIRECT_URL` setting. As you can see, adding social authentication to your site is pretty straightforward.

Authentication using Twitter

For social authentication using Twitter, add the following line to the `AUTHENTICATION_BACKENDS` setting in the `settings.py` file of your project:

```
'social_core.backends.twitter.TwitterOAuth',
```

You will need to create a new application in your Twitter account. Open `https://developer.twitter.com/en/apps/create` in your browser. You will be asked several questions to create a Twitter developer account if you haven't done that yet. Once you have a developer account, when creating a new application, you will see the following form:

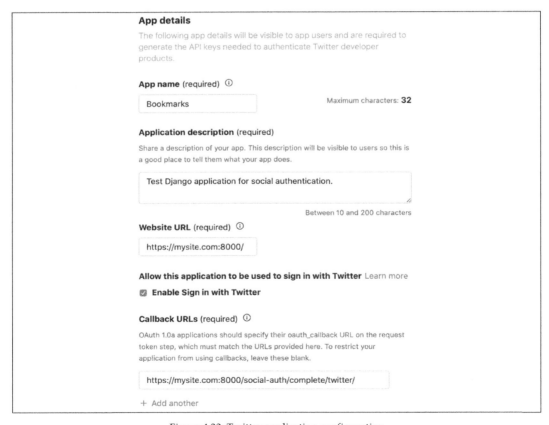

Figure 4.33: Twitter application configuration

Enter the details of your application, including the following settings:

- **Website**: `https://mysite.com:8000/`
- **Callback URL**: `https://mysite.com:8000/social-auth/complete/twitter/`

Make sure that you activate **Enable Sign in with Twitter**. Then, click on **Create**. You will see the application details. Click on the **Keys and tokens** tab. You should see the following information:

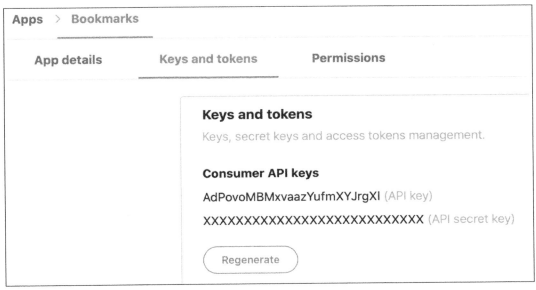

Figure 4.34: Twitter application API keys

Copy the **API key** and **API secret key** into the following settings in the `settings.py` file of your project:

```
SOCIAL_AUTH_TWITTER_KEY = 'XXX' # Twitter API Key
SOCIAL_AUTH_TWITTER_SECRET = 'XXX' # Twitter API Secret
```

Now edit the `registration/login.html` template and add the following code to the `<ul>` element:

```
<li class="twitter">
  <a href="{% url "social:begin" "twitter" %}">Login with Twitter</a>
</li>
```

Open `https://mysite.com:8000/account/login/` in your browser and click on the **Log in with Twitter** link. You will be redirected to Twitter, and it will ask you to authorize the application as follows:

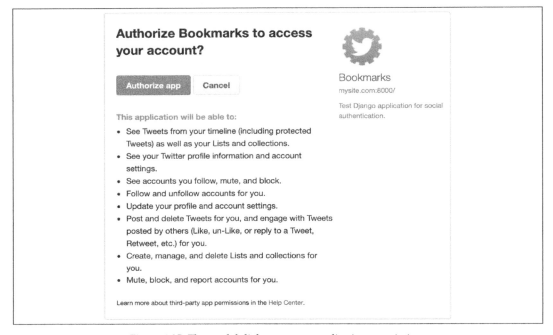

Figure 4.35: The modal dialog to grant application permissions

Click on the **Authorize app** button. You will be logged in and redirected to the dashboard page of your site.

Authentication using Google

Google offers social authentication using OAuth2. You can read about Google's OAuth2 implementation at `https://developers.google.com/identity/protocols/OAuth2`.

To implement authentication using Google, add the following line to the `AUTHENTICATION_BACKENDS` setting in the `settings.py` file of your project:

```
'social_core.backends.google.GoogleOAuth2',
```

First, you will need to create an API key in your Google Developer Console. Open `https://console.developers.google.com/apis/credentials` in your browser. Click on **Select a project** and then on **New project** create a new project, as follows:

Figure 4.36: The Google project creation form

After the project is created, under **Credentials** click on **CREATE CREDENTIALS** and choose **OAuth client ID**, as follows:

Figure 4.37: Google API creation of API credentials

Google will ask you to configure the consent screen first:

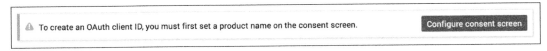

Figure 4.38: The alert to configure the OAuth consent screen

The preceding page is the page that will be shown to users to give their consent to access your site with their Google account. Click on the **Configure consent screen** button. You will be redirected to the following screen:

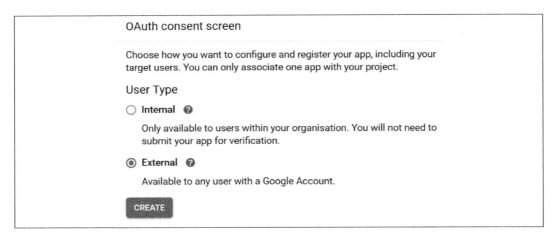

Figure 4.39: User type selection in the Google OAuth consent screen setup

Choose **External** for **User Type** and click on the **CREATE** button. You will see the following screen:

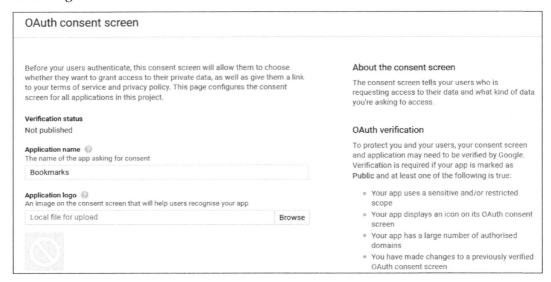

Figure 4.40: Google OAuth consent screen setup

Fill in the form with the following information:

- **Application name**: Enter `Bookmarks`
- **Authorised domains**: Enter `mysite.com`

Click on the **Save** button. The consent screen for your application will be configured and you will see the details of your application consent screen, as follows:

Figure 4.41: Google OAuth consent screen details

In the menu on the left sidebar, click on **Credentials** and click again on **CREATE CREDENTIALS** and then on **OAuth client ID**.

As the next step, enter the following information:

- **Application type**: Select **Web application**
- **Name**: Enter `Bookmarks`
- **Authorised redirect URIs**: Add `https://mysite.com:8000/social-auth/complete/google-oauth2/`

The form should look like this:

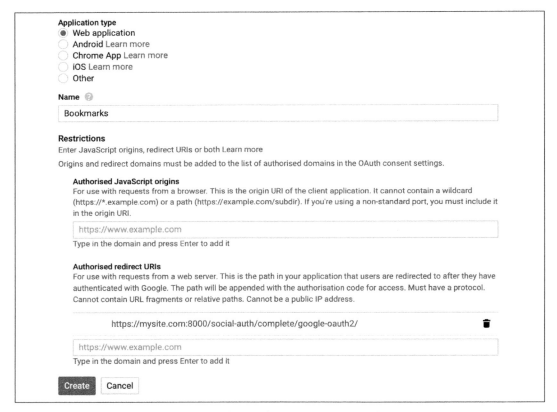

Figure 4.42: The Google application creation form

Click on the **Create** button. You will get the **Client ID** and **Client Secret** keys. Add them to your `settings.py` file, like this:

```
SOCIAL_AUTH_GOOGLE_OAUTH2_KEY = 'XXX' # Google Consumer Key
SOCIAL_AUTH_GOOGLE_OAUTH2_SECRET = 'XXX' # Google Consumer Secret
```

In the left-hand menu of the Google Developers Console, under the **APIs & Services** section, click on the **Library** item. You will see a list that contains all Google APIs.

Click on **Google+ API** and then click on the **ENABLE** button on the following page:

Figure 4.43: The Google+ API block

Edit the `registration/login.html` template and add the following code to the `<ul>` element:

```
<li class="google">
  <a href="{% url "social:begin" "google-oauth2" %}">Login with
Google</a>
</li>
```

Open `https://mysite.com:8000/account/login/` in your browser. The login page should now look as follows:

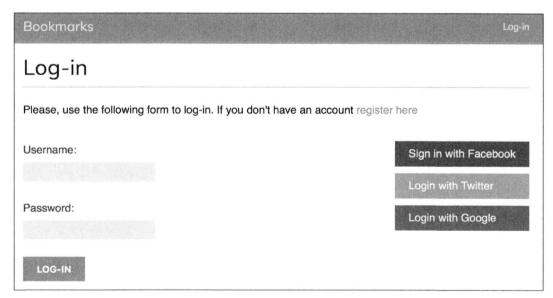

Figure 4.44: The login page including buttons for Twitter and Google authentication

Click on the **Login with Google** button. You will be logged in and redirected to the dashboard page of your website.

You have now added social authentication to your project. You can easily implement social authentication with other popular online services using Python Social Auth.

Summary

In this chapter, you learned how to build an authentication system into your site. You implemented all the necessary views for users to register, log in, log out, edit their password, and reset their password. You built a model for custom user profiles and you created a custom authentication backend to let users log in to your site using their email address. You also added social authentication to your site so that users can use their existing Facebook, Twitter, or Google account to log in.

In the next chapter, you will learn how to create an image bookmarking system, generate image thumbnails, and build AJAX views.

5
Sharing Content on Your Website

In the previous chapter, you built user registration and authentication into your website. You learned how to create a custom profile model for your users and you added social authentication to your site with major social networks.

In this chapter, you will learn how to create a JavaScript bookmarklet to share content from other sites on your website, and you will implement AJAX features into your project using jQuery and Django.

This chapter will cover the following points:

- Creating many-to-many relationships
- Customizing behavior for forms
- Using jQuery with Django
- Building a jQuery bookmarklet
- Generating image thumbnails using `easy-thumbnails`
- Implementing AJAX views and integrating them with jQuery
- Creating custom decorators for views
- Building AJAX pagination

Creating an image bookmarking website

In this chapter, you will learn how to allow users to bookmark and share images that they find on other websites and on your site. For this, you will need to do the following tasks:

1. Define a model to store images and their information
2. Create a form and a view to handle image uploads
3. Build a system for users to be able to post images that they find on external websites

First, create a new application inside your `bookmarks` project directory with the following command:

django-admin startapp images

Add the new application to the INSTALLED_APPS setting in the `settings.py` file, as follows:

```
INSTALLED_APPS = [
    # ...
    'images.apps.ImagesConfig',
]
```

You have activated the `images` application in the project.

Building the image model

Edit the `models.py` file of the `images` application and add the following code to it:

```
from django.db import models
from django.conf import settings

class Image(models.Model):
    user = models.ForeignKey(settings.AUTH_USER_MODEL,
                             related_name='images_created',
                             on_delete=models.CASCADE)
    title = models.CharField(max_length=200)
    slug = models.SlugField(max_length=200,
                            blank=True)
    url = models.URLField()
    image = models.ImageField(upload_to='images/%Y/%m/%d/')
    description = models.TextField(blank=True)
    created = models.DateField(auto_now_add=True,
                               db_index=True)
```

```
def __str__(self):
    return self.title
```

This is the model that you will use to store images retrieved from different sites. Let's take a look at the fields of this model:

- user: This indicates the User object that bookmarked this image. This is a foreign key field because it specifies a one-to-many relationship: a user can post multiple images, but each image is posted by a single user. You use CASCADE for the on_delete parameter so that related images are also deleted when a user is deleted.

- title: A title for the image.

- slug: A short label that contains only letters, numbers, underscores, or hyphens to be used for building beautiful SEO-friendly URLs.

- url: The original URL for this image.

- image: The image file.

- description: An optional description for the image.

- created: The date and time that indicate when the object was created in the database. Since you use auto_now_add, this datetime is automatically set when the object is created. You use db_index=True so that Django creates an index in the database for this field.

 Database indexes improve query performance. Consider setting db_index=True for fields that you frequently query using filter(), exclude(), or order_by(). ForeignKey fields or fields with unique=True imply the creation of an index. You can also use Meta.index_together or Meta.indexes to create indexes for multiple fields. You can learn more about database indexes at https://docs.djangoproject.com/en/3.0/ref/models/options/#django.db.models.Options.indexes.

You will override the save() method of the Image model to automatically generate the slug field based on the value of the title field. Import the slugify() function and add a save() method to the Image model, as follows:

```
from django.utils.text import slugify

class Image(models.Model):
    # ...
    def save(self, *args, **kwargs):
        if not self.slug:
            self.slug = slugify(self.title)
        super().save(*args, **kwargs)
```

In the preceding code, you use the `slugify()` function provided by Django to automatically generate the image slug for the given title when no slug is provided. Then, you save the object. By generating slugs automatically, users don't have to manually enter a slug for each image.

Creating many-to-many relationships

Next, you will add another field to the `Image` model to store the users who like an image. You will need a many-to-many relationship in this case because a user might like multiple images and each image can be liked by multiple users.

Add the following field to the `Image` model:

```
users_like = models.ManyToManyField(settings.AUTH_USER_MODEL,
                                     related_name='images_liked',
                                     blank=True)
```

When you define a `ManyToManyField`, Django creates an intermediary join table using the primary keys of both models. The `ManyToManyField` can be defined in either of the two related models.

As with `ForeignKey` fields, the `related_name` attribute of `ManyToManyField` allows you to name the relationship from the related object back to this one. The `ManyToManyField` fields provide a many-to-many manager that allows you to retrieve related objects, such as `image.users_like.all()`, or get them from a `user` object, such as `user.images_liked.all()`.

You can learn more about many-to-many relationships at `https://docs.djangoproject.com/en/3.0/topics/db/examples/many_to_many/`.

Open the command line and run the following command to create an initial migration:

python manage.py makemigrations images

You should see the following output:

```
Migrations for 'images':
  images/migrations/0001_initial.py
    - Create model Image
```

Now run the following command to apply your migration:

python manage.py migrate images

You will get an output that includes the following line:

```
Applying images.0001_initial... OK
```

The `Image` model is now synced to the database.

Registering the image model in the administration site

Edit the `admin.py` file of the `images` application and register the `Image` model into the administration site, as follows:

```
from django.contrib import admin
from .models import Image

@admin.register(Image)
class ImageAdmin(admin.ModelAdmin):
    list_display = ['title', 'slug', 'image', 'created']
    list_filter = ['created']
```

Start the development server with the following command:

```
python manage.py runserver_plus --cert-file cert.crt
```

Open `https://127.0.0.1:8000/admin/` in your browser, and you will see the `Image` model in the administration site, like this:

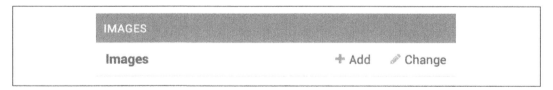

Figure 5.1: The IMAGES block on the Django administration site index page

Posting content from other websites

You will allow users to bookmark images from external websites. The user will provide the URL of the image, a title, and an optional description. Your application will download the image and create a new `Image` object in the database.

Let's start by building a form to submit new images. Create a new `forms.py` file inside the `Images` application directory and add the following code to it:

```
from django import forms
```

```
from .models import Image

class ImageCreateForm(forms.ModelForm):
    class Meta:
        model = Image
        fields = ('title', 'url', 'description')
        widgets = {
            'url': forms.HiddenInput,
        }
```

As you will notice in the preceding code, this form is a `ModelForm` form built from the `Image` model, including only the `title`, `url`, and `description` fields. Users will not enter the image URL directly in the form. Instead, you will provide them with a JavaScript tool to choose an image from an external site, and your form will receive its URL as a parameter. You override the default widget of the `url` field to use a `HiddenInput` widget. This widget is rendered as an HTML `input` element with a `type="hidden"` attribute. You use this widget because you don't want this field to be visible to users.

Cleaning form fields

In order to verify that the provided image URL is valid, you will check that the filename ends with a `.jpg` or `.jpeg` extension to only allow JPEG files. As you saw in the previous chapter, Django allows you to define form methods to clean specific fields using the `clean_<fieldname>()` convention. This method is executed for each field, if present, when you call `is_valid()` on a form instance. In the clean method, you can alter the field's value or raise any validation errors for this specific field when needed. Add the following method to `ImageCreateForm`:

```
def clean_url(self):
    url = self.cleaned_data['url']
    valid_extensions = ['jpg', 'jpeg']
    extension = url.rsplit('.', 1)[1].lower()
    if extension not in valid_extensions:
        raise forms.ValidationError('The given URL does not ' \
                                    'match valid image extensions.')
    return url
```

In the preceding code, you define a `clean_url()` method to clean the `url` field. The code works as follows:

1. You get the value of the `url` field by accessing the `cleaned_data` dictionary of the form instance.

2. You split the URL to get the file extension and check whether it is one of the valid extensions. If the extension is invalid, you raise `ValidationError` and the form instance will not be validated. Here, you are performing a very simple validation. You could use more advanced methods to check whether the given URL provides a valid image file.

In addition to validating the given URL, you also need to download the image file and save it. You could, for example, use the view that handles the form to download the image file. Instead, let's take a more general approach by overriding the `save()` method of your model form to perform this task every time the form is saved.

Overriding the save() method of a ModelForm

As you know, `ModelForm` provides a `save()` method to save the current model instance to the database and return the object. This method receives a Boolean `commit` parameter, which allows you to specify whether the object has to be persisted to the database. If `commit` is `False`, the `save()` method will return a model instance but will not save it to the database. You will override the `save()` method of your form in order to retrieve the given image and save it.

Add the following imports at the top of the `forms.py` file:

```
from urllib import request
from django.core.files.base import ContentFile
from django.utils.text import slugify
```

Then, add the following `save()` method to the `ImageCreateForm` form:

```
def save(self, force_insert=False,
              force_update=False,
              commit=True):
    image = super().save(commit=False)
    image_url = self.cleaned_data['url']
    name = slugify(image.title)
    extension = image_url.rsplit('.', 1)[1].lower()
    image_name = f'{name}.{extension}'

    # download image from the given URL
    response = request.urlopen(image_url)
    image.image.save(image_name,
                     ContentFile(response.read()),
                     save=False)
    if commit:
        image.save()
    return image
```

You override the `save()` method, keeping the parameters required by `ModelForm`. The preceding code can be explained as follows:

1. You create a new `image` instance by calling the `save()` method of the form with `commit=False`.

2. You get the URL from the `cleaned_data` dictionary of the form.

3. You generate the image name by combining the `image` title slug with the original file extension.

4. You use the Python `urllib` module to download the image and then call the `save()` method of the image field, passing it a `ContentFile` object that is instantiated with the downloaded file content. In this way, you save the file to the media directory of your project. You pass the `save=False` parameter to avoid saving the object to the database yet.

5. In order to maintain the same behavior as the `save()` method you override, you save the form to the database only when the `commit` parameter is `True`.

In order to use the `urllib` to retrieve images from URLs served through HTTPS, you need to install the Certifi Python package. Certifi is a collection of root certificates for validating the trustworthiness of SSL/TLS certificates.

Install `certifi` with the following command:

```
pip install --upgrade certifi
```

You will need a view for handling the form. Edit the `views.py` file of the `images` application and add the following code to it:

```python
from django.shortcuts import render, redirect
from django.contrib.auth.decorators import login_required
from django.contrib import messages
from .forms import ImageCreateForm


@login_required
def image_create(request):
    if request.method == 'POST':
        # form is sent
        form = ImageCreateForm(data=request.POST)
        if form.is_valid():
            # form data is valid
            cd = form.cleaned_data
            new_item = form.save(commit=False)

            # assign current user to the item
            new_item.user = request.user
```

```
                    new_item.save()
                    messages.success(request, 'Image added successfully')

                    # redirect to new created item detail view
                    return redirect(new_item.get_absolute_url())
            else:
                # build form with data provided by the bookmarklet via GET
                form = ImageCreateForm(data=request.GET)

        return render(request,
                      'images/image/create.html',
                      {'section': 'images',
                       'form': form})
```

In the preceding code, you use the login_required decorator for the image_create view to prevent access for unauthenticated users. This is how this view works:

1. You expect initial data via GET in order to create an instance of the form. This data will consist of the url and title attributes of an image from an external website and will be provided via GET by the JavaScript tool that you will create later. For now, you just assume that this data will be there initially.

2. If the form is submitted, you check whether it is valid. If the form data is valid, you create a new Image instance, but prevent the object from being saved to the database yet by passing commit=False to the form's save() method.

3. You assign the current user to the new image object. This is how you can know who uploaded each image.

4. You save the image object to the database.

5. Finally, you create a success message using the Django messaging framework and redirect the user to the canonical URL of the new image. You haven't yet implemented the get_absolute_url() method of the Image model; you will do that later.

Create a new urls.py file inside the images application and add the following code to it:

```
from django.urls import path
from . import views

app_name = 'images'

urlpatterns = [
    path('create/', views.image_create, name='create'),
]
```

Edit the main `urls.py` file of the `bookmarks` project to include the patterns for the `images` application, as follows:

```python
urlpatterns = [
    path('admin/', admin.site.urls),
    path('account/', include('account.urls')),
    path('social-auth/',
        include('social_django.urls', namespace='social')),
    path('images/', include('images.urls', namespace='images')),
]
```

Finally, you need to create a template to render the form. Create the following directory structure inside the `images` application directory:

```
templates/
  images/
    image/
      create.html
```

Edit the new `create.html` template and add the following code to it:

```html
{% extends "base.html" %}

{% block title %}Bookmark an image{% endblock %}

{% block content %}
  <h1>Bookmark an image</h1>
  <img src="{{ request.GET.url }}" class="image-preview">
  <form method="post">
    {{ form.as_p }}
    {% csrf_token %}
    <input type="submit" value="Bookmark it!">
  </form>
{% endblock %}
```

Run the development server with `runserver_plus` and open `https://127.0.0.1:8000/images/create/?title=...&url=...` in your browser, including the `title` and `url` GET parameters, providing an existing JPEG image URL in the latter. For example, you can use the following URL: `https://127.0.0.1:8000/images/create/?title=%20Django%20and%20 Duke&url=https://upload.wikimedia.org/wikipedia/commons/8/85/Django_ Reinhardt_and_Duke_Ellington_%28Gottlieb%29.jpg`.

You will see the form with an image preview, like the following:

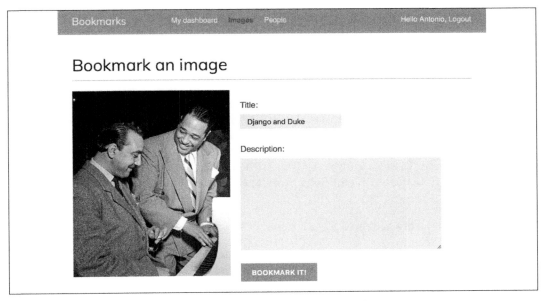

Figure 5.2: The create a new image bookmark page

Add a description and click on the **BOOKMARK IT!** button. A new `Image` object will be saved in your database. However, you will get an error that indicates that the `Image` model has no `get_absolute_url()` method, as follows:

AttributeError at /images/create/

'Image' object has no attribute 'get_absolute_url'

Figure 5.3: An error showing that the Image object has no attribute get_absolute_url

Don't worry about this error for now; you are going to add a `get_absolute_url` method to the `Image` model later.

Open `https://127.0.0.1:8000/admin/images/image/` in your browser and verify that the new `image` object has been saved, like this:

Figure 5.4: The administration site image list page showing the Image object created

Building a bookmarklet with jQuery

A bookmarklet is a bookmark stored in a web browser that contains JavaScript code to extend the browser's functionality. When you click on the bookmark, the JavaScript code is executed on the website being displayed in the browser. This is very useful for building tools that interact with other websites.

Some online services, such as Pinterest, implement their own bookmarklets to let users share content from other sites onto their platform. Let's create a bookmarklet in a similar way for your website, using jQuery to build your bookmarklet. jQuery is a popular JavaScript library that allows you to develop client-side functionality faster. You can read more about jQuery on its official website: https://jquery.com/.

This is how your users will add a bookmarklet to their browser and use it:

1. The user drags a link from your site to their browser's bookmarks. The link contains JavaScript code in its href attribute. This code will be stored in the bookmark.

2. The user navigates to any website and clicks on the bookmark. The JavaScript code of the bookmark is executed.

Since the JavaScript code will be stored as a bookmark, you will not be able to update it later. This is an important drawback that you can solve by implementing a launcher script to load the actual JavaScript bookmarklet from a URL. Your users will save this launcher script as a bookmark, and you will be able to update the code of the bookmarklet at any time. This is the approach that you will take to build your bookmarklet. Let's start!

Create a new template under images/templates/ and name it bookmarklet_ launcher.js. This will be the launcher script. Add the following JavaScript code to this file:

```
(function(){
    if (window.myBookmarklet !== undefined){
        myBookmarklet();
    }
    else {
        document.body.appendChild(document.createElement('script')).
src='https://127.0.0.1:8000/static/js/bookmarklet.js?r='+Math.
floor(Math.random()*9999999999999999999);
    }
})();
```

The preceding script discovers whether the bookmarklet has already been loaded by checking whether the myBookmarklet variable is defined. By doing so, you avoid loading it again if the user clicks on the bookmarklet repeatedly. If myBookmarklet is not defined, you load another JavaScript file by adding a <script> element to the document. The script tag loads the bookmarklet.js script using a random number as a parameter to prevent loading the file from the browser's cache. The actual bookmarklet code resides in the bookmarklet.js static file. This allows you to update your bookmarklet code without requiring your users to update the bookmark they previously added to their browser.

Let's add the bookmarklet launcher to the dashboard pages so that your users can copy it to their bookmarks. Edit the account/dashboard.html template of the account application and make it look like the following:

```
{% extends "base.html" %}

{% block title %}Dashboard{% endblock %}

{% block content %}
  <h1>Dashboard</h1>

  {% with total_images_created=request.user.images_created.count %}
    <p>Welcome to your dashboard. You have bookmarked
{{ total_images_created }} image{{ total_images_created|
pluralize }}.</p>
  {% endwith %}

  <p>Drag the following button to your bookmarks toolbar to bookmark
images from other websites → <a href="javascript:{% include
"bookmarklet_launcher.js" %}" class="button">Bookmark it</a></p>

  <p>You can also <a href="{% url "edit" %}">edit your profile</a>
or <a href="{% url "password_change" %}">change your password</a>.</p>
{% endblock %}
```

Make sure that no template tag is split into multiple lines; Django doesn't support multiple line tags.

The dashboard now displays the total number of images bookmarked by the user. You use the {% with %} template tag to set a variable with the total number of images bookmarked by the current user. You include a link with an href attribute that contains the bookmarklet launcher script. You will include this JavaScript code from the bookmarklet_launcher.js template.

Open `https://127.0.0.1:8000/account/` in your browser. You should see the following page:

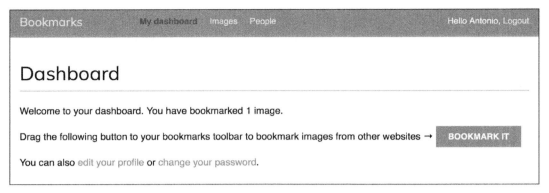

Figure 5.5: The dashboard page, including the total images bookmarked and the button for the bookmarklet

Now create the following directories and files inside the `images` application directory:

```
static/
  js/
    bookmarklet.js
```

You will find a `static/css/` directory under the `images` application directory in the code that comes along with this chapter. Copy the `css/` directory into the `static/` directory of your code. You can find the contents of the directory at `https://github.com/PacktPublishing/Django-3-by-Example/tree/master/Chapter05/bookmarks/images/static`.

The `css/bookmarklet.css` file provides the styles for your JavaScript bookmarklet.

Edit the `bookmarklet.js` static file and add the following JavaScript code to it:

```javascript
(function(){
  var jquery_version = '3.4.1';
  var site_url = 'https://127.0.0.1:8000/';
  var static_url = site_url + 'static/';
  var min_width = 100;
  var min_height = 100;

  function bookmarklet(msg) {
    // Here goes our bookmarklet code
  };

  // Check if jQuery is loaded
```

```
if(typeof window.jQuery != 'undefined') {
  bookmarklet();
} else {
  // Check for conflicts
  var conflict = typeof window.$ != 'undefined';
  // Create the script and point to Google API
  var script = document.createElement('script');
  script.src = '//ajax.googleapis.com/ajax/libs/jquery/' +
    jquery_version + '/jquery.min.js';
  // Add the script to the 'head' for processing
  document.head.appendChild(script);
  // Create a way to wait until script loading
  var attempts = 15;
  (function(){
    // Check again if jQuery is undefined
    if(typeof window.jQuery == 'undefined') {
      if(--attempts > 0) {
        // Calls himself in a few milliseconds
        window.setTimeout(arguments.callee, 250)
      } else {
        // Too much attempts to load, send error
        alert('An error occurred while loading jQuery')
      }
    } else {
      bookmarklet();
    }
  })();
}
})()
```

This is the main jQuery loader script. It takes care of using jQuery if it has already been loaded on the current website. If jQuery is not loaded, the script loads jQuery from Google's **content delivery network (CDN)**, which hosts popular JavaScript frameworks. When jQuery is loaded, it executes the `bookmarklet()` function that will contain your bookmarklet code. Also, set some variables at the top of the file:

- `jquery_version`: The jQuery version to load

- `site_url` and `static_url`: The base URL for your website and the base URL for static files

- `min_width` and `min_height`: The minimum width and height in pixels for the images that your bookmarklet will try to find on the site

Now let's implement the `bookmarklet` function. Edit the `bookmarklet()` function to make it look like this:

```
function bookmarklet(msg) {
   // load CSS
   var css = jQuery('<link>');
   css.attr({
      rel: 'stylesheet',
      type: 'text/css',
      href: static_url + 'css/bookmarklet.css?r=' + Math.floor(Math.
random()*9999999999999999999)
   });
   jQuery('head').append(css);

   // load HTML
   box_html = '<div id="bookmarklet"><a href="#" id="close">&times;</
a><h1>Select an image to bookmark:</h1><div class="images"></div></
div>';
   jQuery('body').append(box_html);

   // close event
   jQuery('#bookmarklet #close').click(function(){
      jQuery('#bookmarklet').remove();
   });
};
```

The preceding code works as follows:

1. You load the `bookmarklet.css` stylesheet using a random number as a parameter to prevent the browser from returning a cached file.

2. You add custom HTML to the document `<body>` element of the current website. This consists of a `<div>` element that will contain the images found on the current website.

3. You add an event that removes your HTML from the document when the user clicks on the close link of your HTML block. You use the `#bookmarklet #close` selector to find the HTML element with an ID named `close`, which has a parent element with an ID named `bookmarklet`. jQuery selectors allow you to find HTML elements. A jQuery selector returns all elements found by the given CSS selector. You can find a list of jQuery selectors at `https://api.jquery.com/category/selectors/`.

After loading the CSS styles and the HTML code for the bookmarklet, you will need to find the images on the website. Add the following JavaScript code at the bottom of the `bookmarklet()` function:

```
// find images and display them
jQuery.each(jQuery('img[src$="jpg"]'), function(index, image) {
  if (jQuery(image).width() >= min_width && jQuery(image).height()
  >= min_height)
  {
    image_url = jQuery(image).attr('src');
    jQuery('#bookmarklet .images').append('<a href="#"><img src="'+
    image_url +'" /></a>');
  }
});
```

The preceding code uses the `img[src$="jpg"]` selector to find all `<img>` HTML elements whose `src` attribute finishes with a `jpg` string. This means that you will search all JPEG images displayed on the current website. You iterate over the results using the `each()` method of jQuery. You add the images with a size larger than the one specified with the `min_width` and `min_height` variables to your `<div class="images">` HTML container.

For security reasons, your browser will prevent you from running the bookmarklet over HTTP on a site served through HTTPS. You will need to be able to load the bookmarklet on any site, including sites secured through HTTPS. To run your development server using an auto-generated SSL/TLS certificate, you will use RunServerPlus from Django Extensions, which you installed in the previous chapter.

Run the RunServerPlus development server with the following command:

`python manage.py runserver_plus --cert-file cert.crt`

Open `https://127.0.0.1:8000/account/` in your browser. Log in with an existing user and then drag the **BOOKMARK IT** button to the bookmarks toolbar of your browser, as follows:

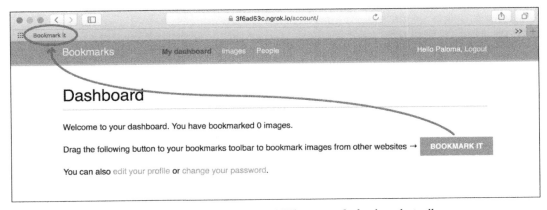

Figure 5.6: Adding the BOOKMARK IT button to the bookmarks toolbar

Open a website of your own choice in your browser and click on your bookmarklet. You will see that a new white box appears on the website, displaying all JPEG images found with dimensions higher than 100×100 pixels. It should look like the following example:

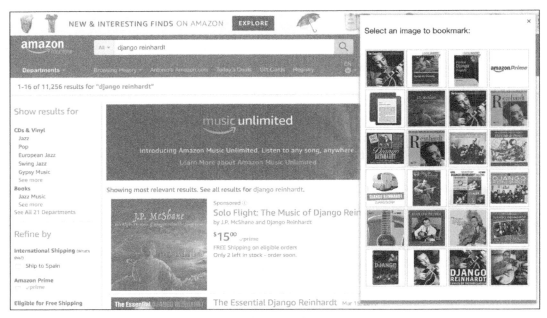

Figure 5.7: The bookmarklet loaded on an external website

The HTML container includes the images that can be bookmarked. You want the user to click on the desired image and bookmark it. Edit the `js/bookmarklet.js` static file and add the following code at the bottom of the `bookmarklet()` function:

```
// when an image is selected open URL with it
jQuery('#bookmarklet .images a').click(function(e){
  selected_image = jQuery(this).children('img').attr('src');
  // hide bookmarklet
  jQuery('#bookmarklet').hide();
  // open new window to submit the image
  window.open(site_url +'images/create/?url='
              + encodeURIComponent(selected_image)
              + '&title='
              + encodeURIComponent(jQuery('title').text()),
              '_blank');
});
```

The preceding code works as follows:

1. You attach a `click()` event to each image's link element.

2. When a user clicks on an image, you set a new variable called `selected_image` that contains the URL of the selected image.

3. You hide the bookmarklet and open a new browser window with the URL for bookmarking a new image on your site. You pass the content of the `<title>` element of the website and the selected image URL as GET parameters.

Open a new URL with your browser and click on your bookmarklet again to display the image selection box. If you click on an image, you will be redirected to the image create page, passing the title of the website and the URL of the selected image as GET parameters:

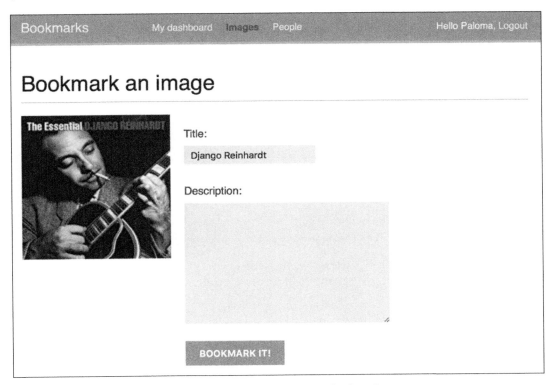

Figure 5.8: Adding a new image bookmark

Congratulations! This is your first JavaScript bookmarklet, and it is fully integrated into your Django project.

Creating a detail view for images

Let's now create a simple detail view to display an image that has been saved into your site. Open the `views.py` file of the `images` application and add the following code to it:

```
from django.shortcuts import get_object_or_404
from .models import Image

def image_detail(request, id, slug):
    image = get_object_or_404(Image, id=id, slug=slug)
    return render(request,
                  'images/image/detail.html',
                  {'section': 'images',
                   'image': image})
```

This is a simple view to display an image. Edit the `urls.py` file of the `images` application and add the following URL pattern:

```
path('detail/<int:id>/<slug:slug>/',
     views.image_detail, name='detail'),
```

Edit the `models.py` file of the `images` application and add the `get_absolute_url()` method to the `Image` model, as follows:

```
from django.urls import reverse

class Image(models.Model):
    # ...
    def get_absolute_url(self):
        return reverse('images:detail', args=[self.id, self.slug])
```

Remember that the common pattern for providing canonical URLs for objects is to define a `get_absolute_url()` method in the model.

Finally, create a template inside the `/images/image/` template directory of the images application and name it `detail.html`. Add the following code to it:

```
{% extends "base.html" %}

{% block title %}{{ image.title }}{% endblock %}

{% block content %}
  <h1>{{ image.title }}</h1>
  <img src="{{ image.image.url }}" class="image-detail">
  {% with total_likes=image.users_like.count %}
    <div class="image-info">
      <div>
        <span class="count">
          {{ total_likes }} like{{ total_likes|pluralize }}
        </span>
      </div>
      {{ image.description|linebreaks }}
    </div>
    <div class="image-likes">
      {% for user in image.users_like.all %}
        <div>
          <img src="{{ user.profile.photo.url }}">
          <p>{{ user.first_name }}</p>
        </div>
      {% empty %}
        Nobody likes this image yet.
      {% endfor %}
    </div>
  {% endwith %}
{% endblock %}
```

This is the template to display the detail view of a bookmarked image. You make use of the `{% with %}` tag to store the result of the QuerySet, counting all user likes in a new variable called `total_likes`. By doing so, you avoid evaluating the same QuerySet twice. You also include the image description and iterate over `image.users_like.all` to display all the users who like this image.

Whenever you need to repeat a query in your template, use the
{% with %} template tag to avoid additional database queries.

Next, bookmark a new image using the bookmarklet. You will be redirected to the image detail page after you post the image. The page will include a success message, as follows:

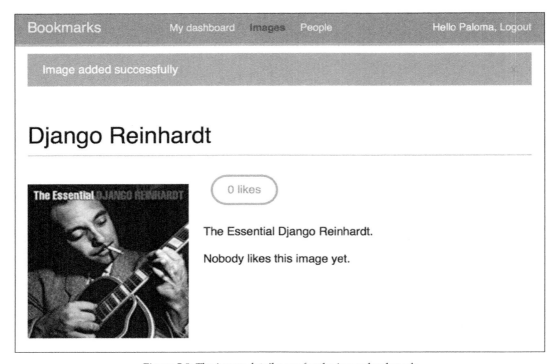

Figure 5.9: The image detail page for the image bookmark

Creating image thumbnails using easy-thumbnails

You are displaying the original image on the detail page, but dimensions for different images may vary considerably. Also, the original files for some images may be huge, and loading them might take too long. The best way to display optimized images in a uniform way is to generate thumbnails. Let's use a Django application called easy-thumbnails for this purpose.

Open the terminal and install `easy-thumbnails` using the following command:

```
pip install easy-thumbnails==2.7
```

Edit the `settings.py` file of the bookmarks project and add `easy_thumbnails` to the `INSTALLED_APPS` setting, as follows:

```
INSTALLED_APPS = [
    # ...
    'easy_thumbnails',
]
```

Then, run the following command to sync the application with your database:

```
python manage.py migrate
```

You should see an output that includes the following lines:

```
Applying easy_thumbnails.0001_initial... OK
Applying easy_thumbnails.0002_thumbnaildimensions... OK
```

The `easy-thumbnails` application offers you different ways to define image thumbnails. The application provides a `{% thumbnail %}` template tag to generate thumbnails in templates and a custom `ImageField` if you want to define thumbnails in your models. Let's use the template tag approach. Edit the `images/image/detail.html` template and consider the following line:

```
<img src="{{ image.image.url }}" class="image-detail">
```

The following lines should replace the preceding one:

```
{% load thumbnail %}
<a href="{{ image.image.url }}">
  <img src="{% thumbnail image.image 300x0 %}" class="image-detail">
</a>
```

You define a thumbnail with a fixed width of `300` pixels and a flexible height to maintain the aspect ratio by using the value `0`. The first time a user loads this page, a thumbnail image is created. The thumbnail is stored in the same directory of the original file. The location is defined by the `MEDIA_ROOT` setting and the `upload_to` attribute of the `image` field of the `Image` model.

The generated thumbnail is served in the following requests. Start the development server and access the image detail page for an existing image. The thumbnail will be generated and displayed on the site. If you check the URL of the generated image, you will see that the original filename is followed by additional details of the settings used to create the thumbnail; for example, `filename.jpg.300x0_q85.jpg`. `85` is the value for the default JPEG quality used by the library to generate the thumbnail.

You can use a different quality value using the `quality` parameter. To set the highest JPEG quality, you can use the value `100`, like this `{% thumbnail image.image 300x0 quality=100 %}`.

The `easy-thumbnails` application offers several options to customize your thumbnails, including cropping algorithms and different effects that can be applied. If you have any difficulty generating thumbnails, you can add `THUMBNAIL_DEBUG = True` to the `settings.py` file in order to obtain debug information. You can read the full documentation of `easy-thumbnails` at `https://easy-thumbnails.readthedocs.io/`.

Adding AJAX actions with jQuery

Now let's add AJAX actions to your application. AJAX comes from Asynchronous JavaScript and XML, encompassing a group of techniques to make asynchronous HTTP requests. It consists of sending and retrieving data from the server asynchronously, without reloading the whole page. Despite the name, XML is not required. You can send or retrieve data in other formats, such as JSON, HTML, or plain text.

You are going to add a link to the image detail page to let users click on it in order to like an image. You will perform this action with an AJAX call to avoid reloading the whole page.

First, create a view for users to like/unlike images. Edit the `views.py` file of the `images` application and add the following code to it:

```
from django.http import JsonResponse
from django.views.decorators.http import require_POST


@login_required
@require_POST
def image_like(request):
    image_id = request.POST.get('id')
    action = request.POST.get('action')
    if image_id and action:
        try:
            image = Image.objects.get(id=image_id)
            if action == 'like':
                image.users_like.add(request.user)
            else:
                image.users_like.remove(request.user)
            return JsonResponse({'status':'ok'})
        except:
```

```
          pass
    return JsonResponse({'status':'error'})
```

You use two decorators for your view. The `login_required` decorator prevents users who are not logged in from accessing this view. The `require_POST` decorator returns an `HttpResponseNotAllowed` object (status code `405`) if the HTTP request is not done via `POST`. This way, you only allow `POST` requests for this view.

Django also provides a `require_GET` decorator to only allow `GET` requests and a `require_http_methods` decorator to which you can pass a list of allowed methods as an argument.

In this view, you use two `POST` parameters:

- `image_id`: The ID of the `image` object on which the user is performing the action
- `action`: The action that the user wants to perform, which you assume to be a string with the value `like` or `unlike`

You use the manager provided by Django for the `users_like` many-to-many field of the `Image` model in order to add or remove objects from the relationship using the `add()` or `remove()` methods. Calling `add()`, that is, passing an object that is already present in the related object set, does not duplicate it. Calling `remove()` and passing an object that is not in the related object set does nothing. Another useful method of many-to-many managers is `clear()`, which removes all objects from the related object set.

Finally, you use the `JsonResponse` class provided by Django, which returns an HTTP response with an `application/json` content type, converting the given object into a JSON output.

Edit the `urls.py` file of the `images` application and add the following URL pattern to it:

```
path('like/', views.image_like, name='like'),
```

Loading jQuery

You will need to add the AJAX functionality to your image detail template. In order to use jQuery in your templates, you will include it in the `base.html` template of your project first. Edit the `base.html` template of the `account` application and include the following code before the closing `</body>` HTML tag:

```html
<script src="https://ajax.googleapis.com/ajax/libs/jquery/3.4.1/
jquery.min.js"></script>
<script>
  $(document).ready(function(){
```

```
        {% block domready %}
        {% endblock %}
    });
</script>
```

You load the jQuery framework from Google's CDN. You can also download jQuery from `https://jquery.com/` and add it to the `static` directory of your application instead.

You add a `<script>` tag to include JavaScript code. `$(document).ready()` is a jQuery function that takes a handler that is executed when the **Document Object Model (DOM)** hierarchy has been fully constructed. The DOM is created by the browser when a web page is loaded, and it is constructed as a tree of objects. By including your code inside this function, you will make sure that all HTML elements that you are going to interact with are loaded in the DOM. Your code will only be executed once the DOM is ready.

Inside the document-ready handler function, you include a Django template block called `domready`, in which templates that extend the base template will be able to include specific JavaScript. Don't get confused by the JavaScript code and Django template tags. The Django template language is rendered on the server side, outputting the final HTML document, and JavaScript is executed on the client side. In some cases, it is useful to generate JavaScript code dynamically using Django, to be able to use the results of QuerySets or server-side calculations to define variables in JavaScript.

The examples in this chapter include JavaScript code in Django templates. The preferred way to include JavaScript code is by loading `.js` files, which are served as static files, especially when they are large scripts.

Cross-site request forgery in AJAX requests

You learned about **cross-site request forgery (CSRF)** in *Chapter 2, Enhancing Your Blog with Advanced Features*. With CSRF protection active, Django checks for a CSRF token in all POST requests. When you submit forms, you can use the `{% csrf_token %}` template tag to send the token along with the form. However, it is a bit inconvenient for AJAX requests to pass the CSRF token as POST data with every POST request. Therefore, Django allows you to set a custom X-CSRFToken header in your AJAX requests with the value of the CSRF token. This enables you to set up jQuery or any other JavaScript library to automatically set the X-CSRFToken header in every request.

In order to include the token in all requests, you need to take the following steps:

1. Retrieve the CSRF token from the `csrftoken` cookie, which is set if CSRF protection is active

2. Send the token in the AJAX request using the X-CSRFToken header

You can find more information about CSRF protection and AJAX at `https://docs.djangoproject.com/en/3.0/ref/csrf/#ajax`.

Edit the last code you included in your `base.html` template and make it look like the following:

```
<script src="https://ajax.googleapis.com/ajax/libs/jquery/3.4.1/
jquery.min.js"></script>
<script src="https://cdn.jsdelivr.net/npm/js-cookie@2.2.1/src/
js.cookie.min.js"></script>
<script>
  var csrftoken = Cookies.get('csrftoken');
  function csrfSafeMethod(method) {
    // these HTTP methods do not require CSRF protection
    return (/^(GET|HEAD|OPTIONS|TRACE)$/.test(method));
  }
  $.ajaxSetup({
    beforeSend: function(xhr, settings) {
      if (!csrfSafeMethod(settings.type) && !this.crossDomain) {
        xhr.setRequestHeader("X-CSRFToken", csrftoken);
      }
    }
  });
  $(document).ready(function(){
    {% block domready %}
    {% endblock %}
  });
</script>
```

The preceding code is as follows:

1. You load the JS Cookie plugin from a public CDN so that you can easily interact with cookies. JS Cookie is a lightweight JavaScript API for handling cookies. You can learn more about it at `https://github.com/js-cookie/js-cookie`.

2. You read the value of the `csrftoken` cookie with `Cookies.get()`.

3. You define the `csrfSafeMethod()` function to check whether an HTTP method is safe. Safe methods don't require CSRF protection—these are GET, HEAD, OPTIONS, and TRACE.

4. You set up jQuery AJAX requests using `$.ajaxSetup()`. Before each AJAX request is performed, you check whether the request method is safe and that the current request is not cross-domain. If the request is unsafe, you set the X-CSRFToken header with the value obtained from the cookie. This setup will apply to all AJAX requests performed with jQuery.

The CSRF token will be included in all AJAX requests that use unsafe HTTP methods, such as POST or PUT.

Performing AJAX requests with jQuery

Edit the `images/image/detail.html` template of the `images` application and consider the following line:

```
{% with total_likes=image.users_like.count %}
```

Replace the preceding line with the following one:

```
{% with total_likes=image.users_like.count users_like=image.users_like.all %}
```

Make sure that the template tag is split into multiple lines.

Replace the line that defines the `for` loop:

```
{% for user in image.users_like.all %}
```

with the following one:

```
{% for user in users_like %}
```

Then, modify the `<div>` element with the `image-info` class, as follows:

```
<div class="image-info">
  <div>
    <span class="count">
      <span class="total">{{ total_likes }}</span>
      like{{ total_likes|pluralize }}
    </span>
    <a href="#" data-id="{{ image.id }}" data-action="{% if
    request.user in users_like %}un{% endif %}like"
    class="like button">
      {% if request.user not in users_like %}
        Like
      {% else %}
        Unlike
      {% endif %}
    </a>
  </div>
  {{ image.description|linebreaks }}
</div>
```

First, you add another variable to the `{% with %}` template tag in order to store the results of the `image.users_like.all` query and avoid executing it twice. You use the variable for the `for` loop that iterates over the users that like this image.

You display the total number of users who like the image and include a link to like/ unlike the image. You check whether the user is in the related object set of `users_ like` to display either *like* or *unlike*, based on the current relationship between the user and this image. You add the following attributes to the `<a>` HTML element:

- `data-id`: The ID of the image displayed.

- `data-action`: The action to run when the user clicks on the link. This can be `like` or `unlike`.

> Any attribute on any HTML element whose attribute name starts with `data-` is a data attribute. Data attributes are used to store custom data for your application.

You will send the value of both attributes in the AJAX request to the `image_like` view. When a user clicks on the `like`/`unlike` link, you will perform the following actions on the client side:

1. Call the AJAX view, passing the image ID and the action parameters to it
2. If the AJAX request is successful, update the `data-action` attribute of the `<a>` HTML element with the opposite action (`like` / `unlike`), and modify its display text accordingly
3. Update the total number of `likes` that is displayed

Add the `domready` block at the bottom of the `images/image/detail.html` template with the following JavaScript code:

```
{% block domready %}
  $('a.like').click(function(e){
    e.preventDefault();
    $.post('{% url "images:like" %}',
      {
        id: $(this).data('id'),
        action: $(this).data('action')
      },
      function(data){
        if (data['status'] == 'ok')
        {
          var previous_action = $('a.like').data('action');

          // toggle data-action
          $('a.like').data('action', previous_action == 'like' ?
          'unlike' : 'like');
```

```
            // toggle link text
            $('a.like').text(previous_action == 'like' ? 'Unlike' :
            'Like');

            // update total likes
            var previous_likes = parseInt($('span.count .total').
text());
            $('span.count .total').text(previous_action == 'like' ?
            previous_likes + 1 : previous_likes - 1);
        }
      }
    );
  });
{% endblock %}
```

The preceding code works as follows:

1. You use the `$('a.like')` jQuery selector to find all `<a>` elements of the HTML document with the `like` class.

2. You define a handler function for the `click` event. This function will be executed every time the user clicks on the `like/unlike` link.

3. Inside the handler function, you use `e.preventDefault()` to avoid the default behavior of the `<a>` element. This will prevent the link from taking you anywhere.

4. You use `$.post()` to perform an asynchronous POST request to the server. jQuery also provides a `$.get()` method to perform GET requests and a low-level `$.ajax()` method.

5. You use Django's `{% url %}` template tag to build the URL for the AJAX request.

6. You build the POST parameters dictionary to send in the request. The parameters are the ID and `action` parameters expected by your Django view. You retrieve these values from the `<a>` element's `data-id` and `data-action` attributes.

7. You define a callback function that is executed when the HTTP response is received; it takes a `data` attribute that contains the content of the response.

8. You access the `status` attribute of the data received and check whether it equals `ok`. If the returned data is as expected, you toggle the `data-action` attribute of the link and its text. This allows the user to undo their action.

9. You increase or decrease the total likes count by one, depending on the action performed.

Open the image detail page in your browser for an image that you have uploaded. You should be able to see the following initial likes count and the **LIKE** button, as follows:

Figure 5.10: The likes count and LIKE button in the image detail template

Click on the **LIKE** button. You will note that the total likes count increases by one and the button text changes to **UNLIKE**, as follows:

Figure 5.11: The likes count and button after clicking the LIKE button

If you click on the **UNLIKE** button, the action is performed, and then the button's text changes back to **LIKE**, and the total count changes accordingly.

When programming JavaScript, especially when performing AJAX requests, it is recommended that you use a tool for debugging JavaScript and HTTP requests. Most modern browsers include developer tools to debug JavaScript. Usually, you can right-click anywhere on the website and click on **Inspect Element** to access the web developer tools.

Creating custom decorators for your views

Let's restrict your AJAX views to allow only requests generated via AJAX. The Django request object provides an `is_ajax()` method that checks whether the request is being made with `XMLHttpRequest`, which means that it is an AJAX request. This value is set in the `HTTP_X_REQUESTED_WITH` HTTP header, which is included in AJAX requests by most JavaScript libraries.

Next, you will create a decorator for checking the `HTTP_X_REQUESTED_WITH` header in your views. A decorator is a function that takes another function and extends the behavior of the latter without explicitly modifying it. If the concept of decorators is foreign to you, you might want to take a look at `https://www.python.org/dev/peps/pep-0318/` before you continue reading.

Since your decorator will be generic and could be applied to any view, you will create a `common` Python package in your project. Create the following directory and files inside the `bookmarks` project directory:

```
common/
    __init__.py
    decorators.py
```

Edit the `decorators.py` file and add the following code to it:

```
from django.http import HttpResponseBadRequest

def ajax_required(f):
    def wrap(request, *args, **kwargs):
        if not request.is_ajax():
            return HttpResponseBadRequest()
        return f(request, *args, **kwargs)
    wrap.__doc__=f.__doc__
    wrap.__name__=f.__name__
    return wrap
```

The preceding code is your custom `ajax_required` decorator. It defines a `wrap` function that returns an `HttpResponseBadRequest` object (HTTP 400 code) if the request is not AJAX. Otherwise, it returns the decorated function.

Now you can edit the `views.py` file of the `images` application and add this decorator to your `image_like` AJAX view, as follows:

```
from common.decorators import ajax_required

@ajax_required
@login_required
@require_POST
def image_like(request):
    # ...
```

If you try to access `https://127.0.0.1:8000/images/like/` directly with your browser, you will get an HTTP 400 response.

> Build custom decorators for your views if you find that you are repeating the same checks in multiple views.

Adding AJAX pagination to your list views

Next, you need to list all bookmarked images on your website. You will use AJAX pagination to build an infinite scroll functionality. Infinite scroll is achieved by loading the next results automatically when the user scrolls to the bottom of the page.

Let's implement an image list view that will handle both standard browser requests and AJAX requests, including pagination. When the user initially loads the image list page, you will display the first page of images. When they scroll to the bottom of the page, you will load the following page of items via AJAX and append it to the bottom of the main page.

The same view will handle both standard and AJAX pagination. Edit the `views.py` file of the `images` application and add the following code to it:

```python
from django.http import HttpResponse
from django.core.paginator import Paginator, EmptyPage, \
                                   PageNotAnInteger


@login_required
def image_list(request):
    images = Image.objects.all()
    paginator = Paginator(images, 8)
    page = request.GET.get('page')
    try:
        images = paginator.page(page)
    except PageNotAnInteger:
        # If page is not an integer deliver the first page
        images = paginator.page(1)
    except EmptyPage:
        if request.is_ajax():
            # If the request is AJAX and the page is out of range
            # return an empty page
            return HttpResponse('')
        # If page is out of range deliver last page of results
        images = paginator.page(paginator.num_pages)
    if request.is_ajax():
        return render(request,
                      'images/image/list_ajax.html',
                      {'section': 'images', 'images': images})
    return render(request,
                  'images/image/list.html',
                  {'section': 'images', 'images': images})
```

In this view, you create a QuerySet to return all images from the database. Then, you build a `Paginator` object to paginate the results, retrieving eight images per page. You get an `EmptyPage` exception if the requested page is out of range. If this is the case and the request is done via AJAX, you return an empty `HttpResponse` that will help you to stop the AJAX pagination on the client side. You render the results to two different templates:

- For AJAX requests, you render the `list_ajax.html` template. This template will only contain the images of the requested page.

- For standard requests, you render the `list.html` template. This template will extend the `base.html` template to display the whole page and will include the `list_ajax.html` template to include the list of images.

Edit the `urls.py` file of the `images` application and add the following URL pattern to it:

```
path('', views.image_list, name='list'),
```

Finally, you need to create the templates mentioned here. Inside the `images/image/` template directory, create a new template and name it `list_ajax.html`. Add the following code to it:

```
{% load thumbnail %}

{% for image in images %}
  <div class="image">
    <a href="{{ image.get_absolute_url }}">
      {% thumbnail image.image 300x300 crop="smart" as im %}
      <a href="{{ image.get_absolute_url }}">
        <img src="{{ im.url }}">
      </a>
    </a>
    <div class="info">
      <a href="{{ image.get_absolute_url }}" class="title">
        {{ image.title }}
      </a>
    </div>
  </div>
{% endfor %}
```

The preceding template displays the list of images. You will use it to return results for AJAX requests. In this code, you iterate over images and generate a square thumbnail for each image. You normalize the size of the thumbnails to `300x300` pixels. You also use the `smart` cropping option. This option indicates that the image has to be incrementally cropped down to the requested size by removing slices from the edges with the least entropy.

Create another template in the same directory and name it `list.html`. Add the following code to it:

```
{% extends "base.html" %}

{% block title %}Images bookmarked{% endblock %}

{% block content %}
  <h1>Images bookmarked</h1>
  <div id="image-list">
    {% include "images/image/list_ajax.html" %}
  </div>
{% endblock %}
```

The list template extends the `base.html` template. To avoid repeating code, you include the `list_ajax.html` template for displaying images. The `list.html` template will hold the JavaScript code for loading additional pages when scrolling to the bottom of the page.

Add the following code to the `list.html` template:

```
{% block domready %}
  var page = 1;
  var empty_page = false;
  var block_request = false;

  $(window).scroll(function() {
    var margin = $(document).height() - $(window).height() - 200;
    if($(window).scrollTop() > margin && empty_page == false &&
    block_request == false) {
     block_request = true;
      page += 1;
      $.get('?page=' + page, function(data) {
        if(data == '') {
          empty_page = true;
        }
        else {
          block_request = false;
          $('#image-list').append(data);
        }
      });
    }
  });
{% endblock %}
```

The preceding code provides the infinite scroll functionality. You include the JavaScript code in the `domready` block that you defined in the `base.html` template. The code is as follows:

1. You define the following variables:
   - `page`: Stores the current page number.
   - `empty_page`: Allows you to know whether the user is on the last page and retrieves an empty page. As soon as you get an empty page, you will stop sending additional AJAX requests because you will assume that there are no more results.
   - `block_request`: Prevents you from sending additional requests while an AJAX request is in progress.

2. You use `$(window).scroll()` to capture the scroll event and also to define a handler function for it.

3. You calculate the `margin` variable to get the difference between the total document height and the window height, because that's the height of the remaining content for the user to scroll. You subtract a value of 200 from the result so that you load the next page when the user is closer than 200 pixels to the bottom of the page.

4. You only send an AJAX request if no other AJAX request is being done (`block_request` has to be `false`) and the user didn't get to the last page of results (`empty_page` is also `false`).

5. You set `block_request` to `true` to avoid a situation where the scroll event triggers additional AJAX requests, and increase the `page` counter by one, in order to retrieve the next page.

6. You perform an AJAX GET request using `$.get()` and receive the HTML response in a variable called `data`. The following are the two scenarios:
   - **The response has no content**: You got to the end of the results, and there are no more pages to load. You set `empty_page` to `true` to prevent additional AJAX requests.
   - **The response contains data**: You append the data to the HTML element with the `image-list` ID. The page content expands vertically, appending results when the user approaches the bottom of the page.

Open `https://127.0.0.1:8000/images/` in your browser. You will see the list of images that you have bookmarked so far. It should look similar to this:

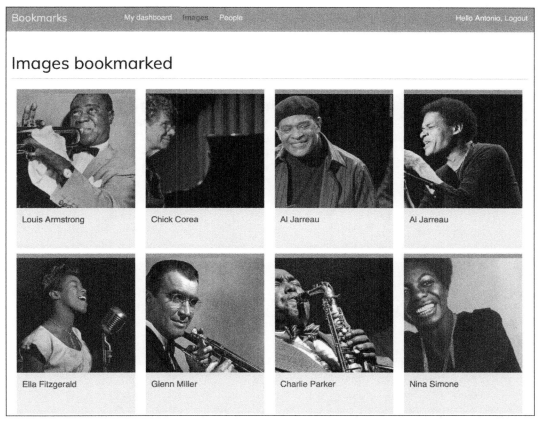

Figure 5.12: The image list page with AJAX pagination

Scroll to the bottom of the page to load additional pages. Ensure that you have bookmarked more than eight images using the bookmarklet, because that's the number of images you are displaying per page. Remember that you can use Firebug or a similar tool to track the AJAX requests and debug your JavaScript code.

Finally, edit the `base.html` template of the `account` application and add the URL for the images item of the main menu, as follows:

```
<li {% if section == "images" %}class="selected"{% endif %}>
  <a href="{% url "images:list" %}">Images</a>
</li>
```

Now you can access the image list from the main menu.

Summary

In this chapter, you created models with many-to-many relationships and learned how to customize the behavior of forms. You used jQuery with Django to build a JavaScript bookmarklet to share images from other websites into your site. This chapter has also covered the creation of image thumbnails using the easy-thumbnails library. Finally, you implemented AJAX views with jQuery and added AJAX pagination to the image list view.

In the next chapter, you will learn how to build a follow system and an activity stream. You will work with generic relations, signals, and denormalization. You will also learn how to use Redis with Django.

6

Tracking User Actions

In the previous chapter, you implemented AJAX views into your project using jQuery and built a JavaScript bookmarklet to share content from other websites on your platform.

In this chapter, you will learn how to build a follow system and create a user activity stream. You will also discover how Django signals work and integrate Redis's fast I/O storage into your project to store item views.

This chapter will cover the following points:

- Building a follow system
- Creating many-to-many relationships with an intermediary model
- Creating an activity stream application
- Adding generic relations to models
- Optimizing QuerySets for related objects
- Using signals for denormalizing counts
- Storing item views in Redis

Building a follow system

Let's build a follow system in your project. This means that your users will be able to follow each other and track what other users share on the platform. The relationship between users is a many-to-many relationship: a user can follow multiple users and they, in turn, can be followed by multiple users.

Creating many-to-many relationships with an intermediary model

In previous chapters, you created many-to-many relationships by adding the `ManyToManyField` to one of the related models and letting Django create the database table for the relationship. This is suitable for most cases, but sometimes you may need to create an intermediary model for the relationship. Creating an intermediary model is necessary when you want to store additional information for the relationship, for example, the date when the relationship was created, or a field that describes the nature of the relationship.

Let's create an intermediary model to build relationships between users. There are two reasons for using an intermediary model:

- You are using the `User` model provided by Django and you want to avoid altering it
- You want to store the time when the relationship was created

Edit the `models.py` file of your `account` application and add the following code to it:

```python
class Contact(models.Model):
    user_from = models.ForeignKey('auth.User',
                                  related_name='rel_from_set',
                                  on_delete=models.CASCADE)
    user_to = models.ForeignKey('auth.User',
                                related_name='rel_to_set',
                                on_delete=models.CASCADE)
    created = models.DateTimeField(auto_now_add=True,
                                   db_index=True)

    class Meta:
        ordering = ('-created',)

    def __str__(self):
        return f'{self.user_from} follows {self.user_to}'
```

The preceding code shows the `Contact` model that you will use for user relationships. It contains the following fields:

- `user_from`: A `ForeignKey` for the user who creates the relationship
- `user_to`: A `ForeignKey` for the user being followed
- `created`: A `DateTimeField` field with `auto_now_add=True` to store the time when the relationship was created

A database index is automatically created on the `ForeignKey` fields. You use `db_index=True` to create a database index for the `created` field. This will improve query performance when ordering QuerySets by this field.

Using the ORM, you could create a relationship for a user, `user1`, following another user, `user2`, like this:

```
user1 = User.objects.get(id=1)
user2 = User.objects.get(id=2)
Contact.objects.create(user_from=user1, user_to=user2)
```

The related managers, `rel_from_set` and `rel_to_set`, will return a QuerySet for the `Contact` model. In order to access the end side of the relationship from the `User` model, it would be desirable for `User` to contain a `ManyToManyField`, as follows:

```
following = models.ManyToManyField('self',
                                    through=Contact,
                                    related_name='followers',
                                    symmetrical=False)
```

In the preceding example, you tell Django to use your custom intermediary model for the relationship by adding `through=Contact` to the `ManyToManyField`. This is a many-to-many relationship from the `User` model to itself; you refer to `'self'` in the `ManyToManyField` field to create a relationship to the same model.

> When you need additional fields in a many-to-many relationship, create a custom model with a `ForeignKey` for each side of the relationship. Add a `ManyToManyField` in one of the related models and indicate to Django that your intermediary model should be used by including it in the `through` parameter.

If the `User` model was part of your application, you could add the previous field to the model. However, you can't alter the `User` class directly because it belongs to the `django.contrib.auth` application. Let's take a slightly different approach by adding this field dynamically to the `User` model.

Edit the `models.py` file of the `account` application and add the following lines:

```
from django.contrib.auth import get_user_model

# Add following field to User dynamically
user_model = get_user_model()
user_model.add_to_class('following',
                    models.ManyToManyField('self',
                        through=Contact,
                        related_name='followers',
                        symmetrical=False))
```

In the preceding code, you retrieve the user model by using the generic function `get_user_model()`, which is provided by Django. You use the `add_to_class()` method of Django models to monkey patch the `User` model. Be aware that using `add_to_class()` is not the recommended way of adding fields to models. However, you take advantage of using it in this case to avoid creating a custom user model, keeping all the advantages of Django's built-in `User` model.

You also simplify the way that you retrieve related objects using the Django ORM with `user.followers.all()` and `user.following.all()`. You use the intermediary `Contact` model and avoid complex queries that would involve additional database joins, as would have been the case had you defined the relationship in your custom `Profile` model. The table for this many-to-many relationship will be created using the `Contact` model. Thus, the `ManyToManyField`, added dynamically, will not imply any database changes for the Django `User` model.

Keep in mind that, in most cases, it is preferable to add fields to the `Profile` model you created before, instead of monkey patching the `User` model. Ideally, you shouldn't alter the existing Django `User` model. Django allows you to use custom user models. If you want to use your custom user model, take a look at the documentation at `https://docs.djangoproject.com/en/3.0/topics/auth/customizing/#specifying-a-custom-user-model`.

Note that the relationship includes `symmetrical=False`. When you define a `ManyToManyField` in the model creating a relationship with itself, Django forces the relationship to be symmetrical. In this case, you are setting `symmetrical=False` to define a non-symmetrical relationship (if I follow you, it doesn't mean that you automatically follow me).

 When you use an intermediary model for many-to-many relationships, some of the related manager's methods are disabled, such as `add()`, `create()`, or `remove()`. You need to create or delete instances of the intermediary model instead.

Run the following command to generate the initial migrations for the `account` application:

```
python manage.py makemigrations account
```

You will obtain the following output:

```
Migrations for 'account':
  account/migrations/0002_contact.py
    - Create model Contact
```

Now, run the following command to sync the application with the database:

```
python manage.py migrate account
```

You should see an output that includes the following line:

```
Applying account.0002_contact... OK
```

The Contact model is now synced to the database, and you are able to create relationships between users. However, your site doesn't offer a way to browse users or see a particular user's profile yet. Let's build list and detail views for the User model.

Creating list and detail views for user profiles

Open the views.py file of the account application and add the following code to it:

```python
from django.shortcuts import get_object_or_404
from django.contrib.auth.models import User

@login_required
def user_list(request):
    users = User.objects.filter(is_active=True)
    return render(request,
                  'account/user/list.html',
                  {'section': 'people',
                   'users': users})


@login_required
def user_detail(request, username):
    user = get_object_or_404(User,
                             username=username,
                             is_active=True)
    return render(request,
                  'account/user/detail.html',
                  {'section': 'people',
                   'user': user})
```

These are simple list and detail views for User objects. The user_list view gets all active users. The Django User model contains an is_active flag to designate whether the user account is considered active. You filter the query by is_active=True to return only active users. This view returns all results, but you can improve it by adding pagination in the same way as you did for the image_list view.

The `user_detail` view uses the `get_object_or_404()` shortcut to retrieve the active user with the given username. The view returns an HTTP `404` response if no active user with the given username is found.

Edit the `urls.py` file of the `account` application, and add a URL pattern for each view, as follows:

```
urlpatterns = [
    # ...
    path('users/', views.user_list, name='user_list'),
    path('users/<username>/', views.user_detail, name='user_detail'),
]
```

You will use the `user_detail` URL pattern to generate the canonical URL for users. You have already defined a `get_absolute_url()` method in a model to return the canonical URL for each object. Another way to specify the URL for a model is by adding the `ABSOLUTE_URL_OVERRIDES` setting to your project.

Edit the `settings.py` file of your project and add the following code to it:

```
from django.urls import reverse_lazy

ABSOLUTE_URL_OVERRIDES = {
    'auth.user': lambda u: reverse_lazy('user_detail',
                                        args=[u.username])
}
```

Django adds a `get_absolute_url()` method dynamically to any models that appear in the `ABSOLUTE_URL_OVERRIDES` setting. This method returns the corresponding URL for the given model specified in the setting. You return the `user_detail` URL for the given user. Now, you can use `get_absolute_url()` on a `User` instance to retrieve its corresponding URL.

Open the Python shell with the `python manage.py shell` command and run the following code to test it:

```
>>> from django.contrib.auth.models import User
>>> user = User.objects.latest('id')
>>> str(user.get_absolute_url())
'/account/users/ellington/'
```

The returned URL is as expected.

You will need to create templates for the views that you just built. Add the following directory and files to the `templates/account/` directory of the `account` application:

```
/user/
    detail.html
    list.html
```

Edit the `account/user/list.html` template and add the following code to it:

```
{% extends "base.html" %}
{% load thumbnail %}

{% block title %}People{% endblock %}

{% block content %}
  <h1>People</h1>
  <div id="people-list">
    {% for user in users %}
      <div class="user">
        <a href="{{ user.get_absolute_url }}">
          <img src="{% thumbnail user.profile.photo 180x180 %}">
        </a>
        <div class="info">
          <a href="{{ user.get_absolute_url }}" class="title">
            {{ user.get_full_name }}
          </a>
        </div>
      </div>
    {% endfor %}
  </div>
{% endblock %}
```

The preceding template allows you to list all the active users on the site. You iterate over the given users and use the `{% thumbnail %}` template tag from easy-thumbnails to generate profile image thumbnails.

Open the `base.html` template of your project and include the `user_list` URL in the `href` attribute of the following menu item:

```
<li {% if section == "people" %}class="selected"{% endif %}>
  <a href="{% url "user_list" %}">People</a>
</li>
```

Start the development server with the `python manage.py runserver` command and open `http://127.0.0.1:8000/account/users/` in your browser. You should see a list of users like the following one:

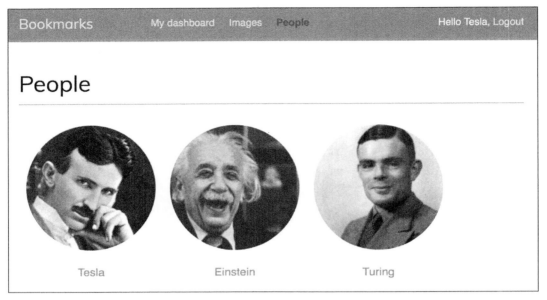

Figure 6.1: The user list page with profile image thumbnails

Remember that if you have any difficulty generating thumbnails, you can add `THUMBNAIL_DEBUG = True` to your `settings.py` file in order to obtain debug information in the shell.

Edit the `account/user/detail.html` template of the `account` application and add the following code to it:

```
{% extends "base.html" %}
{% load thumbnail %}

{% block title %}{{ user.get_full_name }}{% endblock %}

{% block content %}
  <h1>{{ user.get_full_name }}</h1>
```

```
<div class="profile-info">
   <img src="{% thumbnail user.profile.photo 180x180 %}" class="user-
detail">
   </div>
   {% with total_followers=user.followers.count %}
      <span class="count">
         <span class="total">{{ total_followers }}</span>
         follower{{ total_followers|pluralize }}
      </span>
      <a href="#" data-id="{{ user.id }}" data-action="{% if request.
user in user.followers.all %}un{% endif %}follow" class="follow
button">
         {% if request.user not in user.followers.all %}
            Follow
         {% else %}
            Unfollow
         {% endif %}
      </a>
      <div id="image-list" class="image-container">
         {% include "images/image/list_ajax.html" with images=user.
images_created.all %}
      </div>
   {% endwith %}
{% endblock %}
```

Make sure that no template tag is split into multiple lines; Django doesn't support multiple line tags.

In the `detail` template, you display the user profile and use the `{% thumbnail %}` template tag to display the profile image. You show the total number of followers and a link to follow or unfollow the user. You perform an AJAX request to follow/ unfollow a particular user. You add `data-id` and `data-action` attributes to the `<a>` HTML element, including the user ID and the initial action to perform when the link element is clicked – `follow` or `unfollow`, which depends on the user requesting the page being a follower of this other user or not, as the case may be. You display the images bookmarked by the user, including the `images/image/list_ajax.html` template.

Open your browser again and click on a user who has bookmarked some images. You will see profile details, as follows:

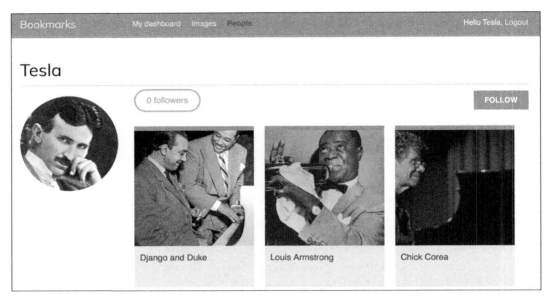

Figure 6.2: The user detail page

Building an AJAX view to follow users

Let's create a simple view to follow/unfollow a user using AJAX. Edit the `views.py` file of the `account` application and add the following code to it:

```
from django.http import JsonResponse
from django.views.decorators.http import require_POST
from common.decorators import ajax_required
from .models import Contact

@ajax_required
@require_POST
@login_required
def user_follow(request):
    user_id = request.POST.get('id')
    action = request.POST.get('action')
    if user_id and action:
        try:
            user = User.objects.get(id=user_id)
            if action == 'follow':
                Contact.objects.get_or_create(
```

```
                         user_from=request.user,
                         user_to=user)
              else:
                  Contact.objects.filter(user_from=request.user,
                                         user_to=user).delete()
              return JsonResponse({'status':'ok'})
         except User.DoesNotExist:
              return JsonResponse({'status':'error'})
     return JsonResponse({'status':'error'})
```

The `user_follow` view is quite similar to the `image_like` view that you created before. Since you are using a custom intermediary model for the user's many-to-many relationship, the default `add()` and `remove()` methods of the automatic manager of `ManyToManyField` are not available. You use the intermediary `Contact` model to create or delete user relationships.

Edit the `urls.py` file of the `account` application and add the following URL pattern to it:

```
    path('users/follow/', views.user_follow, name='user_follow'),
```

Ensure that you place the preceding pattern before the `user_detail` URL pattern. Otherwise, any requests to `/users/follow/` will match the regular expression of the `user_detail` pattern and that view will be executed instead. Remember that in every HTTP request, Django checks the requested URL against each pattern in order of appearance and stops at the first match.

Edit the `user/detail.html` template of the `account` application and append the following code to it:

```
{% block domready %}
  $('a.follow').click(function(e){
    e.preventDefault();
    $.post('{% url "user_follow" %}',
      {
        id: $(this).data('id'),
        action: $(this).data('action')
      },
      function(data){
        if (data['status'] == 'ok') {
          var previous_action = $('a.follow').data('action');

          // toggle data-action
          $('a.follow').data('action',
            previous_action == 'follow' ? 'unfollow' : 'follow');
          // toggle link text
```

```
        $('a.follow').text(
          previous_action == 'follow' ? 'Unfollow' : 'Follow');

        // update total followers
        var previous_followers = parseInt(
          $('span.count .total').text());
        $('span.count .total').text(previous_action == 'follow' ?
        previous_followers + 1 : previous_followers - 1);
      }
    }
  );
});
{% endblock %}
```

The preceding code is the JavaScript code to perform the AJAX request to follow or unfollow a particular user and also to toggle the follow/unfollow link. You use jQuery to perform the AJAX request and set both the data-action attribute and the text of the HTML <a> element based on its previous value. When the AJAX action is performed, you also update the total followers count displayed on the page.

Open the user detail page of an existing user and click on the **FOLLOW** link to test the functionality you just built. You will see that the followers count is increased:

Figure 6.3: The followers count and follow/unfollow button

Building a generic activity stream application

Many social websites display an activity stream to their users so that they can track what other users do on the platform. An activity stream is a list of recent activities performed by a user or a group of users. For example, Facebook's News Feed is an activity stream. Sample actions can be *user X bookmarked image Y* or *user X is now following user Y*.

You are going to build an activity stream application so that every user can see the recent interactions of the users they follow. To do so, you will need a model to save the actions performed by users on the website and a simple way to add actions to the feed.

Create a new application named `actions` inside your project with the following command:

```
python manage.py startapp actions
```

Add the new application to `INSTALLED_APPS` in the `settings.py` file of your project to activate the application in your project:

```
INSTALLED_APPS = [
    # ...
    'actions.apps.ActionsConfig',
]
```

Edit the `models.py` file of the `actions` application and add the following code to it:

```
from django.db import models

class Action(models.Model):
    user = models.ForeignKey('auth.User',
                             related_name='actions',
                             db_index=True,
                             on_delete=models.CASCADE)
    verb = models.CharField(max_length=255)
    created = models.DateTimeField(auto_now_add=True,
                                   db_index=True)

    class Meta:
        ordering = ('-created',)
```

The preceding code shows the `Action` model that will be used to store user activities. The fields of this model are as follows:

- `user`: The user who performed the action; this is a `ForeignKey` to the Django `User` model.

- `verb`: The verb describing the action that the user has performed.

- `created`: The date and time when this action was created. You use `auto_now_add=True` to automatically set this to the current datetime when the object is saved for the first time in the database.

With this basic model, you can only store actions, such as *user X did something*. You need an extra `ForeignKey` field in order to save actions that involve a `target` object, such as *user X bookmarked image Y* or *user X is now following user Y*. As you already know, a normal `ForeignKey` can point to only one model. Instead, you will need a way for the action's `target` object to be an instance of an existing model. This is what the Django `contenttypes` framework will help you to do.

Using the contenttypes framework

Django includes a `contenttypes` framework located at `django.contrib.contenttypes`. This application can track all models installed in your project and provides a generic interface to interact with your models.

The `django.contrib.contenttypes` application is included in the INSTALLED_APPS setting by default when you create a new project using the `startproject` command. It is used by other `contrib` packages, such as the authentication framework and the administration application.

The `contenttypes` application contains a `ContentType` model. Instances of this model represent the actual models of your application, and new instances of `ContentType` are automatically created when new models are installed in your project. The `ContentType` model has the following fields:

- `app_label`: This indicates the name of the application that the model belongs to. This is automatically taken from the `app_label` attribute of the model `Meta` options. For example, your `Image` model belongs to the `images` application.

- `model`: The name of the model class.

- `name`: This indicates the human-readable name of the model. This is automatically taken from the `verbose_name` attribute of the model `Meta` options.

Let's take a look at how you can interact with `ContentType` objects. Open the shell using the `python manage.py shell` command. You can obtain the `ContentType` object corresponding to a specific model by performing a query with the `app_label` and `model` attributes, as follows:

```
>>> from django.contrib.contenttypes.models import ContentType
>>> image_type = ContentType.objects.get(app_label='images',
model='image')
>>> image_type
<ContentType: images | image>
```

You can also retrieve the model class from a `ContentType` object by calling its `model_class()` method:

```
>>> image_type.model_class()
<class 'images.models.Image'>
```

It's also common to get the ContentType object for a particular model class, as follows:

```
>>> from images.models import Image
>>> ContentType.objects.get_for_model(Image)
<ContentType: images | image>
```

These are just some examples of using contenttypes. Django offers more ways to work with them. You can find the official documentation about the contenttypes framework at https://docs.djangoproject.com/en/3.0/ref/contrib/contenttypes/.

Adding generic relations to your models

In generic relations, ContentType objects play the role of pointing to the model used for the relationship. You will need three fields to set up a generic relation in a model:

- A ForeignKey field to ContentType: This will tell you the model for the relationship
- A field to store the primary key of the related object: This will usually be a PositiveIntegerField to match Django's automatic primary key fields
- A field to define and manage the generic relation using the two previous fields: The contenttypes framework offers a GenericForeignKey field for this purpose

Edit the models.py file of the actions application and make it look like this:

```
from django.db import models
from django.contrib.contenttypes.models import ContentType
from django.contrib.contenttypes.fields import GenericForeignKey


class Action(models.Model):
    user = models.ForeignKey('auth.User',
                             related_name='actions',
                             db_index=True,
                             on_delete=models.CASCADE)
    verb = models.CharField(max_length=255)
    target_ct = models.ForeignKey(ContentType,
                                  blank=True,
                                  null=True,
                                  related_name='target_obj',
                                  on_delete=models.CASCADE)
    target_id = models.PositiveIntegerField(null=True,
                                            blank=True,
```

```
                                             db_index=True)
        target = GenericForeignKey('target_ct', 'target_id')
        created = models.DateTimeField(auto_now_add=True,
                                       db_index=True)

        class Meta:
            ordering = ('-created',)
```

You have added the following fields to the Action model:

- target_ct: A ForeignKey field that points to the ContentType model
- target_id: A PositiveIntegerField for storing the primary key of the related object
- target: A GenericForeignKey field to the related object based on the combination of the two previous fields

Django does not create any field in the database for GenericForeignKey fields. The only fields that are mapped to database fields are target_ct and target_id. Both fields have blank=True and null=True attributes, so that a target object is not required when saving Action objects.

 You can make your applications more flexible by using generic relations instead of foreign keys.

Run the following command to create initial migrations for this application:

```
python manage.py makemigrations actions
```

You should see the following output:

```
Migrations for 'actions':
  actions/migrations/0001_initial.py
    - Create model Action
```

Then, run the next command to sync the application with the database:

```
python manage.py migrate
```

The output of the command should indicate that the new migrations have been applied, as follows:

```
Applying actions.0001_initial... OK
```

Let's add the `Action` model to the administration site. Edit the `admin.py` file of the `actions` application and add the following code to it:

```python
from django.contrib import admin
from .models import Action

@admin.register(Action)
class ActionAdmin(admin.ModelAdmin):
    list_display = ('user', 'verb', 'target', 'created')
    list_filter = ('created',)
    search_fields = ('verb',)
```

You just registered the `Action` model in the administration site. Run the `python manage.py runserver` command to start the development server and open `http://127.0.0.1:8000/admin/actions/action/add/` in your browser. You should see the page for creating a new `Action` object, as follows:

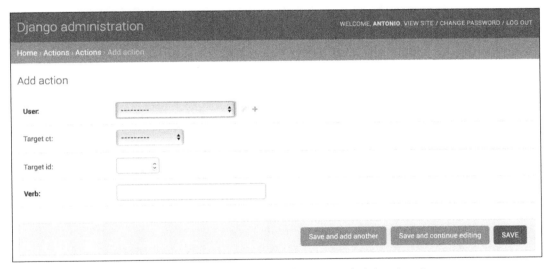

Figure 6.4: The add action page on the Django administration site

As you will notice in the preceding screenshot, only the `target_ct` and `target_id` fields that are mapped to actual database fields are shown. The `GenericForeignKey` field does not appear in the form. The `target_ct` field allows you to select any of the registered models of your Django project. You can restrict the content types to choose from a limited set of models using the `limit_choices_to` attribute in the `target_ct` field; the `limit_choices_to` attribute allows you to restrict the content of `ForeignKey` fields to a specific set of values.

Create a new file inside the `actions` application directory and name it `utils.py`. You need to define a shortcut function that will allow you to create new `Action` objects in a simple way. Edit the new `utils.py` file and add the following code to it:

```
from django.contrib.contenttypes.models import ContentType
from .models import Action

def create_action(user, verb, target=None):
    action = Action(user=user, verb=verb, target=target)
    action.save()
```

The `create_action()` function allows you to create actions that optionally include a `target` object. You can use this function anywhere in your code as a shortcut to add new actions to the activity stream.

Avoiding duplicate actions in the activity stream

Sometimes, your users might click several times on the **LIKE** or **UNLIKE** button or perform the same action multiple times in a short period of time. This will easily lead to storing and displaying duplicate actions. To avoid this, let's improve the `create_action()` function to skip obvious duplicated actions.

Edit the `utils.py` file of the `actions` application, as follows:

```
import datetime
from django.utils import timezone
from django.contrib.contenttypes.models import ContentType
from .models import Action

def create_action(user, verb, target=None):
    # check for any similar action made in the last minute
    now = timezone.now()
    last_minute = now - datetime.timedelta(seconds=60)
    similar_actions = Action.objects.filter(user_id=user.id,
                                            verb= verb,
                                            created__gte=last_minute)
    if target:
        target_ct = ContentType.objects.get_for_model(target)
        similar_actions = similar_actions.filter(
                                            target_ct=target_ct,
                                            target_id=target.id)
    if not similar_actions:
        # no existing actions found
```

```
        action = Action(user=user, verb=verb, target=target)
        action.save()
        return True
    return False
```

You have changed the `create_action()` function to avoid saving duplicate actions and return Boolean to tell you whether the action was saved. This is how you avoid duplicates:

- First, you get the current time using the `timezone.now()` method provided by Django. This method does the same as `datetime.datetime.now()` but returns a timezone-aware object. Django provides a setting called `USE_TZ` to enable or disable timezone support. The default `settings.py` file created using the `startproject` command includes `USE_TZ=True`.

- You use the `last_minute` variable to store the datetime from one minute ago and retrieve any identical actions performed by the user since then.

- You create an `Action` object if no identical action already exists in the last minute. You return `True` if an `Action` object was created, or `False` otherwise.

Adding user actions to the activity stream

It's time to add some actions to your views to build the activity stream for your users. You will store an action for each of the following interactions:

- A user bookmarks an image
- A user likes an image
- A user creates an account
- A user starts following another user

Edit the `views.py` file of the `images` application and add the following import:

```
from actions.utils import create_action
```

In the `image_create` view, add `create_action()` after saving the image, like this:

```
new_item.save()
create_action(request.user, 'bookmarked image', new_item)
```

In the `image_like` view, add `create_action()` after adding the user to the `users_like` relationship, as follows:

```
image.users_like.add(request.user)
create_action(request.user, 'likes', image)
```

Now, edit the `views.py` file of the `account` application and add the following import:

```
from actions.utils import create_action
```

In the `register` view, add `create_action()` after creating the `Profile` object, as follows:

```
Profile.objects.create(user=new_user)
create_action(new_user, 'has created an account')
```

In the `user_follow` view, add `create_action()`:

```
Contact.objects.get_or_create(user_from=request.user,
                              user_to=user)
create_action(request.user, 'is following', user)
```

As you can see in the preceding code, thanks to your `Action` model and your helper function, it's very easy to save new actions to the activity stream.

Displaying the activity stream

Finally, you need a way to display the activity stream for each user. You will include the activity stream in the user's dashboard. Edit the `views.py` file of the `account` application. Import the `Action` model and modify the `dashboard` view, as follows:

```
from actions.models import Action

@login_required
def dashboard(request):
    # Display all actions by default
    actions = Action.objects.exclude(user=request.user)
    following_ids = request.user.following.values_list('id',
                                                       flat=True)
    if following_ids:
        # If user is following others, retrieve only their actions
        actions = actions.filter(user_id__in=following_ids)
    actions = actions[:10]

    return render(request,
                  'account/dashboard.html',
                  {'section': 'dashboard',
                   'actions': actions})
```

In the preceding view, you retrieve all actions from the database, excluding the ones performed by the current user. By default, you retrieve the latest actions performed by all users on the platform. If the user is following other users, you restrict the query to retrieve only the actions performed by the users they follow. Finally, you limit the result to the first 10 actions returned. You don't use `order_by()` in the QuerySet because you rely on the default ordering that you provided in the `Meta` options of the `Action` model. Recent actions will come first since you set `ordering = ('-created',)` in the `Action` model.

Optimizing QuerySets that involve related objects

Every time you retrieve an `Action` object, you will usually access its related `User` object and the user's related `Profile` object. The Django ORM offers a simple way to retrieve related objects at the same time, thereby avoiding additional queries to the database.

Using select_related()

Django offers a QuerySet method called `select_related()` that allows you to retrieve related objects for one-to-many relationships. This translates to a single, more complex QuerySet, but you avoid additional queries when accessing the related objects. The `select_related` method is for `ForeignKey` and `OneToOne` fields. It works by performing a SQL `JOIN` and including the fields of the related object in the `SELECT` statement.

To take advantage of `select_related()`, edit the following line of the preceding code:

```
actions = actions[:10]
```

Also, add `select_related` to the fields that you will use, like this:

```
actions = actions.select_related('user', 'user__profile')[:10]
```

You use `user__profile` to join the `Profile` table in a single SQL query. If you call `select_related()` without passing any arguments to it, it will retrieve objects from all `ForeignKey` relationships. Always limit `select_related()` to the relationships that will be accessed afterward.

 Using `select_related()` carefully can vastly improve execution time.

Using prefetch_related()

`select_related()` will help you to boost performance for retrieving related objects in one-to-many relationships. However, `select_related()` doesn't work for many-to-many or many-to-one relationships (`ManyToMany` or reverse `ForeignKey` fields). Django offers a different QuerySet method called `prefetch_related` that works for many-to-many and many-to-one relationships in addition to the relationships supported by `select_related()`. The `prefetch_related()` method performs a separate lookup for each relationship and joins the results using Python. This method also supports the prefetching of `GenericRelation` and `GenericForeignKey`.

Edit the `views.py` file of the `account` application and complete your query by adding `prefetch_related()` to it for the target `GenericForeignKey` field, as follows:

```
actions = actions.select_related('user', 'user__profile')\
                  .prefetch_related('target')[:10]
```

This query is now optimized for retrieving the user actions, including related objects.

Creating templates for actions

Let's now create the template to display a particular `Action` object. Create a new directory inside the `actions` application directory and name it `templates`. Add the following file structure to it:

```
actions/
    action/
        detail.html
```

Edit the `actions/action/detail.html` template file and add the following lines to it:

```
{% load thumbnail %}

{% with user=action.user profile=action.user.profile %}
<div class="action">
  <div class="images">
    {% if profile.photo %}
      {% thumbnail user.profile.photo "80x80" crop="100%" as im %}
      <a href="{{ user.get_absolute_url }}">
        <img src="{{ im.url }}" alt="{{ user.get_full_name }}"
        class="item-img">
      </a>
    {% endif %}
```

```
    {% if action.target %}
      {% with target=action.target %}
        {% if target.image %}
          {% thumbnail target.image "80x80" crop="100%" as im %}
          <a href="{{ target.get_absolute_url }}">
            <img src="{{ im.url }}" class="item-img">
          </a>
        {% endif %}
      {% endwith %}
    {% endif %}
  </div>
  <div class="info">
    <p>
      <span class="date">{{ action.created|timesince }} ago</span>
      <br />
      <a href="{{ user.get_absolute_url }}">
        {{ user.first_name }}
      </a>
      {{ action.verb }}
      {% if action.target %}
        {% with target=action.target %}
          <a href="{{ target.get_absolute_url }}">{{ target }}</a>
        {% endwith %}
      {% endif %}
    </p>
  </div>
</div>
{% endwith %}
```

This is the template used to display an `Action` object. First, you use the `{% with %}` template tag to retrieve the user performing the action and the related `Profile` object. Then, you display the image of the `target` object if the `Action` object has a related `target` object. Finally, you display the link to the user who performed the action, the verb, and the `target` object, if any.

Edit the `account/dashboard.html` template of the `account` application and append the following code to the bottom of the `content` block:

```
<h2>What's happening</h2>
<div id="action-list">
  {% for action in actions %}
    {% include "actions/action/detail.html" %}
  {% endfor %}
</div>
```

Open `http://127.0.0.1:8000/account/` in your browser. Log in as an existing user and perform several actions so that they get stored in the database. Then, log in using another user, follow the previous user, and take a look at the generated action stream on the dashboard page. It should look like the following:

What's happening

3 minutes ago

Einstein **likes** Alternating electric current generator

5 minutes ago

Einstein **bookmarked image** Turing Machine

2 days, 2 hours ago

Tesla **likes** Chick Corea

Figure 6.5: The activity stream for the current user

You just created a complete activity stream for your users, and you can easily add new user actions to it. You can also add infinite scroll functionality to the activity stream by implementing the same AJAX paginator that you used for the `image_list` view.

Using signals for denormalizing counts

There are some cases when you may want to denormalize your data. Denormalization is making data redundant in such a way that it optimizes read performance. For example, you might be copying related data to an object to avoid expensive read queries to the database when retrieving the related data. You have to be careful about denormalization and only start using it when you really need it. The biggest issue you will find with denormalization is that it's difficult to keep your denormalized data updated.

Let's take a look at an example of how to improve your queries by denormalizing counts. You will denormalize data from your `Image` model and use Django signals to keep the data updated.

Working with signals

Django comes with a signal dispatcher that allows receiver functions to get notified when certain actions occur. Signals are very useful when you need your code to do something every time something else happens. Signals allow you to decouple logic: you can capture a certain action, regardless of the application or code that triggered that action, and implement logic that gets executed whenever that action occurs. For example, you can build a signal receiver function that gets executed every time a `User` object is saved. You can also create your own signals so that others can get notified when an event happens.

Django provides several signals for models located at `django.db.models.signals`. Some of these signals are as follows:

- `pre_save` and `post_save` are sent before or after calling the `save()` method of a model
- `pre_delete` and `post_delete` are sent before or after calling the `delete()` method of a model or QuerySet
- `m2m_changed` is sent when a `ManyToManyField` on a model is changed

These are just a subset of the signals provided by Django. You can find a list of all built-in signals at `https://docs.djangoproject.com/en/3.0/ref/signals/`.

Let's say you want to retrieve images by popularity. You can use the Django aggregation functions to retrieve images ordered by the number of users who like them. Remember that you used Django aggregation functions in *Chapter 3, Extending Your Blog Application*. The following code will retrieve images according to their number of likes:

```
from django.db.models import Count
from images.models import Image

images_by_popularity = Image.objects.annotate(
    total_likes=Count('users_like')).order_by('-total_likes')
```

However, ordering images by counting their total `likes` is more expensive in terms of performance than ordering them by a field that stores total counts. You can add a field to the `Image` model to denormalize the total number of likes to boost performance in queries that involve this field. The issue is how to keep this field updated.

Edit the `models.py` file of the `images` application and add the following `total_likes` field to the `Image` model:

```
class Image(models.Model):
    # ...
    total_likes = models.PositiveIntegerField(db_index=True,
                                              default=0)
```

The `total_likes` field will allow you to store the total count of users who like each image. Denormalizing counts is useful when you want to filter or order QuerySets by them.

 There are several ways to improve performance that you have to take into account before denormalizing fields. Consider database indexes, query optimization, and caching before starting to denormalize your data.

Run the following command to create the migrations for adding the new field to the database table:

```
python manage.py makemigrations images
```

You should see the following output:

```
Migrations for 'images':
  images/migrations/0002_image_total_likes.py
    - Add field total_likes to image
```

Then, run the following command to apply the migration:

```
python manage.py migrate images
```

The output should include the following line:

```
Applying images.0002_image_total_likes... OK
```

You need to attach a `receiver` function to the `m2m_changed` signal. Create a new file inside the `images` application directory and name it `signals.py`. Add the following code to it:

```
from django.db.models.signals import m2m_changed
from django.dispatch import receiver
from .models import Image

@receiver(m2m_changed, sender=Image.users_like.through)
def users_like_changed(sender, instance, **kwargs):
```

```
instance.total_likes = instance.users_like.count()
instance.save()
```

First, you register the `users_like_changed` function as a receiver function using the `receiver()` decorator. You attach it to the `m2m_changed` signal. Then, you connect the function to `Image.users_like.through` so that the function is only called if the `m2m_changed` signal has been launched by this sender. There is an alternate method for registering a receiver function; it consists of using the `connect()` method of the `Signal` object.

 Django signals are synchronous and blocking. Don't confuse signals with asynchronous tasks. However, you can combine both to launch asynchronous tasks when your code gets notified by a signal. You will learn to create asynchronous tasks with Celery in *Chapter 7, Building an Online Shop*.

You have to connect your receiver function to a signal so that it gets called every time the signal is sent. The recommended method for registering your signals is by importing them in the `ready()` method of your application configuration class. Django provides an application registry that allows you to configure and introspect your applications.

Application configuration classes

Django allows you to specify configuration classes for your applications. When you create an application using the `startapp` command, Django adds an `apps.py` file to the application directory, including a basic application configuration that inherits from the `AppConfig` class.

The application configuration class allows you to store metadata and the configuration for the application, and it provides introspection for the application. You can find more information about application configurations at `https://docs.djangoproject.com/en/3.0/ref/applications/`.

In order to register your signal `receiver` functions, when you use the `receiver()` decorator, you just need to import the `signals` module of your application inside the `ready()` method of the application configuration class. This method is called as soon as the application registry is fully populated. Any other initializations for your application should also be included in this method.

Edit the `apps.py` file of the `images` application and make it look like this:

```
from django.apps import AppConfig

class ImagesConfig(AppConfig):
```

```
name = 'images'

def ready(self):
    # import signal handlers
    import images.signals
```

You import the signals for this application in the `ready()` method so that they are imported when the `images` application is loaded.

Run the development server with the following command:

python manage.py runserver

Open your browser to view an image detail page and click on the **LIKE** button. Go back to the administration site, navigate to the edit image URL, such as `http://127.0.0.1:8000/admin/images/image/1/change/`, and take a look at the `total_likes` attribute. You should see that the `total_likes` attribute is updated with the total number of users who like the image, as follows:

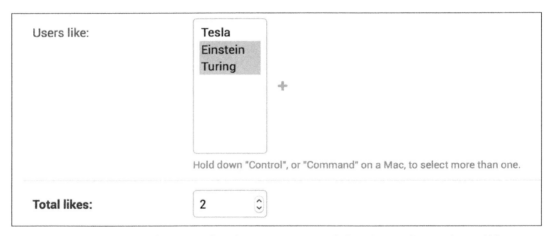

Figure 6.6: The image edit page on the administration site, including denormalization for total likes

Now, you can use the `total_likes` attribute to order images by popularity or display the value anywhere, avoiding using complex queries to calculate it. Consider the following query to get images ordered according to their likes count:

```
from django.db.models import Count

images_by_popularity = Image.objects.annotate(
    likes=Count('users_like')).order_by('-likes')
```

The preceding query can now be written as follows:

```
images_by_popularity = Image.objects.order_by('-total_likes')
```

This results in a less expensive SQL query. This is just an example of how to use Django signals.

 Use signals with caution since they make it difficult to know the control flow. In many cases, you can avoid using signals if you know which receivers need to be notified.

You will need to set initial counts for the rest of the `Image` objects to match the current status of the database. Open the shell with the `python manage.py shell` command and run the following code:

```
from images.models import Image
for image in Image.objects.all():
    image.total_likes = image.users_like.count()
    image.save()
```

The likes count for each image is now up to date.

Using Redis for storing item views

Redis is an advanced key/value database that allows you to save different types of data. It also has extremely fast I/O operations. Redis stores everything in memory, but the data can be persisted by dumping the dataset to disk every once in a while, or by adding each command to a log. Redis is very versatile compared to other key/value stores: it provides a set of powerful commands and supports diverse data structures, such as strings, hashes, lists, sets, ordered sets, and even bitmaps or HyperLogLogs.

Although SQL is best suited to schema-defined persistent data storage, Redis offers numerous advantages when dealing with rapidly changing data, volatile storage, or when a quick cache is needed. Let's take a look at how Redis can be used to build a new functionality into your project.

Installing Redis

If you are using Linux or macOS, download the latest Redis version from `https://redis.io/download`. Unzip the `tar.gz` file, enter the `redis` directory, and compile Redis using the `make` command, as follows:

```
cd redis-5.0.8
make
```

Redis is now installed on your machine. If you are using Windows, the preferred method to install Redis is to enable the **Windows Subsystem for Linux (WSL)** and install it in the Linux system. You can read instructions on enabling WSL and installing Redis at `https://redislabs.com/blog/redis-on-windows-10/`.

After installing Redis, use the following shell command to start the Redis server:

```
src/redis-server
```

You should see an output that ends with the following lines:

```
# Server initialized
* Ready to accept connections
```

By default, Redis runs on port 6379. You can specify a custom port using the `--port` flag, for example, `redis-server --port 6655`.

Keep the Redis server running and open another shell. Start the Redis client with the following command:

```
src/redis-cli
```

You will see the Redis client shell prompt, like this:

```
127.0.0.1:6379>
```

The Redis client allows you to execute Redis commands directly from the shell. Let's try some commands. Enter the SET command in the Redis shell to store a value in a key:

```
127.0.0.1:6379> SET name "Peter"
OK
```

The preceding command creates a `name` key with the string value `"Peter"` in the Redis database. The `OK` output indicates that the key has been saved successfully.

Next, retrieve the value using the GET command, as follows:

```
127.0.0.1:6379> GET name
"Peter"
```

You can also check whether a key exists using the EXISTS command. This command returns 1 if the given key exists, and 0 otherwise:

```
127.0.0.1:6379> EXISTS name
(integer) 1
```

You can set the time for a key to expire using the EXPIRE command, which allows you to set time-to-live in seconds. Another option is using the EXPIREAT command, which expects a Unix timestamp. Key expiration is useful for using Redis as a cache or to store volatile data:

```
127.0.0.1:6379> GET name
"Peter"
127.0.0.1:6379> EXPIRE name 2
(integer) 1
```

Wait for two seconds and try to get the same key again:

```
127.0.0.1:6379> GET name
(nil)
```

The (nil) response is a null response and means that no key has been found. You can also delete any key using the DEL command, as follows:

```
127.0.0.1:6379> SET total 1
OK
127.0.0.1:6379> DEL total
(integer) 1
127.0.0.1:6379> GET total
(nil)
```

These are just basic commands for key operations. You can take a look at all Redis commands at https://redis.io/commands and all Redis data types at https://redis.io/topics/data-types.

Using Redis with Python

You will need Python bindings for Redis. Install redis-py via pip using the following command:

```
pip install redis==3.4.1
```

You can find the redis-py documentation at https://redis-py.readthedocs.io/.

The redis-py package interacts with Redis, providing a Python interface that follows the Redis command syntax. Open the Python shell and execute the following code:

```
>>> import redis
>>> r = redis.Redis(host='localhost', port=6379, db=0)
```

The preceding code creates a connection with the Redis database. In Redis, databases are identified by an integer index instead of a database name. By default, a client is connected to the database 0. The number of available Redis databases is set to 16, but you can change this in the redis.conf configuration file.

Next, set a key using the Python shell:

```
>>> r.set('foo', 'bar')
True
```

The command returns True, indicating that the key has been successfully created. Now you can retrieve the key using the get() command:

```
>>> r.get('foo')
b'bar'
```

As you will note from the preceding code, the methods of Redis follow the Redis command syntax.

Let's integrate Redis into your project. Edit the settings.py file of the bookmarks project and add the following settings to it:

```
REDIS_HOST = 'localhost'
REDIS_PORT = 6379
REDIS_DB = 0
```

These are the settings for the Redis server and the database that you will use for your project.

Storing item views in Redis

Let's find a way to store the total number of times an image has been viewed. If you implement this using the Django ORM, it will involve a SQL UPDATE query every time an image is displayed. If you use Redis instead, you just need to increment a counter stored in memory, resulting in a much better performance and less overhead.

Edit the `views.py` file of the `images` application and add the following code to it after the existing `import` statements:

```
import redis
from django.conf import settings


# connect to redis
r = redis.Redis(host=settings.REDIS_HOST,
                port=settings.REDIS_PORT,
                db=settings.REDIS_DB)
```

With the preceding code, you establish the Redis connection in order to use it in your views. Edit the `views.py` file of the `images` application and modify the `image_detail` view, like this:

```
def image_detail(request, id, slug):
    image = get_object_or_404(Image, id=id, slug=slug)
    # increment total image views by 1
    total_views = r.incr(f'image:{image.id}:views')
    return render(request,
                  'images/image/detail.html',
                  {'section': 'images',
                   'image': image,
                   'total_views': total_views})
```

In this view, you use the `incr` command that increments the value of a given key by 1. If the key doesn't exist, the `incr` command creates it. The `incr()` method returns the final value of the key after performing the operation. You store the value in the `total_views` variable and pass it in the template context. You build the Redis key using a notation, such as `object-type:id:field` (for example, `image:33:id`).

 The convention for naming Redis keys is to use a colon sign as a separator for creating namespaced keys. By doing so, the key names are especially verbose and related keys share part of the same schema in their names.

Edit the `images/image/detail.html` template of the `images` application and add the following code to it after the existing `<span class="count">` element:

```
<span class="count">
  {{ total_views }} view{{ total_views|pluralize }}
</span>
```

Now, open an image detail page in your browser and reload it several times. You will see that each time the view is processed, the total views displayed is incremented by 1. Take a look at the following example:

Figure 6.7: The image detail page, including the count of likes and views

Great! You have successfully integrated Redis into your project to store item counts.

Storing a ranking in Redis

Let's build something more complex with Redis. You will create a ranking of the most viewed images in your platform. For building this ranking, you will use Redis sorted sets. A sorted set is a non-repeating collection of strings in which every member is associated with a score. Items are sorted by their score.

Edit the `views.py` file of the `images` application and make the `image_detail` view look as follows:

```python
def image_detail(request, id, slug):
    image = get_object_or_404(Image, id=id, slug=slug)
    # increment total image views by 1
    total_views = r.incr(f'image:{image.id}:views')
    # increment image ranking by 1
    r.zincrby('image_ranking', 1, image.id)
    return render(request,
                  'images/image/detail.html',
                  {'section': 'images',
                   'image': image,
                   'total_views': total_views})
```

You use the `zincrby()` command to store image views in a sorted set with the `image:ranking` key. You will store the image `id` and a related score of `1`, which will be added to the total score of this element in the sorted set. This will allow you to keep track of all image views globally and have a sorted set ordered by the total number of views.

Now, create a new view to display the ranking of the most viewed images. Add the following code to the `views.py` file of the `images` application:

```
@login_required
def image_ranking(request):
    # get image ranking dictionary
    image_ranking = r.zrange('image_ranking', 0, -1,
                             desc=True)[:10]
    image_ranking_ids = [int(id) for id in image_ranking]
    # get most viewed images
    most_viewed = list(Image.objects.filter(
                          id__in=image_ranking_ids))
    most_viewed.sort(key=lambda x: image_ranking_ids.index(x.id))
    return render(request,
                  'images/image/ranking.html',
                  {'section': 'images',
                   'most_viewed': most_viewed})
```

The `image_ranking` view works like this:

1. You use the `zrange()` command to obtain the elements in the sorted set. This command expects a custom range according to the lowest and highest score. Using `0` as the lowest and `-1` as the highest score, you are telling Redis to return all elements in the sorted set. You also specify `desc=True` to retrieve the elements ordered by descending score. Finally, you slice the results using `[:10]` to get the first 10 elements with the highest score.

2. You build a list of returned image IDs and store it in the `image_ranking_ids` variable as a list of integers. You retrieve the `Image` objects for those IDs and force the query to be executed using the `list()` function. It is important to force the QuerySet execution because you will use the `sort()` list method on it (at this point, you need a list of objects instead of a QuerySet).

3. You sort the `Image` objects by their index of appearance in the image ranking. Now you can use the `most_viewed` list in your template to display the 10 most viewed images.

Create a new `ranking.html` template inside the `images/image/` template directory of the `images` application and add the following code to it:

```
{% extends "base.html" %}

{% block title %}Images ranking{% endblock %}

{% block content %}
  <h1>Images ranking</h1>
  <ol>
    {% for image in most_viewed %}
      <li>
        <a href="{{ image.get_absolute_url }}">
          {{ image.title }}
        </a>
      </li>
    {% endfor %}
  </ol>
{% endblock %}
```

The template is pretty straightforward. You iterate over the `Image` objects contained in the `most_viewed` list and display their names, including a link to the image detail page.

Finally, you need to create a URL pattern for the new view. Edit the `urls.py` file of the `images` application and add the following pattern to it:

```
path('ranking/', views.image_ranking, name='ranking'),
```

Run the development server, access your site in your web browser, and load the image detail page multiple times for different images. Then, access `http://127.0.0.1:8000/images/ranking/` from your browser. You should be able to see an image ranking, as follows:

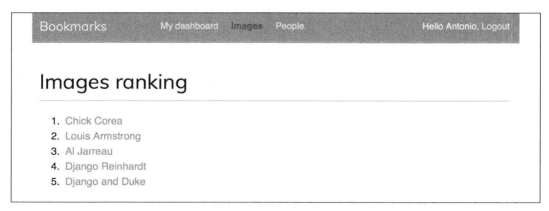

Figure 6.8: The ranking page built with data retrieved from Redis

Great! You just created a ranking with Redis.

Next steps with Redis

Redis is not a replacement for your SQL database, but it does offer fast in-memory storage that is more suitable for certain tasks. Add it to your stack and use it when you really feel it's needed. The following are some scenarios in which Redis could be useful:

- **Counting**: As you have seen, it is very easy to manage counters with Redis. You can use `incr()` and `incrby()` for counting stuff.
- **Storing latest items**: You can add items to the start/end of a list using `lpush()` and `rpush()`. Remove and return the first/last element using `lpop()` / `rpop()`. You can trim the list's length using `ltrim()` to maintain its length.
- **Queues**: In addition to `push` and `pop` commands, Redis offers the blocking of queue commands.
- **Caching**: Using `expire()` and `expireat()` allows you to use Redis as a cache. You can also find third-party Redis cache backends for Django.
- **Pub/sub**: Redis provides commands for subscribing/unsubscribing and sending messages to channels.
- **Rankings and leaderboards**: Redis sorted sets with scores make it very easy to create leaderboards.
- **Real-time tracking**: Redis's fast I/O makes it perfect for real-time scenarios.

Summary

In this chapter, you built a follow system using many-to-many relationships with an intermediary model. You also created an activity stream using generic relations and you optimized QuerySets to retrieve related objects. This chapter then introduced you to Django signals, and you created a signal receiver function to denormalize related object counts. We covered application configuration classes, which you used to load your signal handlers. You also learned how to install and configure Redis in your Django project. Finally, you used Redis in your project to store item views, and you built an image ranking with Redis.

In the next chapter, you will learn how to build an online shop. You will create a product catalog and build a shopping cart using sessions. You will also discover how to launch asynchronous tasks using Celery.

7
Building an Online Shop

In the previous chapter, you created a follow system and built a user activity stream. You also learned how Django signals work and integrated Redis into your project to count image views.

In this chapter, you will start a new Django project that consists of a fully featured online shop. This chapter and the following two chapters will show you how to build the essential functionalities of an e-commerce platform. Your online shop will enable clients to browse products, add them to the cart, apply discount codes, go through the checkout process, pay with a credit card, and obtain an invoice. You will also implement a recommendation engine to recommend products to your customers, and you will use internationalization to offer your site in multiple languages.

In this chapter, you will learn how to:

- Create a product catalog
- Build a shopping cart using Django sessions
- Create custom context processors
- Manage customer orders
- Configure Celery in your project with RabbitMQ as a message broker
- Send asynchronous notifications to customers using Celery
- Monitor Celery using Flower

Creating an online shop project

Let's start with a new Django project to build an online shop. Your users will be able to browse through a product catalog and add products to a shopping cart. Finally, they will be able to check out the cart and place an order. This chapter will cover the following functionalities of an online shop:

- Creating the product catalog models, adding them to the administration site, and building the basic views to display the catalog
- Building a shopping cart system using Django sessions to allow users to keep selected products while they browse the site
- Creating the form and functionality to place orders on the site
- Sending an asynchronous email confirmation to users when they place an order

Open a shell, create a virtual environment for the new project, and activate it with the following commands:

```
mkdir env
python3 -m venv env/myshop
source env/myshop/bin/activate
```

Install Django in your virtual environment with the following command:

```
pip install "Django==3.0.*"
```

Start a new project called myshop with an application called shop by opening a shell and running the following commands:

```
django-admin startproject myshop
cd myshop/
django-admin startapp shop
```

Edit the settings.py file of your project and add the shop application to the INSTALLED_APPS setting as follows:

```
INSTALLED_APPS = [
    # ...
    'shop.apps.ShopConfig',
]
```

Your application is now active for this project. Let's define the models for the product catalog.

Creating product catalog models

The catalog of your shop will consist of products that are organized into different categories. Each product will have a name, an optional description, an optional image, a price, and its availability.

Edit the `models.py` file of the `shop` application that you just created and add the following code:

```python
from django.db import models

class Category(models.Model):
    name = models.CharField(max_length=200,
                            db_index=True)
    slug = models.SlugField(max_length=200,
                            unique=True)

    class Meta:
        ordering = ('name',)
        verbose_name = 'category'
        verbose_name_plural = 'categories'

    def __str__(self):
        return self.name

class Product(models.Model):
    category = models.ForeignKey(Category,
                                 related_name='products',
                                 on_delete=models.CASCADE)
    name = models.CharField(max_length=200, db_index=True)
    slug = models.SlugField(max_length=200, db_index=True)
    image = models.ImageField(upload_to='products/%Y/%m/%d',
                              blank=True)
    description = models.TextField(blank=True)
    price = models.DecimalField(max_digits=10, decimal_places=2)
    available = models.BooleanField(default=True)
    created = models.DateTimeField(auto_now_add=True)
    updated = models.DateTimeField(auto_now=True)

    class Meta:
        ordering = ('name',)
        index_together = (('id', 'slug'),)

    def __str__(self):
        return self.name
```

These are the `Category` and `Product` models. The `Category` model consists of a `name` field and a unique `slug` field (`unique` implies the creation of an index). The `Product` model fields are as follows:

- `category`: A `ForeignKey` to the `Category` model. This is a one-to-many relationship: a product belongs to one category and a category contains multiple products.

- `name`: The name of the product.

- `slug`: The slug for this product to build beautiful URLs.

- `image`: An optional product image.

- `description`: An optional description of the product.

- `price`: This field uses Python's `decimal.Decimal` type to store a fixed-precision decimal number. The maximum number of digits (including the decimal places) is set using the `max_digits` attribute and decimal places with the `decimal_places` attribute.

- `available`: A Boolean value that indicates whether the product is available or not. It will be used to enable/disable the product in the catalog.

- `created`: This field stores when the object was created.

- `updated`: This field stores when the object was last updated.

For the `price` field, you use `DecimalField` instead of `FloatField` to avoid rounding issues.

 Always use `DecimalField` to store monetary amounts. `FloatField` uses Python's `float` type internally, whereas `DecimalField` uses Python's `Decimal` type. By using the `Decimal` type, you will avoid `float` rounding issues.

In the `Meta` class of the `Product` model, you use the `index_together` meta option to specify an index for the `id` and `slug` fields together. You define this index because you plan to query products by both `id` and `slug`. Both fields are indexed together to improve performance for queries that utilize the two fields.

Since you are going to deal with images in your models, open the shell and install `Pillow` with the following command:

```
pip install Pillow==7.0.0
```

Now run the next command to create initial migrations for your project:

```
python manage.py makemigrations
```

You will see the following output:

```
Migrations for 'shop':
  shop/migrations/0001_initial.py
    - Create model Category
    - Create model Product
```

Run the next command to sync the database:

```
python manage.py migrate
```

You will see output that includes the following line:

```
Applying shop.0001_initial... OK
```

The database is now synced with your models.

Registering catalog models on the administration site

Let's add your models to the administration site so that you can easily manage categories and products. Edit the `admin.py` file of the `shop` application and add the following code to it:

```
from django.contrib import admin
from .models import Category, Product

@admin.register(Category)
class CategoryAdmin(admin.ModelAdmin):
    list_display = ['name', 'slug']
    prepopulated_fields = {'slug': ('name',)}

@admin.register(Product)
class ProductAdmin(admin.ModelAdmin):
    list_display = ['name', 'slug', 'price',
                    'available', 'created', 'updated']
    list_filter = ['available', 'created', 'updated']
    list_editable = ['price', 'available']
    prepopulated_fields = {'slug': ('name',)}
```

Remember that you use the `prepopulated_fields` attribute to specify fields where the value is automatically set using the value of other fields. As you have seen before, this is convenient for generating slugs.

You use the `list_editable` attribute in the `ProductAdmin` class to set the fields that can be edited from the list display page of the administration site. This will allow you to edit multiple rows at once. Any field in `list_editable` must also be listed in the `list_display` attribute, since only the fields displayed can be edited.

Now create a superuser for your site using the following command:

```
python manage.py createsuperuser
```

Start the development server with the command `python manage.py runserver`. Open `http://127.0.0.1:8000/admin/shop/product/add/` in your browser and log in with the user that you just created. Add a new category and product using the administration interface. The product change list page of the administration page will then look like this:

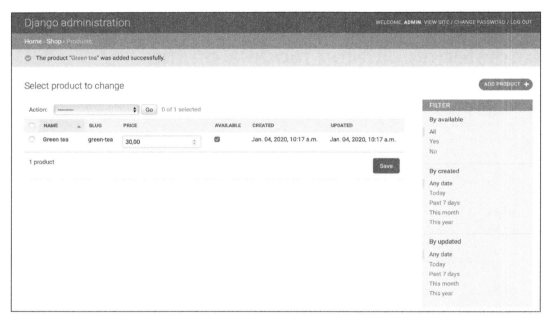

Figure 7.1: The product change list page

Building catalog views

In order to display the product catalog, you need to create a view to list all the products or filter products by a given category. Edit the `views.py` file of the `shop` application and add the following code to it:

```python
from django.shortcuts import render, get_object_or_404
from .models import Category, Product
```

```
def product_list(request, category_slug=None):
    category = None
    categories = Category.objects.all()
    products = Product.objects.filter(available=True)
    if category_slug:
        category = get_object_or_404(Category, slug=category_slug)
        products = products.filter(category=category)
    return render(request,
                  'shop/product/list.html',
                  {'category': category,
                   'categories': categories,
                   'products': products})
```

In the preceding code, you filter the QuerySet with `available=True` to retrieve only available products. You use an optional `category_slug` parameter to optionally filter products by a given category.

You also need a view to retrieve and display a single product. Add the following view to the `views.py` file:

```
def product_detail(request, id, slug):
    product = get_object_or_404(Product,
                                id=id,
                                slug=slug,
                                available=True)
    return render(request,
                  'shop/product/detail.html',
                  {'product': product})
```

The `product_detail` view expects the `id` and `slug` parameters in order to retrieve the `Product` instance. You can get this instance just through the ID, since it's a unique attribute. However, you include the slug in the URL to build SEO-friendly URLs for products.

After building the product list and detail views, you have to define URL patterns for them. Create a new file inside the `shop` application directory and name it `urls.py`. Add the following code to it:

```
from django.urls import path
from . import views

app_name = 'shop'

urlpatterns = [
    path('', views.product_list, name='product_list'),
```

```
        path('<slug:category_slug>/', views.product_list,
            name='product_list_by_category'),
        path('<int:id>/<slug:slug>/', views.product_detail,
            name='product_detail'),
]
```

These are the URL patterns for your product catalog. You have defined two different URL patterns for the product_list view: a pattern named product_list, which calls the product_list view without any parameters, and a pattern named product_list_by_category, which provides a category_slug parameter to the view for filtering products according to a given category. You added a pattern for the product_detail view, which passes the id and slug parameters to the view in order to retrieve a specific product.

Edit the urls.py file of the myshop project to make it look like this:

```
from django.contrib import admin
from django.urls import path, include

urlpatterns = [
    path('admin/', admin.site.urls),
    path('', include('shop.urls', namespace='shop')),
]
```

In the main URL patterns of the project, you include URLs for the shop application under a custom namespace named shop.

Next, edit the models.py file of the shop application, import the reverse() function, and add a get_absolute_url() method to the Category and Product models as follows:

```
from django.urls import reverse
# ...
class Category(models.Model):
    # ...
    def get_absolute_url(self):
        return reverse('shop:product_list_by_category',
                        args=[self.slug])

class Product(models.Model):
    # ...
    def get_absolute_url(self):
        return reverse('shop:product_detail',
                        args=[self.id, self.slug])
```

As you already know, `get_absolute_url()` is the convention to retrieve the URL for a given object. Here, you use the URL patterns that you just defined in the `urls.py` file.

Creating catalog templates

Now you need to create templates for the product list and detail views. Create the following directory and file structure inside the `shop` application directory:

```
templates/
    shop/
        base.html
        product/
            list.html
            detail.html
```

You need to define a base template and then extend it in the product list and detail templates. Edit the `shop/base.html` template and add the following code to it:

```html
{% load static %}
<!DOCTYPE html>
<html>
  <head>
    <meta charset="utf-8" />
    <title>{% block title %}My shop{% endblock %}</title>
    <link href="{% static "css/base.css" %}" rel="stylesheet">
  </head>
  <body>
    <div id="header">
      <a href="/" class="logo">My shop</a>
    </div>
    <div id="subheader">
      <div class="cart">
        Your cart is empty.
      </div>
    </div>
    <div id="content">
      {% block content %}
      {% endblock %}
    </div>
  </body>
</html>
```

This is the base template that you will use for your shop. In order to include the CSS styles and images that are used by the templates, you need to copy the static files that accompany this chapter, which are located in the `static/` directory of the `shop` application. Copy them to the same location in your project. You can find the contents of the directory at `https://github.com/PacktPublishing/Django-3-by-Example/tree/master/Chapter07/myshop/shop/static`.

Edit the `shop/product/list.html` template and add the following code to it:

```
{% extends "shop/base.html" %}
{% load static %}

{% block title %}
  {% if category %}{{ category.name }}{% else %}Products{% endif %}
{% endblock %}

{% block content %}
  <div id="sidebar">
    <h3>Categories</h3>
    <ul>
      <li {% if not category %}class="selected"{% endif %}>
        <a href="{% url "shop:product_list" %}">All</a>
      </li>
      {% for c in categories %}
        <li {% if category.slug == c.slug %}class="selected"
        {% endif %}>
          <a href="{{ c.get_absolute_url }}">{{ c.name }}</a>
        </li>
      {% endfor %}
    </ul>
  </div>
  <div id="main" class="product-list">
    <h1>{% if category %}{{ category.name }}{% else %}Products
    {% endif %}</h1>
    {% for product in products %}
      <div class="item">
        <a href="{{ product.get_absolute_url }}">
          <img src="{% if product.image %}{{ product.image.url }}{%
else %}{% static "img/no_image.png" %}{% endif %}">
        </a>
        <a href="{{ product.get_absolute_url }}">{{ product.name }}</
a>
        <br>
        ${{ product.price }}
      </div>
```

```
        {% endfor %}
    </div>
{% endblock %}
```

Make sure that no template tag is split into multiple lines.

This is the product list template. It extends the `shop/base.html` template and uses the `categories` context variable to display all the categories in a sidebar, and `products` to display the products of the current page. The same template is used for both listing all available products and listing products filtered by a category. Since the `image` field of the `Product` model can be blank, you need to provide a default image for the products that don't have an image. The image is located in your static files directory with the relative path `img/no_image.png`.

Since you are using `ImageField` to store product images, you need the development server to serve uploaded image files.

Edit the `settings.py` file of `myshop` and add the following settings:

```
MEDIA_URL = '/media/'
MEDIA_ROOT = os.path.join(BASE_DIR, 'media/')
```

`MEDIA_URL` is the base URL that serves media files uploaded by users. `MEDIA_ROOT` is the local path where these files reside, which you build by dynamically prepending the `BASE_DIR` variable.

For Django to serve the uploaded media files using the development server, edit the main `urls.py` file of `myshop` and add the following code to it:

```
from django.conf import settings
from django.conf.urls.static import static

urlpatterns = [
    # ...
]
if settings.DEBUG:
    urlpatterns += static(settings.MEDIA_URL,
                          document_root=settings.MEDIA_ROOT)
```

Remember that you only serve static files this way during development. In a production environment, you should never serve static files with Django; the Django development server doesn't serve static files in an efficient manner. *Chapter 14, Going Live*, will teach you how to serve static files in a production environment.

Add a couple of products to your shop using the administration site and open `http://127.0.0.1:8000/` in your browser. You will see the product list page, which will look similar to this:

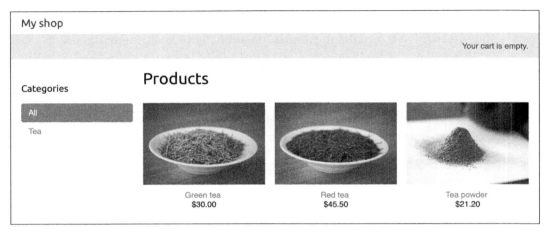

Figure 7.2: The product list page

If you create a product using the administration site and don't upload any image for it, the default `no_image.png` image will be displayed instead:

Figure 7.3: The product list displaying a default image for products that have no image

Edit the `shop/product/detail.html` template and add the following code to it:

```
{% extends "shop/base.html" %}
{% load static %}

{% block title %}
  {{ product.name }}
{% endblock %}

{% block content %}
  <div class="product-detail">
```

```
<img src="{% if product.image %}{{ product.image.url }}{% else %}
{% static "img/no_image.png" %}{% endif %}">
<h1>{{ product.name }}</h1>
<h2>
  <a href="{{ product.category.get_absolute_url }}">
    {{ product.category }}
  </a>
</h2>
<p class="price">${{ product.price }}</p>
{{ product.description|linebreaks }}
  </div>
{% endblock %}
```

In the preceding code, you call the `get_absolute_url()` method on the related category object to display the available products that belong to the same category.

Now open `http://127.0.0.1:8000/` in your browser and click on any product to see the product detail page. It will look as follows:

Figure 7.4: The product detail page

You have now created a basic product catalog.

Building a shopping cart

After building the product catalog, the next step is to create a shopping cart so that users can pick the products that they want to purchase. A shopping cart allows users to select products and set the amount they want to order, and then store this information temporarily while they browse the site, until they eventually place an order. The cart has to be persisted in the session so that the cart items are maintained during a user's visit.

You will use Django's session framework to persist the cart. The cart will be kept in the session until it finishes or the user checks out of the cart. You will also need to build additional Django models for the cart and its items.

Using Django sessions

Django provides a session framework that supports anonymous and user sessions. The session framework allows you to store arbitrary data for each visitor. Session data is stored on the server side, and cookies contain the session ID unless you use the cookie-based session engine. The session middleware manages the sending and receiving of cookies. The default session engine stores session data in the database, but you can choose other session engines.

To use sessions, you have to make sure that the MIDDLEWARE setting of your project contains `'django.contrib.sessions.middleware.SessionMiddleware'`. This middleware manages sessions. It's added by default to the MIDDLEWARE setting when you create a new project using the `startproject` command.

The session middleware makes the current session available in the `request` object. You can access the current session using `request.session`, treating it like a Python dictionary to store and retrieve session data. The `session` dictionary accepts any Python object by default that can be serialized to JSON. You can set a variable in the session like this:

```
request.session['foo'] = 'bar'
```

Retrieve a session key as follows:

```
request.session.get('foo')
```

Delete a key you previously stored in the session as follows:

```
del request.session['foo']
```

When users log in to the site, their anonymous session is lost and a new session is created for authenticated users. If you store items in an anonymous session that you need to keep after the user logs in, you will have to copy the old session data into the new session. You can do this by retrieving the session data before you log in the user using the `login()` function of the Django authentication system and storing it in the session after that.

Session settings

There are several settings you can use to configure sessions for your project. The most important is SESSION_ENGINE. This setting allows you to set the place where sessions are stored. By default, Django stores sessions in the database using the Session model of the django.contrib.sessions application.

Django offers the following options for storing session data:

- **Database sessions**: Session data is stored in the database. This is the default session engine.

- **File-based sessions**: Session data is stored in the filesystem.

- **Cached sessions**: Session data is stored in a cache backend. You can specify cache backends using the CACHES setting. Storing session data in a cache system provides the best performance.

- **Cached database sessions**: Session data is stored in a write-through cache and database. Reads only use the database if the data is not already in the cache.

- **Cookie-based sessions**: Session data is stored in the cookies that are sent to the browser.

 For better performance use a cache-based session engine. Django supports Memcached out of the box and you can find third-party cache backends for Redis and other cache systems.

You can customize sessions with specific settings. Here are some of the important session-related settings:

- SESSION_COOKIE_AGE: The duration of session cookies in seconds. The default value is 1209600 (two weeks).

- SESSION_COOKIE_DOMAIN: The domain used for session cookies. Set this to mydomain.com to enable cross-domain cookies or use None for a standard domain cookie.

- SESSION_COOKIE_SECURE: A Boolean indicating that the cookie should only be sent if the connection is an HTTPS connection.

- SESSION_EXPIRE_AT_BROWSER_CLOSE: A Boolean indicating that the session has to expire when the browser is closed.

- SESSION_SAVE_EVERY_REQUEST: A Boolean that, if True, will save the session to the database on every request. The session expiration is also updated each time it's saved.

You can see all the session settings and their default values at `https://docs.djangoproject.com/en/3.0/ref/settings/#sessions`.

Session expiration

You can choose to use browser-length sessions or persistent sessions using the `SESSION_EXPIRE_AT_BROWSER_CLOSE` setting. This is set to `False` by default, forcing the session duration to the value stored in the `SESSION_COOKIE_AGE` setting. If you set `SESSION_EXPIRE_AT_BROWSER_CLOSE` to `True`, the session will expire when the user closes the browser, and the `SESSION_COOKIE_AGE` setting will not have any effect.

You can use the `set_expiry()` method of `request.session` to overwrite the duration of the current session.

Storing shopping carts in sessions

You need to create a simple structure that can be serialized to JSON for storing cart items in a session. The cart has to include the following data for each item contained in it:

- The ID of a `Product` instance
- The quantity selected for the product
- The unit price for the product

Since product prices may vary, let's take the approach of storing the product's price along with the product itself when it's added to the cart. By doing so, you use the current price of the product when users add it to their cart, no matter whether the product's price is changed afterwards. This means that the price that the item has when the client adds it to the cart is maintained for that client in the session until checkout is completed or the session finishes.

Next, you have to build functionality to create shopping carts and associate them with sessions. This has to work as follows:

- When a cart is needed, you check whether a custom session key is set. If no cart is set in the session, you create a new cart and save it in the cart session key.
- For successive requests, you perform the same check and get the cart items from the cart session key. You retrieve the cart items from the session and their related `Product` objects from the database.

Edit the `settings.py` file of your project and add the following setting to it:

```
CART_SESSION_ID = 'cart'
```

This is the key that you are going to use to store the cart in the user session. Since Django sessions are managed per visitor, you can use the same cart session key for all sessions.

Let's create an application for managing shopping carts. Open the terminal and create a new application, running the following command from the project directory:

python manage.py startapp cart

Then, edit the `settings.py` file of your project and add the new application to the `INSTALLED_APPS` setting, as follows:

```
INSTALLED_APPS = [
    # ...
    'shop.apps.ShopConfig',
    'cart.apps.CartConfig',
]
```

Create a new file inside the `cart` application directory and name it `cart.py`. Add the following code to it:

```
from decimal import Decimal
from django.conf import settings
from shop.models import Product


class Cart(object):

    def __init__(self, request):
        """
        Initialize the cart.
        """
        self.session = request.session
        cart = self.session.get(settings.CART_SESSION_ID)
        if not cart:
            # save an empty cart in the session
            cart = self.session[settings.CART_SESSION_ID] = {}
        self.cart = cart
```

This is the `Cart` class that will allow you to manage the shopping cart. You require the cart to be initialized with a `request` object. You store the current session using `self.session = request.session` to make it accessible to the other methods of the `Cart` class.

First, you try to get the cart from the current session using `self.session.get(settings.CART_SESSION_ID)`. If no cart is present in the session, you create an empty cart by setting an empty dictionary in the session.

You will build your `cart` dictionary with product IDs as keys, and for each product key, a dictionary will be a value that includes quantity and price. By doing this, you can guarantee that a product will not be added more than once to the cart. This way, you can also simplify retrieving cart items.

Let's create a method to add products to the cart or update their quantity. Add the following `add()` and `save()` methods to the `Cart` class:

```python
class Cart(object):
    # ...
    def add(self, product, quantity=1, override_quantity=False):
        """
        Add a product to the cart or update its quantity.
        """
        product_id = str(product.id)
        if product_id not in self.cart:
            self.cart[product_id] = {'quantity': 0,
                                     'price': str(product.price)}
        if override_quantity:
            self.cart[product_id]['quantity'] = quantity
        else:
            self.cart[product_id]['quantity'] += quantity
        self.save()

    def save(self):
        # mark the session as "modified" to make sure it gets saved
        self.session.modified = True
```

The `add()` method takes the following parameters as input:

- `product`: The `product` instance to add or update in the cart.

- `quantity`: An optional integer with the product quantity. This defaults to `1`.

- `override_quantity`: This is a Boolean that indicates whether the quantity needs to be overridden with the given quantity (`True`), or whether the new quantity has to be added to the existing quantity (`False`).

You use the product ID as a key in the cart's content dictionary. You convert the product ID into a string because Django uses JSON to serialize session data, and JSON only allows string key names. The product ID is the key, and the value that you persist is a dictionary with quantity and price figures for the product. The product's price is converted from decimal into a string in order to serialize it. Finally, you call the `save()` method to save the cart in the session.

The `save()` method marks the session as modified using `session.modified = True`. This tells Django that the session has changed and needs to be saved.

You also need a method for removing products from the cart. Add the following method to the `Cart` class:

```
class Cart(object):
    # ...
    def remove(self, product):
        """
        Remove a product from the cart.
        """
        product_id = str(product.id)
        if product_id in self.cart:
            del self.cart[product_id]
            self.save()
```

The `remove()` method removes a given product from the `cart` dictionary and calls the `save()` method to update the cart in the session.

You will have to iterate through the items contained in the cart and access the related `Product` instances. To do so, you can define an `__iter__()` method in your class. Add the following method to the `Cart` class:

```
class Cart(object):
    # ...
    def __iter__(self):
        """
        Iterate over the items in the cart and get the products
        from the database.
        """
        product_ids = self.cart.keys()
        # get the product objects and add them to the cart
        products = Product.objects.filter(id__in=product_ids)

        cart = self.cart.copy()
        for product in products:
            cart[str(product.id)]['product'] = product

        for item in cart.values():
            item['price'] = Decimal(item['price'])
            item['total_price'] = item['price'] * item['quantity']
            yield item
```

In the __iter__() method, you retrieve the Product instances that are present in the cart to include them in the cart items. You copy the current cart in the cart variable and add the Product instances to it. Finally, you iterate over the cart items, converting each item's price back into decimal, and adding a total_price attribute to each item. This __iter__() method will allow you to easily iterate over the items in the cart in views and templates.

You also need a way to return the number of total items in the cart. When the len() function is executed on an object, Python calls its __len__() method to retrieve its length. Next, you are going to define a custom __len__() method to return the total number of items stored in the cart.

Add the following __len__() method to the Cart class:

```python
class Cart(object):
    # ...
    def __len__(self):
        """
        Count all items in the cart.
        """
        return sum(item['quantity'] for item in self.cart.values())
```

You return the sum of the quantities of all the cart items.

Add the following method to calculate the total cost of the items in the cart:

```python
class Cart(object):
    # ...
    def get_total_price(self):
        return sum(Decimal(item['price']) * item['quantity'] for item
in self.cart.values())
```

Finally, add a method to clear the cart session:

```python
class Cart(object):
    # ...
    def clear(self):
        # remove cart from session
        del self.session[settings.CART_SESSION_ID]
        self.save()
```

Your Cart class is now ready to manage shopping carts.

Creating shopping cart views

Now that you have a `Cart` class to manage the cart, you need to create the views to add, update, or remove items from it. You need to create the following views:

- A view to add or update items in the cart that can handle current and new quantities
- A view to remove items from the cart
- A view to display cart items and totals

Adding items to the cart

In order to add items to the cart, you need a form that allows the user to select a quantity. Create a `forms.py` file inside the `cart` application directory and add the following code to it:

```
from django import forms

PRODUCT_QUANTITY_CHOICES = [(i, str(i)) for i in range(1, 21)]

class CartAddProductForm(forms.Form):
    quantity = forms.TypedChoiceField(
                            choices=PRODUCT_QUANTITY_CHOICES,
                            coerce=int)
    override = forms.BooleanField(required=False,
                            initial=False,
                            widget=forms.HiddenInput)
```

You will use this form to add products to the cart. Your `CartAddProductForm` class contains the following two fields:

- `quantity`: This allows the user to select a quantity between one and 20. You use a `TypedChoiceField` field with `coerce=int` to convert the input into an integer.

- `override`: This allows you to indicate whether the quantity has to be added to any existing quantity in the cart for this product (`False`), or whether the existing quantity has to be overridden with the given quantity (`True`). You use a `HiddenInput` widget for this field, since you don't want to display it to the user.

Let's create a view for adding items to the cart. Edit the `views.py` file of the `cart` application and add the following code to it:

```
from django.shortcuts import render, redirect, get_object_or_404
from django.views.decorators.http import require_POST
from shop.models import Product
from .cart import Cart
from .forms import CartAddProductForm


@require_POST
def cart_add(request, product_id):
    cart = Cart(request)
    product = get_object_or_404(Product, id=product_id)
    form = CartAddProductForm(request.POST)
    if form.is_valid():
        cd = form.cleaned_data
        cart.add(product=product,
                 quantity=cd['quantity'],
                 override_quantity=cd['override'])
    return redirect('cart:cart_detail')
```

This is the view for adding products to the cart or updating quantities for existing products. You use the `require_POST` decorator to allow only POST requests. The view receives the product ID as a parameter. You retrieve the `Product` instance with the given ID and validate `CartAddProductForm`. If the form is valid, you either add or update the product in the cart. The view redirects to the `cart_detail` URL, which will display the contents of the cart. You are going to create the `cart_detail` view shortly.

You also need a view to remove items from the cart. Add the following code to the `views.py` file of the `cart` application:

```
@require_POST
def cart_remove(request, product_id):
    cart = Cart(request)
    product = get_object_or_404(Product, id=product_id)
    cart.remove(product)
    return redirect('cart:cart_detail')
```

The `cart_remove` view receives the product ID as a parameter. You use the `require_POST` decorator to allow only POST requests. You retrieve the `Product` instance with the given ID and remove the product from the cart. Then, you redirect the user to the `cart_detail` URL.

Finally, you need a view to display the cart and its items. Add the following view to the `views.py` file of the `cart` application:

```
def cart_detail(request):
    cart = Cart(request)
    return render(request, 'cart/detail.html', {'cart': cart})
```

The `cart_detail` view gets the current cart to display it.

You have created views to add items to the cart, update quantities, remove items from the cart, and display the cart's contents. Let's add URL patterns for these views. Create a new file inside the `cart` application directory and name it `urls.py`. Add the following URLs to it:

```
from django.urls import path
from . import views

app_name = 'cart'

urlpatterns = [
    path('', views.cart_detail, name='cart_detail'),
    path('add/<int:product_id>/', views.cart_add, name='cart_add'),
    path('remove/<int:product_id>/', views.cart_remove,
                                     name='cart_remove'),
]
```

Edit the main `urls.py` file of the `myshop` project and add the following URL pattern to include the cart URLs:

```
urlpatterns = [
    path('admin/', admin.site.urls),
    path('cart/', include('cart.urls', namespace='cart')),
    path('', include('shop.urls', namespace='shop')),
]
```

Make sure that you include this URL pattern before the `shop.urls` pattern, since it's more restrictive than the latter.

Building a template to display the cart

The `cart_add` and `cart_remove` views don't render any templates, but you need to create a template for the `cart_detail` view to display cart items and totals.

Create the following file structure inside the `cart` application directory:

```
templates/
    cart/
        detail.html
```

Edit the `cart/detail.html` template and add the following code to it:

```
{% extends "shop/base.html" %}
{% load static %}

{% block title %}
  Your shopping cart
{% endblock %}

{% block content %}
  <h1>Your shopping cart</h1>
  <table class="cart">
    <thead>
      <tr>
        <th>Image</th>
        <th>Product</th>
        <th>Quantity</th>
        <th>Remove</th>
        <th>Unit price</th>
        <th>Price</th>
      </tr>
    </thead>
    <tbody>
      {% for item in cart %}
        {% with product=item.product %}
          <tr>
            <td>
              <a href="{{ product.get_absolute_url }}">
                <img src="{% if product.image %}{{ product.image.url
}}
                {% else %}{% static "img/no_image.png" %}{% endif %}">
              </a>
            </td>
            <td>{{ product.name }}</td>
            <td>{{ item.quantity }}</td>
            <td>
              <form action="{% url "cart:cart_remove" product.id %}"
method="post">
                <input type="submit" value="Remove">
                {% csrf_token %}
              </form>
            </td>
            <td class="num">${{ item.price }}</td>
            <td class="num">${{ item.total_price }}</td>
          </tr>
        {% endwith %}
      {% endfor %}
```

```
      <tr class="total">
        <td>Total</td>
        <td colspan="4"></td>
        <td class="num">${{ cart.get_total_price }}</td>
      </tr>
    </tbody>
  </table>
  <p class="text-right">
    <a href="{% url "shop:product_list" %}" class="button
    light">Continue shopping</a>
    <a href="#" class="button">Checkout</a>
  </p>
{% endblock %}
```

Make sure that no template tag is split into multiple lines.

This is the template that is used to display the cart's contents. It contains a table with the items stored in the current cart. You allow users to change the quantity of the selected products using a form that is posted to the cart_add view. You also allow users to remove items from the cart by providing a **Remove** button for each of them. Finally, you use an HTML form with an action attribute that points to the cart_remove URL including the product ID.

Adding products to the cart

Now you need to add an **Add to cart** button to the product detail page. Edit the views.py file of the shop application and add CartAddProductForm to the product_detail view, as follows:

```python
from cart.forms import CartAddProductForm


def product_detail(request, id, slug):
    product = get_object_or_404(Product, id=id,
                                         slug=slug,
                                         available=True)

    cart_product_form = CartAddProductForm()
    return render(request,
                  'shop/product/detail.html',
                  {'product': product,
                   'cart_product_form': cart_product_form})
```

Edit the shop/product/detail.html template of the shop application, and add the following form to the product price as follows:

```html
<p class="price">${{ product.price }}</p>
<form action="{% url "cart:cart_add" product.id %}" method="post">
```

```
    {{ cart_product_form }}
    {% csrf_token %}
    <input type="submit" value="Add to cart">
</form>
{{ product.description|linebreaks }}
```

Make sure that the development server is running with the command `python manage.py runserver`. Now open `http://127.0.0.1:8000/` in your browser and navigate to a product's detail page. It will contain a form to choose a quantity before adding the product to the cart. The page will look like this:

Figure 7.5: The product detail page, including the add to cart form

Choose a quantity and click on the **Add to cart** button. The form is submitted to the `cart_add` view via `POST`. The view adds the product to the cart in the session, including its current price and the selected quantity. Then, it redirects the user to the cart detail page, which will look like the following screenshot:

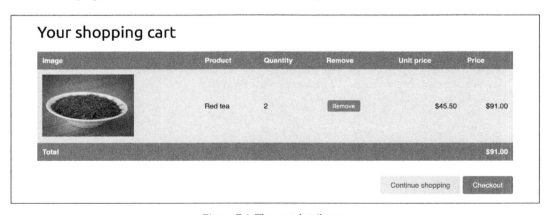

Figure 7.6: The cart detail page

Updating product quantities in the cart

When users see the cart, they might want to change product quantities before placing an order. You are going to allow users to change quantities from the cart detail page.

Edit the `views.py` file of the `cart` application and change the `cart_detail` view to this:

```python
def cart_detail(request):
    cart = Cart(request)
    for item in cart:
        item['update_quantity_form'] = CartAddProductForm(initial={
                                'quantity': item['quantity'],
                                'override': True})
    return render(request, 'cart/detail.html', {'cart': cart})
```

You create an instance of `CartAddProductForm` for each item in the cart to allow changing product quantities. You initialize the form with the current item quantity and set the `override` field to `True` so that when you submit the form to the `cart_add` view, the current quantity is replaced with the new one.

Now edit the `cart/detail.html` template of the `cart` application and find the following line:

```html
<td>{{ item.quantity }}</td>
```

Replace the previous line with the following code:

```html
<td>
  <form action="{% url "cart:cart_add" product.id %}" method="post">
    {{ item.update_quantity_form.quantity }}
    {{ item.update_quantity_form.override }}
    <input type="submit" value="Update">
    {% csrf_token %}
  </form>
</td>
```

Make sure that the development server is running with the command `python manage.py runserver`. Open `http://127.0.0.1:8000/cart/` in your browser.

You will see a form to edit the quantity for each cart item, as follows:

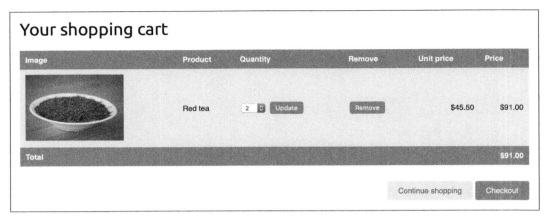

Figure 7.7: The cart detail page, including the form to update product quantities

Change the quantity of an item and click on the **Update** button to test the new functionality. You can also remove an item from the cart by clicking the **Remove** button.

Creating a context processor for the current cart

You might have noticed that the message **Your cart is empty** is displayed in the header of the site, even when the cart contains items. You should display the total number of items in the cart and the total cost instead. Since this has to be displayed on all pages, you need to build a context processor to include the current cart in the request context, regardless of the view that processes the request.

Context processors

A context processor is a Python function that takes the request object as an argument and returns a dictionary that gets added to the request context. Context processors come in handy when you need to make something available globally to all templates.

By default, when you create a new project using the startproject command, your project contains the following template context processors in the context_processors option inside the TEMPLATES setting:

- `django.template.context_processors.debug`: This sets the Boolean `debug` and `sql_queries` variables in the context, representing the list of SQL queries executed in the request

- `django.template.context_processors.request`: This sets the `request` variable in the context

- `django.contrib.auth.context_processors.auth`: This sets the `user` variable in the request

- `django.contrib.messages.context_processors.messages`: This sets a `messages` variable in the context containing all the messages that have been generated using the messages framework

Django also enables `django.template.context_processors.csrf` to avoid **cross-site request forgery (CSRF)** attacks. This context processor is not present in the settings, but it is always enabled and can't be turned off for security reasons.

You can see the list of all built-in context processors at `https://docs.djangoproject.com/en/3.0/ref/templates/api/#built-in-template-context-processors`.

Setting the cart into the request context

Let's create a context processor to set the current cart into the request context. With it, you will be able to access the cart in any template.

Create a new file inside the `cart` application directory and name it `context_processors.py`. Context processors can reside anywhere in your code, but creating them here will keep your code well organized. Add the following code to the file:

```
from .cart import Cart


def cart(request):
    return {'cart': Cart(request)}
```

In your context processor, you instantiate the cart using the `request` object and make it available for the templates as a variable named `cart`.

Edit the `settings.py` file of your project and add `cart.context_processors.cart` to the `context_processors` option inside the `TEMPLATES` setting, as follows:

```
TEMPLATES = [
    {
        'BACKEND': 'django.template.backends.django.DjangoTemplates',
        'DIRS': [],
        'APP_DIRS': True,
        'OPTIONS': {
```

```
            'context_processors': [
                # ...
                'cart.context_processors.cart',
            ],
        },
    },
]
```

The `cart` context processor will be executed every time a template is rendered using Django's `RequestContext`. The `cart` variable will be set in the context of your templates. You can read more about `RequestContext` at `https://docs.djangoproject.com/en/3.0/ref/templates/api/#django.template.RequestContext`.

 Context processors are executed in all the requests that use `RequestContext`. You might want to create a custom template tag instead of a context processor if your functionality is not needed in all templates, especially if it involves database queries.

Next, edit the `shop/base.html` template of the `shop` application and find the following lines:

```html
<div class="cart">
  Your cart is empty.
</div>
```

Replace the previous lines with the following code:

```html
<div class="cart">
  {% with total_items=cart|length %}
    {% if total_items > 0 %}
      Your cart:
      <a href="{% url "cart:cart_detail" %}">
        {{ total_items }} item{{ total_items|pluralize }},
        ${{ cart.get_total_price }}
      </a>
    {% else %}
      Your cart is empty.
    {% endif %}
  {% endwith %}
</div>
```

Reload your server using the command `python manage.py runserver`. Open `http://127.0.0.1:8000/` in your browser and add some products to the cart.

In the header of the website, you can now see the total number of items in the cart and the total cost, as follows:

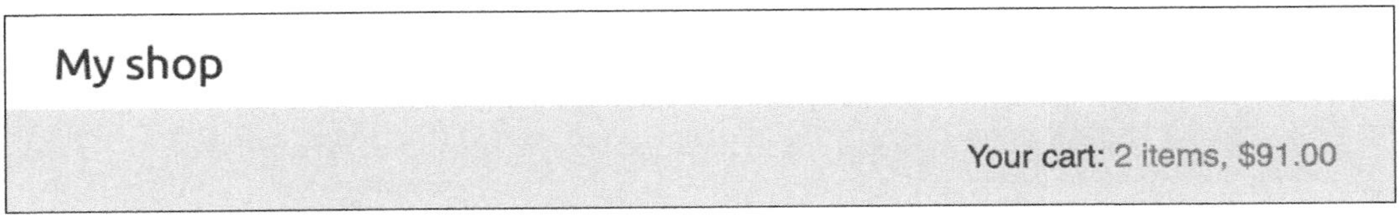

My shop

Your cart: 2 items, $91.00

Figure 7.8: The site header displaying current items in the cart

Registering customer orders

When a shopping cart is checked out, you need to save an order into the database. Orders will contain information about customers and the products they are buying.

Create a new application for managing customer orders using the following command:

```
python manage.py startapp orders
```

Edit the settings.py file of your project and add the new application to the INSTALLED_APPS setting, as follows:

```
INSTALLED_APPS = [
    # ...
    'orders.apps.OrdersConfig',
]
```

You have activated the orders application.

Creating order models

You will need a model to store the order details and a second model to store items bought, including their price and quantity. Edit the models.py file of the orders application and add the following code to it:

```
from django.db import models
from shop.models import Product


class Order(models.Model):
    first_name = models.CharField(max_length=50)
    last_name = models.CharField(max_length=50)
    email = models.EmailField()
    address = models.CharField(max_length=250)
    postal_code = models.CharField(max_length=20)
```

```
        city = models.CharField(max_length=100)
        created = models.DateTimeField(auto_now_add=True)
        updated = models.DateTimeField(auto_now=True)
        paid = models.BooleanField(default=False)

        class Meta:
            ordering = ('-created',)

        def __str__(self):
            return f'Order {self.id}'

        def get_total_cost(self):
            return sum(item.get_cost() for item in self.items.all())


    class OrderItem(models.Model):
        order = models.ForeignKey(Order,
                                  related_name='items',
                                  on_delete=models.CASCADE)
        product = models.ForeignKey(Product,
                                    related_name='order_items',
                                    on_delete=models.CASCADE)
        price = models.DecimalField(max_digits=10, decimal_places=2)
        quantity = models.PositiveIntegerField(default=1)

        def __str__(self):
            return str(self.id)

        def get_cost(self):
            return self.price * self.quantity
```

The `Order` model contains several fields to store customer information and a `paid` Boolean field, which defaults to `False`. Later on, you are going to use this field to differentiate between paid and unpaid orders. You also define a `get_total_cost()` method to obtain the total cost of the items bought in this order.

The `OrderItem` model allows you to store the product, quantity, and price paid for each item. You include `get_cost()` to return the cost of the item.

Run the next command to create initial migrations for the `orders` application:

```
python manage.py makemigrations
```

You will see the following output:

```
Migrations for 'orders':
  orders/migrations/0001_initial.py
    - Create model Order
    - Create model OrderItem
```

Run the following command to apply the new migration:

```
python manage.py migrate
```

Your order models are now synced to the database.

Including order models in the administration site

Let's add the order models to the administration site. Edit the `admin.py` file of the `orders` application to make it look like this:

```python
from django.contrib import admin
from .models import Order, OrderItem

class OrderItemInline(admin.TabularInline):
    model = OrderItem
    raw_id_fields = ['product']

@admin.register(Order)
class OrderAdmin(admin.ModelAdmin):
    list_display = ['id', 'first_name', 'last_name', 'email',
                    'address', 'postal_code', 'city', 'paid',
                    'created', 'updated']
    list_filter = ['paid', 'created', 'updated']
    inlines = [OrderItemInline]
```

You use a `ModelInline` class for the `OrderItem` model to include it as an *inline* in the `OrderAdmin` class. An inline allows you to include a model on the same edit page as its related model.

Run the development server with the command `python manage.py runserver`, and then open `http://127.0.0.1:8000/admin/orders/order/add/` in your browser. You will see the following page:

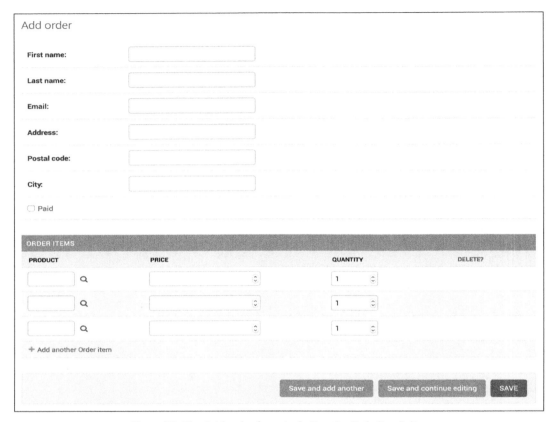

Figure 7.9: The Add order form, including the OrderItemInline

Creating customer orders

You will use the order models that you created to persist the items contained in the shopping cart when the user finally places an order. A new order will be created following these steps:

- Present a user with an order form to fill in their data
- Create a new `Order` instance with the data entered, and create an associated `OrderItem` instance for each item in the cart
- Clear all the cart's contents and redirect the user to a success page

First, you need a form to enter the order details. Create a new file inside the `orders` application directory and name it `forms.py`. Add the following code to it:

```
from django import forms
from .models import Order


class OrderCreateForm(forms.ModelForm):
    class Meta:
        model = Order
        fields = ['first_name', 'last_name', 'email', 'address',
                  'postal_code', 'city']
```

This is the form that you are going to use to create new `Order` objects. Now you need a view to handle the form and create a new order. Edit the `views.py` file of the `orders` application and add the following code to it:

```
from django.shortcuts import render
from .models import OrderItem
from .forms import OrderCreateForm
from cart.cart import Cart


def order_create(request):
    cart = Cart(request)
    if request.method == 'POST':
        form = OrderCreateForm(request.POST)
        if form.is_valid():
            order = form.save()
            for item in cart:
                OrderItem.objects.create(order=order,
                                         product=item['product'],
                                         price=item['price'],
                                         quantity=item['quantity'])

            # clear the cart
            cart.clear()
            return render(request,
                          'orders/order/created.html',
                          {'order': order})
    else:
        form = OrderCreateForm()
    return render(request,
                  'orders/order/create.html',
                  {'cart': cart, 'form': form})
```

In the `order_create` view, you obtain the current cart from the session with `cart = Cart(request)`. Depending on the request method, you perform the following tasks:

- **GET request**: Instantiates the `OrderCreateForm` form and renders the `orders/order/create.html` template.

- **POST request**: Validates the data sent in the request. If the data is valid, you create a new order in the database using `order = form.save()`. You iterate over the cart items and create an `OrderItem` for each of them. Finally, you clear the cart's contents and render the template `orders/order/created.html`.

Create a new file inside the `orders` application directory and name it `urls.py`. Add the following code to it:

```
from django.urls import path
from . import views

app_name = 'orders'

urlpatterns = [
    path('create/', views.order_create, name='order_create'),
]
```

This is the URL pattern for the `order_create` view. Edit the `urls.py` file of myshop and include the following pattern. Remember to place it before the `shop.urls` pattern:

```
path('orders/', include('orders.urls', namespace='orders')),
```

Edit the `cart/detail.html` template of the `cart` application and locate this line:

```
<a href="#" class="button">Checkout</a>
```

Add the `order_create` URL as follows:

```
<a href="{% url "orders:order_create" %}" class="button">
  Checkout
</a>
```

Users can now navigate from the cart detail page to the order form.

You still need to define templates for placing orders. Create the following file structure inside the `orders` application directory:

```
templates/
    orders/
        order/
            create.html
            created.html
```

Edit the `orders/order/create.html` template and include the following code:

```
{% extends "shop/base.html" %}

{% block title %}
  Checkout
{% endblock %}

{% block content %}
  <h1>Checkout</h1>

  <div class="order-info">
    <h3>Your order</h3>
    <ul>
      {% for item in cart %}
        <li>
          {{ item.quantity }}x {{ item.product.name }}
          <span>${{ item.total_price }}</span>
        </li>
      {% endfor %}
    </ul>
    <p>Total: ${{ cart.get_total_price }}</p>
  </div>

  <form method="post" class="order-form">
    {{ form.as_p }}
    <p><input type="submit" value="Place order"></p>
    {% csrf_token %}
  </form>
{% endblock %}
```

This template displays the cart items, including totals and the form to place an order.

Edit the `orders/order/created.html` template and add the following code:

```
{% extends "shop/base.html" %}

{% block title %}
  Thank you
{% endblock %}

{% block content %}
  <h1>Thank you</h1>
  <p>Your order has been successfully completed. Your order number is
  <strong>{{ order.id }}</strong>.</p>
{% endblock %}
```

This is the template that you render when the order is successfully created.

Start the web development server to load new files. Open `http://127.0.0.1:8000/` in your browser, add a couple of products to the cart, and continue to the checkout page. You will see a page like the one following:

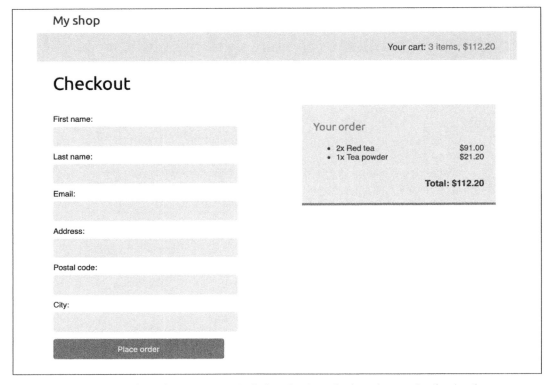

Figure 7.10: The order create page, including the chart checkout form and order details

Fill in the form with valid data and click on the **Place order** button. The order will be created and you will see a success page like this:

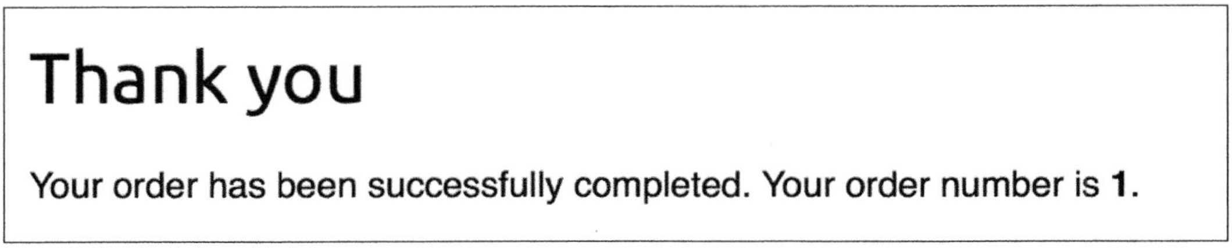

Thank you

Your order has been successfully completed. Your order number is **1**.

Figure 7.11: The order created template displaying the order number

Now open the administration site at `http://127.0.0.1:8000/admin/orders/ order/`. You will see that the order has been successfully created.

Launching asynchronous tasks with Celery

Everything you execute in a view affects response times. In many situations, you might want to return a response to the user as quickly as possible and let the server execute some process asynchronously. This is especially relevant for time-consuming processes or processes subject to failure, which might need a retry policy. For example, a video sharing platform allows users to upload videos but requires a long time to transcode uploaded videos. The site might return a response to users to inform them that the transcoding will start soon, and start transcoding the video asynchronously. Another example is sending emails to users. If your site sends email notifications from a view, the **Simple Mail Transfer Protocol** (**SMTP**) connection might fail or slow down the response. Launching asynchronous tasks is essential to avoid blocking the code execution.

Celery is a distributed task queue that can process vast amounts of messages. Using Celery, not only can you create asynchronous tasks easily and let them be executed by workers as soon as possible, but you can also schedule them to run at a specific time.

You can find the Celery documentation at `http://docs.celeryproject.org/en/ latest/index.html`.

Installing Celery

Let's install Celery and integrate it into your project. Install Celery via `pip` using the following command:

```
pip install celery==4.4.2
```

Celery requires a message broker in order to handle requests from an external source. A message broker is used to translate messages to a formal messaging protocol and manage message queues for multiple receivers, providing reliable storage and guaranteed message delivery. You use a message broker to send messages to Celery workers, which process tasks as they receive them.

Installing RabbitMQ

There are several options for a message broker for Celery, including key/value stores such as Redis, or an actual message system such as RabbitMQ. Let's configure Celery with RabbitMQ, since it's the recommended message worker for Celery. RabbitMQ is lightweight, it supports multiple messaging protocols, and it can be used when scalability and high availability are required.

If you are using Linux, you can install RabbitMQ from the shell using the following command:

```
apt-get install rabbitmq
```

If you need to install RabbitMQ on macOS or Windows, you can find standalone versions at https://www.rabbitmq.com/download.html. On this site, you can also find detailed installation guides for different Linux distributions, other operating systems, and containers.

After installing it, launch RabbitMQ using the following command from the shell:

```
rabbitmq-server
```

You will see output that ends with the following line:

```
Starting broker... completed with 10 plugins.
```

RabbitMQ is running and ready to receive messages.

Adding Celery to your project

You have to provide a configuration for the Celery instance. Create a new file next to the settings.py file of myshop and name it celery.py. This file will contain the Celery configuration for your project. Add the following code to it:

```
import os
from celery import Celery

# set the default Django settings module for the 'celery' program.
os.environ.setdefault('DJANGO_SETTINGS_MODULE', 'myshop.settings')

app = Celery('myshop')

app.config_from_object('django.conf:settings', namespace='CELERY')
app.autodiscover_tasks()
```

In this code, you do the following:

- You set the DJANGO_SETTINGS_MODULE variable for the Celery command-line program.

- You create an instance of the application with `app = Celery('myshop')`.

- You load any custom configuration from your project settings using the `config_from_object()` method. The `namespace` attribute specifies the prefix that Celery-related settings will have in your `settings.py` file. By setting the `CELERY` namespace, all Celery settings need to include the `CELERY_` prefix in their name (for example, `CELERY_BROKER_URL`).

- Finally, you tell Celery to auto-discover asynchronous tasks for your applications. Celery will look for a `tasks.py` file in each application directory of applications added to `INSTALLED_APPS` in order to load asynchronous tasks defined in it.

You need to import the `celery` module in the `__init__.py` file of your project to make sure it is loaded when Django starts. Edit the `myshop/__init__.py` file and add the following code to it:

```
# import celery
from .celery import app as celery_app
```

Now you can start programming asynchronous tasks for your applications.

 The `CELERY_ALWAYS_EAGER` setting allows you to execute tasks locally in a synchronous way, instead of sending them to the queue. This is useful for running unit tests or executing the application in your local environment without running Celery.

Adding asynchronous tasks to your application

Next, you are going to create an asynchronous task to send an email notification to your users when they place an order. The convention is to include asynchronous tasks for your application in a `tasks` module within your application directory.

Create a new file inside the `orders` application and name it `tasks.py`. This is the place where Celery will look for asynchronous tasks. Add the following code to it:

```
from celery import task
from django.core.mail import send_mail
from .models import Order

@task
def order_created(order_id):
    """
```

```
    Task to send an e-mail notification when an order is
    successfully created.
    """
    order = Order.objects.get(id=order_id)
    subject = f'Order nr. {order.id}'
    message = f'Dear {order.first_name},\n\n' \
              f'You have successfully placed an order.' \
              f'Your order ID is {order.id}.'
    mail_sent = send_mail(subject,
                          message,
                          'admin@myshop.com',
                          [order.email])
    return mail_sent
```

You define the `order_created` task by using the `task` decorator. As you can see, a Celery task is just a Python function decorated with `@task`. Your `task` function receives an `order_id` parameter. It's always recommended to only pass IDs to task functions and lookup objects when the task is executed. You use the `send_mail()` function provided by Django to send an email notification to the user who placed the order.

You learned how to configure Django to use your SMTP server in *Chapter 2, Enhancing Your Blog with Advanced Features*. If you don't want to set up email settings, you can tell Django to write emails to the console by adding the following setting to the `settings.py` file:

```
EMAIL_BACKEND = 'django.core.mail.backends.console.EmailBackend'
```

 Use asynchronous tasks not only for time-consuming processes, but also for other processes that do not take so much time to be executed but which are subject to connection failures or require a retry policy.

Now you have to add the task to your `order_create` view. Edit the `views.py` file of the `orders` application, import the task, and call the `order_created` asynchronous task after clearing the cart, as follows:

```
from .tasks import order_created

def order_create(request):
    # ...
```

```
if request.method == 'POST':
    # ...
    if form.is_valid():
        # ...
        cart.clear()
        # launch asynchronous task
        order_created.delay(order.id)
    # ...
```

You call the `delay()` method of the task to execute it asynchronously. The task will be added to the queue and will be executed by a worker as soon as possible.

Open another shell and start the Celery worker from your project directory, using the following command:

```
celery -A myshop worker -l info
```

The Celery worker is now running and ready to process tasks. Make sure that the Django development server is also running.

Open `http://127.0.0.1:8000/` in your browser, add some products to your shopping cart, and complete an order. In the shell, you started the Celery worker and you will see an output similar to this one:

```
[2020-01-04 17:43:11,462: INFO/MainProcess] Received task: orders.tasks.
order_created[e990ddae-2e30-4e36-b0e4-78bbd4f2738e]

...

[2020-01-04 17:43:11,685: INFO/ForkPoolWorker-4] Task orders.tasks.
order_created[e990ddae-2e30-4e36-b0e4-78bbd4f2738e] succeeded in
0.02019841300789267s: 1
```

The task has been executed and an email notification for your order has been sent or displayed in the Celery worker output if you are using the console email backend.

Monitoring Celery

You might want to monitor the asynchronous tasks that are executed. Flower is a web-based tool for monitoring Celery. You can install Flower using this command:

```
pip install flower==0.9.3
```

Once installed, you can launch Flower by running the following command from your project directory:

```
celery -A myshop flower
```

Open `http://localhost:5555/dashboard` in your browser. You will be able to see the active Celery workers and asynchronous task statistics:

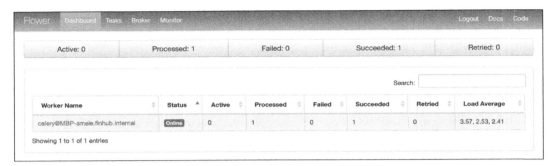

Figure 7.12: The Flower dashboard

You can find the documentation for Flower at `https://flower.readthedocs.io/`.

Summary

In this chapter, you created a basic shop application. You made a product catalog and built a shopping cart using sessions. You implemented a custom context processor to make the cart available to your templates and created a form for placing orders. You also learned how to launch asynchronous tasks with Celery.

In the next chapter, you will discover how to integrate a payment gateway into your shop, add custom actions to the administration site, export data in CSV format, and generate PDF files dynamically.

8

Managing Payments and Orders

In the previous chapter, you created a basic online shop with a product catalog and a shopping cart. You also learned how to launch asynchronous tasks with Celery.

In this chapter, you will learn how to integrate a payment gateway into your site to let users pay by credit card. You will also extend the administration site with different features.

In this chapter, you will:

- Integrate a payment gateway into your project
- Export orders to CSV files
- Create custom views for the administration site
- Generate PDF invoices dynamically

Integrating a payment gateway

A payment gateway allows you to process payments online. Using a payment gateway, you can manage customers' orders and delegate payment processing to a reliable, secure third party. You won't have to worry about processing credit cards in your own system.

There are several payment gateway providers to choose from. You are going to integrate Braintree, which is used by popular online services such as Uber and Airbnb.

Braintree provides an API that allows you to process online payments with multiple payment methods, such as credit card, PayPal, Google Pay, and Apple Pay. You can learn more about Braintree at `https://www.braintreepayments.com/`.

Braintree provides different integration options. The simplest is the *Drop-in* integration, which contains a preformatted payment form. However, in order to customize the behavior and experience of your checkout, you are going to use the advanced *Hosted Fields* integration. You can learn more about this integration at `https://developers.braintreepayments.com/guides/hosted-fields/overview/javascript/v3`.

Certain payment fields on the checkout page, such as the credit card number, CVV number, or expiration date, must be hosted securely. The Hosted Fields integration hosts the checkout fields on the payment gateway's domain and renders an iframe to present the fields to users. This provides you with the ability to customize the look and feel of the payment form, while ensuring that you are compliant with **Payment Card Industry (PCI)** requirements. Since you can customize the look and feel of the form fields, users won't notice the iframe.

Creating a Braintree sandbox account

You need a Braintree account to integrate the payment gateway into your site. Let's create a sandbox account to test the Braintree API. Open `https://www.braintreepayments.com/sandbox` in your browser. You will see a form like the following one:

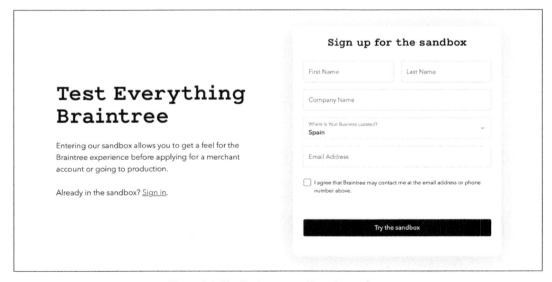

Figure 8.1: The Braintree sandbox signup form

Fill in the details to create a new sandbox account. You will receive an email from Braintree with a link. Follow the link and complete your account setup. Once you are done, log in at `https://sandbox.braintreegateway.com/login`. Your merchant ID and public/private keys will be displayed like this:

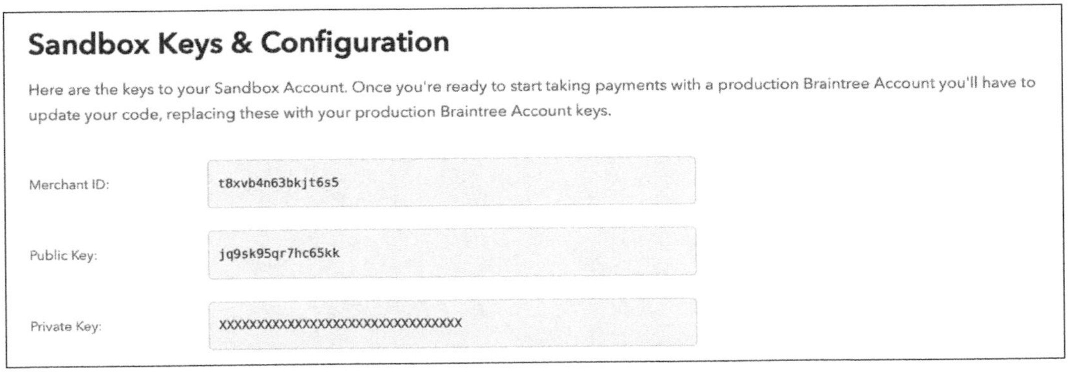

Sandbox Keys & Configuration

Here are the keys to your Sandbox Account. Once you're ready to start taking payments with a production Braintree Account you'll have to update your code, replacing these with your production Braintree Account keys.

Merchant ID:	t8xvb4n63bkjt6s5
Public Key:	jq9sk95qr7hc65kk
Private Key:	XXXXXXXXXXXXXXXXXXXXXXXXXXXXXX

Figure 8.2: The Braintree sandbox merchant ID and public/private keys

You will need this information to authenticate requests to the Braintree API. Always keep your private key secret.

Installing the Braintree Python module

Braintree provides a Python module that simplifies dealing with its API. You are going to integrate the payment gateway into your project using the `braintree` module.

Install the `braintree` module from the shell using the following command:

```
pip install braintree==3.59.0
```

Add the following settings to the `settings.py` file of your project:

```python
# Braintree settings
BRAINTREE_MERCHANT_ID = 'XXX'  # Merchant ID
BRAINTREE_PUBLIC_KEY = 'XXX'   # Public Key
BRAINTREE_PRIVATE_KEY = 'XXX'  # Private key

import braintree

BRAINTREE_CONF = braintree.Configuration(
    braintree.Environment.Sandbox,
    BRAINTREE_MERCHANT_ID,
    BRAINTREE_PUBLIC_KEY,
    BRAINTREE_PRIVATE_KEY
)
```

Replace the `BRAINTREE_MERCHANT_ID`, `BRAINTREE_PUBLIC_KEY`, and `BRAINTREE_PRIVATE_KEY` values with the ones for your account.

 You use `Environment.Sandbox` for integrating the sandbox. Once you go live and create a real account, you will need to change this to `Environment.Production`. Braintree will provide you with a new merchant ID and private/public keys for the production environment. In *Chapter 14*, *Going Live*, you will learn how to configure settings for multiple environments.

Let's integrate the payment gateway into the checkout process.

Integrating the payment gateway

The checkout process will work as follows:

1. Add items to the shopping cart
2. Check out the shopping cart
3. Enter credit card details and pay

You are going to create a new application to manage payments. Create a new application in your project using the following command:

```
python manage.py startapp payment
```

Edit the `settings.py` file of your project and add the new application to the `INSTALLED_APPS` setting, as follows:

```
INSTALLED_APPS = [
    # ...
    'payment.apps.PaymentConfig',
]
```

The `payment` application is now active.

After clients place an order, you need to redirect them to the payment process. Edit the `views.py` file of the `orders` application and include the following imports:

```
from django.urls import reverse
from django.shortcuts import render, redirect
```

In the same file, find the following lines of the `order_create` view:

```
# launch asynchronous task
order_created.delay(order.id)
```

```
return render(request,
              'orders/order/created.html',
              locals())
```

Replace them with the following:

```
# launch asynchronous task
order_created.delay(order.id)
# set the order in the session
request.session['order_id'] = order.id
# redirect for payment
return redirect(reverse('payment:process'))
```

With this code, after successfully creating an order, you set the order ID in the current session using the `order_id` session key. Then, you redirect the user to the `payment:process` URL, which you are going to implement later. Remember that you need to run Celery in order for the `order_created` task to be queued and executed.

Every time an order is created in Braintree, a unique transaction identifier is generated. You will add a new field to the `Order` model of the `orders` application to store the transaction ID. This will allow you to link each order with its related Braintree transaction.

Edit the `models.py` file of the `orders` application and add the following field to the `Order` model:

```
class Order(models.Model):
    # ...
    braintree_id = models.CharField(max_length=150, blank=True)
```

Let's sync this field with the database. Use the following command to generate migrations:

```
python manage.py makemigrations
```

You will see the following output:

```
Migrations for 'orders':
  orders/migrations/0002_order_braintree_id.py
    - Add field braintree_id to order
```

Apply the migration to the database with the following command:

```
python manage.py migrate
```

You will see output that ends with the following line:

```
Applying orders.0002_order_braintree_id... OK
```

The model changes are now synced with the database. Now you are able to store the Braintree transaction ID for each order. Let's integrate the payment gateway.

Integrating Braintree using Hosted Fields

The Hosted Fields integration allows you to create your own payment form using custom styles and layouts. An iframe is added dynamically to the page using the Braintree JavaScript **software development kit (SDK)**. The iframe includes the Hosted Fields payment form. When the customer submits the form, Hosted Fields collects the card details securely and attempts to tokenize them. If tokenization succeeds, you can send the generated token nonce to your view to make a transaction using the Python `braintree` module. A token nonce is a secure, one-time-use reference to payment information. It allows you to send sensitive payment information to Braintree without touching the raw data.

Let's create a view for processing payments. The whole checkout process will work as follows:

1. In the view, a client token is generated using the `braintree` Python module. This token is used in the next step to instantiate the Braintree JavaScript client; it's not the payment token nonce.

2. The view renders the checkout template. The template loads the Braintree JavaScript SDK using the client token and generates the iframe with the hosted payment form fields.

3. Users enter their credit card details and submit the form. A payment token nonce is generated with the Braintree JavaScript client. You send the token to your view with a POST request.

4. The payment view receives the token nonce and you use it to generate a transaction using the `braintree` Python module.

Let's start with the payment checkout view. Edit the `views.py` file of the `payment` application and add the following code to it:

```python
import braintree
from django.shortcuts import render, redirect, get_object_or_404
from django.conf import settings
from orders.models import Order

# instantiate Braintree payment gateway
gateway = braintree.BraintreeGateway(settings.BRAINTREE_CONF)

def payment_process(request):
    order_id = request.session.get('order_id')
```

```
order = get_object_or_404(Order, id=order_id)
total_cost = order.get_total_cost()

if request.method == 'POST':
    # retrieve nonce
    nonce = request.POST.get('payment_method_nonce', None)
    # create and submit transaction
    result = gateway.transaction.sale({
        'amount': f'{total_cost:.2f}',
        'payment_method_nonce': nonce,
        'options': {
            'submit_for_settlement': True
        }
    })
    if result.is_success:
        # mark the order as paid
        order.paid = True
        # store the unique transaction id
        order.braintree_id = result.transaction.id
        order.save()
        return redirect('payment:done')
    else:
        return redirect('payment:canceled')
else:
    # generate token
    client_token = gateway.client_token.generate()
    return render(request,
                  'payment/process.html',
                  {'order': order,
                   'client_token': client_token})
```

In the previous code, you import the `braintree` module and create an instance of the Braintree gateway using `BraintreeGateway()`, with the configuration defined in the `BRAINTREE_CONF` setting of the project.

The `payment_process` view manages the checkout process. In this view, you take the following actions:

1. You get the current order from the `order_id` session key, which was stored previously in the session by the `order_create` view.

2. You retrieve the `Order` object for the given ID or raise an `Http404` exception if it is not found.

3. When the view is loaded with a POST request, you retrieve the `payment_method_nonce` to generate a new transaction using `gateway.transaction.sale()`. You pass the following parameters to it:

    ○ `amount`: The total amount to charge the customer. This is a string with the total amount formatted with two decimal places.

    ○ `payment_method_nonce`: The token nonce generated by Braintree for the payment. It will be generated in the template using the Braintree JavaScript SDK.

    ○ `options`: You send the `submit_for_settlement` option with `True` so that the transaction is automatically submitted for settlement.

4. If the transaction is successfully processed, you mark the order as paid by setting its `paid` attribute to `True` and store the unique transaction ID returned by the gateway in the `braintree_id` attribute. You redirect the user to the `payment:done` URL if the payment is successful; otherwise, you redirect them to `payment:canceled`.

5. If the view was loaded with a GET request, generate a client token with `gateway.client_token.generate()` that you will use in the template to instantiate the Braintree JavaScript client.

Let's create basic views to redirect users when their payment has been successful, or when it has been canceled for any reason. Add the following code to the `views.py` file of the `payment` application:

```python
def payment_done(request):
    return render(request, 'payment/done.html')


def payment_canceled(request):
    return render(request, 'payment/canceled.html')
```

Create a new file inside the `payment` application directory and name it `urls.py`. Add the following code to it:

```python
from django.urls import path
from . import views

app_name = 'payment'

urlpatterns = [
    path('process/', views.payment_process, name='process'),
    path('done/', views.payment_done, name='done'),
    path('canceled/', views.payment_canceled, name='canceled'),
]
```

These are the URLs for the payment workflow. You have included the following URL patterns:

- `process`: The view that processes the payment
- `done`: The view to redirect the user if the payment is successful
- `canceled`: The view to redirect the user if the payment is not successful

Edit the main `urls.py` file of the `myshop` project and include the URL patterns for the `payment` application, as follows:

```
urlpatterns = [
    # ...
    path('payment/', include('payment.urls', namespace='payment')),
    path('', include('shop.urls', namespace='shop')),
]
```

Remember to place the new path before the `shop.urls` pattern to avoid an unintended pattern match with a pattern defined in `shop.urls`. Remember that Django runs through each URL pattern in order and stops at the first one that matches the requested URL.

Create the following file structure inside the `payment` application directory:

```
templates/
    payment/
        process.html
        done.html
        canceled.html
```

Edit the `payment/process.html` template and add the following code to it:

```
{% extends "shop/base.html" %}

{% block title %}Pay by credit card{% endblock %}

{% block content %}
  <h1>Pay by credit card</h1>
  <form id="payment" method="post">

    <label for="card-number">Card Number</label>
    <div id="card-number" class="field"></div>

    <label for="cvv">CVV</label>
    <div id="cvv" class="field"></div>

    <label for="expiration-date">Expiration Date</label>
```

```
      <div id="expiration-date" class="field"></div>

      <input type="hidden" id="nonce" name="payment_method_nonce"
value="">
      {% csrf_token %}
      <input type="submit" value="Pay">
   </form>
   <!-- includes the Braintree JS client SDK -->
   <script src="https://js.braintreegateway.com/web/3.44.2/js/client.
min.js"></script>
   <script src="https://js.braintreegateway.com/web/3.44.2/js/hosted-
fields.min.js"></script>
   <script>
     var form = document.querySelector('#payment');
     var submit = document.querySelector('input[type="submit"]');

     braintree.client.create({
       authorization: '{{ client_token }}'
     }, function (clientErr, clientInstance) {
       if (clientErr) {
         console.error(clientErr);
         return;
       }

       braintree.hostedFields.create({
         client: clientInstance,
         styles: {
           'input': {'font-size': '13px'},
           'input.invalid': {'color': 'red'},
           'input.valid': {'color': 'green'}
         },
         fields: {
           number: {selector: '#card-number'},
           cvv: {selector: '#cvv'},
           expirationDate: {selector: '#expiration-date'}
         }
       }, function (hostedFieldsErr, hostedFieldsInstance) {
         if (hostedFieldsErr) {
           console.error(hostedFieldsErr);
           return;
         }

         submit.removeAttribute('disabled');
```

```
      form.addEventListener('submit', function (event) {
        event.preventDefault();

        hostedFieldsInstance.tokenize(function (tokenizeErr,
payload) {
          if (tokenizeErr) {
            console.error(tokenizeErr);
            return;
          }
          // set nonce to send to the server
          document.getElementById('nonce').value = payload.nonce;
          // submit form
          document.getElementById('payment').submit();
        });
      }, false);
    });
  });
  </script>
{% endblock %}
```

This is the template that displays the payment form and processes the payment. You define `<div>` containers instead of `<input>` elements for the credit card input fields: the credit card number, CVV number, and expiration date. This is how you specify the fields that the Braintree JavaScript client will render in the iframe. You also include an `<input>` element named payment_method_nonce that you will use to send the token nonce to your view once it is generated by the Braintree JavaScript client.

In your template, you load the Braintree JavaScript SDK `client.min.js` and the Hosted Fields component `hosted-fields.min.js`. Then, you execute the following JavaScript code:

1. You instantiate the Braintree JavaScript client with the `braintree.client.create()` method, using the `client_token` generated by the payment_process view.

2. You instantiate the Hosted Fields component with the `braintree.hostedFields.create()` method.

3. You specify custom CSS styles for the `input` fields.

4. You specify the `id` selectors for the fields `card-number`, `cvv`, and `expiration-date`.

5. You use `form.addEventListener()` to add an event listener for the `submit` action of the form; this is a function that waits for the `submit` action and gets executed when it occurs. When the form is submitted, the fields are tokenized using the Braintree SDK and the token nonce is set in the `payment_method_nonce` field. Then, the form is submitted so that your view receives the nonce to process the payment.

Edit the `payment/done.html` template and add the following code to it:

```
{% extends "shop/base.html" %}

{% block title %}Payment successful{% endblock %}

{% block content %}
  <h1>Your payment was successful</h1>
  <p>Your payment has been processed successfully.</p>
{% endblock %}
```

This is the template for the page that the user is redirected to following a successful payment.

Edit the `payment/canceled.html` template and add the following code to it:

```
{% extends "shop/base.html" %}

{% block title %}Payment canceled{% endblock %}

{% block content %}
  <h1>Your payment has not been processed</h1>
  <p>There was a problem processing your payment.</p>
{% endblock %}
```

This is the template for the page that the user is redirected to when the transaction is not successful. Let's try the payment process.

Testing payments

Open a shell and run RabbitMQ with the following command:

```
rabbitmq-server
```

Open another shell and start the Celery worker from your project directory with the following command:

```
celery -A myshop worker -l info
```

Open one more shell and start the development server with this command:

```
python manage.py runserver
```

Open `http://127.0.0.1:8000/` in your browser, add some products to the shopping cart, and fill in the checkout form. When you click the **Place order** button, the order will be persisted to the database, the order ID will be saved in the current session, and you will be redirected to the payment process page.

The payment process page retrieves the order from the session and renders the Hosted Fields form in an iframe, as follows:

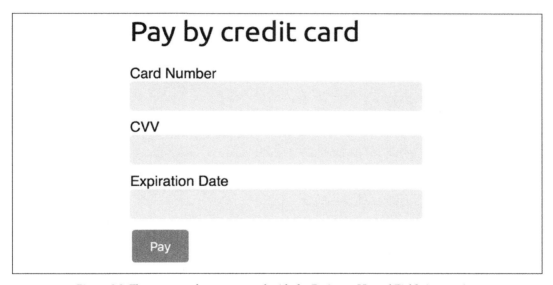

Figure 8.3: The payment from generated with the Braintree Hosted Fields integration

You can take a look at the HTML source code to see the generated HTML.

Braintree provides a list of successful and unsuccessful credit cards so that you can test all possible scenarios. You can find the list of credit cards for testing at `https://developers.braintreepayments.com/guides/credit-cards/testing-go-live/python`. You are going to use the VISA test card `4111 1111 1111 1111`, which returns a successful purchase. You are going to use CVV `123` and any future expiration date, such as `12/28`. Enter the credit card details as follows:

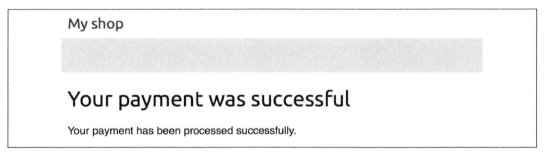

Figure 8.4: The payment form with the valid test credit card details

Click on the **Pay** button. You will see the following page:

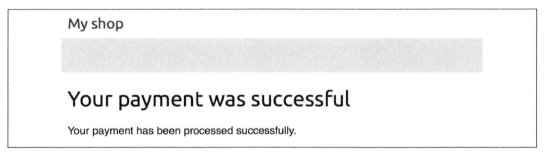

Figure 8.5: The successful payment page

The transaction has been successfully processed. Now you can log in to your account at `https://sandbox.braintreegateway.com/login`. Under **Transactions**, you will be able to see the transaction:

Figure 8.6: The transaction stored in the Braintree panel

Next, open `http://127.0.0.1:8000/admin/orders/order/` in your browser. The order should now be marked as paid and contain the related Braintree transaction ID:

Figure 8.7: The Paid and Braintree id fields of the order that has been processed

Congratulations! You have implemented a payment gateway to process credit cards.

Note that the `payment_process` view does not handle transaction declines. Braintree provides you with the processor response codes that are returned by the credit card processor. These are especially useful to know why a transaction might have been declined. You can obtain a response code using `result.transaction.processor_response_code` and its associated response text using `result.transaction.processor_response_text`. You can find the list of payment authorization responses at `https://developers.braintreepayments.com/reference/general/processor-responses/authorization-responses`.

Going live

Once you have tested your environment, you can create a real Braintree account at `https://www.braintreepayments.com`. Once you are ready to move into production, remember to change your live environment credentials in the `settings.py` file of your project and use `braintree.Environment.Production` to set up your environment. All steps to go live are summarized at `https://developers.braintreepayments.com/start/go-live/python`. In addition to this, you can read *Chapter 14, Going Live*, to learn how to configure project settings for multiple environments.

Exporting orders to CSV files

Sometimes, you might want to export the information contained in a model to a file so that you can import it in another system. One of the most widely used formats to export/import data is **comma-separated values (CSV)**. A CSV file is a plain text file consisting of a number of records. There is usually one record per line and some delimiter character, usually a literal comma, separating the record fields. You are going to customize the administration site to be able to export orders to CSV files.

Adding custom actions to the administration site

Django offers a wide range of options to customize the administration site. You are going to modify the object list view to include a custom administration action. You can implement custom administration actions to allow staff users to apply actions to multiple elements at once in the change list view.

An administration action works as follows: a user selects objects from the administration object list page with checkboxes, then they select an action to perform on all of the selected items, and execute the actions. The following screenshot shows where actions are located in the administration site:

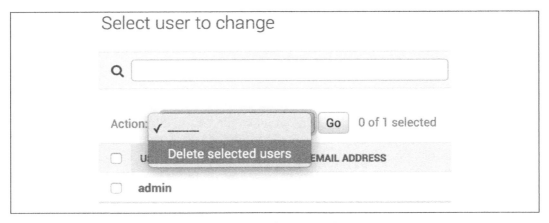

Figure 8.8: The dropdown menu for Django administration actions

You can create a custom action by writing a regular function that receives the following parameters:

- The current `ModelAdmin` being displayed
- The current request object as an `HttpRequest` instance
- A QuerySet for the objects selected by the user

This function will be executed when the action is triggered from the administration site.

You are going to create a custom administration action to download a list of orders as a CSV file. Edit the `admin.py` file of the `orders` application and add the following code before the `OrderAdmin` class:

```
import csv
import datetime
from django.http import HttpResponse

def export_to_csv(modeladmin, request, queryset):
    opts = modeladmin.model._meta
    content_disposition = 'attachment; filename={opts.verbose_name}.
csv'
    response = HttpResponse(content_type='text/csv')
    response['Content-Disposition'] = content_disposition
    writer = csv.writer(response)

    fields = [field for field in opts.get_fields() if not \
    field.many_to_many and not field.one_to_many]
    # Write a first row with header information
    writer.writerow([field.verbose_name for field in fields])
    # Write data rows
    for obj in queryset:
        data_row = []
        for field in fields:
            value = getattr(obj, field.name)
            if isinstance(value, datetime.datetime):
                value = value.strftime('%d/%m/%Y')
            data_row.append(value)
        writer.writerow(data_row)
    return response
export_to_csv.short_description = 'Export to CSV'
```

In this code, you perform the following tasks:

1. You create an instance of `HttpResponse`, specifying the `text/csv` content type, to tell the browser that the response has to be treated as a CSV file. You also add a `Content-Disposition` header to indicate that the HTTP response contains an attached file.

2. You create a CSV `writer` object that will write to the `response` object.

3. You get the `model` fields dynamically using the `get_fields()` method of the model `_meta` options. You exclude many-to-many and one-to-many relationships.

4. You write a header row including the field names.

5. You iterate over the given QuerySet and write a row for each object returned by the QuerySet. You take care of formatting `datetime` objects because the output value for CSV has to be a string.

6. You customize the display name for the action in the actions dropdown element of the administration site by setting a `short_description` attribute on the function.

You have created a generic administration action that can be added to any `ModelAdmin` class.

Finally, add the new `export_to_csv` administration action to the `OrderAdmin` class, as follows:

```
class OrderAdmin(admin.ModelAdmin):
    # ...
    actions = [export_to_csv]
```

Start the development server with the command `python manage.py runserver` and open `http://127.0.0.1:8000/admin/orders/order/` in your browser. The resulting administration action should look like this:

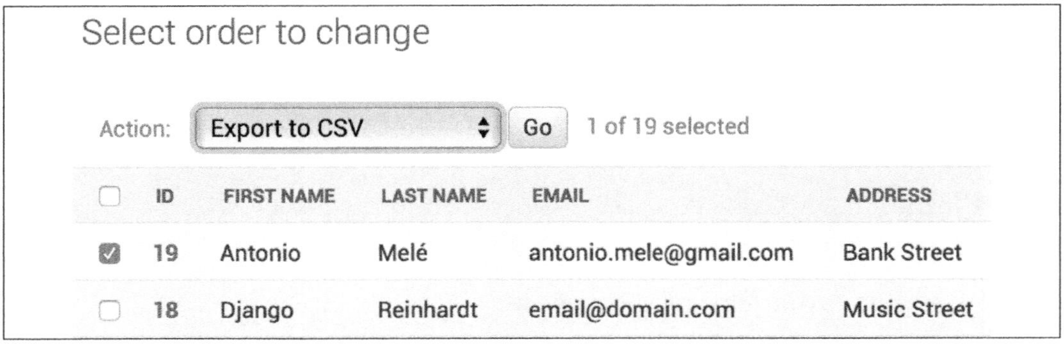

Figure 8.9: Using the custom Export to CSV administration action

Select some orders and choose the **Export to CSV** action from the select box, then click the **Go** button. Your browser will download the generated CSV file named `order.csv`. Open the downloaded file using a text editor. You should see content with the following format, including a header row and a row for each `Order` object you selected:

```
ID,first name,last name,email,address,postal code,city,created,
updated,paid,braintree id
3,Antonio,Melé,antonio.mele@gmail.com,Bank Street,WS J11,London,04/01/
2020,04/01/2020,True,2bwkx5b6
...
```

As you can see, creating administration actions is pretty straightforward. You can learn more about generating CSV files with Django at `https://docs. djangoproject.com/en/3.0/howto/outputting-csv/`.

Extending the administration site with custom views

Sometimes, you may want to customize the administration site beyond what is possible through configuring `ModelAdmin`, creating administration actions, and overriding administration templates. You might want to implement additional functionalities that are not available in existing administration views or templates. If this is the case, you need to create a custom administration view. With a custom view, you can build any functionality you want; you just have to make sure that only staff users can access your view and that you maintain the administration look and feel by making your template extend an administration template.

Let's create a custom view to display information about an order. Edit the `views.py` file of the `orders` application and add the following code to it:

```python
from django.contrib.admin.views.decorators import staff_member_required
from django.shortcuts import get_object_or_404
from .models import Order


@staff_member_required
def admin_order_detail(request, order_id):
    order = get_object_or_404(Order, id=order_id)
    return render(request,
                  'admin/orders/order/detail.html',
                  {'order': order})
```

The `staff_member_required` decorator checks that both the `is_active` and `is_staff` fields of the user requesting the page are set to `True`. In this view, you get the `Order` object with the given ID and render a template to display the order.

Next, edit the `urls.py` file of the `orders` application and add the following URL pattern to it:

```
path('admin/order/<int:order_id>/', views.admin_order_detail,
    name='admin_order_detail'),
```

Create the following file structure inside the `templates/` directory of the `orders` application:

```
admin/
    orders/
        order/
            detail.html
```

Edit the `detail.html` template and add the following content to it:

```
{% extends "admin/base_site.html" %}

{% block title %}
  Order {{ order.id }} {{ block.super }}
{% endblock %}

{% block breadcrumbs %}
  <div class="breadcrumbs">
    <a href="{% url "admin:index" %}">Home</a> &rsaquo;
    <a href="{% url "admin:orders_order_changelist" %}">Orders</a>
    &rsaquo;
    <a href="{% url "admin:orders_order_change" order.id %}">Order {{
order.id }}</a>
    &rsaquo; Detail
  </div>
{% endblock %}

{% block content %}
<h1>Order {{ order.id }}</h1>
<ul class="object-tools">
  <li>
    <a href="#" onclick="window.print();">Print order</a>
  </li>
</ul>
<table>
  <tr>
    <th>Created</th>
    <td>{{ order.created }}</td>
  </tr>
  <tr>
```

```
      <th>Customer</th>
      <td>{{ order.first_name }} {{ order.last_name }}</td>
    </tr>
    <tr>
      <th>E-mail</th>
      <td><a href="mailto:{{ order.email }}">{{ order.email }}</a></td>
    </tr>
    <tr>
      <th>Address</th>
    <td>
      {{ order.address }},
      {{ order.postal_code }} {{ order.city }}
    </td>
    </tr>
    <tr>
      <th>Total amount</th>
      <td>${{ order.get_total_cost }}</td>
    </tr>
    <tr>
      <th>Status</th>
      <td>{% if order.paid %}Paid{% else %}Pending payment{% endif %}</
td>
    </tr>
</table>

<div class="module">
  <h2>Items bought</h2>
  <table style="width:100%">
    <thead>
      <tr>
        <th>Product</th>
        <th>Price</th>
        <th>Quantity</th>
        <th>Total</th>
      </tr>
    </thead>
    <tbody>
      {% for item in order.items.all %}
        <tr class="row{% cycle "1" "2" %}">
          <td>{{ item.product.name }}</td>
          <td class="num">${{ item.price }}</td>
          <td class="num">{{ item.quantity }}</td>
          <td class="num">${{ item.get_cost }}</td>
        </tr>
```

```
        {% endfor %}
        <tr class="total">
          <td colspan="3">Total</td>
          <td class="num">${{ order.get_total_cost }}</td>
        </tr>
      </tbody>
    </table>
  </div>
{% endblock %}
```

Make sure that no template tag is split into multiple lines.

This is the template to display the details of an order on the administration site. This template extends the `admin/base_site.html` template of Django's administration site, which contains the main HTML structure and CSS styles. You use the blocks defined in the parent template to include your own content. You display information about the order and the items bought.

When you want to extend an administration template, you need to know its structure and identify existing blocks. You can find all administration templates at `https://github.com/django/django/tree/3.0/django/contrib/admin/templates/admin`.

You can also override an administration template if you need to. To do so, copy a template into your `templates/` directory, keeping the same relative path and filename. Django's administration site will use your custom template instead of the default one.

Finally, let's add a link to each `Order` object in the list display page of the administration site. Edit the `admin.py` file of the `orders` application and add the following code to it, above the `OrderAdmin` class:

```
from django.urls import reverse
from django.utils.safestring import mark_safe

def order_detail(obj):
    url = reverse('orders:admin_order_detail', args=[obj.id])
    return mark_safe(f'<a href="{url}">View</a>')
```

This is a function that takes an `Order` object as an argument and returns an HTML link for the `admin_order_detail` URL. Django escapes HTML output by default. You have to use the `mark_safe` function to avoid auto-escaping.

 Avoid using `mark_safe` on input that has come from the user to avoid **cross-site scripting** (**XSS**). XSS enables attackers to inject client-side scripts into web content viewed by other users.

Then, edit the `OrderAdmin` class to display the link:

```
class OrderAdmin(admin.ModelAdmin):
    list_display = ['id',
                    'first_name',
                    # ...
                    'updated',
                    order_detail]
```

Start the development server with the command `python manage.py runserver` and open `http://127.0.0.1:8000/admin/orders/order/` in your browser. Each row includes a **View** link, as follows:

PAID	CREATED	▼	UPDATED	ORDER DETAIL
✓	Jan. 4, 2020, 7:19 p.m.		Jan. 4, 2020, 7:19 p.m.	View

Figure 8.10: The View link included in each order row

Click on the **View** link for any order to load the custom order detail page. You should see a page like the following one:

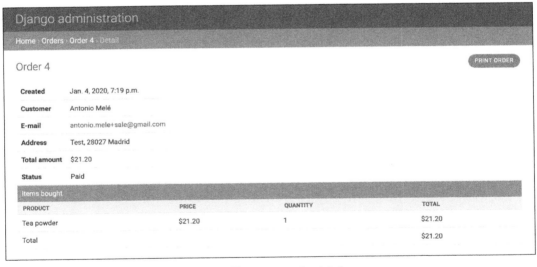

Figure 8.11: The custom order detail page

Generating PDF invoices dynamically

Now that you have a complete checkout and payment system, you can generate a PDF invoice for each order. There are several Python libraries to generate PDF files. One popular library to generate PDFs with Python code is ReportLab. You can find information about how to output PDF files with ReportLab at `https://docs.djangoproject.com/en/3.0/howto/outputting-pdf/`.

In most cases, you will have to add custom styles and formatting to your PDF files. You will find it more convenient to render an HTML template and convert it into a PDF file, keeping Python away from the presentation layer. You are going to follow this approach and use a module to generate PDF files with Django. You will use WeasyPrint, which is a Python library that can generate PDF files from HTML templates.

Installing WeasyPrint

First, install WeasyPrint's dependencies for your operating system from `https://weasyprint.readthedocs.io/en/latest/install.html`. Then, install WeasyPrint via `pip` using the following command:

```
pip install WeasyPrint==51
```

Creating a PDF template

You need an HTML document as input for WeasyPrint. You are going to create an HTML template, render it using Django, and pass it to WeasyPrint to generate the PDF file.

Create a new template file inside the `templates/orders/order/` directory of the `orders` application and name it `pdf.html`. Add the following code to it:

```html
<html>
<body>
  <h1>My Shop</h1>
  <p>
    Invoice no. {{ order.id }}</br>
    <span class="secondary">
      {{ order.created|date:"M d, Y" }}
    </span>
  </p>

  <h3>Bill to</h3>
  <p>
```

```
      {{ order.first_name }} {{ order.last_name }}<br>
      {{ order.email }}<br>
      {{ order.address }}<br>
      {{ order.postal_code }}, {{ order.city }}
    </p>

    <h3>Items bought</h3>
    <table>
      <thead>
        <tr>
          <th>Product</th>
          <th>Price</th>
          <th>Quantity</th>
          <th>Cost</th>
        </tr>
      </thead>
      <tbody>
        {% for item in order.items.all %}
          <tr class="row{% cycle "1" "2" %}">
            <td>{{ item.product.name }}</td>
            <td class="num">${{ item.price }}</td>
            <td class="num">{{ item.quantity }}</td>
            <td class="num">${{ item.get_cost }}</td>
          </tr>
        {% endfor %}
        <tr class="total">
          <td colspan="3">Total</td>
          <td class="num">${{ order.get_total_cost }}</td>
        </tr>
      </tbody>
    </table>

    <span class="{% if order.paid %}paid{% else %}pending{% endif %}">
      {% if order.paid %}Paid{% else %}Pending payment{% endif %}
    </span>
  </body>
</html>
```

This is the template for the PDF invoice. In this template, you display all order details and an HTML `<table>` element including the products. You also include a message to display whether the order has been paid.

Rendering PDF files

You are going to create a view to generate PDF invoices for existing orders using the administration site. Edit the `views.py` file inside the `orders` application directory and add the following code to it:

```python
from django.conf import settings
from django.http import HttpResponse
from django.template.loader import render_to_string
import weasyprint

@staff_member_required
def admin_order_pdf(request, order_id):
    order = get_object_or_404(Order, id=order_id)
    html = render_to_string('orders/order/pdf.html',
                            {'order': order})
    response = HttpResponse(content_type='application/pdf')
    response['Content-Disposition'] = f'filename=order_{order.id}.pdf'
    weasyprint.HTML(string=html).write_pdf(response,
        stylesheets=[weasyprint.CSS(
            settings.STATIC_ROOT + 'css/pdf.css')])
    return response
```

This is the view to generate a PDF invoice for an order. You use the `staff_member_required` decorator to make sure only staff users can access this view.

You get the `Order` object with the given ID and you use the `render_to_string()` function provided by Django to render `orders/order/pdf.html`. The rendered HTML is saved in the `html` variable.

Then, you generate a new `HttpResponse` object specifying the `application/pdf` content type and including the `Content-Disposition` header to specify the filename. You use WeasyPrint to generate a PDF file from the rendered HTML code and write the file to the `HttpResponse` object.

You use the static file `css/pdf.css` to add CSS styles to the generated PDF file. Then, you load it from the local path by using the `STATIC_ROOT` setting. Finally, you return the generated response.

If you are missing the CSS styles, remember to copy the static files located in the `static/` directory of the `shop` application to the same location of your project.

You can find the contents of the directory at `https://github.com/PacktPublishing/Django-3-by-Example/tree/master/Chapter08/myshop/shop/static`.

Since you need to use the `STATIC_ROOT` setting, you have to add it to your project. This is the project's path where static files reside. Edit the `settings.py` file of the `myshop` project and add the following setting:

```python
STATIC_ROOT = os.path.join(BASE_DIR, 'static/')
```

Then, run the following command:

```
python manage.py collectstatic
```

You should see output that ends likes this:

```
133 static files copied to 'code/myshop/static'.
```

The `collectstatic` command copies all static files from your applications into the directory defined in the `STATIC_ROOT` setting. This allows each application to provide its own static files using a `static/` directory containing them. You can also provide additional static files sources in the `STATICFILES_DIRS` setting. All of the directories specified in the `STATICFILES_DIRS` list will also be copied to the `STATIC_ROOT` directory when `collectstatic` is executed. Whenever you execute `collectstatic` again, you will be asked if you want to override the existing static files.

Edit the `urls.py` file inside the `orders` application directory and add the following URL pattern to it:

```python
urlpatterns = [
    # ...
    path('admin/order/<int:order_id>/pdf/',
        views.admin_order_pdf,
        name='admin_order_pdf'),
]
```

Now you can edit the administration list display page for the `Order` model to add a link to the PDF file for each result. Edit the `admin.py` file inside the `orders` application and add the following code above the `OrderAdmin` class:

```python
def order_pdf(obj):
    url = reverse('orders:admin_order_pdf', args=[obj.id])
    return mark_safe(f'<a href="{url}">PDF</a>')
order_pdf.short_description = 'Invoice'
```

If you specify a `short_description` attribute for your callable, Django will use it for the name of the column.

Add `order_pdf` to the `list_display` attribute of the `OrderAdmin` class, as follows:

```python
class OrderAdmin(admin.ModelAdmin):
    list_display = ['id',
                    # ...
                    order_detail,
                    order_pdf]
```

Ensure the development server is started. Open `http://127.0.0.1:8000/admin/` `orders/order/` in your browser. Each row should now include a **PDF** link, like this:

UPDATED	ORDER DETAIL	INVOICE
Jan. 4, 2020, 7:19 p.m.	View	PDF

Figure 8.12: The PDF link included in each order row

Click on the **PDF** link for any order. You should see a generated PDF file like the following one for orders that have not been paid yet:

Figure 8.13: The PDF invoice of an unpaid order

For paid orders, you will see the following PDF file:

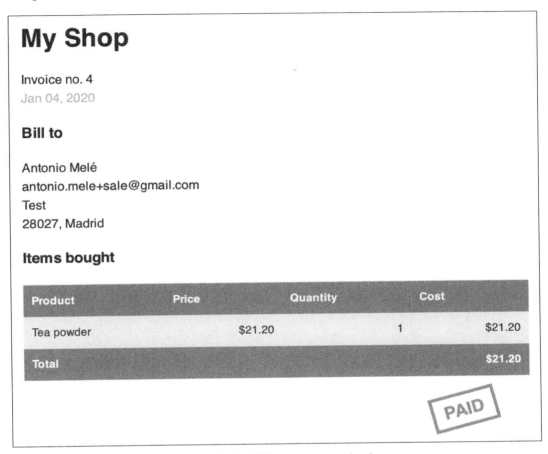

Figure 8.14: The PDF invoice of a paid order

Sending PDF files by email

When a payment is successful, you will send an automatic email to your customer including the generated PDF invoice. You will create an asynchronous task to perform this action.

Create a new file inside the `payment` application directory and name it `tasks.py`. Add the following code to it:

```
from io import BytesIO
from celery import task
import weasyprint
```

```
from django.template.loader import render_to_string
from django.core.mail import EmailMessage
from django.conf import settings
from orders.models import Order

@task
def payment_completed(order_id):
    """
    Task to send an e-mail notification when an order is
    successfully created.
    """
    order = Order.objects.get(id=order_id)

    # create invoice e-mail
    subject = f'My Shop - EE Invoice no. {order.id}'
    message = 'Please, find attached the invoice for your recent
purchase.'
    email = EmailMessage(subject,
                         message,
                         'admin@myshop.com',
                         [order.email])
    # generate PDF
    html = render_to_string('orders/order/pdf.html', {'order': order})
    out = BytesIO()
    stylesheets=[weasyprint.CSS(settings.STATIC_ROOT + 'css/pdf.css')]
    weasyprint.HTML(string=html).write_pdf(out,
                                           stylesheets=stylesheets)
    # attach PDF file
    email.attach(f'order_{order.id}.pdf',
                 out.getvalue(),
                 'application/pdf')
    # send e-mail
    email.send()
```

You define the payment_completed task by using the @task decorator. In this task, you use the EmailMessage class provided by Django to create an email object. Then, you render the template into the html variable. You generate the PDF file from the rendered template and output it to a BytesIO instance, which is an in-memory bytes buffer. Then, you attach the generated PDF file to the EmailMessage object using the attach() method, including the contents of the out buffer. Finally, you send the email.

Remember to set up your **Simple Mail Transfer Protocol (SMTP)** settings in
the `settings.py` file of the project to send emails. You can refer to *Chapter 2,
Enhancing Your Blog with Advanced Features,* to see a working example of an SMTP
configuration. If you don't want to set up email settings, you can tell Django to write
emails to the console by adding the following setting to the `settings.py` file:

```
EMAIL_BACKEND = 'django.core.mail.backends.console.EmailBackend'
```

Let's add the `payment_completed` task to the view. Edit the `views.py` file of the
`payment` application and modify it to make it look like this:

```
import braintree
from django.shortcuts import render, redirect, get_object_or_404
from django.conf import settings
from orders.models import Order
from .tasks import payment_completed

# instantiate Braintree payment gateway
gateway = braintree.BraintreeGateway(settings.BRAINTREE_CONF)

def payment_process(request):
    order_id = request.session.get('order_id')
    order = get_object_or_404(Order, id=order_id)
    total_cost = order.get_total_cost()

    if request.method == 'POST':
        # retrieve nonce
        nonce = request.POST.get('payment_method_nonce', None)
        # create and submit transaction
        result = gateway.transaction.sale({
            'amount': f'{total_cost:.2f}',
            'payment_method_nonce': nonce,
            'options': {
                'submit_for_settlement': True
            }
        })
        if result.is_success:
            # mark the order as paid
            order.paid = True
            # store the unique transaction id
            order.braintree_id = result.transaction.id
            order.save()
            # launch asynchronous task
            payment_completed.delay(order.id)
            return redirect('payment:done')
```

```
        else:
            return redirect('payment:canceled')
    else:
        # generate token
        client_token = gateway.client_token.generate()
        return render(request,
                      'payment/process.html',
                      {'order': order,
                       'client_token': client_token})

def payment_done(request):
    return render(request, 'payment/done.html')

def payment_canceled(request):
    return render(request, 'payment/canceled.html')
```

You call the `payment_completed` task when a payment is successfully completed. Then, you call the `delay()` method of the task to execute it asynchronously. The task will be added to the queue and will be executed by a Celery worker as soon as possible.

Now you can complete a new payment process in order to receive the PDF invoice into your email.

Summary

In this chapter, you integrated the Braintree payment gateway into your project using the Hosted Fields integration. You built a custom administration action to export orders to CSV. You also customized the Django administration site using custom views and templates. Finally, you learned how to generate PDF files with WeasyPrint and how to send them by email.

The next chapter will give you an insight into the internationalization and localization of Django projects. You will also create a coupon system using Django sessions and build a product recommendation engine with Redis.

9

Extending Your Shop

In the previous chapter, you learned how to integrate a payment gateway into your shop. You also learned how to generate CSV and PDF files.

In this chapter, you will add a coupon system to your shop. You will also learn how internationalization and localization work, and you will build a recommendation engine.

This chapter will cover the following points:

- Creating a coupon system to apply discounts
- Adding internationalization to your project
- Using Rosetta to manage translations
- Translating models using `django-parler`
- Building a product recommendation engine

Creating a coupon system

Many online shops give out coupons to customers that can be redeemed for discounts on their purchases. An online coupon usually consists of a code that is given to users and is valid for a specific time frame.

You are going to create a coupon system for your shop. Your coupons will be valid for customers in a certain time frame. The coupons will not have any limitations in terms of the number of times they can be redeemed, and they will be applied to the total value of the shopping cart. For this functionality, you will need to create a model to store the coupon code, a valid time frame, and the discount to apply.

Create a new application inside the `myshop` project using the following command:

```
python manage.py startapp coupons
```

Edit the `settings.py` file of `myshop` and add the application to the `INSTALLED_APPS` setting, as follows:

```
INSTALLED_APPS = [
    # ...
    'coupons.apps.CouponsConfig',
]
```

The new application is now active in your Django project.

Building the coupon model

Let's start by creating the `Coupon` model. Edit the `models.py` file of the `coupons` application and add the following code to it:

```
from django.db import models
from django.core.validators import MinValueValidator, \
                                    MaxValueValidator


class Coupon(models.Model):
    code = models.CharField(max_length=50,
                            unique=True)
    valid_from = models.DateTimeField()
    valid_to = models.DateTimeField()
    discount = models.IntegerField(
                validators=[MinValueValidator(0),
                            MaxValueValidator(100)])
    active = models.BooleanField()

    def __str__(self):
        return self.code
```

This is the model that you are going to use to store coupons. The `Coupon` model contains the following fields:

- `code`: The code that users have to enter in order to apply the coupon to their purchase.
- `valid_from`: The datetime value that indicates when the coupon becomes valid.

- `valid_to`: The datetime value that indicates when the coupon becomes invalid.
- `discount`: The discount rate to apply (this is a percentage, so it takes values from 0 to 100). You use validators for this field to limit the minimum and maximum accepted values.
- `active`: A Boolean that indicates whether the coupon is active.

Run the following command to generate the initial migration for the `coupons` application:

```
python manage.py makemigrations
```

The output should include the following lines:

```
Migrations for 'coupons':
  coupons/migrations/0001_initial.py:
    - Create model Coupon
```

Then, execute the next command to apply migrations:

```
python manage.py migrate
```

You should see an output that includes the following line:

```
Applying coupons.0001_initial... OK
```

The migrations are now applied in the database. Let's add the `Coupon` model to the administration site. Edit the `admin.py` file of the `coupons` application and add the following code to it:

```python
from django.contrib import admin
from .models import Coupon

@admin.register(Coupon)
class CouponAdmin(admin.ModelAdmin):
    list_display = ['code', 'valid_from', 'valid_to',
                    'discount', 'active']
    list_filter = ['active', 'valid_from', 'valid_to']
    search_fields = ['code']
```

The `Coupon` model is now registered in the administration site. Ensure that your local server is running with the command `python manage.py runserver`. Open `http://127.0.0.1:8000/admin/coupons/coupon/add/` in your browser.

You should see the following form:

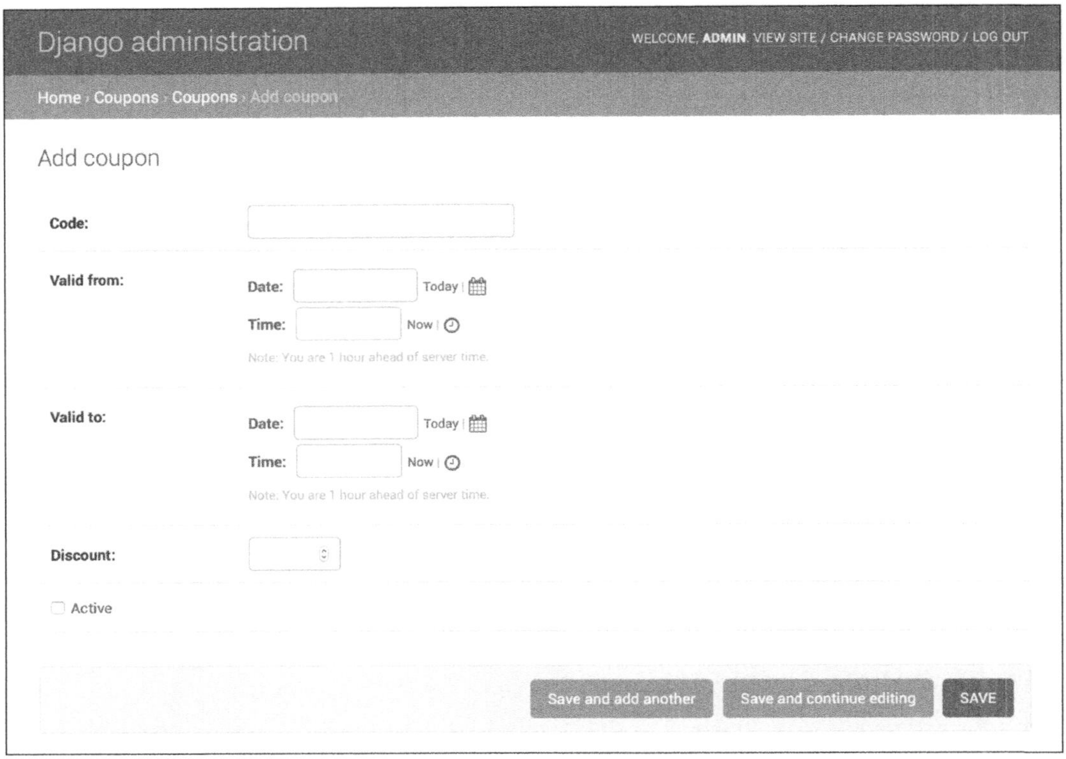

Figure 9.1: The Add coupon form

Fill in the form to create a new coupon that is valid for the current date and make sure that you check the **Active** checkbox and click the **SAVE** button.

Applying a coupon to the shopping cart

You can store new coupons and make queries to retrieve existing coupons. Now you need a way for customers to apply coupons to their purchases. The functionality to apply a coupon would be as follows:

1. The user adds products to the shopping cart.

2. The user can enter a coupon code in a form displayed on the shopping cart detail page.

3. When the user enters a coupon code and submits the form, you look for an existing coupon with the given code that is currently valid. You have to check that the coupon code matches the one entered by the user, that the `active` attribute is `True`, and that the current datetime is between the `valid_from` and `valid_to` values.

4. If a coupon is found, you save it in the user's session and display the cart, including the discount applied to it and the updated total amount.

5. When the user places an order, you save the coupon to the given order.

Create a new file inside the `coupons` application directory and name it `forms.py`. Add the following code to it:

```python
from django import forms

class CouponApplyForm(forms.Form):
    code = forms.CharField()
```

This is the form that you are going to use for the user to enter a coupon code. Edit the `views.py` file inside the `coupons` application and add the following code to it:

```python
from django.shortcuts import render, redirect
from django.utils import timezone
from django.views.decorators.http import require_POST
from .models import Coupon
from .forms import CouponApplyForm

@require_POST
def coupon_apply(request):
    now = timezone.now()
    form = CouponApplyForm(request.POST)
    if form.is_valid():
        code = form.cleaned_data['code']
        try:
            coupon = Coupon.objects.get(code__iexact=code,
                                        valid_from__lte=now,
                                        valid_to__gte=now,
                                        active=True)
            request.session['coupon_id'] = coupon.id
        except Coupon.DoesNotExist:
            request.session['coupon_id'] = None
    return redirect('cart:cart_detail')
```

The `coupon_apply` view validates the coupon and stores it in the user's session. You apply the `require_POST` decorator to this view to restrict it to `POST` requests. In the view, you perform the following tasks:

1. You instantiate the `CouponApplyForm` form using the posted data and check that the form is valid.

2. If the form is valid, you get the `code` entered by the user from the form's `cleaned_data` dictionary. You try to retrieve the `Coupon` object with the given code. You use the `iexact` field lookup to perform a case-insensitive exact match. The coupon has to be currently active (`active=True`) and valid for the current datetime. You use Django's `timezone.now()` function to get the current timezone-aware datetime and you compare it with the `valid_from` and `valid_to` fields performing `lte` (less than or equal to) and `gte` (greater than or equal to) field lookups, respectively.

3. You store the coupon ID in the user's session.

4. You redirect the user to the `cart_detail` URL to display the cart with the coupon applied.

You need a URL pattern for the `coupon_apply` view. Create a new file inside the `coupons` application directory and name it `urls.py`. Add the following code to it:

```
from django.urls import path
from . import views

app_name = 'coupons'

urlpatterns = [
    path('apply/', views.coupon_apply, name='apply'),
]
```

Then, edit the main `urls.py` of the `myshop` project and include the `coupons` URL patterns, as follows:

```
urlpatterns = [
    # ...
    path('coupons/', include('coupons.urls', namespace='coupons')),
    path('', include('shop.urls', namespace='shop')),
]
```

Remember to place this pattern before the `shop.urls` pattern.

Now, edit the `cart.py` file of the `cart` application. Include the following import:

```
from coupons.models import Coupon
```

Add the following code to the end of the `__init__()` method of the `Cart` class to initialize the coupon from the current session:

```
class Cart(object):
    def __init__(self, request):
        # ...
        # store current applied coupon
        self.coupon_id = self.session.get('coupon_id')
```

In this code, you try to get the `coupon_id` session key from the current session and store its value in the `Cart` object. Add the following methods to the `Cart` object:

```
class Cart(object):
    # ...
    @property
    def coupon(self):
        if self.coupon_id:
            try:
                return Coupon.objects.get(id=self.coupon_id)
            except Coupon.DoesNotExist:
                pass
        return None

    def get_discount(self):
        if self.coupon:
            return (self.coupon.discount / Decimal(100)) \
                * self.get_total_price()
        return Decimal(0)

    def get_total_price_after_discount(self):
        return self.get_total_price() - self.get_discount()
```

These methods are as follows:

- `coupon()`: You define this method as a `property`. If the cart contains a `coupon_id` attribute, the `Coupon` object with the given ID is returned.

- `get_discount()`: If the cart contains a coupon, you retrieve its discount rate and return the amount to be deducted from the total amount of the cart.

- `get_total_price_after_discount()`: You return the total amount of the cart after deducting the amount returned by the `get_discount()` method.

The `Cart` class is now prepared to handle a coupon applied to the current session and apply the corresponding discount.

Let's include the coupon system in the cart's detail view. Edit the `views.py` file of the `cart` application and add the following import at the top of the file:

```
from coupons.forms import CouponApplyForm
```

Further down, edit the `cart_detail` view and add the new form to it, as follows:

```
def cart_detail(request):
    cart = Cart(request)
    for item in cart:
        item['update_quantity_form'] = CartAddProductForm(initial={
                                'quantity': item['quantity'],
                                'override': True})
    coupon_apply_form = CouponApplyForm()

    return render(request,
                  'cart/detail.html',
                  {'cart': cart,
                   'coupon_apply_form': coupon_apply_form})
```

Edit the `cart/detail.html` template of the `cart` application and locate the following lines:

```
<tr class="total">
  <td>Total</td>
  <td colspan="4"></td>
  <td class="num">${{ cart.get_total_price }}</td>
</tr>
```

Replace them with the following:

```
{% if cart.coupon %}
  <tr class="subtotal">
    <td>Subtotal</td>
    <td colspan="4"></td>
    <td class="num">${{ cart.get_total_price|floatformat:2 }}</td>
  </tr>
  <tr>
    <td>
      "{{ cart.coupon.code }}" coupon
      ({{ cart.coupon.discount }}% off)
    </td>
    <td colspan="4"></td>
    <td class="num neg">
      - ${{ cart.get_discount|floatformat:2 }}
    </td>
  </tr>
{% endif %}
<tr class="total">
  <td>Total</td>
  <td colspan="4"></td>
  <td class="num">
    ${{ cart.get_total_price_after_discount|floatformat:2 }}
  </td>
</tr>
```

This is the code for displaying an optional coupon and its discount rate. If the cart contains a coupon, you display a first row, including the total amount of the cart as the subtotal. Then, you use a second row to display the current coupon applied to the cart. Finally, you display the total price, including any discount, by calling the `get_total_price_after_discount()` method of the `cart` object.

In the same file, include the following code after the `</table>` HTML tag:

```
<p>Apply a coupon:</p>
<form action="{% url "coupons:apply" %}" method="post">
  {{ coupon_apply_form }}
  <input type="submit" value="Apply">
  {% csrf_token %}
</form>
```

This will display the form to enter a coupon code and apply it to the current cart.

Open `http://127.0.0.1:8000/` in your browser, add a product to the cart, and apply the coupon you created by entering its code in the form. You should see that the cart displays the coupon discount as follows:

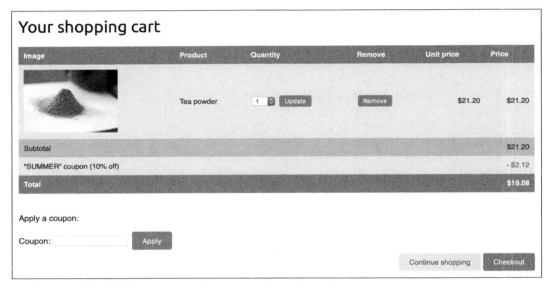

Figure 9.2: The cart detail page, including coupon details and a form to apply a coupon

Let's add the coupon to the next step of the purchase process. Edit the `orders/order/create.html` template of the `orders` application and locate the following lines:

```
<ul>
  {% for item in cart %}
    <li>
      {{ item.quantity }}x {{ item.product.name }}
      <span>${{ item.total_price }}</span>
    </li>
  {% endfor %}
</ul>
```

Replace them with the following code:

```
<ul>
  {% for item in cart %}
    <li>
      {{ item.quantity }}x {{ item.product.name }}
      <span>${{ item.total_price|floatformat:2 }}</span>
```

```
    </li>
  {% endfor %}
  {% if cart.coupon %}
    <li>
      "{{ cart.coupon.code }}" ({{ cart.coupon.discount }}% off)
      <span class="neg">- ${{ cart.get_discount|floatformat:2 }}</
span>
    </li>
  {% endif %}
</ul>
```

The order summary should now include the coupon applied, if there is one. Now find the following line:

```
<p>Total: ${{ cart.get_total_price }}</p>
```

Replace it with the following:

```
<p>Total: ${{ cart.get_total_price_after_discount|floatformat:2 }}</p>
```

By doing this, the total price will also be calculated by applying the discount of the coupon.

Open `http://127.0.0.1:8000/orders/create/` in your browser. You should see that the order summary includes the applied coupon, as follows:

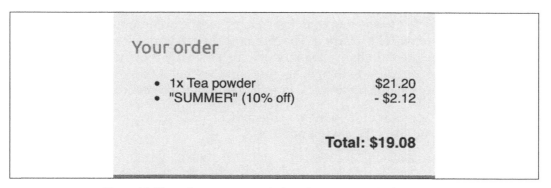

Figure 9.3: The order summary, including the coupon applied to the cart

Users can now apply coupons to their shopping cart. However, you still need to store coupon information in the order that it is created when users check out the cart.

Applying coupons to orders

You are going to store the coupon that was applied to each order. First, you need to modify the `Order` model to store the related `Coupon` object, if there is one.

Edit the `models.py` file of the `orders` application and add the following imports to it:

```
from decimal import Decimal
from django.core.validators import MinValueValidator, \
                                   MaxValueValidator
from coupons.models import Coupon
```

Then, add the following fields to the `Order` model:

```
class Order(models.Model):
    # ...
    coupon = models.ForeignKey(Coupon,
                               related_name='orders',
                               null=True,
                               blank=True,
                               on_delete=models.SET_NULL)
    discount = models.IntegerField(default=0,
                                   validators=[MinValueValidator(0),
                                   MaxValueValidator(100)])
```

These fields allow you to store an optional coupon for the order and the discount percentage applied with the coupon. The discount is stored in the related `Coupon` object, but you include it in the `Order` model to preserve it if the coupon is modified or deleted. You set `on_delete` to `models.SET_NULL` so that if the coupon gets deleted, the `coupon` field is set to `Null`, but the discount is preserved.

You need to create a migration to include the new fields of the `Order` model. Run the following command from the command line:

```
python manage.py makemigrations
```

You should see an output like the following:

```
Migrations for 'orders':
  orders/migrations/0003_auto_20191213_1618.py:
    - Add field coupon to order
    - Add field discount to order
```

Apply the new migration with the following command:

```
python manage.py migrate orders
```

You should see a confirmation indicating that the new migration has been applied. The Order model field changes are now synced with the database.

Go back to the models.py file and change the get_total_cost() method of the Order model, as follows:

```
class Order(models.Model):
    # ...
    def get_total_cost(self):
        total_cost = sum(item.get_cost() for item in self.items.all())
        return total_cost - total_cost * \
            (self.discount / Decimal(100))
```

The get_total_cost() method of the Order model will now take into account the discount applied, if there is one.

Edit the views.py file of the orders application and modify the order_create view to save the related coupon and its discount when creating a new order. Find the following line:

```
order = form.save()
```

Replace it with the following:

```
order = form.save(commit=False)
if cart.coupon:
    order.coupon = cart.coupon
    order.discount = cart.coupon.discount
order.save()
```

In the new code, you create an Order object using the save() method of the OrderCreateForm form. You avoid saving it to the database yet by using commit=False. If the cart contains a coupon, you store the related coupon and the discount that was applied. Then, you save the order object to the database.

Make sure that the development server is running with the command python manage.py runserver. Open http://127.0.0.1:8000/ in your browser and complete a purchase using the coupon you created.

When you finish a successful purchase, you can go to `http://127.0.0.1:8000/admin/orders/order/` and check that the `order` object contains the coupon and the applied discount, as follows:

Figure 9.4: The order edit form, including the coupon and discount applied

You can also modify the administration order detail template and the order PDF invoice to display the applied coupon in the same way you did for the cart.

Next, you are going to add internationalization to your project.

Adding internationalization and localization

Django offers full internationalization and localization support. It allows you to translate your application into multiple languages and it handles locale-specific formatting for dates, times, numbers, and timezones. Let's clarify the difference between internationalization and localization. **Internationalization** (frequently abbreviated to **i18n**) is the process of adapting software for the potential use of different languages and locales, so that it isn't hardwired to a specific language or locale. **Localization** (abbreviated to **l10n**) is the process of actually translating the software and adapting it to a particular locale. Django itself is translated into more than 50 languages using its internationalization framework.

Internationalization with Django

The internationalization framework allows you to easily mark strings for translation, both in Python code and in your templates. It relies on the GNU gettext toolset to generate and manage message files. A **message file** is a plain text file that represents a language. It contains a part, or all, of the translation strings found in your application and their respective translations for a single language. Message files have the `.po` extension. Once the translation is done, message files are compiled to offer rapid access to translated strings. The compiled translation files have the `.mo` extension.

Internationalization and localization settings

Django provides several settings for internationalization. The following settings are the most relevant ones:

- `USE_I18N`: A Boolean that specifies whether Django's translation system is enabled. This is `True` by default.

- `USE_L10N`: A Boolean indicating whether localized formatting is enabled. When active, localized formats are used to represent dates and numbers. This is `False` by default.

- `USE_TZ`: A Boolean that specifies whether datetimes are timezone-aware. When you create a project with the `startproject` command, this is set to `True`.

- `LANGUAGE_CODE`: The default language code for the project. This is in standard language ID format, for example, `'en-us'` for American English, or `'en-gb'` for British English. This setting requires `USE_I18N` to be set to `True` in order to take effect. You can find a list of valid language IDs at `http://www.i18nguy.com/unicode/language-identifiers.html`.

- `LANGUAGES`: A tuple that contains available languages for the project. They come in two tuples of a **language code** and **language name**. You can see the list of available languages at `django.conf.global_settings`. When you choose which languages your site will be available in, you set `LANGUAGES` to a subset of that list.

- `LOCALE_PATHS`: A list of directories where Django looks for message files containing translations for the project.

- `TIME_ZONE`: A string that represents the timezone for the project. This is set to `'UTC'` when you create a new project using the `startproject` command. You can set it to any other timezone, such as `'Europe/Madrid'`.

These are some of the internationalization and localization settings available. You can find the full list at `https://docs.djangoproject.com/en/3.0/ref/ settings/#globalization-i18n-l10n`.

Internationalization management commands

Django includes the following management commands to manage translations:

- `makemessages`: This runs over the source tree to find all strings marked for translation and creates or updates the `.po` message files in the `locale` directory. A single `.po` file is created for each language.

- `compilemessages`: This compiles the existing `.po` message files to `.mo` files that are used to retrieve translations.

You will need the gettext toolkit to be able to create, update, and compile message files. Most Linux distributions include the gettext toolkit. If you are using macOS, probably the simplest way to install it is via Homebrew, at `https:// brew.sh/`, with the command `brew install gettext`. You might also need to force link it with the command `brew link --force gettext`. For Windows, follow the steps at `https://docs.djangoproject.com/en/3.0/topics/i18n/ translation/#gettext-on-windows`.

How to add translations to a Django project

Let's take a look at the process of internationalizing your project. You will need to do the following:

1. Mark strings for translation in your Python code and your templates
2. Run the `makemessages` command to create or update message files that include all translation strings from your code
3. Translate the strings contained in the message files and compile them using the `compilemessages` management command

How Django determines the current language

Django comes with a middleware that determines the current language based on the request data. This is the `LocaleMiddleware` middleware that resides in `django. middleware.locale.LocaleMiddleware` performs the following tasks:

1. If you are using `i18n_patterns`, that is, you are using translated URL patterns, it looks for a language prefix in the requested URL to determine the current language.

2. If no language prefix is found, it looks for an existing LANGUAGE_SESSION_ KEY in the current user's session.

3. If the language is not set in the session, it looks for an existing cookie with the current language. A custom name for this cookie can be provided in the LANGUAGE_COOKIE_NAME setting. By default, the name for this cookie is django_language.

4. If no cookie is found, it looks for the Accept-Language HTTP header of the request.

5. If the Accept-Language header does not specify a language, Django uses the language defined in the LANGUAGE_CODE setting.

By default, Django will use the language defined in the LANGUAGE_CODE setting unless you are using LocaleMiddleware. The process described here only applies when using this middleware.

Preparing your project for internationalization

Let's prepare your project to use different languages. You are going to create an English and a Spanish version for your shop. Edit the settings.py file of your project and add the following LANGUAGES setting to it. Place it next to the LANGUAGE_ CODE setting:

```
LANGUAGES = (
    ('en', 'English'),
    ('es', 'Spanish'),
)
```

The LANGUAGES setting contains two tuples that consist of a language code and a name. Language codes can be locale-specific, such as en-us or en-gb, or generic, such as en. With this setting, you specify that your application will only be available in English and Spanish. If you don't define a custom LANGUAGES setting, the site will be available in all the languages that Django is translated into.

Make your LANGUAGE_CODE setting look as follows:

```
LANGUAGE_CODE = 'en'
```

Add 'django.middleware.locale.LocaleMiddleware' to the MIDDLEWARE setting. Make sure that this middleware comes after SessionMiddleware because LocaleMiddleware needs to use session data. It also has to be placed before CommonMiddleware because the latter needs an active language to resolve the requested URL. The MIDDLEWARE setting should now look as follows:

```
MIDDLEWARE = [
```

```
        'django.middleware.security.SecurityMiddleware',
        'django.contrib.sessions.middleware.SessionMiddleware',
        'django.middleware.locale.LocaleMiddleware',
        'django.middleware.common.CommonMiddleware',
        # ...
    ]
```

 The order of middleware classes is very important because each middleware can depend on data set by other middleware executed previously. Middleware is applied for requests in order of appearance in MIDDLEWARE, and in reverse order for responses.

Create the following directory structure inside the main project directory, next to the `manage.py` file:

```
locale/
    en/
    es/
```

The `locale` directory is the place where message files for your application will reside. Edit the `settings.py` file again and add the following setting to it:

```
LOCALE_PATHS = (
    os.path.join(BASE_DIR, 'locale/'),
)
```

The `LOCALE_PATHS` setting specifies the directories where Django has to look for translation files. Locale paths that appear first have the highest precedence.

When you use the `makemessages` command from your project directory, message files will be generated in the `locale/` path you created. However, for applications that contain a `locale/` directory, message files will be generated in that directory.

Translating Python code

To translate literals in your Python code, you can mark strings for translation using the `gettext()` function included in `django.utils.translation`. This function translates the message and returns a string. The convention is to import this function as a shorter alias named _ (underscore character).

You can find all the documentation about translations at `https://docs.djangoproject.com/en/3.0/topics/i18n/translation/`.

Standard translations

The following code shows how to mark a string for translation:

```
from django.utils.translation import gettext as _
output = _('Text to be translated.')
```

Lazy translations

Django includes **lazy** versions for all of its translation functions, which have the suffix _lazy(). When using the lazy functions, strings are translated when the value is accessed, rather than when the function is called (this is why they are translated **lazily**). The lazy translation functions come in handy when strings marked for translation are in paths that are executed when modules are loaded.

 Using gettext_lazy() instead of gettext() means that strings are translated when the value is accessed. Django offers a lazy version for all translation functions.

Translations including variables

The strings marked for translation can include placeholders to include variables in the translations. The following code is an example of a translation string with a placeholder:

```
from django.utils.translation import gettext as _
month = _('April')
day = '14'
output = _('Today is %(month)s %(day)s') % {'month': month,
                                             'day': day}
```

By using placeholders, you can reorder the text variables. For example, an English translation of the previous example might be *today is April 14*, while the Spanish one might be *hoy es 14 de Abril*. Always use string interpolation instead of positional interpolation when you have more than one parameter for the translation string. By doing so, you will be able to reorder the placeholder text.

Plural forms in translations

For plural forms, you can use ngettext() and ngettext_lazy(). These functions translate singular and plural forms depending on an argument that indicates the number of objects. The following example shows how to use them:

```
output = ngettext('there is %(count)d product',
                  'there are %(count)d products',
                  count) % {'count': count}
```

Now that you know the basics about translating literals in your Python code, it's time to apply translations to your project.

Translating your own code

Edit the `settings.py` file of your project, import the `gettext_lazy()` function, and change the LANGUAGES setting as follows to translate the language names:

```
from django.utils.translation import gettext_lazy as _

LANGUAGES = (
    ('en', _('English')),
    ('es', _('Spanish')),
)
```

Here, you use the `gettext_lazy()` function instead of `gettext()` to avoid a circular import, thus translating the languages' names when they are accessed.

Open the shell and run the following command from your project directory:

django-admin makemessages --all

You should see the following output:

processing locale es

processing locale en

Take a look at the `locale/` directory. You should see a file structure like the following:

```
en/
    LC_MESSAGES/
        django.po
es/
    LC_MESSAGES/
        django.po
```

A `.po` message file has been created for each language. Open `es/LC_MESSAGES/django.po` with a text editor. At the end of the file, you should be able to see the following:

```
#: myshop/settings.py:118
msgid "English"
msgstr ""

#: myshop/settings.py:119
msgid "Spanish"
msgstr ""
```

Each translation string is preceded by a comment showing details about the file and the line where it was found. Each translation includes two strings:

- `msgid`: The translation string as it appears in the source code.
- `msgstr`: The language translation, which is empty by default. This is where you have to enter the actual translation for the given string.

Fill in the `msgstr` translations for the given `msgid` string, as follows:

```
#: myshop/settings.py:118
msgid "English"
msgstr "Inglés"

#: myshop/settings.py:119
msgid "Spanish"
msgstr "Español"
```

Save the modified message file, open the shell, and run the following command:

```
django-admin compilemessages
```

If everything goes well, you should see an output like the following:

```
processing file django.po in myshop/locale/en/LC_MESSAGES
processing file django.po in myshop/locale/es/LC_MESSAGES
```

The output gives you information about the message files that are being compiled. Take a look at the `locale` directory of the `myshop` project again. You should see the following files:

```
en/
    LC_MESSAGES/
        django.mo
        django.po
es/
    LC_MESSAGES/
        django.mo
        django.po
```

You can see that a `.mo` compiled message file has been generated for each language.

You have translated the language names themselves. Now, let's translate the model field names that are displayed in the site. Edit the `models.py` file of the `orders` application and add names marked for translation for the `Order` model fields as follows:

```
from django.utils.translation import gettext_lazy as _
```

```
class Order(models.Model):
    first_name = models.CharField(_('first name'),
                                  max_length=50)
    last_name = models.CharField(_('last name'),
                                 max_length=50)
    email = models.EmailField(_('e-mail'))
    address = models.CharField(_('address'),
                               max_length=250)
    postal_code = models.CharField(_('postal code'),
                                   max_length=20)
    city = models.CharField(_('city'),
                            max_length=100)
    # ...
```

You have added names for the fields that are displayed when a user is placing a new order. These are `first_name`, `last_name`, `email`, `address`, `postal_code`, and `city`. Remember that you can also use the `verbose_name` attribute to name the fields.

Create the following directory structure inside the `orders` application directory:

```
locale/
    en/
    es/
```

By creating a `locale` directory, translation strings of this application will be stored in a message file under this directory instead of the main messages file. In this way, you can generate separate translation files for each application.

Open the shell from the project directory and run the following command:

```
django-admin makemessages --all
```

You should see the following output:

```
processing locale es
```

```
processing locale en
```

Open the `locale/es/LC_MESSAGES/django.po` file of the `order` application using a text editor. You will see the translation strings for the `Order` model. Fill in the following `msgstr` translations for the given `msgid` strings:

```
#: orders/models.py:11
msgid "first name"
msgstr "nombre"

#: orders/models.py:12
```

```
msgid "last name"
msgstr "apellidos"

#: orders/models.py:13
msgid "e-mail"
msgstr "e-mail"

#: orders/models.py:13
msgid "address"
msgstr "dirección"

#: orders/models.py:14
msgid "postal code"
msgstr "código postal"

#: orders/models.py:15
msgid "city"
msgstr "ciudad"
```

After you have finished adding the translations, save the file.

Besides a text editor, you can use Poedit to edit translations. Poedit is a software for editing translations that uses gettext. It is available for Linux, Windows, and macOS. You can download Poedit from https://poedit.net/.

Let's also translate the forms of your project. The OrderCreateForm of the orders application does not have to be translated, since it is a ModelForm and it uses the verbose_name attribute of the Order model fields for the form field labels. You are going to translate the forms of the cart and coupons applications.

Edit the forms.py file inside the cart application directory and add a label attribute to the quantity field of the CartAddProductForm, and then mark this field for translation, as follows:

```
from django import forms
from django.utils.translation import gettext_lazy as _

PRODUCT_QUANTITY_CHOICES = [(i, str(i)) for i in range(1, 21)]

class CartAddProductForm(forms.Form):
    quantity = forms.TypedChoiceField(
                            choices=PRODUCT_QUANTITY_CHOICES,
                            coerce=int,
                            label=_('Quantity'))
    override = forms.BooleanField(required=False,
                            initial=False,
                            widget=forms.HiddenInput)
```

Edit the `forms.py` file of the `coupons` application and translate the `CouponApplyForm` form, as follows:

```python
from django import forms
from django.utils.translation import gettext_lazy as _

class CouponApplyForm(forms.Form):
    code = forms.CharField(label=_('Coupon'))
```

You have added a label to the `code` field and marked it for translation.

Translating templates

Django offers the `{% trans %}` and `{% blocktrans %}` template tags to translate strings in templates. In order to use the translation template tags, you have to add `{% load i18n %}` at the top of your template to load them.

The {% trans %} template tag

The `{% trans %}` template tag allows you to mark a literal for translation. Internally, Django executes `gettext()` on the given text. This is how to mark a string for translation in a template:

```
{% trans "Text to be translated" %}
```

You can use `as` to store the translated content in a variable that you can use throughout your template. The following example stores the translated text in a variable called `greeting`:

```
{% trans "Hello!" as greeting %}
<h1>{{ greeting }}</h1>
```

The `{% trans %}` tag is useful for simple translation strings, but it can't handle content for translation that includes variables.

The {% blocktrans %} template tag

The `{% blocktrans %}` template tag allows you to mark content that includes literals and variable content using placeholders. The following example shows you how to use the `{% blocktrans %}` tag, including a `name` variable in the content for translation:

```
{% blocktrans %}Hello {{ name }}!{% endblocktrans %}
```

You can use `with` to include template expressions, such as accessing object attributes or applying template filters to variables. You always have to use placeholders for these. You can't access expressions or object attributes inside the `blocktrans` block. The following example shows you how to use `with` to include an object attribute to which the `capfirst` filter is applied:

```
{% blocktrans with name=user.name|capfirst %}
  Hello {{ name }}!
{% endblocktrans %}
```

 Use the `{% blocktrans %}` tag instead of `{% trans %}` when you need to include variable content in your translation string.

Translating the shop templates

Edit the `shop/base.html` template of the `shop` application. Make sure that you load the `i18n` tag at the top of the template and mark strings for translation, as follows:

```
{% load i18n %}
{% load static %}
<!DOCTYPE html>
<html>
<head>
  <meta charset="utf-8" />
  <title>
    {% block title %}{% trans "My shop" %}{% endblock %}
  </title>
  <link href="{% static "css/base.css" %}" rel="stylesheet">
</head>
<body>
  <div id="header">
    <a href="/" class="logo">{% trans "My shop" %}</a>
  </div>
  <div id="subheader">
    <div class="cart">
      {% with total_items=cart|length %}
        {% if total_items > 0 %}
          {% trans "Your cart" %}:
          <a href="{% url "cart:cart_detail" %}">
            {% blocktrans with total=cart.get_total_price count
items=total_items %}
              {{ items }} item, ${{ total }}
```

```
            {% plural %}
               {{ items }} items, ${{ total }}
            {% endblocktrans %}
          </a>
        {% else %}
          {% trans "Your cart is empty." %}
        {% endif %}
      {% endwith %}
    </div>
  </div>
  <div id="content">
    {% block content %}
    {% endblock %}
  </div>
</body>
</html>
```

Make sure that no template tag is split across multiple lines.

Notice the `{% blocktrans %}` tag to display the cart's summary. The cart's summary was previously as follows:

```
{{ total_items }} item{{ total_items|pluralize }},
${{ cart.get_total_price }}
```

You changed it and now you use `{% blocktrans with ... %}` to set up the placeholder `total` with the value of `cart.get_total_price` (the object method called here). You also use `count`, which allows you to set a variable for counting objects for Django to select the right plural form. You set the `items` variable to count objects with the value of `total_items`. This allows you to set a translation for the singular and plural forms, which you separate with the `{% plural %}` tag within the `{% blocktrans %}` block. The resulting code is:

```
{% blocktrans with total=cart.get_total_price count items=total_items
%}
   {{ items }} item, ${{ total }}
{% plural %}
   {{ items }} items, ${{ total }}
{% endblocktrans %}
```

Next, edit the `shop/product/detail.html` template of the `shop` application and load the `i18n` tags at the top of it, but after the `{% extends %}` tag, which always has to be the first tag in the template:

```
{% load i18n %}
```

Then, find the following line:

```
<input type="submit" value="Add to cart">
```

Replace it with the following:

```
<input type="submit" value="{% trans "Add to cart" %}">
```

Now, translate the `orders` application template. Edit the `orders/order/create.html` template of the `orders` application and mark text for translation, as follows:

```
{% extends "shop/base.html" %}
{% load i18n %}

{% block title %}
  {% trans "Checkout" %}
{% endblock %}

{% block content %}
  <h1>{% trans "Checkout" %}</h1>

  <div class="order-info">
    <h3>{% trans "Your order" %}</h3>
    <ul>
      {% for item in cart %}
        <li>
          {{ item.quantity }}x {{ item.product.name }}
          <span>${{ item.total_price }}</span>
        </li>
      {% endfor %}
      {% if cart.coupon %}
        <li>
          {% blocktrans with code=cart.coupon.code discount=cart.coupon.discount %}
            "{{ code }}" ({{ discount }}% off)
          {% endblocktrans %}
          <span class="neg">- ${{ cart.get_discount|floatformat:2 }}</span>
        </li>
      {% endif %}
    </ul>
    <p>{% trans "Total" %}: ${{ cart.get_total_price_after_discount|floatformat:2 }}</p>
  </div>

  <form method="post" class="order-form">
    {{ form.as_p }}
    <p><input type="submit" value="{% trans "Place order" %}"></p>
```

```
    {% csrf_token %}
  </form>
{% endblock %}
```

Make sure that no template tag is split across multiple lines. Take a look at the following files in the code that accompanies this chapter to see how strings have been marked for translation:

- The `shop` application: Template `shop/product/list.html`
- The `orders` application: Template `orders/order/created.html`
- The `cart` application: Template `cart/detail.html`

You can find the source code for this chapter at `https://github.com/PacktPublishing/Django-3-by-Example/tree/master/Chapter09`.

Let's update the message files to include the new translation strings. Open the shell and run the following command:

```
django-admin makemessages --all
```

The `.po` files are inside the `locale` directory of the `myshop` project and you'll see that the `orders` application now contains all the strings that you marked for translation.

Edit the `.po` translation files of the project and the `orders` application, and include Spanish translations in the `msgstr`. You can also use the translated `.po` files in the source code that accompanies this chapter.

Run the following command to compile the translation files:

```
django-admin compilemessages
```

You will see the following output:

```
processing file django.po in myshop/locale/en/LC_MESSAGES
processing file django.po in myshop/locale/es/LC_MESSAGES
processing file django.po in myshop/orders/locale/en/LC_MESSAGES
processing file django.po in myshop/orders/locale/es/LC_MESSAGES
```

A `.mo` file containing compiled translations has been generated for each `.po` translation file.

Using the Rosetta translation interface

Rosetta is a third-party application that allows you to edit translations using the same interface as the Django administration site. Rosetta makes it easy to edit `.po` files and it updates compiled translation files. Let's add it to your project.

Install Rosetta via `pip` using this command:

```
pip install django-rosetta==0.9.3
```

Then, add `'rosetta'` to the `INSTALLED_APPS` setting in your project's `settings.py` file, as follows:

```
INSTALLED_APPS = [
    # ...
    'rosetta',
]
```

You need to add Rosetta's URLs to your main URL configuration. Edit the main `urls.py` file of your project and add the following URL pattern to it:

```
urlpatterns = [
    # ...
    path('rosetta/', include('rosetta.urls')),
    path('', include('shop.urls', namespace='shop')),
]
```

Make sure you place it before the `shop.urls` pattern to avoid an undesired pattern match.

Open `http://127.0.0.1:8000/admin/` and log in with a superuser. Then, navigate to `http://127.0.0.1:8000/rosetta/` in your browser. In the **Filter** menu, click **THIRD PARTY** to display all the available message files, including those that belong to the `orders` application. You should see a list of existing languages, as follows:

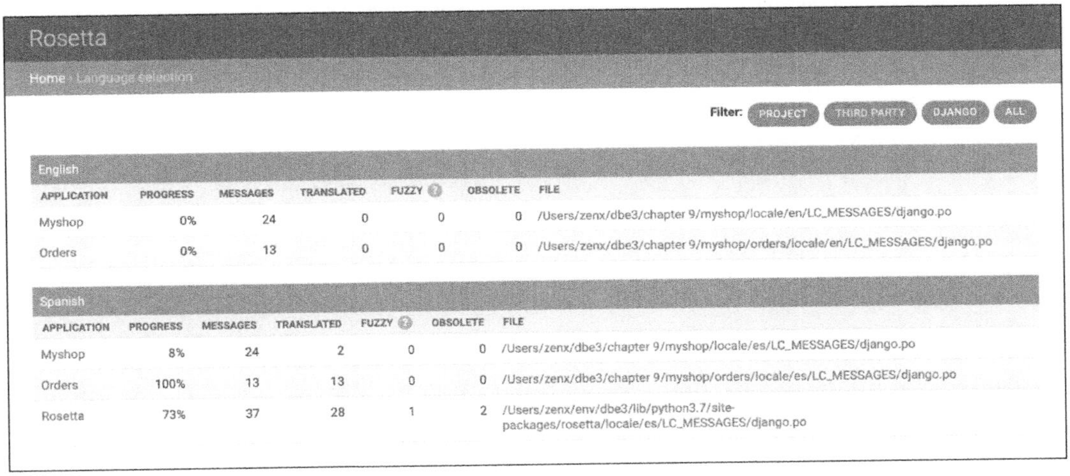

Figure 9.5: The Rosetta administration interface

Click the **Myshop** link under the **Spanish** section to edit the Spanish translations. You should see a list of translation strings, as follows:

Figure 9.6: Editing Spanish translations using Rosetta

You can enter the translations under the **SPANISH** column. The **OCCURRENCE(S)** column displays the files and line of code where each translation string was found.

Translations that include placeholders will appear as follows:

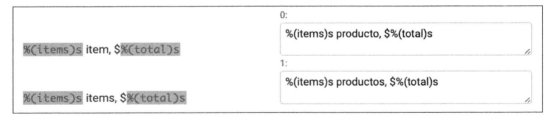

Figure 9.7: Translations including placeholders

Rosetta uses a different background color to display placeholders. When you translate content, make sure that you keep placeholders untranslated. For example, take the following string:

```
%(items)s items, $%(total)s
```

It is translated into Spanish as follows:

```
%(items)s productos, $%(total)s
```

You can take a look at the source code that comes along with this chapter to use the same Spanish translations for your project.

When you finish editing translations, click the **Save and translate next block** button to save the translations to the `.po` file. Rosetta compiles the message file when you save translations, so there is no need for you to run the `compilemessages` command. However, Rosetta requires write access to the `locale` directories to write the message files. Make sure that the directories have valid permissions.

If you want other users to be able to edit translations, open `http://127.0.0.1:8000/admin/auth/group/add/` in your browser and create a new group named `translators`. Then, access `http://127.0.0.1:8000/admin/auth/user/` to edit the users to whom you want to grant permissions so that they can edit translations. When editing a user, under the **Permissions** section, add the `translators` group to the **Chosen Groups** for each user. Rosetta is only available to superusers or users who belong to the `translators` group.

You can read Rosetta's documentation at `https://django-rosetta.readthedocs.io/`.

 When you add new translations to your production environment, if you serve Django with a real web server, you will have to reload your server after running the `compilemessages` command, or after saving the translations with Rosetta, for changes to take effect.

Fuzzy translations

You might have noticed that there is a **FUZZY** column in Rosetta. This is not a Rosetta feature; it is provided by gettext. If the fuzzy flag is active for a translation, it will not be included in the compiled message files. This flag marks translation strings that need to be reviewed by a translator. When `.po` files are updated with new translation strings, it is possible that some translation strings will automatically be flagged as fuzzy. This happens when gettext finds some `msgid` that has been slightly modified. gettext pairs it with what it thinks was the old translation and flags it as fuzzy for review. The translator should then review fuzzy translations, remove the fuzzy flag, and compile the translation file again.

URL patterns for internationalization

Django offers internationalization capabilities for URLs. It includes two main features for internationalized URLs:

- **Language prefix in URL patterns**: Adding a language prefix to URLs to serve each language version under a different base URL
- **Translated URL patterns**: Translating URL patterns so that every URL is different for each language

A reason for translating URLs is to optimize your site for search engines. By adding a language prefix to your patterns, you will be able to index a URL for each language instead of a single URL for all of them. Furthermore, by translating URLs into each language, you will provide search engines with URLs that will rank better for each language.

Adding a language prefix to URL patterns

Django allows you to add a language prefix to your URL patterns. For example, the English version of your site can be served under a path starting /en/, and the Spanish version under /es/. To use languages in URL patterns, you have to use the LocaleMiddleware provided by Django. The framework will use it to identify the current language from the requested URL. You added it previously to the MIDDLEWARE setting of your project, so you don't need to do it now.

Let's add a language prefix to your URL patterns. Edit the main urls.py file of the myshop project and add i18n_patterns(), as follows:

```
from django.conf.urls.i18n import i18n_patterns

urlpatterns = i18n_patterns(
 path('admin/', admin.site.urls),
 path('cart/', include('cart.urls', namespace='cart')),
 path('orders/', include('orders.urls', namespace='orders')),
 path('payment/', include('payment.urls', namespace='payment')),
 path('coupons/', include('coupons.urls', namespace='coupons')),
 path('rosetta/', include('rosetta.urls')),
 path('', include('shop.urls', namespace='shop')),
)
```

You can combine non-translatable standard URL patterns and patterns under i18n_patterns so that some patterns include a language prefix and others don't. However, it's better to use translated URLs only to avoid the possibility that a carelessly translated URL matches a non-translated URL pattern.

Run the development server and open `http://127.0.0.1:8000/` in your browser. Django will perform the steps described previously in the *How Django determines the current language* section to determine the current language, and it will redirect you to the requested URL, including the language prefix. Take a look at the URL in your browser; it should now look like `http://127.0.0.1:8000/en/`. The current language is the one set by the `Accept-Language` header of your browser if it is Spanish or English; otherwise, it is the default `LANGUAGE_CODE` (English) defined in your settings.

Translating URL patterns

Django supports translated strings in URL patterns. You can use a different translation for each language for a single URL pattern. You can mark URL patterns for translation in the same way as you would with literals, using the `gettext_lazy()` function.

Edit the main `urls.py` file of the `myshop` project and add translation strings to the regular expressions of the URL patterns for the `cart`, `orders`, `payment`, and `coupons` applications, as follows:

```python
from django.utils.translation import gettext_lazy as _

urlpatterns = i18n_patterns(
 path(_('admin/'), admin.site.urls),
 path(_('cart/'), include('cart.urls', namespace='cart')),
 path(_('orders/'), include('orders.urls', namespace='orders')),
 path(_('payment/'), include('payment.urls', namespace='payment')),
 path(_('coupons/'), include('coupons.urls', namespace='coupons')),
 path('rosetta/', include('rosetta.urls')),
 path('', include('shop.urls', namespace='shop')),
)
```

Edit the `urls.py` file of the `orders` application and mark URL patterns for translation, as follows:

```python
from django.utils.translation import gettext_lazy as _

urlpatterns = [
    path(_('create/'), views.order_create, name='order_create'),
    # ...
]
```

Edit the `urls.py` file of the `payment` application and change the code to the following:

```python
from django.utils.translation import gettext_lazy as _
```

```
urlpatterns = [
    path(_('process/'), views.payment_process, name='process'),
    path(_('done/'), views.payment_done, name='done'),
    path(_('canceled/'), views.payment_canceled, name='canceled'),
]
```

You don't need to translate the URL patterns of the `shop` application, since they are built with variables and do not include any other literals.

Open the shell and run the next command to update the message files with the new translations:

django-admin makemessages --all

Make sure the development server is running. Open `http://127.0.0.1:8000/en/rosetta/` in your browser and click the **Myshop** link under the **Spanish** section. Now you will see the URL patterns for translation. You can click on **Untranslated only** to only see the strings that have not been translated yet. You can now translate the URLs.

Allowing users to switch language

Since you are serving content that is available in multiple languages, you should let your users switch the site's language. You are going to add a language selector to your site. The language selector will consist of a list of available languages displayed using links.

Edit the `shop/base.html` template of the `shop` application and locate the following lines:

```
<div id="header">
  <a href="/" class="logo">{% trans "My shop" %}</a>
</div>
```

Replace them with the following code:

```
<div id="header">
  <a href="/" class="logo">{% trans "My shop" %}</a>
  {% get_current_language as LANGUAGE_CODE %}
  {% get_available_languages as LANGUAGES %}
  {% get_language_info_list for LANGUAGES as languages %}
  <div class="languages">
    <p>{% trans "Language" %}:</p>
    <ul class="languages">
      {% for language in languages %}
        <li>
```

```
        <a href="/{{ language.code }}/"
        {% if language.code == LANGUAGE_CODE %} class="selected"{%
endif %}>
            {{ language.name_local }}
        </a>
      </li>
    {% endfor %}
  </ul>
  </div>
</div>
```

Make sure that no template tag is split into multiple lines.

This is how you build your language selector:

1. You load the internationalization tags using {% load i18n %}

2. You use the {% get_current_language %} tag to retrieve the current language

3. You get the languages defined in the LANGUAGES setting using the {% get_available_languages %} template tag

4. You use the tag {% get_language_info_list %} to provide easy access to the language attributes

5. You build an HTML list to display all available languages and you add a selected class attribute to the current active language

In the code for the language selector, you used the template tags provided by i18n, based on the languages available in the settings of your project. Now open http://127.0.0.1:8000/ in your browser and take a look. You should see the language selector in the top right-hand corner of the site, as follows:

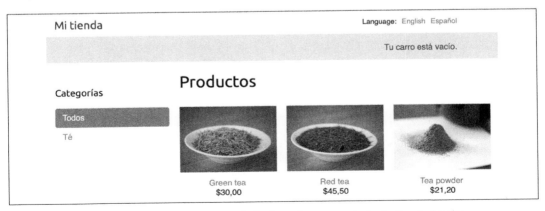

Figure 9.8: The product list page, including a language selector in the site header

Users can now easily switch to their preferred language by clicking on it.

Translating models with django-parler

Django does not provide a solution for translating models out of the box. You have to implement your own solution to manage content stored in different languages, or use a third-party module for model translation. There are several third-party applications that allow you to translate model fields. Each of them takes a different approach to storing and accessing translations. One of these applications is django-parler. This module offers a very effective way to translate models and it integrates smoothly with Django's administration site.

django-parler generates a separate database table for each model that contains translations. This table includes all the translated fields and a foreign key for the original object that the translation belongs to. It also contains a language field, since each row stores the content for a single language.

Installing django-parler

Install `django-parler` via `pip` using the following command:

```
pip install django-parler==2.0.1
```

Edit the `settings.py` file of your project and add `'parler'` to the `INSTALLED_APPS` setting, as follows:

```
INSTALLED_APPS = [
    # ...
    'parler',
]
```

Also, add the following code to your settings:

```
PARLER_LANGUAGES = {
    None: (
        {'code': 'en'},
        {'code': 'es'},
    ),
    'default': {
        'fallback': 'en',
        'hide_untranslated': False,
    }
}
```

This setting defines the available languages, en and es, for django-parler. You specify the default language en and indicate that django-parler should not hide untranslated content.

Translating model fields

Let's add translations for your product catalog. django-parler provides a TranslatableModel model class and a TranslatedFields wrapper to translate model fields. Edit the models.py file inside the shop application directory and add the following import:

```
from parler.models import TranslatableModel, TranslatedFields
```

Then, modify the Category model to make the name and slug fields translatable, as follows:

```
class Category(TranslatableModel):
    translations = TranslatedFields(
        name = models.CharField(max_length=200,
                                db_index=True),
        slug = models.SlugField(max_length=200,
                                db_index=True,
                                unique=True)
    )
```

The Category model now inherits from TranslatableModel instead of models.Model and both the name and slug fields are included in the TranslatedFields wrapper.

Edit the Product model to add translations for the name, slug, and description fields, as follows:

```
class Product(TranslatableModel):
    translations = TranslatedFields(
        name = models.CharField(max_length=200, db_index=True),
        slug = models.SlugField(max_length=200, db_index=True),
        description = models.TextField(blank=True)
    )
    category = models.ForeignKey(Category,
                                 related_name='products')
    image = models.ImageField(upload_to='products/%Y/%m/%d',
                              blank=True)
    price = models.DecimalField(max_digits=10, decimal_places=2)
    available = models.BooleanField(default=True)
    created = models.DateTimeField(auto_now_add=True)
    updated = models.DateTimeField(auto_now=True)
```

`django-parler` manages translations by generating another model for each translatable model. In the following schema, you can see the fields of the `Product` model and what the generated `ProductTranslation` model will look like:

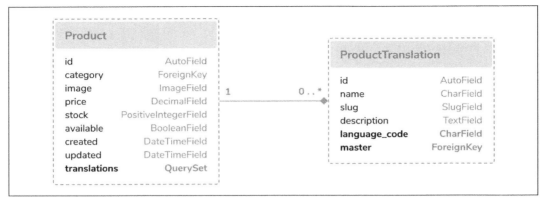

Figure 9.9: The Product model and related ProductTranslation model generated by django-parler

The `ProductTranslation` model generated by `django-parler` includes the name, slug, and description translatable fields, a `language_code` field, and a `ForeignKey` for the master `Product` object. There is a one-to-many relationship from `Product` to `ProductTranslation`. A `ProductTranslation` object will exist for each available language of each `Product` object.

Since Django uses a separate table for translations, there are some Django features that you can't use. It is not possible to use a default ordering by a translated field. You can filter by translated fields in queries, but you can't include a translatable field in the `ordering` Meta options.

Edit the `models.py` file of the `shop` application and comment out the `ordering` attribute of the `Category` Meta class:

```
class Category(TranslatableModel):
    # ...
    class Meta:
        # ordering = ('name',)
        verbose_name = 'category'
        verbose_name_plural = 'categories'
```

You also have to comment out the `ordering` and `index_together` attributes of the `Product` Meta class. The current version of `django-parler` does not provide support to validate `index_together`. Comment out the `Product` Meta class, as follows:

```
class Product(TranslatableModel):
    # ...
```

```
# class Meta:
#     ordering = ('-name',)
#     index_together = (('id', 'slug'),)
```

You can read more about the `django-parler` module's compatibility with Django at `https://django-parler.readthedocs.io/en/latest/compatibility.html`.

Integrating translations into the administration site

`django-parler` integrates smoothly with the Django administration site. It includes a `TranslatableAdmin` class that overrides the `ModelAdmin` class provided by Django to manage model translations.

Edit the `admin.py` file of the `shop` application and add the following import to it:

```
from parler.admin import TranslatableAdmin
```

Modify the `CategoryAdmin` and `ProductAdmin` classes to inherit from `TranslatableAdmin` instead of `ModelAdmin`. `django-parler` doesn't support the `prepopulated_fields` attribute, but it does support the `get_prepopulated_fields()` method that provides the same functionality. Let's change this accordingly. Edit the `admin.py` file to make it look as follows:

```
from django.contrib import admin
from parler.admin import TranslatableAdmin
from .models import Category, Product

@admin.register(Category)
class CategoryAdmin(TranslatableAdmin):
    list_display = ['name', 'slug']

    def get_prepopulated_fields(self, request, obj=None):
        return {'slug': ('name',)}

@admin.register(Product)
class ProductAdmin(TranslatableAdmin):
    list_display = ['name', 'slug', 'price',
                    'available', 'created', 'updated']
    list_filter = ['available', 'created', 'updated']
    list_editable = ['price', 'available']

    def get_prepopulated_fields(self, request, obj=None):
        return {'slug': ('name',)}
```

You have adapted the administration site to work with the new translated models. You can now sync the database with the model changes that you made.

Creating migrations for model translations

Open the shell and run the following command to create a new migration for the model translations:

```
python manage.py makemigrations shop --name "translations"
```

You will see the following output:

```
Migrations for 'shop':
  shop/migrations/0002_translations.py
    - Change Meta options on category
    - Change Meta options on product
    - Remove field name from category
    - Remove field slug from category
    - Alter index_together for product (0 constraint(s))
    - Remove field description from product
    - Remove field name from product
    - Remove field slug from product
    - Create model ProductTranslation
    - Create model CategoryTranslation
```

This migration automatically includes the `CategoryTranslation` and `ProductTranslation` models created dynamically by `django-parler`. It's important to note that this migration deletes the previous existing fields from your models. This means that you will lose that data and will need to set your categories and products again in the administration site after running it.

Edit the file `migrations/0002_translations.py` of the `shop` application and replace the two occurrences of the following line:

```
bases=(parler.models.TranslatedFieldsModelMixin, models.Model),
```

with the following one:

```
bases=(parler.models.TranslatableModel, models.Model),
```

This is a fix for a minor issue found in the `django-parler` version you are using. This change is necessary to prevent the migration from failing when applying it. This issue is related to creating translations for existing fields in the model and will probably be fixed in newer `django-parler` versions.

Run the following command to apply the migration:

```
python manage.py migrate shop
```

You will see an output that ends with the following line:

```
Applying shop.0002_translations... OK
```

Your models are now synchronized with the database.

Run the development server using `python manage.py runserver` and open `http://127.0.0.1:8000/en/admin/shop/category/` in your browser. You will see that existing categories lost their name and slug due to deleting those fields and using the translatable models generated by `django-parler` instead. Click on a category to edit it. You will see that the **Change category** page includes two different tabs, one for English and one for Spanish translations:

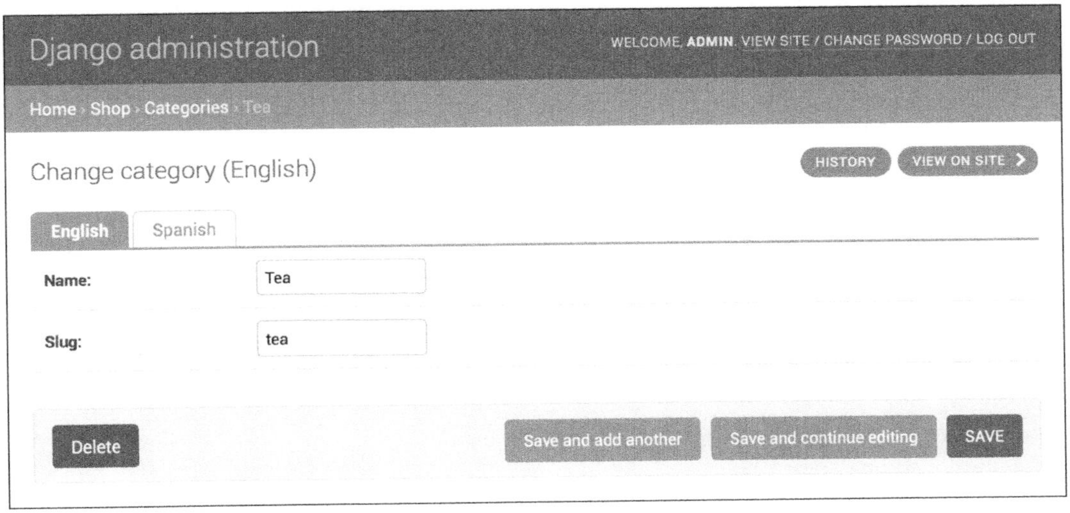

Figure 9.10: The category edit form, including language tabs added by django-parler

Make sure that you fill in a name and slug for all existing categories. Also, add a Spanish translation for each of them and click the **SAVE** button. Make sure that you save the changes before you switch tab or you will lose them.

After completing the data for existing categories, open `http://127.0.0.1:8000/en/admin/shop/product/` and edit each of the products, providing an English and Spanish name, a slug, and a description.

Adapting views for translations

You have to adapt your `shop` views to use translation QuerySets. Run the following command to open the Python shell:

```
python manage.py shell
```

Let's take a look at how you can retrieve and query translation fields. To get the object with translatable fields translated in a specific language, you can use Django's `activate()` function, as follows:

```
>>> from shop.models import Product
>>> from django.utils.translation import activate
>>> activate('es')
>>> product=Product.objects.first()
>>> product.name
'Té verde'
```

Another way to do this is by using the `language()` manager provided by django-parler, as follows:

```
>>> product=Product.objects.language('en').first()
>>> product.name
'Green tea'
```

When you access translated fields, they are resolved using the current language. You can set a different current language for an object to access that specific translation, as follows:

```
>>> product.set_current_language('es')
>>> product.name
'Té verde'
>>> product.get_current_language()
'es'
```

When performing a QuerySet using `filter()`, you can filter using the related translation objects with the `translations__` syntax, as follows:

```
>>> Product.objects.filter(translations__name='Green tea')
<TranslatableQuerySet [<Product: Té verde>]>
```

Let's adapt the product catalog views. Edit the `views.py` file of the `shop` application and, in the `product_list` view, find the following line:

```
    category = get_object_or_404(Category, slug=category_slug)
```

Replace it with the following ones:

```
language = request.LANGUAGE_CODE
category = get_object_or_404(Category,
                            translations__language_code=language,
                            translations__slug=category_slug)
```

Then, edit the `product_detail` view and find the following lines:

```
product = get_object_or_404(Product,
                            id=id,
                            slug=slug,
                            available=True)
```

Replace them with the following code:

```
language = request.LANGUAGE_CODE
product = get_object_or_404(Product,
                            id=id,
                            translations__language_code=language,
                            translations__slug=slug,
                            available=True)
```

The `product_list` and `product_detail` views are now adapted to retrieve objects using translated fields. Run the development server and open `http://127.0.0.1:8000/es/` in your browser. You should see the product list page, including all products translated into Spanish:

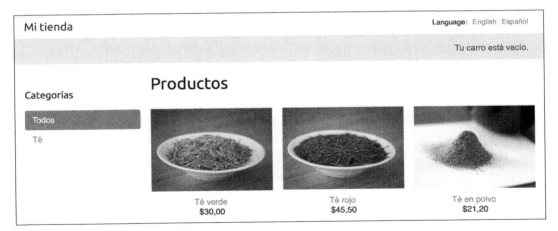

Figure 9.11: The Spanish version of the product list page

Now, each product's URL is built using the `slug` field translated into the current language. For example, the URL for a product in Spanish is `http://127.0.0.1:8000/es/2/te-rojo/`, whereas in English, the URL is `http://127.0.0.1:8000/en/2/red-tea/`. If you navigate to a product detail page, you will see the translated URL and the contents of the selected language, as shown in the following example:

Figure 9.12: The Spanish version of the product detail page

If you want to know more about `django-parler`, you can find the full documentation at `https://django-parler.readthedocs.io/en/latest/`.

You have learned how to translate Python code, templates, URL patterns, and model fields. To complete the internationalization and localization process, you need to use localized formatting for dates, times, and numbers as well.

Format localization

Depending on the user's locale, you might want to display dates, times, and numbers in different formats. Localized formatting can be activated by changing the USE_L10N setting to `True` in the `settings.py` file of your project.

When USE_L10N is enabled, Django will try to use a locale-specific format whenever it outputs a value in a template. You can see that decimal numbers in the English version of your site are displayed with a dot separator for decimal places, while in the Spanish version, they are displayed using a comma. This is due to the locale formats specified for the `es` locale by Django. You can take a look at the Spanish formatting configuration at `https://github.com/django/django/blob/stable/3.0.x/django/conf/locale/es/formats.py`.

Normally, you will set the USE_L10N setting to True and let Django apply the format localization for each locale. However, there might be situations in which you don't want to use localized values. This is especially relevant when outputting JavaScript or JSON that has to provide a machine-readable format.

Django offers a {% localize %} template tag that allows you to turn on/off localization for template fragments. This gives you control over localized formatting. You will have to load the l10n tags to be able to use this template tag. The following is an example of how to turn localization on and off in a template:

```
{% load l10n %}

{% localize on %}
  {{ value }}
{% endlocalize %}

{% localize off %}
  {{ value }}
{% endlocalize %}
```

Django also offers the localize and unlocalize template filters to force or avoid the localization of a value. These filters can be applied as follows:

```
{{ value|localize }}
{{ value|unlocalize }}
```

You can also create custom format files to specify locale formatting. You can find further information about format localization at https://docs.djangoproject.com/en/3.0/topics/i18n/formatting/.

Using django-localflavor to validate form fields

django-localflavor is a third-party module that contains a collection of utils, such as form fields or model fields, that are specific for each country. It's very useful for validating local regions, local phone numbers, identity card numbers, social security numbers, and so on. The package is organized into a series of modules named after ISO 3166 country codes.

Install django-localflavor using the following command:

```
pip install django-localflavor==3.0.1
```

Edit the `settings.py` file of your project and add `localflavor` to the `INSTALLED_APPS` setting, as follows:

```
INSTALLED_APPS = [
    # ...
    'localflavor',
]
```

You are going to add the United States' zip code field so that a valid United States zip code is required to create a new order.

Edit the `forms.py` file of the `orders` application and make it look as follows:

```
from django import forms
from localflavor.us.forms import USZipCodeField
from .models import Order

class OrderCreateForm(forms.ModelForm):
    postal_code = USZipCodeField()
    class Meta:
        model = Order
        fields = ['first_name', 'last_name', 'email', 'address',
                  'postal_code', 'city']
```

You import the `USZipCodeField` field from the `us` package of `localflavor` and use it for the `postal_code` field of the `OrderCreateForm` form.

Run the development server and open `http://127.0.0.1:8000/en/orders/create/` in your browser. Fill in all fields, enter a three-letter zip code, and then submit the form. You will get the following validation error that is raised by `USZipCodeField`:

```
Enter a zip code in the format XXXXX or XXXXX-XXXX.
```

This is just a brief example of how to use a custom field from `localflavor` in your own project for validation purposes. The local components provided by `localflavor` are very useful for adapting your application to specific countries. You can read the `django-localflavor` documentation and see all available local components for each country at `https://django-localflavor.readthedocs.io/en/latest/`.

Next, you are going to build a recommendation engine into your shop.

Building a recommendation engine

A recommendation engine is a system that predicts the preference or rating that a user would give to an item. The system selects relevant items for a user based on their behavior and the knowledge it has about them. Nowadays, recommendation systems are used in many online services. They help users by selecting the stuff they might be interested in from the vast amount of available data that is irrelevant to them. Offering good recommendations enhances user engagement. E-commerce sites also benefit from offering relevant product recommendations by increasing their average revenue per user.

You are going to create a simple, yet powerful, recommendation engine that suggests products that are usually bought together. You will suggest products based on historical sales, thus identifying products that are usually bought together. You are going to suggest complementary products in two different scenarios:

- **Product detail page**: You will display a list of products that are usually bought with the given product. This will be displayed as *users who bought this also bought X, Y, Z*. You need a data structure that allows you to store the number of times that each product has been bought together with the product being displayed.
- **Cart detail page**: Based on the products users add to the cart, you are going to suggest products that are usually bought together with these ones. In this case, the score you calculate to obtain related products has to be aggregated.

You are going to use Redis to store products that are purchased together. Remember that you already used Redis in *Chapter 6, Tracking User Actions*. If you haven't installed Redis yet, you can find installation instructions in that chapter.

Recommending products based on previous purchases

You will recommend products to users based on what they have added to the cart. You are going to store a key in Redis for each product bought on your site. The product key will contain a Redis sorted set with scores. You will increment the score by 1 for each product bought together every time a new purchase is completed. The sorted set will allow you to give scores to products that are bought together.

Remember to install `redis-py` in your environment using the following command:

```
pip install redis==3.4.1
```

Edit the `settings.py` file of your project and add the following settings to it:

```
REDIS_HOST = 'localhost'
REDIS_PORT = 6379
REDIS_DB = 1
```

These are the settings required to establish a connection with the Redis server. Create a new file inside the `shop` application directory and name it `recommender.py`. Add the following code to it:

```python
import redis
from django.conf import settings
from .models import Product

# connect to redis
r = redis.Redis(host=settings.REDIS_HOST,
                port=settings.REDIS_PORT,
                db=settings.REDIS_DB)


class Recommender(object):

    def get_product_key(self, id):
        return f'product:{id}:purchased_with'

    def products_bought(self, products):
        product_ids = [p.id for p in products]
        for product_id in product_ids:
            for with_id in product_ids:
                # get the other products bought with each product
                if product_id != with_id:
                    # increment score for product purchased together
                    r.zincrby(self.get_product_key(product_id),
                              1,
                              with_id)
```

This is the `Recommender` class that will allow you to store product purchases and retrieve product suggestions for a given product or products.

The `get_product_key()` method receives an ID of a `Product` object and builds the Redis key for the sorted set where related products are stored, which looks like `product:[id]:purchased_with`.

The `products_bought()` method receives a list of `Product` objects that have been bought together (that is, belong to the same order).

In this method, you perform the following tasks:

1. You get the product IDs for the given `Product` objects.

2. You iterate over the product IDs. For each ID, you iterate again over the product IDs and skip the same product so that you get the products that are bought together with each product.

3. You get the Redis product key for each product bought using the `get_product_id()` method. For a product with an ID of 33, this method returns the key `product:33:purchased_with`. This is the key for the sorted set that contains the product IDs of products that were bought together with this one.

4. You increment the score of each product ID contained in the sorted set by 1. The score represents the times another product has been bought together with the given product.

You now have a method to store and score the products that were bought together. Next, you need a method to retrieve the products that were bought together for a list of given products. Add the following `suggest_products_for()` method to the `Recommender` class:

```python
def suggest_products_for(self, products, max_results=6):
    product_ids = [p.id for p in products]
    if len(products) == 1:
        # only 1 product
        suggestions = r.zrange(
                        self.get_product_key(product_ids[0]),
                        0, -1, desc=True)[:max_results]
    else:
        # generate a temporary key
        flat_ids = ''.join([str(id) for id in product_ids])
        tmp_key = f'tmp_{flat_ids}'
        # multiple products, combine scores of all products
        # store the resulting sorted set in a temporary key
        keys = [self.get_product_key(id) for id in product_ids]
        r.zunionstore(tmp_key, keys)
        # remove ids for the products the recommendation is for
        r.zrem(tmp_key, *product_ids)
        # get the product ids by their score, descendant sort
        suggestions = r.zrange(tmp_key, 0, -1,
                                desc=True)[:max_results]
        # remove the temporary key
        r.delete(tmp_key)
    suggested_products_ids = [int(id) for id in suggestions]
```

```
    # get suggested products and sort by order of appearance
    suggested_products = list(Product.objects.filter(id__in=suggested_
products_ids))
    suggested_products.sort(key=lambda x: suggested_products_ids.
index(x.id))
    return suggested_products
```

The `suggest_products_for()` method receives the following parameters:

- `products`: This is a list of `Product` objects to get recommendations for. It can contain one or more products.

- `max_results`: This is an integer that represents the maximum number of recommendations to return.

In this method, you perform the following actions:

1. You get the product IDs for the given `Product` objects.

2. If only one product is given, you retrieve the ID of the products that were bought together with the given product, ordered by the total number of times that they were bought together. To do so, you use Redis' ZRANGE command. You limit the number of results to the number specified in the `max_results` attribute (6 by default).

3. If more than one product is given, you generate a temporary Redis key built with the IDs of the products.

4. You combine and sum all scores for the items contained in the sorted set of each of the given products. This is done using the Redis ZUNIONSTORE command. The ZUNIONSTORE command performs a union of the sorted sets with the given keys, and stores the aggregated sum of scores of the elements in a new Redis key. You can read more about this command at https:// redis.io/commands/ZUNIONSTORE. You save the aggregated scores in the temporary key.

5. Since you are aggregating scores, you might obtain the same products you are getting recommendations for. You remove them from the generated sorted set using the ZREM command.

6. You retrieve the IDs of the products from the temporary key, ordered by their score using the ZRANGE command. You limit the number of results to the number specified in the `max_results` attribute. Then, you remove the temporary key.

7. Finally, you get the `Product` objects with the given IDs and you order the products in the same order as them.

For practical purposes, let's also add a method to clear the recommendations. Add the following method to the Recommender class:

```
def clear_purchases(self):
    for id in Product.objects.values_list('id', flat=True):
        r.delete(self.get_product_key(id))
```

Let's try your recommendation engine. Make sure you include several Product objects in the database and initialize the Redis server using the following command from the shell in your Redis directory:

src/redis-server

Open another shell and run the following command to open the Python shell:

python manage.py shell

Make sure that you have at least four different products in your database. Retrieve four different products by their names:

```
>>> from shop.models import Product
>>> black_tea = Product.objects.get(translations__name='Black tea')
>>> red_tea = Product.objects.get(translations__name='Red tea')
>>> green_tea = Product.objects.get(translations__name='Green tea')
>>> tea_powder = Product.objects.get(translations__name='Tea powder')
```

Then, add some test purchases to the recommendation engine:

```
>>> from shop.recommender import Recommender
>>> r = Recommender()
>>> r.products_bought([black_tea, red_tea])
>>> r.products_bought([black_tea, green_tea])
>>> r.products_bought([red_tea, black_tea, tea_powder])
>>> r.products_bought([green_tea, tea_powder])
>>> r.products_bought([black_tea, tea_powder])
>>> r.products_bought([red_tea, green_tea])
```

You have stored the following scores:

```
black_tea:  red_tea (2), tea_powder (2), green_tea (1)
red_tea:    black_tea (2), tea_powder (1), green_tea (1)
green_tea:  black_tea (1), tea_powder (1), red_tea(1)
tea_powder: black_tea (2), red_tea (1), green_tea (1)
```

Let's activate a language to retrieve translated products and get product recommendations to buy together with a given single product:

```
>>> from django.utils.translation import activate
>>> activate('en')
>>> r.suggest_products_for([black_tea])
[<Product: Tea powder>, <Product: Red tea>, <Product: Green tea>]
>>> r.suggest_products_for([red_tea])
[<Product: Black tea>, <Product: Tea powder>, <Product: Green tea>]
>>> r.suggest_products_for([green_tea])
[<Product: Black tea>, <Product: Tea powder>, <Product: Red tea>]
>>> r.suggest_products_for([tea_powder])
[<Product: Black tea>, <Product: Red tea>, <Product: Green tea>]
```

You can see that the order for recommended products is based on their score. Let's get recommendations for multiple products with aggregated scores:

```
>>> r.suggest_products_for([black_tea, red_tea])
[<Product: Tea powder>, <Product: Green tea>]
>>> r.suggest_products_for([green_tea, red_tea])
[<Product: Black tea>, <Product: Tea powder>]
>>> r.suggest_products_for([tea_powder, black_tea])
[<Product: Red tea>, <Product: Green tea>]
```

You can see that the order of the suggested products matches the aggregated scores. For example, products suggested for black_tea and red_tea are tea_powder (2+1) and green_tea (1+1).

You have verified that your recommendation algorithm works as expected. Let's now display recommendations for products on your site.

Edit the `views.py` file of the `shop` application. Add the functionality to retrieve a maximum of four recommended products in the `product_detail` view, as follows:

```python
from .recommender import Recommender

def product_detail(request, id, slug):
    language = request.LANGUAGE_CODE
    product = get_object_or_404(Product,
                                id=id,
                                translations__language_code=language,
                                translations__slug=slug,
                                available=True)
    cart_product_form = CartAddProductForm()

    r = Recommender()
    recommended_products = r.suggest_products_for([product], 4)

    return render(request,
                  'shop/product/detail.html',
                  {'product': product,
                   'cart_product_form': cart_product_form,
                   'recommended_products': recommended_products})
```

Edit the `shop/product/detail.html` template of the `shop` application and add the following code after `{{ product.description|linebreaks }}`:

```html
{% if recommended_products %}
  <div class="recommendations">
    <h3>{% trans "People who bought this also bought" %}</h3>
    {% for p in recommended_products %}
      <div class="item">
        <a href="{{ p.get_absolute_url }}">
          <img src="{% if p.image %}{{ p.image.url }}{% else %}
          {% static  "img/no_image.png" %}{% endif %}">
        </a>
        <p><a href="{{ p.get_absolute_url }}">{{ p.name }}</a></p>
      </div>
    {% endfor %}
  </div>
{% endif %}
```

Run the development server and open `http://127.0.0.1:8000/en/` in your browser. Click on any product to view its details. You should see that recommended products are displayed below the product, as shown in the following screenshot:

Figure 9.13: The product detail page, including recommended products

You are also going to include product recommendations in the cart. The recommendations will be based on the products that the user has added to the cart.

Edit `views.py` inside the `cart` application, import the `Recommender` class, and edit the `cart_detail` view to make it look as follows:

```
from shop.recommender import Recommender

def cart_detail(request):
    cart = Cart(request)
    for item in cart:
        item['update_quantity_form'] = CartAddProductForm(initial={
```

```
                              'quantity': item['quantity'],
                              'override': True})

        coupon_apply_form = CouponApplyForm()

        r = Recommender()
        cart_products = [item['product'] for item in cart]
        recommended_products = r.suggest_products_for(cart_products,
                                                      max_results=4)


    return render(request,
                  'cart/detail.html',
                  {'cart': cart,
                   'coupon_apply_form': coupon_apply_form,
                   'recommended_products': recommended_products})
```

Edit the `cart/detail.html` template of the `cart` application and add the following code just after the `</table>` HTML tag:

```
{% if recommended_products %}
  <div class="recommendations cart">
    <h3>{% trans "People who bought this also bought" %}</h3>
    {% for p in recommended_products %}
      <div class="item">
        <a href="{{ p.get_absolute_url }}">
          <img src="{% if p.image %}{{ p.image.url }}{% else %}
          {% static "img/no_image.png" %}{% endif %}">
        </a>
        <p><a href="{{ p.get_absolute_url }}">{{ p.name }}</a></p>
      </div>
    {% endfor %}
  </div>
{% endif %}
```

Open `http://127.0.0.1:8000/en/` in your browser and add a couple of products to your cart. When you navigate to `http://127.0.0.1:8000/en/cart/`, you should see the aggregated product recommendations for the items in the cart, as follows:

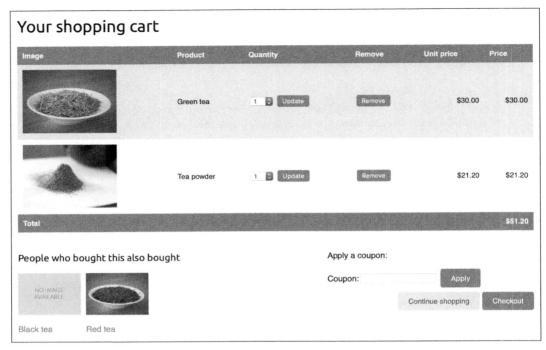

Figure 9.14: The shopping cart detail page, including recommended products

Congratulations! You have built a complete recommendation engine using Django and Redis.

Summary

In this chapter, you created a coupon system using sessions. You also learned the basics of internationalization and localization for Django projects. You marked code and template strings for translation, and you discovered how to generate and compile translation files. You also installed Rosetta in your project to manage translations through a browser interface. You translated URL patterns and you created a language selector to allow users to switch the language of the site. Then, you used `django-parler` to translate models and you used `django-localflavor` to validate localized form fields. Finally, you built a recommendation engine using Redis to recommend products that are usually purchased together.

In the next chapter, you will start a new project. You will build an e-learning platform with Django using class-based views and you will create a custom content management system.

10
Building an E-Learning Platform

In the previous chapter, you added internationalization to your online shop project. You also built a coupon system using sessions and a product recommendation engine using Redis. In this chapter, you will start a new Django project. You will build an e-learning platform with your own **content management system** (**CMS**). Online learning platforms are a great example of applications where you need to provide tools to generate content with flexibility in mind. In this chapter, you will learn how to build the functionality for instructors to create courses and manage the contents of courses in a versatile and efficient manner.

In this chapter, you will learn how to:

- Create fixtures for your models
- Use model inheritance
- Create custom model fields
- Use class-based views and mixins
- Build formsets
- Manage groups and permissions
- Create a CMS

Setting up the e-learning project

Your final practical project will be an e-learning platform. First, create a virtual environment for your new project and activate it with the following commands:

```
mkdir env
python3 -m venv env/educa
source env/educa/bin/activate
```

Install Django in your virtual environment with the following command:

```
pip install "Django==3.0.*"
```

You are going to manage image uploads in your project, so you also need to install `Pillow` with the following command:

```
pip install Pillow==7.0.0
```

Create a new project using the following command:

```
django-admin startproject educa
```

Enter the new `educa` directory and create a new application using the following commands:

```
cd educa
django-admin startapp courses
```

Edit the `settings.py` file of the `educa` project and add `courses` to the `INSTALLED_APPS` setting, as follows:

```
INSTALLED_APPS = [
    'courses.apps.CoursesConfig',
    'django.contrib.admin',
    'django.contrib.auth',
    'django.contrib.contenttypes',
    'django.contrib.sessions',
    'django.contrib.messages',
    'django.contrib.staticfiles',
]
```

The `courses` application is now active for the project. Let's define the models for courses and course contents.

Building the course models

Your e-learning platform will offer courses on various subjects. Each course will be divided into a configurable number of modules, and each module will contain a configurable number of contents. The contents will be of various types: text, file, image, or video. The following example shows what the data structure of your course catalog will look like:

```
Subject 1
  Course 1
    Module 1
      Content 1 (image)
      Content 2 (text)
    Module 2
      Content 3 (text)
      Content 4 (file)
      Content 5 (video)
    ...
```

Let's build the course models. Edit the `models.py` file of the `courses` application and add the following code to it:

```python
from django.db import models
from django.contrib.auth.models import User

class Subject(models.Model):
    title = models.CharField(max_length=200)
    slug = models.SlugField(max_length=200, unique=True)

    class Meta:
        ordering = ['title']

    def __str__(self):
        return self.title

class Course(models.Model):
    owner = models.ForeignKey(User,
                              related_name='courses_created',
                              on_delete=models.CASCADE)
    subject = models.ForeignKey(Subject,
                                related_name='courses',
                                on_delete=models.CASCADE)
    title = models.CharField(max_length=200)
    slug = models.SlugField(max_length=200, unique=True)
    overview = models.TextField()
```

```
        created = models.DateTimeField(auto_now_add=True)

        class Meta:
            ordering = ['-created']

        def __str__(self):
            return self.title


    class Module(models.Model):
        course = models.ForeignKey(Course,
                                   related_name='modules',
                                   on_delete=models.CASCADE)
        title = models.CharField(max_length=200)
        description = models.TextField(blank=True)

        def __str__(self):
            return self.title
```

These are the initial Subject, Course, and Module models. The Course model fields are as follows:

- owner: The instructor who created this course.
- subject: The subject that this course belongs to. It is a ForeignKey field that points to the Subject model.
- title: The title of the course.
- slug: The slug of the course. This will be used in URLs later.
- overview: A TextField column to store an overview of the course.
- created: The date and time when the course was created. It will be automatically set by Django when creating new objects because of auto_now_add=True.

Each course is divided into several modules. Therefore, the Module model contains a ForeignKey field that points to the Course model.

Open the shell and run the following command to create the initial migration for this application:

python manage.py makemigrations

You will see the following output:

Migrations for 'courses':
  courses/migrations/0001_initial.py:

- `Create model Course`
- `Create model Module`
- `Create model Subject`
- `Add field subject to course`

Then, run the following command to apply all migrations to the database:

`python manage.py migrate`

You should see output that includes all applied migrations, including those of Django. The output will contain the following line:

`Applying courses.0001_initial... OK`

The models of your `courses` application have been synced with the database.

Registering the models in the administration site

Let's add the course models to the administration site. Edit the `admin.py` file inside the `courses` application directory and add the following code to it:

```python
from django.contrib import admin
from .models import Subject, Course, Module


@admin.register(Subject)
class SubjectAdmin(admin.ModelAdmin):
    list_display = ['title', 'slug']
    prepopulated_fields = {'slug': ('title',)}


class ModuleInline(admin.StackedInline):
    model = Module


@admin.register(Course)
class CourseAdmin(admin.ModelAdmin):
    list_display = ['title', 'subject', 'created']
    list_filter = ['created', 'subject']
    search_fields = ['title', 'overview']
    prepopulated_fields = {'slug': ('title',)}
    inlines = [ModuleInline]
```

The models for the course application are now registered in the administration site. Remember that you use the `@admin.register()` decorator to register models in the administration site.

Using fixtures to provide initial data for models

Sometimes, you might want to prepopulate your database with hardcoded data. This is useful for automatically including initial data in the project setup, instead of having to add it manually. Django comes with a simple way to load and dump data from the database into files that are called **fixtures**. Django supports fixtures in JSON, XML, or YAML formats. You are going to create a fixture to include several initial Subject objects for your project.

First, create a superuser using the following command:

```
python manage.py createsuperuser
```

Then, run the development server using the following command:

```
python manage.py runserver
```

Open http://127.0.0.1:8000/admin/courses/subject/ in your browser. Create several subjects using the administration site. The list display page should look as follows:

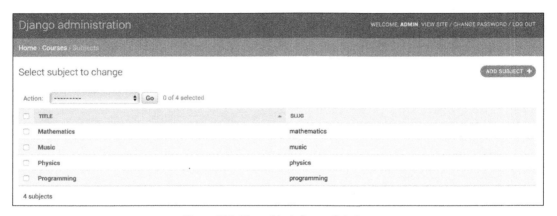

Figure 10.1: The subject change list view

Run the following command from the shell:

```
python manage.py dumpdata courses --indent=2
```

You will see output similar to the following:

```
[
{
  "model": "courses.subject",
```

```
  "pk": 1,
  "fields": {
    "title": "Mathematics",
    "slug": "mathematics"
  }
},
{
  "model": "courses.subject",
  "pk": 2,
  "fields": {
    "title": "Music",
    "slug": "music"
  }
},
{
  "model": "courses.subject",
  "pk": 3,
  "fields": {
    "title": "Physics",
    "slug": "physics"
  }
},
{
  "model": "courses.subject",
  "pk": 4,
  "fields": {
    "title": "Programming",
    "slug": "programming"
  }
}
]
```

The `dumpdata` command dumps data from the database into the standard output, serialized in JSON format by default. The resulting data structure includes information about the model and its fields for Django to be able to load it into the database.

You can limit the output to the models of an application by providing the application names to the command, or specifying single models for outputting data using the `app.Model` format. You can also specify the format using the `--format` flag. By default, `dumpdata` outputs the serialized data to the standard output. However, you can indicate an output file using the `--output` flag. The `--indent` flag allows you to specify indentation. For more information on `dumpdata` parameters, run `python manage.py dumpdata --help`.

Save this dump to a fixtures file in a new `fixtures/` directory in the `courses` application using the following commands:

```
mkdir courses/fixtures

python manage.py dumpdata courses --indent=2 --output=courses/fixtures/
subjects.json
```

Run the development server and use the administration site to remove the subjects you created. Then, load the fixture into the database using the following command:

```
python manage.py loaddata subjects.json
```

All `Subject` objects included in the fixture are loaded into the database.

By default, Django looks for files in the `fixtures/` directory of each application, but you can specify the complete path to the fixture file for the `loaddata` command. You can also use the `FIXTURE_DIRS` setting to tell Django additional directories to look in for fixtures.

 Fixtures are not only useful for setting up initial data, but also for providing sample data for your application or data required for your tests.

You can read about how to use fixtures for testing at `https://docs.djangoproject.com/en/3.0/topics/testing/tools/#fixture-loading`.

If you want to load fixtures in model migrations, take a look at Django's documentation about data migrations. You can find the documentation for migrating data at `https://docs.djangoproject.com/en/3.0/topics/migrations/#data-migrations`.

Creating models for diverse content

You plan to add different types of content to the course modules, such as text, images, files, and videos. Therefore, you need a versatile data model that allows you to store diverse content. In *Chapter 6, Tracking User Actions*, you learned the convenience of using generic relations to create foreign keys that can point to the objects of any model. You are going to create a Content model that represents the modules' contents, and define a generic relation to associate any kind of content.

Edit the models.py file of the courses application and add the following imports:

```
from django.contrib.contenttypes.models import ContentType
from django.contrib.contenttypes.fields import GenericForeignKey
```

Then, add the following code to the end of the file:

```
class Content(models.Model):
    module = models.ForeignKey(Module,
                               related_name='contents',
                               on_delete=models.CASCADE)
    content_type = models.ForeignKey(ContentType,
                                     on_delete=models.CASCADE)
    object_id = models.PositiveIntegerField()
    item = GenericForeignKey('content_type', 'object_id')
```

This is the Content model. A module contains multiple contents, so you define a ForeignKey field that points to the Module model. You also set up a generic relation to associate objects from different models that represent different types of content. Remember that you need three different fields to set up a generic relation. In your Content model, these are:

- content_type: A ForeignKey field to the ContentType model
- object_id: A PositiveIntegerField to store the primary key of the related object
- item: A GenericForeignKey field to the related object combining the two previous fields

Only the content_type and object_id fields have a corresponding column in the database table of this model. The item field allows you to retrieve or set the related object directly, and its functionality is built on top of the other two fields.

You are going to use a different model for each type of content. Your content models will have some common fields, but they will differ in the actual data they can store.

Using model inheritance

Django supports model inheritance. It works in a similar way to standard class inheritance in Python. Django offers the following three options to use model inheritance:

- **Abstract models**: Useful when you want to put some common information into several models.
- **Multi-table model inheritance**: Applicable when each model in the hierarchy is considered a complete model by itself.
- **Proxy models**: Useful when you need to change the behavior of a model, for example, by including additional methods, changing the default manager, or using different meta options.

Let's take a closer look at each of them.

Abstract models

An abstract model is a base class in which you define fields you want to include in all child models. Django doesn't create any database tables for abstract models. A database table is created for each child model, including the fields inherited from the abstract class and the ones defined in the child model.

To mark a model as abstract, you need to include `abstract=True` in its `Meta` class. Django will recognize that it is an abstract model and will not create a database table for it. To create child models, you just need to subclass the abstract model.

The following example shows an abstract `Content` model and a child `Text` model:

```python
from django.db import models

class BaseContent(models.Model):
    title = models.CharField(max_length=100)
    created = models.DateTimeField(auto_now_add=True)

    class Meta:
        abstract = True

class Text(BaseContent):
    body = models.TextField()
```

In this case, Django would create a table for the `Text` model only, including the `title`, `created`, and `body` fields.

Multi-table model inheritance

In multi-table inheritance, each model corresponds to a database table. Django creates a `OneToOneField` field for the relationship between the child model and its parent model. To use multi-table inheritance, you have to subclass an existing model. Django will create a database table for both the original model and the sub-model. The following example shows multi-table inheritance:

```python
from django.db import models

class BaseContent(models.Model):
    title = models.CharField(max_length=100)
    created = models.DateTimeField(auto_now_add=True)

class Text(BaseContent):
    body = models.TextField()
```

Django would include an automatically generated `OneToOneField` field in the `Text` model and create a database table for each model.

Proxy models

A proxy model changes the behavior of a model. Both models operate on the database table of the original model. To create a proxy model, add `proxy=True` to the `Meta` class of the model. The following example illustrates how to create a proxy model:

```python
from django.db import models
from django.utils import timezone

class BaseContent(models.Model):
    title = models.CharField(max_length=100)
    created = models.DateTimeField(auto_now_add=True)

class OrderedContent(BaseContent):
    class Meta:
        proxy = True
        ordering = ['created']

    def created_delta(self):
        return timezone.now() - self.created
```

Here, you define an `OrderedContent` model that is a proxy model for the `Content` model. This model provides a default ordering for QuerySets and an additional `created_delta()` method. Both models, `Content` and `OrderedContent`, operate on the same database table, and objects are accessible via the ORM through either model.

Creating the content models

The `Content` model of your `courses` application contains a generic relation to associate different types of content with it. You will create a different model for each type of content. All content models will have some fields in common and additional fields to store custom data. You are going to create an abstract model that provides the common fields for all content models.

Edit the `models.py` file of the `courses` application and add the following code to it:

```
class ItemBase(models.Model):
    owner = models.ForeignKey(User,
                              related_name='%(class)s_related',
                              on_delete=models.CASCADE)
    title = models.CharField(max_length=250)
    created = models.DateTimeField(auto_now_add=True)
    updated = models.DateTimeField(auto_now=True)

    class Meta:
        abstract = True

    def __str__(self):
        return self.title

class Text(ItemBase):
    content = models.TextField()

class File(ItemBase):
    file = models.FileField(upload_to='files')

class Image(ItemBase):
    file = models.FileField(upload_to='images')

class Video(ItemBase):
    url = models.URLField()
```

In this code, you define an abstract model named `ItemBase`. Therefore, you set `abstract=True` in its `Meta` class.

In this model, you define the `owner`, `title`, `created`, and `updated` fields. These common fields will be used for all types of content.

The `owner` field allows you to store which user created the content. Since this field is defined in an abstract class, you need a different `related_name` for each sub-model. Django allows you to specify a placeholder for the model class name in the `related_name` attribute as `%(class)s`. By doing so, `related_name` for each child model will be generated automatically. Since you use `'%(class)s_related'` as the `related_name`, the reverse relationship for child models will be `text_related`, `file_related`, `image_related`, and `video_related`, respectively.

You have defined four different content models that inherit from the `ItemBase` abstract model. These are as follows:

- `Text`: To store text content
- `File`: To store files, such as PDFs
- `Image`: To store image files
- `Video`: To store videos; you use an `URLField` field to provide a video URL in order to embed it

Each child model contains the fields defined in the `ItemBase` class in addition to its own fields. A database table will be created for the `Text`, `File`, `Image`, and `Video` models, respectively. There will be no database table associated with the `ItemBase` model, since it is an abstract model.

Edit the `Content` model you created previously and modify its `content_type` field, as follows:

```
content_type = models.ForeignKey(ContentType,
                 on_delete=models.CASCADE,
                 limit_choices_to={'model__in':(
                            'text',
                            'video',
                            'image',
                            'file')})
```

You add a `limit_choices_to` argument to limit the `ContentType` objects that can be used for the generic relation. You use the `model__in` field lookup to filter the query to the `ContentType` objects with a `model` attribute that is `'text'`, `'video'`, `'image'`, or `'file'`.

Let's create a migration to include the new models you have added. Run the following command from the command line:

```
python manage.py makemigrations
```

You will see the following output:

```
Migrations for 'courses':
  courses/migrations/0002_content_file_image_text_video.py
    - Create model Video
    - Create model Text
    - Create model Image
    - Create model File
    - Create model Content
```

Then, run the following command to apply the new migration:

```
python manage.py migrate
```

The output you see should end with the following line:

```
Applying courses.0002_content_file_image_text_video... OK
```

You have created models that are suitable for adding diverse content to the course modules. However, there is still something missing in your models: the course modules and contents should follow a particular order. You need a field that allows you to order them easily.

Creating custom model fields

Django comes with a complete collection of model fields that you can use to build your models. However, you can also create your own model fields to store custom data or alter the behavior of existing fields.

You need a field that allows you to define an order for objects. An easy way to specify an order for objects using existing Django fields is by adding a PositiveIntegerField to your models. Using integers, you can easily specify the order of objects. You can create a custom order field that inherits from PositiveIntegerField and provides additional behavior.

There are two relevant functionalities that you will build into your order field:

- **Automatically assign an order value when no specific order is provided**: When saving a new object with no specific order, your field should automatically assign the number that comes after the last existing ordered object. If there are two objects with order 1 and 2 respectively, when saving a third object, you should automatically assign the order 3 to it if no specific order has been provided.

- **Order objects with respect to other fields**: Course modules will be ordered with respect to the course they belong to and module contents with respect to the module they belong to.

Create a new `fields.py` file inside the `courses` application directory and add the following code to it:

```python
from django.db import models
from django.core.exceptions import ObjectDoesNotExist


class OrderField(models.PositiveIntegerField):
    def __init__(self, for_fields=None, *args, **kwargs):
        self.for_fields = for_fields
        super().__init__(*args, **kwargs)

    def pre_save(self, model_instance, add):
        if getattr(model_instance, self.attname) is None:
            # no current value
            try:
                qs = self.model.objects.all()
                if self.for_fields:
                    # filter by objects with the same field values
                    # for the fields in "for_fields"
                    query = {field: getattr(model_instance, field)\
                    for field in self.for_fields}
                    qs = qs.filter(**query)
                # get the order of the last item
                last_item = qs.latest(self.attname)
                value = last_item.order + 1
            except ObjectDoesNotExist:
                value = 0
            setattr(model_instance, self.attname, value)
            return value
        else:
            return super().pre_save(model_instance, add)
```

This is your custom `OrderField`. It inherits from the `PositiveIntegerField` field provided by Django. Your `OrderField` field takes an optional `for_fields` parameter that allows you to indicate the fields that the order has to be calculated with respect to.

Your field overrides the `pre_save()` method of the `PositiveIntegerField` field, which is executed before saving the field into the database. In this method, you perform the following actions:

1. You check whether a value already exists for this field in the model instance. You use `self.attname`, which is the attribute name given to the field in the model. If the attribute's value is different to `None`, you calculate the order you should give it as follows:

    1. You build a QuerySet to retrieve all objects for the field's model. You retrieve the model class the field belongs to by accessing `self.model`.

    2. If there are any field names in the `for_fields` attribute of the field, you filter the QuerySet by the current value of the model fields in `for_fields`. By doing so, you calculate the order with respect to the given fields.

    3. You retrieve the object with the highest order with `last_item = qs.latest(self.attname)` from the database. If no object is found, you assume this object is the first one and assign the order `0` to it.

    4. If an object is found, you add `1` to the highest order found.

    5. You assign the calculated order to the field's value in the model instance using `setattr()` and return it.

2. If the model instance has a value for the current field, you use it instead of calculating it.

 When you create custom model fields, make them generic. Avoid hardcoding data that depends on a specific model or field. Your field should work in any model.

You can find more information about writing custom model fields at `https://docs.djangoproject.com/en/3.0/howto/custom-model-fields/`.

Adding ordering to module and content objects

Let's add the new field to your models. Edit the `models.py` file of the `courses` application, and import the `OrderField` class and a field to the `Module` model, as follows:

```
from .fields import OrderField
```

```
class Module(models.Model):
    # ...
    order = OrderField(blank=True, for_fields=['course'])
```

You name the new field `order`, and specify that the ordering is calculated with respect to the course by setting `for_fields=['course']`. This means that the order for a new module will be assigned by adding 1 to the last module of the same `Course` object.

Now, you can, edit the `__str__()` method of the `Module` model to include its order, as follows:

```
class Module(models.Model):
    # ...
    def __str__(self):
        return f'{self.order}. {self.title}'
```

Module contents also need to follow a particular order. Add an `OrderField` field to the `Content` model, as follows:

```
class Content(models.Model):
    # ...
    order = OrderField(blank=True, for_fields=['module'])
```

This time, you specify that the order is calculated with respect to the `module` field.

Finally, let's add a default ordering for both models. Add the following `Meta` class to the `Module` and `Content` models:

```
class Module(models.Model):
    # ...
    class Meta:
        ordering = ['order']


class Content(models.Model):
    # ...
    class Meta:
        ordering = ['order']
```

The `Module` and `Content` models should now look as follows:

```
class Module(models.Model):
    course = models.ForeignKey(Course,
                               related_name='modules',
                               on_delete=models.CASCADE)
    title = models.CharField(max_length=200)
    description = models.TextField(blank=True)
```

```
        order = OrderField(blank=True, for_fields=['course'])

        class Meta:
            ordering = ['order']

        def __str__(self):
            return f'{self.order}. {self.title}'

    class Content(models.Model):
        module = models.ForeignKey(Module,
                                   related_name='contents',
                                   on_delete=models.CASCADE)
        content_type = models.ForeignKey(ContentType,
                                         on_delete=models.CASCADE,
                                         limit_choices_to={'model__in':(
                                                    'text',
                                                    'video',
                                                    'image',
                                                    'file')})
        object_id = models.PositiveIntegerField()
        item = GenericForeignKey('content_type', 'object_id')
        order = OrderField(blank=True, for_fields=['module'])

        class Meta:
            ordering = ['order']
```

Let's create a new model migration that reflects the new order fields. Open the shell and run the following command:

```
python manage.py makemigrations courses
```

You will see the following output:

```
You are trying to add a non-nullable field 'order' to content without
a default; we can't do that (the database needs something to populate
existing rows).

Please select a fix:

 1) Provide a one-off default now (will be set on all existing rows with
a null value for this column)

 2) Quit, and let me add a default in models.py

Select an option:
```

Django is telling you that you have to provide a default value for the new `order` field for existing rows in the database. If the field had `null=True`, it would accept null values and Django would create the migration automatically instead of asking for a default value. You can specify a default value, or cancel the migration and add a `default` attribute to the `order` field in the `models.py` file before creating the migration.

Enter `1` and press *Enter* to provide a default value for existing records. You will see the following output:

```
Please enter the default value now, as valid Python

The datetime and django.utils.timezone modules are available, so you can do e.g. timezone.now

Type 'exit' to exit this prompt

>>>
```

Enter `0` so that this is the default value for existing records and press *Enter*. Django will ask you for a default value for the `Module` model too. Choose the first option and enter `0` as the default value again. Finally, you will see an output similar to the following one:

```
Migrations for 'courses':

  courses/migrations/0003_auto_20191214_1253.py

    - Change Meta options on content

    - Change Meta options on module

    - Add field order to content

    - Add field order to module
```

Then, apply the new migrations with the following command:

```
python manage.py migrate
```

The output of the command will inform you that the migration was successfully applied, as follows:

```
Applying courses.0003_auto_20191214_1253... OK
```

Let's test your new field. Open the shell with the following command:

```
python manage.py shell
```

Create a new course, as follows:

```
>>> from django.contrib.auth.models import User
>>> from courses.models import Subject, Course, Module
```

```
>>> user = User.objects.last()
>>> subject = Subject.objects.last()
>>> c1 = Course.objects.create(subject=subject, owner=user, title='Course
1', slug='course1')
```

You have created a course in the database. Now, you will add modules to the course and see how their order is automatically calculated. You create an initial module and check its order:

```
>>> m1 = Module.objects.create(course=c1, title='Module 1')
>>> m1.order
0
```

OrderField sets its value to 0, since this is the first Module object created for the given course. You, create a second module for the same course:

```
>>> m2 = Module.objects.create(course=c1, title='Module 2')
>>> m2.order
1
```

OrderField calculates the next order value, adding 1 to the highest order for existing objects. Let's create a third module, forcing a specific order:

```
>>> m3 = Module.objects.create(course=c1, title='Module 3', order=5)
>>> m3.order
5
```

If you specify a custom order, the OrderField field does not interfere and the value given to order is used.

Let's add a fourth module:

```
>>> m4 = Module.objects.create(course=c1, title='Module 4')
>>> m4.order
6
```

The order for this module has been automatically set. Your OrderField field does not guarantee that all order values are consecutive. However, it respects existing order values and always assigns the next order based on the highest existing order.

Let's create a second course and add a module to it:

```
>>> c2 = Course.objects.create(subject=subject, title='Course 2',
slug='course2', owner=user)
>>> m5 = Module.objects.create(course=c2, title='Module 1')
```

```
>>> m5.order
0
```

To calculate the new module's order, the field only takes into consideration existing modules that belong to the same course. Since this is the first module of the second course, the resulting order is 0. This is because you specified for_ fields=['course'] in the order field of the Module model.

Congratulations! You have successfully created your first custom model field.

Creating a CMS

Now that you have created a versatile data model, you are going to build the CMS. The CMS will allow instructors to create courses and manage their contents. You need to provide the following functionality:

- Log in to the CMS
- List the courses created by the instructor
- Create, edit, and delete courses
- Add modules to a course and reorder them
- Add different types of content to each module and reorder them

Adding an authentication system

You are going to use Django's authentication framework in your platform. Both instructors and students will be instances of Django's User model, so they will be able to log in to the site using the authentication views of django.contrib.auth.

Edit the main urls.py file of the educa project and include the login and logout views of Django's authentication framework:

```
from django.contrib import admin
from django.urls import path
from django.contrib.auth import views as auth_views

urlpatterns = [
    path('accounts/login/', auth_views.LoginView.as_view(),
        name='login'),
    path('accounts/logout/', auth_views.LogoutView.as_view(),
        name='logout'),
    path('admin/', admin.site.urls),
]
```

Creating the authentication templates

Create the following file structure inside the `courses` application directory:

```
templates/
    base.html
    registration/
        login.html
        logged_out.html
```

Before building the authentication templates, you need to prepare the base template for your project. Edit the `base.html` template file and add the following content to it:

```
{% load static %}
<!DOCTYPE html>
<html>
<head>
  <meta charset="utf-8" />
  <title>{% block title %}Educa{% endblock %}</title>
  <link href="{% static "css/base.css" %}" rel="stylesheet">
</head>
<body>
  <div id="header">
    <a href="/" class="logo">Educa</a>
    <ul class="menu">
      {% if request.user.is_authenticated %}
        <li><a href="{% url "logout" %}">Sign out</a></li>
      {% else %}
        <li><a href="{% url "login" %}">Sign in</a></li>
      {% endif %}
    </ul>
  </div>
  <div id="content">
    {% block content %}
    {% endblock %}
  </div>

  <script src="https://ajax.googleapis.com/ajax/libs/jquery/3.4.1/
jquery.min.js">
  </script>
  <script>
    $(document).ready(function() {
      {% block domready %}
      {% endblock %}
    });
```

```
    </script>
  </body>
</html>
```

This is the base template that will be extended by the rest of the templates. In this template, you define the following blocks:

- `title`: The block for other templates to add a custom title for each page.
- `content`: The main block for content. All templates that extend the base template should add content to this block.
- `domready`: Located inside the `$(document).ready()` function of jQuery. It allows you to execute code when the **Document Object Model (DOM)** has finished loading.

The CSS styles used in this template are located in the `static/` directory of the `courses` application in the code that comes along with this chapter. Copy the `static/` directory into the same directory of your project to use them. You can find the contents of the directory at `https://github.com/PacktPublishing/Django-3-by-Example/tree/master/Chapter10/educa/courses/static`.

Edit the `registration/login.html` template and add the following code to it:

```
{% extends "base.html" %}

{% block title %}Log-in{% endblock %}

{% block content %}
  <h1>Log-in</h1>
  <div class="module">
    {% if form.errors %}
      <p>Your username and password didn't match. Please try again.</p>
    {% else %}
      <p>Please, use the following form to log-in:</p>
    {% endif %}
    <div class="login-form">
      <form action="{% url 'login' %}" method="post">
        {{ form.as_p }}
        {% csrf_token %}
        <input type="hidden" name="next" value="{{ next }}" />
        <p><input type="submit" value="Log-in"></p>
      </form>
    </div>
  </div>
{% endblock %}
```

This is a standard login template for Django's `login` view.

Edit the `registration/logged_out.html` template and add the following code to it:

```
{% extends "base.html" %}

{% block title %}Logged out{% endblock %}

{% block content %}
  <h1>Logged out</h1>
  <div class="module">
    <p>You have been successfully logged out.
        You can <a href="{% url "login" %}">log-in again</a>.</p>
  </div>
{% endblock %}
```

This is the template that will be displayed to the user after logout. Run the development server with the following command:

python manage.py runserver

Open `http://127.0.0.1:8000/accounts/login/` in your browser. You should see the login page:

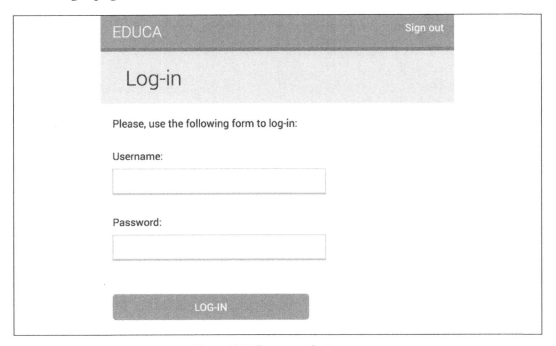

Figure 10.2: The account login page

Creating class-based views

You are going to build views to create, edit, and delete courses. You will use class-based views for this. Edit the `views.py` file of the `courses` application and add the following code to it:

```python
from django.views.generic.list import ListView
from .models import Course

class ManageCourseListView(ListView):
    model = Course
    template_name = 'courses/manage/course/list.html'

    def get_queryset(self):
        qs = super().get_queryset()
        return qs.filter(owner=self.request.user)
```

This is the `ManageCourseListView` view. It inherits from Django's generic `ListView`. You override the `get_queryset()` method of the view to retrieve only courses created by the current user. To prevent users from editing, updating, or deleting courses they didn't create, you will also need to override the `get_queryset()` method in the create, update, and delete views. When you need to provide a specific behavior for several class-based views, it is recommended that you use *mixins*.

Using mixins for class-based views

Mixins are a special kind of multiple inheritance for a class. You can use them to provide common discrete functionality that, when added to other mixins, allows you to define the behavior of a class. There are two main situations to use mixins:

- You want to provide multiple optional features for a class
- You want to use a particular feature in several classes

Django comes with several mixins that provide additional functionality to your class-based views. You can learn more about mixins at `https://docs.djangoproject.com/en/3.0/topics/class-based-views/mixins/`.

You are going to create a mixin class that includes a common behavior, and use it for the course views. Edit the `views.py` file of the `courses` application and modify it as follows:

```python
from django.urls import reverse_lazy
from django.views.generic.list import ListView
from django.views.generic.edit import CreateView, UpdateView, \
                                       DeleteView
```

```
from .models import Course

class OwnerMixin(object):
    def get_queryset(self):
        qs = super().get_queryset()
        return qs.filter(owner=self.request.user)

class OwnerEditMixin(object):
    def form_valid(self, form):
        form.instance.owner = self.request.user
        return super().form_valid(form)

class OwnerCourseMixin(OwnerMixin):
    model = Course
    fields = ['subject', 'title', 'slug', 'overview']
    success_url = reverse_lazy('manage_course_list')

class OwnerCourseEditMixin(OwnerCourseMixin, OwnerEditMixin):
    template_name = 'courses/manage/course/form.html'

class ManageCourseListView(OwnerCourseMixin, ListView):
    template_name = 'courses/manage/course/list.html'

class CourseCreateView(OwnerCourseEditMixin, CreateView):
    pass

class CourseUpdateView(OwnerCourseEditMixin, UpdateView):
    pass

class CourseDeleteView(OwnerCourseMixin, DeleteView):
    template_name = 'courses/manage/course/delete.html'
```

In this code, you create the OwnerMixin and OwnerEditMixin mixins. You will use these mixins together with the ListView, CreateView, UpdateView, and DeleteView views provided by Django. OwnerMixin implements the get_queryset() method, which is used by the views to get the base QuerySet. Your mixin will override this method to filter objects by the owner attribute to retrieve objects that belong to the current user (request.user).

OwnerEditMixin implements the form_valid() method, which is used by views that use Django's ModelFormMixin mixin, that is, views with forms or model forms such as CreateView and UpdateView. form_valid() is executed when the submitted form is valid.

The default behavior for this method is saving the instance (for model forms) and redirecting the user to `success_url`. You override this method to automatically set the current user in the `owner` attribute of the object being saved. By doing so, you set the owner for an object automatically when it is saved.

Your `OwnerMixin` class can be used for views that interact with any model that contains an `owner` attribute.

You also define an `OwnerCourseMixin` class that inherits `OwnerMixin` and provides the following attributes for child views:

- `model`: The model used for QuerySets; it is used by all views.
- `fields`: The fields of the model to build the model form of the `CreateView` and `UpdateView` views.
- `success_url`: Used by `CreateView`, `UpdateView`, and `DeleteView` to redirect the user after the form is successfully submitted or the object is deleted. You use a URL with the name `manage_course_list`, which you are going to create later.

You define an `OwnerCourseEditMixin` mixin with the following attribute:

- `template_name`: The template you will use for the `CreateView` and `UpdateView` views

Finally, you create the following views that subclass `OwnerCourseMixin`:

- `ManageCourseListView`: Lists the courses created by the user. It inherits from `OwnerCourseMixin` and `ListView`. It defines a specific `template_name` attribute for a template to list courses.
- `CourseCreateView`: Uses a model form to create a new `Course` object. It uses the fields defined in `OwnerCourseMixin` to build a model form and also subclasses `CreateView`. It uses the template defined in `OwnerCourseEditMixin`.
- `CourseUpdateView`: Allows the editing of an existing `Course` object. It uses the fields defined in `OwnerCourseMixin` to build a model form and also subclasses `UpdateView`. It uses the template defined in `OwnerCourseEditMixin`.
- `CourseDeleteView`: Inherits from `OwnerCourseMixin` and the generic `DeleteView`. It defines a specific `template_name` attribute for a template to confirm the course deletion.

Working with groups and permissions

You have created the basic views to manage courses. Currently, any user could access these views. You want to restrict these views so that only instructors have the permission to create and manage courses.

Django's authentication framework includes a permission system that allows you to assign permissions to users and groups. You are going to create a group for instructor users and assign permissions to create, update, and delete courses.

Run the development server using the command `python manage.py runserver` and open `http://127.0.0.1:8000/admin/auth/group/add/` in your browser to create a new `Group` object. Add the name `Instructors` and choose all permissions of the `courses` application, except those of the `Subject` model, as follows:

Figure 10.3: The Instructors group permissions

As you can see, there are four different permissions for each model: *can view, can add, can change,* and *can delete*. After choosing permissions for this group, click on the **SAVE** button.

Django creates permissions for models automatically, but you can also create custom permissions. You will learn to create custom permissions in *Chapter 12, Building an API*. You can read more about adding custom permissions at `https://docs.djangoproject.com/en/3.0/topics/auth/customizing/#custom-permissions`.

Open `http://127.0.0.1:8000/admin/auth/user/add/` and create a new user. Edit the user and add it to the **Instructors** group, as follows:

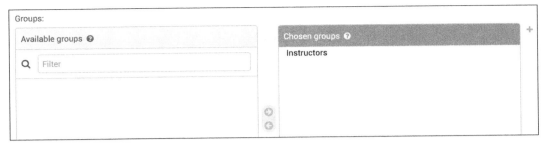

Figure 10.4: User group selection

Users inherit the permissions of the groups they belong to, but you can also add individual permissions to a single user using the administration site. Users that have is_superuser set to True have all permissions automatically.

Restricting access to class-based views

You are going to restrict access to the views so that only users with the appropriate permissions can add, change, or delete Course objects. You are going to use the following two mixins provided by django.contrib.auth to limit access to views:

- LoginRequiredMixin: Replicates the login_required decorator's functionality.
- PermissionRequiredMixin: Grants access to the view to users with a specific permission. Remember that superusers automatically have all permissions.

Edit the views.py file of the courses application and add the following import:

```
from django.contrib.auth.mixins import LoginRequiredMixin, \
                                        PermissionRequiredMixin
```

Make OwnerCourseMixin inherit LoginRequiredMixin and PermissionRequiredMixin, like this:

```
class OwnerCourseMixin(OwnerMixin,
                       LoginRequiredMixin,
                       PermissionRequiredMixin):
    model = Course
    fields = ['subject', 'title', 'slug', 'overview']
    success_url = reverse_lazy('manage_course_list')
```

Then, add a `permission_required` attribute to the course views, as follows:

```
class ManageCourseListView(OwnerCourseMixin, ListView):
    template_name = 'courses/manage/course/list.html'
    permission_required = 'courses.view_course'

class CourseCreateView(OwnerCourseEditMixin, CreateView):
    permission_required = 'courses.add_course'

class CourseUpdateView(OwnerCourseEditMixin, UpdateView):
    permission_required = 'courses.change_course'

class CourseDeleteView(OwnerCourseMixin, DeleteView):
    template_name = 'courses/manage/course/delete.html'
    permission_required = 'courses.delete_course'
```

`PermissionRequiredMixin` checks that the user accessing the view has the permission specified in the `permission_required` attribute. Your views are now only accessible to users with proper permissions.

Let's create URLs for these views. Create a new file inside the `courses` application directory and name it `urls.py`. Add the following code to it:

```
from django.urls import path
from . import views

urlpatterns = [
    path('mine/',
        views.ManageCourseListView.as_view(),
        name='manage_course_list'),
    path('create/',
        views.CourseCreateView.as_view(),
        name='course_create'),
    path('<pk>/edit/',
        views.CourseUpdateView.as_view(),
        name='course_edit'),
    path('<pk>/delete/',
        views.CourseDeleteView.as_view(),
        name='course_delete'),
]
```

These are the URL patterns for the list, create, edit, and delete course views. Edit the main `urls.py` file of the `educa` project and include the URL patterns of the `courses` application, as follows:

```
from django.urls import path, include
```

```
urlpatterns = [
    path('accounts/login/', auth_views.LoginView.as_view(),
        name='login'),
    path('accounts/logout/', auth_views.LogoutView.as_view(),
        name='logout'),
    path('admin/', admin.site.urls),
    path('course/', include('courses.urls')),
]
```

You need to create the templates for these views. Create the following directories and files inside the templates/ directory of the courses application:

```
courses/
    manage/
        course/
            list.html
            form.html
            delete.html
```

Edit the courses/manage/course/list.html template and add the following code to it:

```
{% extends "base.html" %}

{% block title %}My courses{% endblock %}

{% block content %}
  <h1>My courses</h1>

  <div class="module">
    {% for course in object_list %}
      <div class="course-info">
        <h3>{{ course.title }}</h3>
        <p>
          <a href="{% url "course_edit" course.id %}">Edit</a>
          <a href="{% url "course_delete" course.id %}">Delete</a>
        </p>
      </div>
    {% empty %}
      <p>You haven't created any courses yet.</p>
    {% endfor %}
    <p>
      <a href="{% url "course_create" %}" class="button">Create new
course</a>
    </p>
  </div>
{% endblock %}
```

This is the template for the `ManageCourseListView` view. In this template, you list the courses created by the current user. You include links to edit or delete each course, and a link to create new courses.

Run the development server using the command `python manage.py runserver`. Open `http://127.0.0.1:8000/accounts/login/?next=/course/mine/` in your browser and log in with a user belonging to the `Instructors` group. After logging in, you will be redirected to the `http://127.0.0.1:8000/course/mine/` URL and you should see the following page:

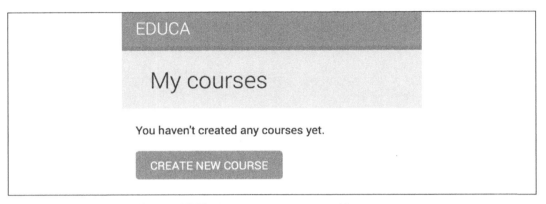

Figure 10.5: The instructor courses page with no courses

This page will display all courses created by the current user.

Let's create the template that displays the form for the create and update course views. Edit the `courses/manage/course/form.html` template and write the following code:

```
{% extends "base.html" %}

{% block title %}
  {% if object %}
    Edit course "{{ object.title }}"
  {% else %}
    Create a new course
  {% endif %}
{% endblock %}

{% block content %}
  <h1>
    {% if object %}
      Edit course "{{ object.title }}"
    {% else %}
```

```
      Create a new course
   {% endif %}
 </h1>
 <div class="module">
   <h2>Course info</h2>
   <form method="post">
     {{ form.as_p }}
     {% csrf_token %}
     <p><input type="submit" value="Save course"></p>
   </form>
 </div>
{% endblock %}
```

The `form.html` template is used for both the `CourseCreateView` and `CourseUpdateView` views. In this template, you check whether an `object` variable is in the context. If `object` exists in the context, you know that you are updating an existing course, and you use it in the page title. Otherwise, you are creating a new `Course` object.

Open `http://127.0.0.1:8000/course/mine/` in your browser and click the **CREATE NEW COURSE** button. You will see the following page:

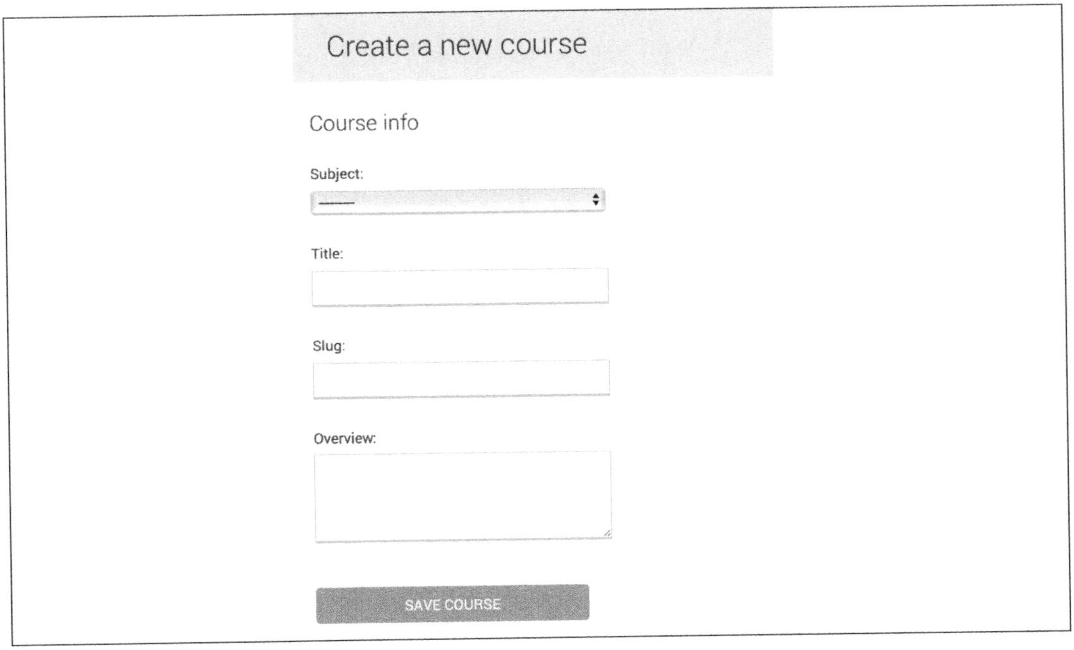

Figure 10.6: The form to create a new course

Fill in the form and click the **SAVE COURSE** button. The course will be saved and you will be redirected to the course list page. It should look as follows:

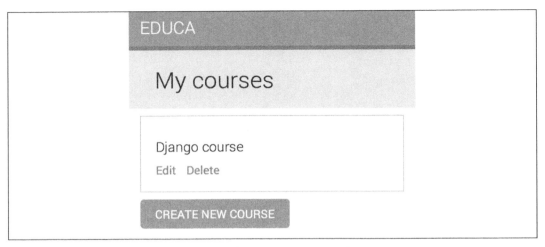

Figure 10.7: The instructor courses page with one course

Then, click the **Edit** link for the course you have just created. You will see the form again, but this time you are editing an existing `Course` object instead of creating one.

Finally, edit the `courses/manage/course/delete.html` template and add the following code:

```
{% extends "base.html" %}

{% block title %}Delete course{% endblock %}

{% block content %}
  <h1>Delete course "{{ object.title }}"</h1>

  <div class="module">
    <form action="" method="post">
      {% csrf_token %}
      <p>Are you sure you want to delete "{{ object }}"?</p>
      <input type="submit" value="Confirm">
    </form>
  </div>
{% endblock %}
```

This is the template for the `CourseDeleteView` view. This view inherits from `DeleteView`, provided by Django, which expects user confirmation to delete an object.

Open the course list in the browser and click the **Delete** link of your course. You should see the following confirmation page:

Figure 10.8: The delete course confirmation page

Click the **CONFIRM** button. The course will be deleted and you will be redirected to the course list page again.

Instructors can now create, edit, and delete courses. Next, you need to provide them with a CMS to add course modules and their contents. You will start by managing course modules.

Managing course modules and their contents

You are going to build a system to manage course modules and their contents. You will need to build forms that can be used for managing multiple modules per course and different types of content for each module. Both modules and their contents will have to follow a specific order and you should be able to reorder them using the CMS.

Using formsets for course modules

Django comes with an abstraction layer to work with multiple forms on the same page. These groups of forms are known as *formsets*. Formsets manage multiple instances of a certain Form or ModelForm. All forms are submitted at once and the formset takes care of the initial number of forms to display, limiting the maximum number of forms that can be submitted and validating all the forms.

Formsets include an `is_valid()` method to validate all forms at once. You can also provide initial data for the forms and specify how many additional empty forms to display. You can learn more about formsets at https://docs.djangoproject.com/ en/3.0/topics/forms/formsets/ and about model formsets at https://docs. djangoproject.com/en/3.0/topics/forms/modelforms/#model-formsets.

Since a course is divided into a variable number of modules, it makes sense to use formsets to manage them. Create a `forms.py` file in the `courses` application directory and add the following code to it:

```python
from django import forms
from django.forms.models import inlineformset_factory
from .models import Course, Module

ModuleFormSet = inlineformset_factory(Course,
                                      Module,
                                      fields=['title',
                                              'description'],
                                      extra=2,
                                      can_delete=True)
```

This is the `ModuleFormSet` formset. You build it using the `inlineformset_ factory()` function provided by Django. Inline formsets are a small abstraction on top of formsets that simplify working with related objects. This function allows you to build a model formset dynamically for the `Module` objects related to a `Course` object.

You use the following parameters to build the formset:

- `fields`: The fields that will be included in each form of the formset.
- `extra`: Allows you to set the number of empty extra forms to display in the formset.
- `can_delete`: If you set this to `True`, Django will include a Boolean field for each form that will be rendered as a checkbox input. It allows you to mark the objects that you want to delete.

Edit the `views.py` file of the `courses` application and add the following code to it:

```python
from django.shortcuts import redirect, get_object_or_404
from django.views.generic.base import TemplateResponseMixin, View
from .forms import ModuleFormSet

class CourseModuleUpdateView(TemplateResponseMixin, View):
    template_name = 'courses/manage/module/formset.html'
    course = None

    def get_formset(self, data=None):
        return ModuleFormSet(instance=self.course,
                             data=data)

    def dispatch(self, request, pk):
        self.course = get_object_or_404(Course,
                                        id=pk,
                                        owner=request.user)
        return super().dispatch(request, pk)

    def get(self, request, *args, **kwargs):
        formset = self.get_formset()
        return self.render_to_response({'course': self.course,
                                        'formset': formset})

    def post(self, request, *args, **kwargs):
        formset = self.get_formset(data=request.POST)
        if formset.is_valid():
            formset.save()
            return redirect('manage_course_list')
        return self.render_to_response({'course': self.course,
                                        'formset': formset})
```

The `CourseModuleUpdateView` view handles the formset to add, update, and delete modules for a specific course. This view inherits from the following mixins and views:

- `TemplateResponseMixin`: This mixin takes charge of rendering templates and returning an HTTP response. It requires a `template_name` attribute that indicates the template to be rendered and provides the `render_to_response()` method to pass it a context and render the template.
- `View`: The basic class-based view provided by Django.

In this view, you implement the following methods:

- `get_formset()`: You define this method to avoid repeating the code to build the formset. You create a `ModuleFormSet` object for the given `Course` object with optional data.
- `dispatch()`: This method is provided by the `View` class. It takes an HTTP request and its parameters and attempts to delegate to a lowercase method that matches the HTTP method used. A GET request is delegated to the `get()` method and a POST request to `post()`, respectively. In this method, you use the `get_object_or_404()` shortcut function to get the `Course` object for the given `id` parameter that belongs to the current user. You include this code in the `dispatch()` method because you need to retrieve the course for both GET and POST requests. You save it into the `course` attribute of the view to make it accessible to other methods.
- `get()`: Executed for GET requests. You build an empty `ModuleFormSet` formset and render it to the template together with the current `Course` object using the `render_to_response()` method provided by `TemplateResponseMixin`.
- `post()`: Executed for POST requests.

  In this method, you perform the following actions:

  1. You build a `ModuleFormSet` instance using the submitted data.
  2. You execute the `is_valid()` method of the formset to validate all of its forms.
  3. If the formset is valid, you save it by calling the `save()` method. At this point, any changes made, such as adding, updating, or marking modules for deletion, are applied to the database. Then, you redirect users to the `manage_course_list` URL. If the formset is not valid, you render the template to display any errors instead.

Edit the `urls.py` file of the `courses` application and add the following URL pattern to it:

```python
path('<pk>/module/',
     views.CourseModuleUpdateView.as_view(),
     name='course_module_update'),
```

Create a new directory inside the `courses/manage/` template directory and name it `module`. Create a `courses/manage/module/formset.html` template and add the following code to it:

```django
{% extends "base.html" %}

{% block title %}
  Edit "{{ course.title }}"
{% endblock %}

{% block content %}
  <h1>Edit "{{ course.title }}"</h1>
  <div class="module">
    <h2>Course modules</h2>
    <form method="post">
      {{ formset }}
      {{ formset.management_form }}
      {% csrf_token %}
      <input type="submit" value="Save modules">
    </form>
  </div>
{% endblock %}
```

In this template, you create a `<form>` HTML element in which you include `formset`. You also include the management form for the formset with the variable `{{ formset.management_form }}`. The management form includes hidden fields to control the initial, total, minimum, and maximum number of forms. You can see that it's very easy to create a formset.

Edit the `courses/manage/course/list.html` template and add the following link for the `course_module_update` URL below the course edit and delete links:

```django
<a href="{% url "course_edit" course.id %}">Edit</a>
<a href="{% url "course_delete" course.id %}">Delete</a>
<a href="{% url "course_module_update" course.id %}">Edit modules</a>
```

You have included the link to edit the course modules.

Open `http://127.0.0.1:8000/course/mine/` in your browser. Create a course and click the **Edit modules** link for it. You should see a formset, as follows:

Figure 10.9: The course edit page, including the formset for course modules

The formset includes a form for each `Module` object contained in the course. After these, two empty extra forms are displayed because you set `extra=2` for `ModuleFormSet`. When you save the formset, Django will include another two extra fields to add new modules.

Adding content to course modules

Now, you need a way to add content to course modules. You have four different types of content: text, video, image, and file. You could consider creating four different views to create content, with one for each model. However, you are going to take a more generic approach and create a view that handles creating or updating the objects of any content model.

Edit the `views.py` file of the `courses` application and add the following code to it:

```
from django.forms.models import modelform_factory
from django.apps import apps
from .models import Module, Content

class ContentCreateUpdateView(TemplateResponseMixin, View):
    module = None
    model = None
    obj = None
    template_name = 'courses/manage/content/form.html'

    def get_model(self, model_name):
        if model_name in ['text', 'video', 'image', 'file']:
            return apps.get_model(app_label='courses',
                                  model_name=model_name)
        return None

    def get_form(self, model, *args, **kwargs):
        Form = modelform_factory(model, exclude=['owner',
                                                 'order',
                                                 'created',
                                                 'updated'])
        return Form(*args, **kwargs)

    def dispatch(self, request, module_id, model_name, id=None):
        self.module = get_object_or_404(Module,
                                        id=module_id,
                                        course__owner=request.user)
        self.model = self.get_model(model_name)
        if id:
            self.obj = get_object_or_404(self.model,
                                         id=id,
                                         owner=request.user)
        return super().dispatch(request, module_id, model_name, id)
```

This is the first part of `ContentCreateUpdateView`. It will allow you to create and update different models' contents. This view defines the following methods:

- `get_model()`: Here, you check that the given model name is one of the four content models: `Text`, `Video`, `Image`, or `File`. Then, you use Django's `apps` module to obtain the actual class for the given model name. If the given model name is not one of the valid ones, you return `None`.

- `get_form()`: You build a dynamic form using the `modelform_factory()` function of the form's framework. Since you are going to build a form for the `Text`, `Video`, `Image`, and `File` models, you use the `exclude` parameter to specify the common fields to exclude from the form and let all other attributes be included automatically. By doing so, you don't have to know which fields to include depending on the model.

- `dispatch()`: It receives the following URL parameters and stores the corresponding module, model, and content object as class attributes:

  - `module_id`: The ID for the module that the content is/will be associated with.

  - `model_name`: The model name of the content to create/update.

  - `id`: The ID of the object that is being updated. It's `None` to create new objects.

Add the following `get()` and `post()` methods to `ContentCreateUpdateView`:

```python
def get(self, request, module_id, model_name, id=None):
    form = self.get_form(self.model, instance=self.obj)
    return self.render_to_response({'form': form,
                                    'object': self.obj})

def post(self, request, module_id, model_name, id=None):
    form = self.get_form(self.model,
                         instance=self.obj,
                         data=request.POST,
                         files=request.FILES)
    if form.is_valid():
        obj = form.save(commit=False)
        obj.owner = request.user
        obj.save()
        if not id:
            # new content
            Content.objects.create(module=self.module,
                                   item=obj)
        return redirect('module_content_list', self.module.id)

    return self.render_to_response({'form': form,
                                    'object': self.obj})
```

These methods are as follows:

- `get()`: Executed when a GET request is received. You build the model form for the `Text`, `Video`, `Image`, or `File` instance that is being updated. Otherwise, you pass no instance to create a new object, since `self.obj` is `None` if no ID is provided.

- `post()`: Executed when a POST request is received. You build the model form, passing any submitted data and files to it. Then, you validate it. If the form is valid, you create a new object and assign `request.user` as its owner before saving it to the database. You check for the `id` parameter. If no ID is provided, you know the user is creating a new object instead of updating an existing one. If this is a new object, you create a Content object for the given module and associate the new content with it.

Edit the `urls.py` file of the `courses` application and add the following URL patterns to it:

```
path('module/<int:module_id>/content/<model_name>/create/',
    views.ContentCreateUpdateView.as_view(),
    name='module_content_create'),

path('module/<int:module_id>/content/<model_name>/<id>/',
    views.ContentCreateUpdateView.as_view(),
    name='module_content_update'),
```

The new URL patterns are as follows:

- `module_content_create`: To create new text, video, image, or file objects and add them to a module. It includes the `module_id` and `model_name` parameters. The first one allows linking the new content object to the given module. The latter specifies the content model to build the form for.

- `module_content_update`: To update an existing text, video, image, or file object. It includes the `module_id` and `model_name` parameters and an `id` parameter to identify the content that is being updated.

Create a new directory inside the `courses/manage/` template directory and name it `content`. Create the template `courses/manage/content/form.html` and add the following code to it:

```
{% extends "base.html" %}

{% block title %}
  {% if object %}
    Edit content "{{ object.title }}"
  {% else %}
    Add new content
  {% endif %}
{% endblock %}

{% block content %}
  <h1>
```

```
    {% if object %}
      Edit content "{{ object.title }}"
    {% else %}
      Add new content
    {% endif %}
  </h1>
  <div class="module">
    <h2>Course info</h2>
    <form action="" method="post" enctype="multipart/form-data">
      {{ form.as_p }}
      {% csrf_token %}
      <p><input type="submit" value="Save content"></p>
    </form>
  </div>
{% endblock %}
```

This is the template for the `ContentCreateUpdateView` view. In this template, you check whether an `object` variable is in the context. If `object` exists in the context, you are updating an existing object. Otherwise, you are creating a new object.

You include `enctype="multipart/form-data"` in the `<form>` HTML element because the form contains a file upload for the `File` and `Image` content models.

Run the development server, open `http://127.0.0.1:8000/course/mine/`, click **Edit modules** for an existing course, and create a module. Open the Python shell with the command `python manage.py shell` and obtain the ID of the most recently created module, as follows:

```
>>> from courses.models import Module
>>> Module.objects.latest('id').id
6
```

Run the development server and open `http://127.0.0.1:8000/course/module/6/content/image/create/` in your browser, replacing the module ID with the one you obtained before. You will see the form to create an `Image` object, as follows:

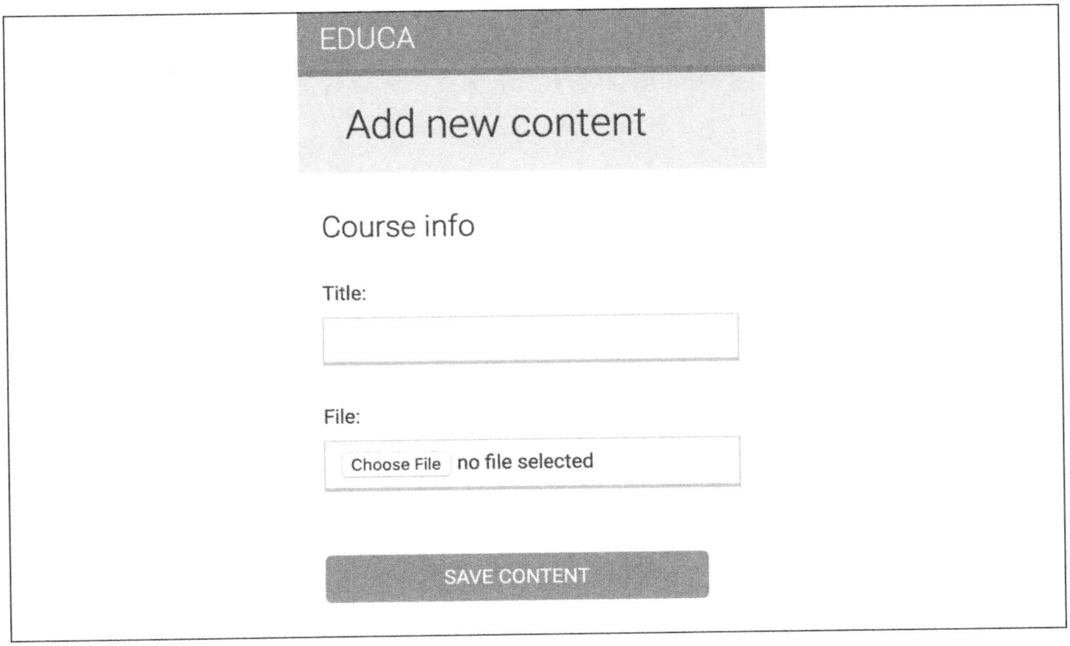

Figure 10.10: The course add image content form

Don't submit the form yet. If you try to do so, it will fail because you haven't defined the `module_content_list` URL yet. You are going to create it in a bit.

You also need a view for deleting content. Edit the `views.py` file of the `courses` application and add the following code:

```
class ContentDeleteView(View):

    def post(self, request, id):
        content = get_object_or_404(Content,
                                    id=id,
                                    module__course__owner=request.user)
        module = content.module
        content.item.delete()
        content.delete()
        return redirect('module_content_list', module.id)
```

The `ContentDeleteView` class retrieves the `Content` object with the given ID. It deletes the related `Text`, `Video`, `Image`, or `File` object. Finally, it deletes the `Content` object and redirects the user to the `module_content_list` URL to list the other contents of the module.

Edit the `urls.py` file of the `courses` application and add the following URL pattern to it:

```
path('content/<int:id>/delete/',
     views.ContentDeleteView.as_view(),
     name='module_content_delete'),
```

Now instructors can create, update, and delete content easily.

Managing modules and their contents

You have built views to create, edit, and delete course modules and their contents. Next, you need a view to display all modules for a course and list the contents of a specific module.

Edit the `views.py` file of the `courses` application and add the following code to it:

```
class ModuleContentListView(TemplateResponseMixin, View):
    template_name = 'courses/manage/module/content_list.html'

    def get(self, request, module_id):
        module = get_object_or_404(Module,
                                   id=module_id,
                                   course__owner=request.user)

        return self.render_to_response({'module': module})
```

This is the `ModuleContentListView` view. This view gets the `Module` object with the given ID that belongs to the current user and renders a template with the given module.

Edit the `urls.py` file of the `courses` application and add the following URL pattern to it:

```
path('module/<int:module_id>/',
     views.ModuleContentListView.as_view(),
     name='module_content_list'),
```

Create a new template inside the `templates/courses/manage/module/` directory and name it `content_list.html`. Add the following code to it:

```
{% extends "base.html" %}

{% block title %}
  Module {{ module.order|add:1 }}: {{ module.title }}
{% endblock %}

{% block content %}
{% with course=module.course %}
  <h1>Course "{{ course.title }}"</h1>
  <div class="contents">
    <h3>Modules</h3>
    <ul id="modules">
      {% for m in course.modules.all %}
        <li data-id="{{ m.id }}" {% if m == module %}
         class="selected"{% endif %}>
          <a href="{% url "module_content_list" m.id %}">
            <span>
              Module <span class="order">{{ m.order|add:1 }}</span>
            </span>
            <br>
            {{ m.title }}
          </a>
        </li>
      {% empty %}
        <li>No modules yet.</li>
      {% endfor %}
    </ul>
    <p><a href="{% url "course_module_update" course.id %}">
    Edit modules</a></p>
  </div>
  <div class="module">
    <h2>Module {{ module.order|add:1 }}: {{ module.title }}</h2>
    <h3>Module contents:</h3>

    <div id="module-contents">
      {% for content in module.contents.all %}
        <div data-id="{{ content.id }}">
          {% with item=content.item %}
            <p>{{ item }}</p>
            <a href="#">Edit</a>
            <form action="{% url "module_content_delete" content.id
%}"
              method="post">
              <input type="submit" value="Delete">
              {% csrf_token %}
            </form>
          {% endwith %}
```

```
        </div>
      {% empty %}
        <p>This module has no contents yet.</p>
      {% endfor %}
    </div>
    <h3>Add new content:</h3>
    <ul class="content-types">
      <li><a href="{% url "module_content_create" module.id "text"
%}">
        Text</a></li>
      <li><a href="{% url "module_content_create" module.id "image"
%}">
        Image</a></li>
      <li><a href="{% url "module_content_create" module.id "video"
%}">
        Video</a></li>
      <li><a href="{% url "module_content_create" module.id "file"
%}">
        File</a></li>
    </ul>
  </div>
{% endwith %}
{% endblock %}
```

Make sure that no template tag is split into multiple lines.

This is the template that displays all modules for a course and the contents of the selected module. You iterate over the course modules to display them in a sidebar. You iterate over a module's contents and access `content.item` to get the related `Text`, `Video`, `Image`, or `File` object. You also include links to create new text, video, image, or file content.

You want to know which type of object each of the `item` objects is: `Text`, `Video`, `Image`, or `File`. You need the model name to build the URL to edit the object. Besides this, you could display each item in the template differently based on the type of content it is. You can get the model name for an object from the model's `Meta` class by accessing the object's `_meta` attribute. Nevertheless, Django doesn't allow accessing variables or attributes starting with an underscore in templates to prevent retrieving private attributes or calling private methods. You can solve this by writing a custom template filter.

Create the following file structure inside the `courses` application directory:

```
templatetags/
    __init__.py
    course.py
```

Edit the `course.py` module and add the following code to it:

```
from django import template

register = template.Library()

@register.filter
def model_name(obj):
    try:
        return obj._meta.model_name
    except AttributeError:
        return None
```

This is the `model_name` template filter. You can apply it in templates as `object|model_name` to get the model name for an object.

Edit the `templates/courses/manage/module/content_list.html` template and add the following line below the `{% extends %}` template tag:

```
{% load course %}
```

This will load the `course` template tags. Then, find the following lines:

```
<p>{{ item }}</p>
<a href="#">Edit</a>
```

Replace them with the following ones:

```
<p>{{ item }} ({{ item|model_name }})</p>
<a href="{% url "module_content_update" module.id item|model_name
item.id %}">
  Edit
</a>
```

In the preceding code, you display the item model name in the template and also use the model name to build the link to edit the object.

Edit the `courses/manage/course/list.html` template and add a link to the `module_content_list` URL, like this:

```
<a href="{% url "course_module_update" course.id %}">Edit modules</a>
{% if course.modules.count > 0 %}
  <a href="{% url "module_content_list" course.modules.first.id %}">
  Manage contents</a>
{% endif %}
```

The new link allows users to access the contents of the first module of the course, if there are any.

Stop the development server and run it again using the command `python manage.py runserver`. By stopping and running the development server, you make sure that the `course` template tags file gets loaded.

Open `http://127.0.0.1:8000/course/mine/` and click the **Manage contents** link for a course that contains at least one module. You will see a page like the following one:

Figure 10.11: The page to manage course module contents

When you click on a module in the left sidebar, its contents are displayed in the main area. The template also includes links to add new text, video, image, or file content for the module being displayed.

Add a couple of different types of content to the module and take a look at the result. Module contents will appear below **Module contents**:

Figure 10.12: Managing different module contents

Reordering modules and their contents

You need to provide a simple way to reorder course modules and their contents. You will use a JavaScript drag-and-drop widget to let your users reorder the modules of a course by dragging them. When users finish dragging a module, you will launch an asynchronous request (AJAX) to store the new module order.

Using mixins from django-braces

django-braces is a third-party module that contains a collection of generic mixins for Django. These mixins provide additional features for class-based views. You can see a list of all mixins provided by django-braces at https://django-braces.readthedocs.io/.

You will use the following mixins of django-braces:

- CsrfExemptMixin: Used to avoid checking the **cross-site request forgery (CSRF)** token in the POST requests. You need this to perform AJAX POST requests without having to generate a csrf_token.

- JsonRequestResponseMixin: Parses the request data as JSON and also serializes the response as JSON and returns an HTTP response with the application/json content type.

Install django-braces via pip using the following command:

```
pip install django-braces==1.14.0
```

You need a view that receives the new order of module IDs encoded in JSON. Edit the views.py file of the courses application and add the following code to it:

```
from braces.views import CsrfExemptMixin, JsonRequestResponseMixin

class ModuleOrderView(CsrfExemptMixin,
                      JsonRequestResponseMixin,
                      View):
    def post(self, request):
        for id, order in self.request_json.items():
            Module.objects.filter(id=id,
                    course__owner=request.user).update(order=order)
        return self.render_json_response({'saved': 'OK'})
```

This is the ModuleOrderView view.

You can build a similar view to order a module's contents. Add the following code to the `views.py` file:

```
class ContentOrderView(CsrfExemptMixin,
                       JsonRequestResponseMixin,
                       View):
    def post(self, request):
        for id, order in self.request_json.items():
            Content.objects.filter(id=id,
                    module__course__owner=request.user) \
                    .update(order=order)
        return self.render_json_response({'saved': 'OK'})
```

Now, edit the `urls.py` file of the `courses` application and add the following URL patterns to it:

```
path('module/order/',
    views.ModuleOrderView.as_view(),
    name='module_order'),

path('content/order/',
    views.ContentOrderView.as_view(),
    name='content_order'),
```

Finally, you need to implement the drag-and-drop functionality in the template. You will use the jQuery UI library for this. jQuery UI is built on top of jQuery and it provides a set of interface interactions, effects, and widgets. You will use its `sortable` element. First, you need to load jQuery UI in the base template. Open the `base.html` file located in the `templates/` directory of the `courses` application, and add jQuery UI below the script to load jQuery, as follows:

```
<script src="https://ajax.googleapis.com/ajax/libs/jquery/3.4.1/
jquery.min.js"></script>
<script src="https://ajax.googleapis.com/ajax/libs/jqueryui/1.12.1/
jquery-ui.min.js"></script>
```

You load the jQuery UI library just below the jQuery framework. Next, edit the `courses/manage/module/content_list.html` template and add the following code to it at the bottom of the template:

```
{% block domready %}
  $('#modules').sortable({
    stop: function(event, ui) {
      modules_order = {};
      $('#modules').children().each(function(){
        // update the order field
```

```
            $(this).find('.order').text($(this).index() + 1);
            // associate the module's id with its order
            modules_order[$(this).data('id')] = $(this).index();
          });
          $.ajax({
            type: 'POST',
            url: '{% url "module_order" %}',
            contentType: 'application/json; charset=utf-8',
            dataType: 'json',
            data: JSON.stringify(modules_order)
          });
        }
      });

      $('#module-contents').sortable({
        stop: function(event, ui) {
          contents_order = {};
          $('#module-contents').children().each(function(){
            // associate the module's id with its order
            contents_order[$(this).data('id')] = $(this).index();
          });

          $.ajax({
            type: 'POST',
            url: '{% url "content_order" %}',
            contentType: 'application/json; charset=utf-8',
            dataType: 'json',
            data: JSON.stringify(contents_order),
          });
        }
      });
    {% endblock %}
```

This JavaScript code is in the {% block domready %} block and therefore it will be included in the $(document).ready() event of jQuery that you defined in the base.html template. This guarantees that your JavaScript code will be executed once the page has been loaded.

You define a sortable element for the module list in the sidebar and a different one for the module contents list. Both work in a similar manner.

In this code, you perform the following tasks:

1. You define a `sortable` element for the `modules` HTML element. Remember that you use `#modules`, since jQuery uses CSS notation for selectors.

2. You specify a function for the `stop` event. This event is triggered every time the user finishes sorting an element.

3. You create an empty `modules_order` dictionary. The keys for this dictionary will be the module IDs, and the values will be the assigned order for each module.

4. You iterate over the `#module` children elements. You recalculate the displayed order for each module and get its `data-id` attribute, which contains the module's ID. You add the ID as the key of the `modules_order` dictionary and the new index of the module as the value.

5. You launch an AJAX `POST` request to the `content_order` URL, including the serialized JSON data of `modules_order` in the request. The corresponding `ModuleOrderView` takes care of updating the order of the modules.

The `sortable` element to order module contents is quite similar to this one. Go back to your browser and reload the page. Now you will be able to click and drag both modules and their contents to reorder them like the following example:

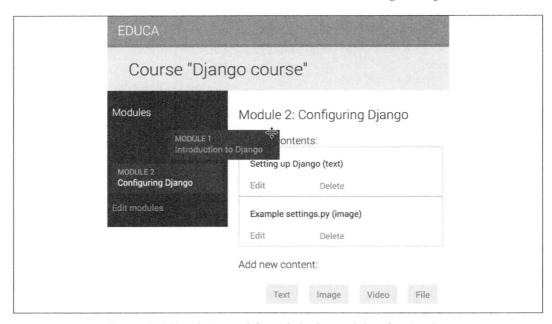

Figure 10.13: Reordering modules with the drag-and-drop functionality

Great! Now you can reorder both course modules and module contents.

Summary

In this chapter, you learned how to use fixtures to provide initial data for models. By using model inheritance, you created a versatile system to manage different types of content for the course modules. You implemented a custom model field to order objects. You also discovered how to use class-based views and mixins. You worked with groups and permissions to restrict access to your views. Finally, you used formsets to manage course modules, and you built a drag-and-drop functionality with jQuery UI to reorder modules and their contents.

In the next chapter, you will create a student registration system. You will also render different kinds of content, and you will learn how to work with Django's cache framework.

11
Rendering and Caching Content

In the previous chapter, you used model inheritance and generic relations to create flexible course content models. You implemented a custom model field, and you built a course management system using class-based views. Finally, you created an AJAX-based drag-and-drop functionality to order course modules and their contents.

In this chapter, you will build the functionality to access course contents, create a student registration system, and manage student enrollment onto courses. You will also learn how to cache data using the Django cache framework.

In this chapter, you will:

- Create public views for displaying course information
- Build a student registration system
- Manage student enrollment onto courses
- Render diverse content for course modules
- Install and configure Memcached
- Cache content using the Django cache framework
- Monitor Memcached using the django-memcache-status

Let's start by creating a course catalog for students to browse existing courses and enroll on them.

Displaying courses

For your course catalog, you have to build the following functionalities:

- List all available courses, optionally filtered by subject
- Display a single course overview

Edit the `views.py` file of the `courses` application and add the following code:

```
from django.db.models import Count
from .models import Subject

class CourseListView(TemplateResponseMixin, View):
    model = Course
    template_name = 'courses/course/list.html'

    def get(self, request, subject=None):
        subjects = Subject.objects.annotate(
                    total_courses=Count('courses'))
        courses = Course.objects.annotate(
                    total_modules=Count('modules'))
        if subject:
            subject = get_object_or_404(Subject, slug=subject)
            courses = courses.filter(subject=subject)
        return self.render_to_response({'subjects': subjects,
                                        'subject': subject,
                                        'courses': courses})
```

This is the `CourseListView` view. It inherits from `TemplateResponseMixin` and `View`. In this view, you perform the following tasks:

1. You retrieve all subjects, using the ORM's `annotate()` method with the `Count()` aggregation function to include the total number of courses for each subject

2. You retrieve all available courses, including the total number of modules contained in each course

3. If a subject slug URL parameter is given, you retrieve the corresponding subject object and limit the query to the courses that belong to the given subject

4. You use the `render_to_response()` method provided by `TemplateResponseMixin` to render the objects to a template and return an HTTP response

Let's create a detail view for displaying a single course overview. Add the following code to the `views.py` file:

```
from django.views.generic.detail import DetailView

class CourseDetailView(DetailView):
    model = Course
    template_name = 'courses/course/detail.html'
```

This view inherits from the generic `DetailView` provided by Django. You specify the `model` and `template_name` attributes. Django's `DetailView` expects a primary key (`pk`) or slug URL parameter to retrieve a single object for the given model. The view renders the template specified in `template_name`, including the `Course` object in the template context variable `object`.

Edit the main `urls.py` file of the `educa` project and add the following URL pattern to it:

```
from courses.views import CourseListView

urlpatterns = [
    # ...
    path('', CourseListView.as_view(), name='course_list'),
]
```

You add the `course_list` URL pattern to the main `urls.py` file of the project because you want to display the list of courses in the URL `http://127.0.0.1:8000/`, and all other URLs for the `courses` application have the `/course/` prefix.

Edit the `urls.py` file of the `courses` application and add the following URL patterns:

```
path('subject/<slug:subject>/',
    views.CourseListView.as_view(),
    name='course_list_subject'),

path('<slug:slug>/',
    views.CourseDetailView.as_view(),
    name='course_detail'),
```

You define the following URL patterns:

- `course_list_subject`: For displaying all courses for a subject
- `course_detail`: For displaying a single course overview

Let's build templates for the `CourseListView` and `CourseDetailView` views.

Create the following file structure inside the `templates/courses/` directory of the `courses` application:

```
course/
    list.html
    detail.html
```

Edit the `courses/course/list.html` template of the `courses` application and write the following code:

```
{% extends "base.html" %}

{% block title %}
  {% if subject %}
    {{ subject.title }} courses
  {% else %}
    All courses
  {% endif %}
{% endblock %}

{% block content %}
  <h1>
    {% if subject %}
      {{ subject.title }} courses
    {% else %}
      All courses
    {% endif %}
  </h1>
  <div class="contents">
    <h3>Subjects</h3>
    <ul id="modules">
      <li {% if not subject %}class="selected"{% endif %}>
        <a href="{% url "course_list" %}">All</a>
      </li>
      {% for s in subjects %}
        <li {% if subject == s %}class="selected"{% endif %}>
          <a href="{% url "course_list_subject" s.slug %}">
            {{ s.title }}
            <br><span>{{ s.total_courses }} courses</span>
          </a>
        </li>
      {% endfor %}
    </ul>
```

```
    </div>
    <div class="module">
      {% for course in courses %}
        {% with subject=course.subject %}
          <h3>
            <a href="{% url "course_detail" course.slug %}">
              {{ course.title }}
            </a>
          </h3>
          <p>
            <a href="{% url "course_list_subject" subject.slug %}">{{
subject }}</a>.
              {{ course.total_modules }} modules.
              Instructor: {{ course.owner.get_full_name }}
          </p>
        {% endwith %}
      {% endfor %}
    </div>
{% endblock %}
```

Make sure that no template tag is split into multiple lines.

This is the template for listing the available courses. You create an HTML list to display all Subject objects and build a link to the course_list_subject URL for each of them. You add a selected HTML class to highlight the current subject if a subject is selected. You iterate over every Course object, displaying the total number of modules and the instructor's name.

Run the development server and open http://127.0.0.1:8000/ in your browser. You should see a page similar to the following one:

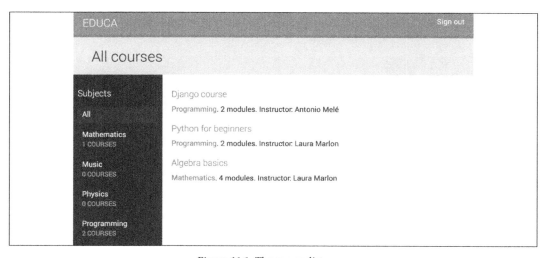

Figure 11.1: The course list page

The left sidebar contains all subjects, including the total number of courses for each of them. You can click any subject to filter the courses displayed.

Edit the `courses/course/detail.html` template and add the following code to it:

```
{% extends "base.html" %}

{% block title %}
  {{ object.title }}
{% endblock %}

{% block content %}
  {% with subject=object.subject %}
    <h1>
      {{ object.title }}
    </h1>
    <div class="module">
      <h2>Overview</h2>
      <p>
        <a href="{% url "course_list_subject" subject.slug %}">
        {{ subject.title }}</a>.
        {{ object.modules.count }} modules.
        Instructor: {{ object.owner.get_full_name }}
      </p>
      {{ object.overview|linebreaks }}
    </div>
  {% endwith %}
{% endblock %}
```

In this template, you display the overview and details for a single course. Open `http://127.0.0.1:8000/` in your browser and click on one of the courses. You should see a page with the following structure:

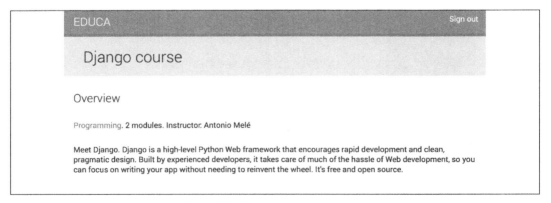

Figure 11.2: The course overview page

You have created a public area for displaying courses. Next, you need to allow users to register as students and enroll on courses.

Adding student registration

Create a new application using the following command:

```
python manage.py startapp students
```

Edit the settings.py file of the educa project and add the new application to the INSTALLED_APPS setting, as follows:

```
INSTALLED_APPS = [
    # ...
    'students.apps.StudentsConfig',
]
```

Creating a student registration view

Edit the views.py file of the students application and write the following code:

```
from django.urls import reverse_lazy
from django.views.generic.edit import CreateView
from django.contrib.auth.forms import UserCreationForm
from django.contrib.auth import authenticate, login

class StudentRegistrationView(CreateView):
    template_name = 'students/student/registration.html'
    form_class = UserCreationForm
    success_url = reverse_lazy('student_course_list')

    def form_valid(self, form):
        result = super().form_valid(form)
        cd = form.cleaned_data
        user = authenticate(username=cd['username'],
                            password=cd['password1'])
        login(self.request, user)
        return result
```

This is the view that allows students to register on your site. You use the generic CreateView, which provides the functionality for creating model objects. This view requires the following attributes:

- template_name: The path of the template to render this view.

- form_class: The form for creating objects, which has to be ModelForm. You use Django's UserCreationForm as the registration form to create User objects.
- success_url: The URL to redirect the user to when the form is successfully submitted. You reverse the URL named student_course_list, which you are going to create in the *Accessing the course contents* section for listing the courses that students are enrolled on.

The form_valid() method is executed when valid form data has been posted. It has to return an HTTP response. You override this method to log the user in after they have successfully signed up.

Create a new file inside the students application directory and name it urls.py. Add the following code to it:

```python
from django.urls import path
from . import views

urlpatterns = [
    path('register/',
        views.StudentRegistrationView.as_view(),
        name='student_registration'),
]
```

Then, edit the main urls.py of the educa project and include the URLs for the students application by adding the following pattern to your URL configuration:

```python
urlpatterns = [
    # ...
    path('students/', include('students.urls')),
]
```

Create the following file structure inside the students application directory:

```
templates/
    students/
        student/
            registration.html
```

Edit the students/student/registration.html template and add the following code to it:

```
{% extends "base.html" %}

{% block title %}
  Sign up
```

```
{% endblock %}

{% block content %}
  <h1>
    Sign up
  </h1>
  <div class="module">
    <p>Enter your details to create an account:</p>
    <form method="post">
      {{ form.as_p }}
      {% csrf_token %}
      <p><input type="submit" value="Create my account"></p>
    </form>
  </div>
{% endblock %}
```

Run the development server and open `http://127.0.0.1:8000/students/register/` in your browser. You should see a registration form like this:

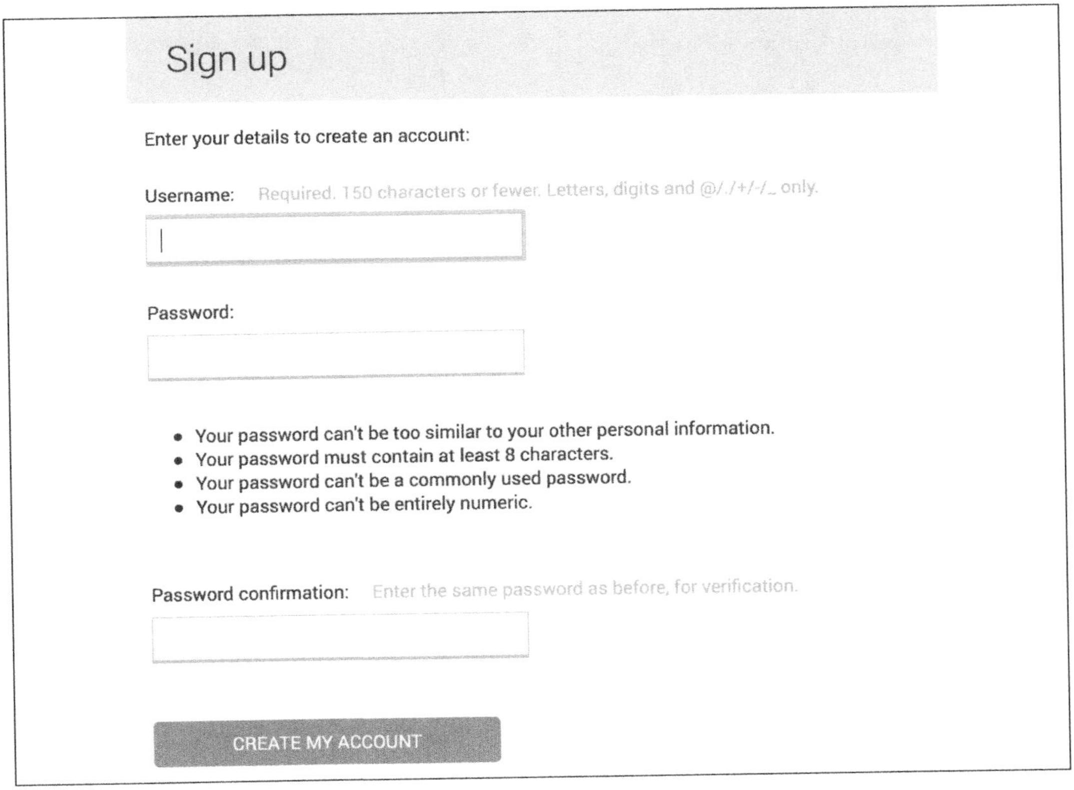

Figure 11.3: The student registration form

Note that the `student_course_list` URL specified in the `success_url` attribute of the `StudentRegistrationView` view doesn't exist yet. If you submit the form, Django won't find the URL to redirect you to after a successful registration. As mentioned, you will create this URL in the *Accessing the course contents* section.

Enrolling on courses

After users create an account, they should be able to enroll on courses. In order to store enrollments, you need to create a many-to-many relationship between the `Course` and `User` models.

Edit the `models.py` file of the `courses` application and add the following field to the `Course` model:

```
students = models.ManyToManyField(User,
                                  related_name='courses_joined',
                                  blank=True)
```

From the shell, execute the following command to create a migration for this change:

```
python manage.py makemigrations
```

You will see output similar to this:

```
Migrations for 'courses':
  courses/migrations/0004_course_students.py
    - Add field students to course
```

Then, execute the next command to apply pending migrations:

```
python manage.py migrate
```

You should see output that ends with the following line:

```
Applying courses.0004_course_students... OK
```

You can now associate students with the courses on which they are enrolled. Let's create the functionality for students to enroll on courses.

Create a new file inside the `students` application directory and name it `forms.py`. Add the following code to it:

```
from django import forms
from courses.models import Course

class CourseEnrollForm(forms.Form):
    course = forms.ModelChoiceField(queryset=Course.objects.all(),
                                    widget=forms.HiddenInput)
```

You are going to use this form for students to enroll on courses. The course field is for the course on which the user will be enrolled; therefore, it's a ModelChoiceField. You use a HiddenInput widget because you are not going to show this field to the user. You are going to use this form in the CourseDetailView view to display a button to enroll.

Edit the views.py file of the students application and add the following code:

```python
from django.views.generic.edit import FormView
from django.contrib.auth.mixins import LoginRequiredMixin
from .forms import CourseEnrollForm


class StudentEnrollCourseView(LoginRequiredMixin, FormView):
    course = None
    form_class = CourseEnrollForm

    def form_valid(self, form):
        self.course = form.cleaned_data['course']
        self.course.students.add(self.request.user)
        return super().form_valid(form)

    def get_success_url(self):
        return reverse_lazy('student_course_detail',
                            args=[self.course.id])
```

This is the StudentEnrollCourseView view. It handles students enrolling on courses. The view inherits from the LoginRequiredMixin mixin so that only logged-in users can access the view. It also inherits from Django's FormView view, since you handle a form submission. You use the CourseEnrollForm form for the form_class attribute and also define a course attribute for storing the given Course object. When the form is valid, you add the current user to the students enrolled on the course.

The get_success_url() method returns the URL that the user will be redirected to if the form was successfully submitted. This method is equivalent to the success_url attribute. Then, you reverse the URL named student_course_detail.

Edit the urls.py file of the students application and add the following URL pattern to it:

```python
path('enroll-course/',
     views.StudentEnrollCourseView.as_view(),
     name='student_enroll_course'),
```

Let's add the enroll button form to the course overview page. Edit the `views.py` file of the `courses` application and modify `CourseDetailView` to make it look as follows:

```python
from students.forms import CourseEnrollForm

class CourseDetailView(DetailView):
    model = Course
    template_name = 'courses/course/detail.html'

    def get_context_data(self, **kwargs):
        context = super().get_context_data(**kwargs)
        context['enroll_form'] = CourseEnrollForm(
                                   initial={'course':self.object})
        return context
```

You use the `get_context_data()` method to include the enrollment form in the context for rendering the templates. You initialize the hidden course field of the form with the current `Course` object so that it can be submitted directly.

Edit the `courses/course/detail.html` template and locate the following line:

```
{{ object.overview|linebreaks }}
```

Replace it with the following code:

```html
{{ object.overview|linebreaks }}
{% if request.user.is_authenticated %}
  <form action="{% url "student_enroll_course" %}" method="post">
    {{ enroll_form }}
    {% csrf_token %}
    <input type="submit" value="Enroll now">
  </form>
{% else %}
  <a href="{% url "student_registration" %}" class="button">
    Register to enroll
  </a>
{% endif %}
```

This is the button for enrolling on courses. If the user is authenticated, you display the enrollment button, including the hidden form that points to the `student_enroll_course` URL. If the user is not authenticated, you display a link to register on the platform.

Make sure that the development server is running, open `http://127.0.0.1:8000/` in your browser, and click a course. If you are logged in, you should see an **ENROLL NOW** button placed below the course overview, as follows:

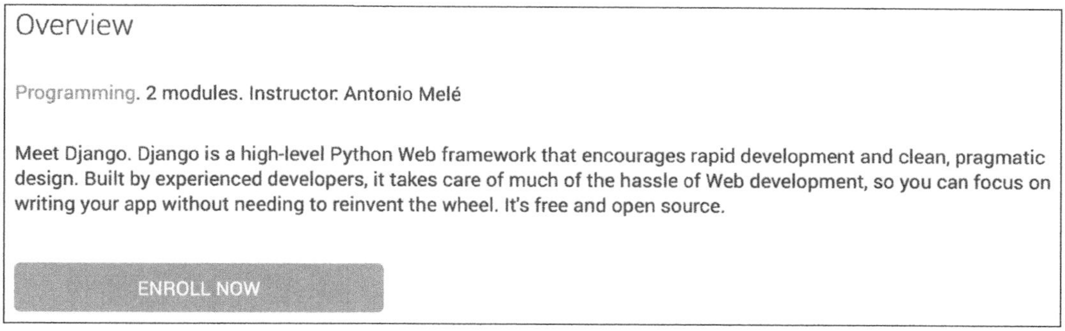

Overview

Programming. 2 modules. Instructor: Antonio Melé

Meet Django. Django is a high-level Python Web framework that encourages rapid development and clean, pragmatic design. Built by experienced developers, it takes care of much of the hassle of Web development, so you can focus on writing your app without needing to reinvent the wheel. It's free and open source.

ENROLL NOW

Figure 11.4: The course overview page, including an ENROLL NOW button

If you are not logged in, you will see a **REGISTER TO ENROLL** button instead.

Accessing the course contents

You need a view for displaying the courses that students are enrolled on, and a view for accessing the actual course contents. Edit the `views.py` file of the `students` application and add the following code to it:

```python
from django.views.generic.list import ListView
from courses.models import Course

class StudentCourseListView(LoginRequiredMixin, ListView):
    model = Course
    template_name = 'students/course/list.html'

    def get_queryset(self):
        qs = super().get_queryset()
        return qs.filter(students__in=[self.request.user])
```

This is the view to see courses that students are enrolled on. It inherits from `LoginRequiredMixin` to make sure that only logged in users can access the view. It also inherits from the generic `ListView` for displaying a list of `Course` objects. You override the `get_queryset()` method to retrieve only the courses that a student is enrolled on; you filter the QuerySet by the student's `ManyToManyField` field to do so.

Then, add the following code to the `views.py` file of the `students` application:

```python
from django.views.generic.detail import DetailView
```

```
class StudentCourseDetailView(DetailView):
    model = Course
    template_name = 'students/course/detail.html'

    def get_queryset(self):
        qs = super().get_queryset()
        return qs.filter(students__in=[self.request.user])

    def get_context_data(self, **kwargs):
        context = super().get_context_data(**kwargs)
        # get course object
        course = self.get_object()
        if 'module_id' in self.kwargs:
            # get current module
            context['module'] = course.modules.get(
                                     id=self.kwargs['module_id'])
        else:
            # get first module
            context['module'] = course.modules.all()[0]
        return context
```

This is the `StudentCourseDetailView` view. You override the `get_queryset()` method to limit the base QuerySet to courses on which the student is enrolled. You also override the `get_context_data()` method to set a course module in the context if the `module_id` URL parameter is given. Otherwise, you set the first module of the course. This way, students will be able to navigate through modules inside a course.

Edit the `urls.py` file of the `students` application and add the following URL patterns to it:

```
path('courses/',
     views.StudentCourseListView.as_view(),
     name='student_course_list'),

path('course/<pk>/',
     views.StudentCourseDetailView.as_view(),
     name='student_course_detail'),

path('course/<pk>/<module_id>/',
     views.StudentCourseDetailView.as_view(),
     name='student_course_detail_module'),
```

Create the following file structure inside the `templates/students/` directory of the `students` application:

```
course/
    detail.html
    list.html
```

Edit the `students/course/list.html` template and add the following code to it:

```
{% extends "base.html" %}

{% block title %}My courses{% endblock %}

{% block content %}
  <h1>My courses</h1>

  <div class="module">
    {% for course in object_list %}
      <div class="course-info">
        <h3>{{ course.title }}</h3>
        <p><a href="{% url "student_course_detail" course.id %}">
        Access contents</a></p>
      </div>
    {% empty %}
      <p>
        You are not enrolled in any courses yet.
        <a href="{% url "course_list" %}">Browse courses</a>
        to enroll in a course.
      </p>
    {% endfor %}
  </div>
{% endblock %}
```

This template displays the courses that the student is enrolled on. Remember that when a new student successfully registers with the platform, they will be redirected to the `student_course_list` URL. Let's also redirect students to this URL when they log in to the platform.

Edit the `settings.py` file of the `educa` project and add the following code to it:

```
from django.urls import reverse_lazy
LOGIN_REDIRECT_URL = reverse_lazy('student_course_list')
```

This is the setting used by the `auth` module to redirect the student after a successful login if no `next` parameter is present in the request. After a successful login, a student will be redirected to the `student_course_list` URL to view the courses that they are enrolled on.

Edit the `students/course/detail.html` template and add the following code to it:

```
{% extends "base.html" %}

{% block title %}
  {{ object.title }}
{% endblock %}

{% block content %}
  <h1>
    {{ module.title }}
  </h1>
  <div class="contents">
    <h3>Modules</h3>
    <ul id="modules">
      {% for m in object.modules.all %}
        <li data-id="{{ m.id }}" {% if m == module %}
class="selected"{% endif %}>
          <a href="{% url "student_course_detail_module" object.id
m.id %}">
            <span>
              Module <span class="order">{{ m.order|add:1 }}</span>
            </span>
            <br>
            {{ m.title }}
          </a>
        </li>
      {% empty %}
        <li>No modules yet.</li>
      {% endfor %}
    </ul>
  </div>
  <div class="module">
    {% for content in module.contents.all %}
      {% with item=content.item %}
        <h2>{{ item.title }}</h2>
        {{ item.render }}
      {% endwith %}
    {% endfor %}
  </div>
{% endblock %}
```

This is the template for enrolled students to access the contents of a course. First, you build an HTML list including all course modules and highlighting the current module. Then, you iterate over the current module contents and access each content item to display it using `{{ item.render }}`. You are going to add the `render()` method to the content models next. This method will take care of rendering the content properly.

Rendering different types of content

You need to provide a way to render each type of content. Edit the `models.py` file of the `courses` application and add the following `render()` method to the `ItemBase` model:

```python
from django.template.loader import render_to_string

class ItemBase(models.Model):
    # ...

    def render(self):
        return render_to_string(
            f'courses/content/{self._meta.model_name}.html',
            {'item': self})
```

This method uses the `render_to_string()` function for rendering a template and returning the rendered content as a string. Each kind of content is rendered using a template named after the content model. You use `self._meta.model_name` to generate the appropriate template name for each content model dynamically. The `render()` method provides a common interface for rendering diverse content.

Create the following file structure inside the `templates/courses/` directory of the `courses` application:

```
content/
    text.html
    file.html
    image.html
    video.html
```

Edit the `courses/content/text.html` template and write this code:

```
{{ item.content|linebreaks }}
```

This is the template to render text content. The `linebreaks` template filter replaces line breaks in plain text with HTML line breaks.

Edit the `courses/content/file.html` template and add the following:

```
<p><a href="{{ item.file.url }}" class="button">Download file</a></p>
```

This is the template to render files. You generate a link to download the file.

Edit the `courses/content/image.html` template and write:

```
<p><img src="{{ item.file.url }}" alt="{{ item.title }}"></p>
```

This is the template to render images. For files uploaded with `ImageField` and `FileField` to work, you need to set up your project to serve media files with the development server.

Edit the `settings.py` file of your project and add the following code to it:

```
MEDIA_URL = '/media/'
MEDIA_ROOT = os.path.join(BASE_DIR, 'media/')
```

Remember that `MEDIA_URL` is the base URL to serve uploaded media files and `MEDIA_ROOT` is the local path where the files are located.

Edit the main `urls.py` file of your project and add the following imports:

```
from django.conf import settings
from django.conf.urls.static import static
```

Then, write the following lines at the end of the file:

```
if settings.DEBUG:
    urlpatterns += static(settings.MEDIA_URL,
                          document_root=settings.MEDIA_ROOT)
```

Your project is now ready to upload and serve media files. The Django development server will be in charge of serving the media files during development (that is, when the `DEBUG` setting is set to `True`). Remember that the development server is not suitable for production use. You will learn how to set up a production environment in *Chapter 14, Going Live*.

You also have to create a template for rendering `Video` objects. You will use `django-embed-video` for embedding video content. `django-embed-video` is a third-party Django application that allows you to embed videos in your templates, from sources such as YouTube or Vimeo, by simply providing their public URL.

Install the package with the following command:

```
pip install django-embed-video==1.3.2
```

Edit the `settings.py` file of your project and add the application to the `INSTALLED_APPS` setting, as follows:

```
INSTALLED_APPS = [
    # ...
    'embed_video',
]
```

You can find the `django-embed-video` application's documentation at `https://django-embed-video.readthedocs.io/en/latest/`.

Edit the `courses/content/video.html` template and write the following code:

```
{% load embed_video_tags %}
{% video item.url "small" %}
```

This is the template to render videos.

Now run the development server and access `http://127.0.0.1:8000/course/mine/` in your browser. Access the site with a user belonging to the `Instructors` group, and add multiple contents to a course. To include video content, you can just copy any YouTube URL, such as `https://www.youtube.com/watch?v=bgV39DlmZ2U`, and include it in the `url` field of the form.

After adding contents to the course, open `http://127.0.0.1:8000/`, click the course, and click on the **ENROLL NOW** button. You should be enrolled on the course and redirected to the `student_course_detail` URL. The following screenshot shows a sample course contents page:

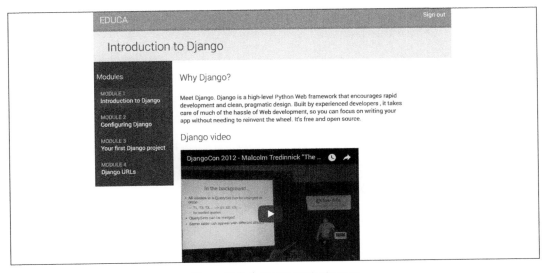

Figure 11.5: A course contents page

Great! You have created a common interface for rendering different types of course contents.

Using the cache framework

HTTP requests to your web application usually entail database access, data processing, and template rendering. This is much more expensive in terms of processing than serving a static website. The overhead in some requests can be significant when your site starts getting more and more traffic. This is where caching becomes precious. By caching queries, calculation results, or rendered content in an HTTP request, you will avoid expensive operations in the following requests. This translates into shorter response times and less processing on the server side.

Django includes a robust cache system that allows you to cache data with different levels of granularity. You can cache a single query, the output of a specific view, parts of rendered template content, or your entire site. Items are stored in the cache system for a default time. You can specify the default timeout for cached data.

This is how you will usually use the cache framework when your application gets an HTTP request:

1. Try to find the requested data in the cache
2. If found, return the cached data
3. If not found, perform the following steps:
   - Perform the query or processing required to obtain the data
   - Save the generated data in the cache
   - Return the data

You can read detailed information about Django's cache system at `https://docs.djangoproject.com/en/3.0/topics/cache/`.

Available cache backends

Django comes with several cache backends. These are the following:

- `backends.memcached.MemcachedCache` or `backends.memcached.PyLibMCCache`: A Memcached backend. Memcached is a fast and efficient memory-based cache server. The backend to use depends on the Memcached Python bindings you choose.

- `backends.db.DatabaseCache`: Use the database as a cache system.

- `backends.filebased.FileBasedCache`: Use the file storage system. This serializes and stores each cache value as a separate file.
- `backends.locmem.LocMemCache`: A local memory cache backend. This the default cache backend.
- `backends.dummy.DummyCache`: A dummy cache backend intended only for development. It implements the cache interface without actually caching anything. This cache is per-process and thread-safe.

 For optimal performance, use a memory-based cache backend such as the Memcached backend.

Installing Memcached

You are going to use the Memcached backend. Memcached runs in memory and it is allotted a specified amount of RAM. When the allotted RAM is full, Memcached starts removing the oldest data to store new data.

Download Memcached from `https://memcached.org/downloads`. If you are using Linux, you can install Memcached using the following command:

```
./configure && make && make test && sudo make install
```

If you are using macOS, you can install Memcached with the Homebrew package manager using the command `brew install memcached`. You can download Homebrew from `https://brew.sh/`.

After installing Memcached, open a shell and start it using the following command:

```
memcached -l 127.0.0.1:11211
```

Memcached will run on port `11211` by default. However, you can specify a custom host and port by using the `-l` option. You can find more information about Memcached at `https://memcached.org`.

After installing Memcached, you have to install its Python bindings. You can do this with the following command:

```
pip install python-memcached==1.59
```

Cache settings

Django provides the following cache settings:

- CACHES: A dictionary containing all available caches for the project
- CACHE_MIDDLEWARE_ALIAS: The cache alias to use for storage
- CACHE_MIDDLEWARE_KEY_PREFIX: The prefix to use for cache keys
- Set a prefix to avoid key collisions if you share the same cache between several sites
- CACHE_MIDDLEWARE_SECONDS: The default number of seconds to cache pages

The caching system for the project can be configured using the CACHES setting. This setting allows you to specify the configuration for multiple caches. Each cache included in the CACHES dictionary can specify the following data:

- BACKEND: The cache backend to use.
- KEY_FUNCTION: A string containing a dotted path to a callable that takes a prefix, version, and key as arguments and returns a final cache key.
- KEY_PREFIX: A string prefix for all cache keys, to avoid collisions.
- LOCATION: The location of the cache. Depending on the cache backend, this might be a directory, a host and port, or a name for the in-memory backend.
- OPTIONS: Any additional parameters to be passed to the cache backend.
- TIMEOUT: The default timeout, in seconds, for storing the cache keys. It is 300 seconds by default, which is five minutes. If set to None, cache keys will not expire.
- VERSION: The default version number for the cache keys. Useful for cache versioning.

Adding Memcached to your project

Let's configure the cache for your project. Edit the settings.py file of the educa project and add the following code to it:

```
CACHES = {
    'default': {
        'BACKEND': 'django.core.cache.backends.memcached.
MemcachedCache',
        'LOCATION': '127.0.0.1:11211',
    }
}
```

You are using the `MemcachedCache` backend. You specify its location using the `address:port` notation. If you have multiple Memcached instances, you can use a list for `LOCATION`.

Monitoring Memcached

In order to monitor Memcached, you will use a third-party package called django-memcache-status. This application displays statistics for your Memcached instances in the administration site. Install it with the following command:

```
pip install django-memcache-status==2.2
```

Edit the `settings.py` file and add `'memcache_status'` to the `INSTALLED_APPS` setting:

```
INSTALLED_APPS = [
    # ...
    'memcache_status',
]
```

Edit the `admin.py` file of the `courses` application and add the following lines to it:

```
# use memcache admin index site
admin.site.index_template = 'memcache_status/admin_index.html'
```

Make sure Memcached is running, start the development server in another shell window and open `http://127.0.0.1:8000/admin/` in your browser. Log in to the administration site using a superuser. You should see the following block on the index page of the administration site:

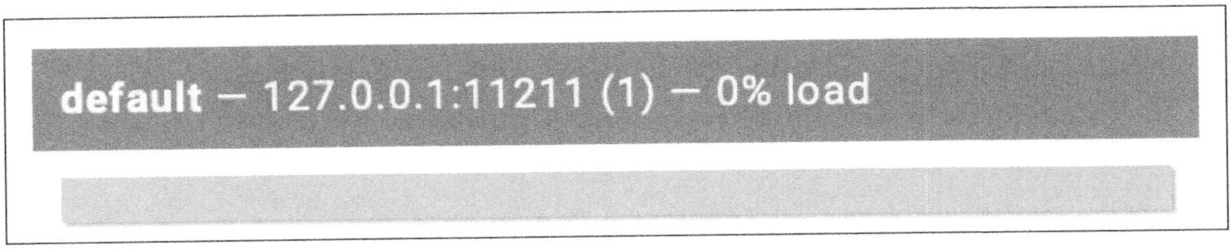

Figure 11.6: The Memcached status block

The block contains a bar graph that shows the cache load. The green color represents free cache, while red indicates used space. If you click the title of the box, it shows detailed statistics of your Memcached instance.

You have set up Memcached for your project and are able to monitor it. Let's start caching data!

Cache levels

Django provides the following levels of caching, listed here by ascending order of granularity:

- **Low-level cache API**: Provides the highest granularity. Allows you to cache specific queries or calculations.
- **Template cache**: Allows you to cache template fragments.
- **Per-view cache**: Provides caching for individual views.
- **Per-site cache**: The highest-level cache. It caches your entire site.

 Think about your cache strategy before implementing caching. Focus first on expensive queries or calculations that are not calculated on a per-user basis.

Using the low-level cache API

The low-level cache API allows you to store objects in the cache with any granularity. It is located at `django.core.cache`. You can import it like this:

```
from django.core.cache import cache
```

This uses the default cache. It's equivalent to `caches['default']`. Accessing a specific cache is also possible via its alias:

```
from django.core.cache import caches
my_cache = caches['alias']
```

Let's take a look at how the cache API works. Open the shell with the command `python manage.py shell` and execute the following code:

```
>>> from django.core.cache import cache
>>> cache.set('musician', 'Django Reinhardt', 20)
```

You access the default cache backend and use `set(key, value, timeout)` to store a key named `'musician'` with a value that is the string `'Django Reinhardt'` for 20 seconds. If you don't specify a timeout, Django uses the default timeout specified for the cache backend in the CACHES setting. Now, execute the following code:

```
>>> cache.get('musician')
'Django Reinhardt'
```

You retrieve the key from the cache. Wait for 20 seconds and execute the same code:

```
>>> cache.get('musician')
```

No value is returned this time. The `'musician'` cache key has expired and the `get()` method returns `None` because the key is not in the cache anymore.

 Always avoid storing a `None` value in a cache key because you won't be able to distinguish between the actual value and a cache miss.

Let's cache a QuerySet with the following code:

```
>>> from courses.models import Subject
>>> subjects = Subject.objects.all()
>>> cache.set('my_subjects', subjects)
```

You perform a QuerySet on the `Subject` model and store the returned objects in the `'my_subjects'` key. Let's retrieve the cached data:

```
>>> cache.get('my_subjects')
<QuerySet [<Subject: Mathematics>, <Subject: Music>, <Subject: Physics>,
<Subject: Programming>]>
```

You are going to cache some queries in your views. Edit the `views.py` file of the `courses` application and add the following import:

```
from django.core.cache import cache
```

In the `get()` method of the `CourseListView`, find the following line:

```
subjects = Subject.objects.annotate(
            total_courses=Count('courses'))
```

Replace it with the following ones:

```
subjects = cache.get('all_subjects')
if not subjects:
    subjects = Subject.objects.annotate(
                total_courses=Count('courses'))
    cache.set('all_subjects', subjects)
```

In this code, you try to get the `all_students` key from the cache using `cache.get()`. This returns `None` if the given key is not found. If no key is found (not cached yet or cached but timed out), you perform the query to retrieve all `Subject` objects and their number of courses, and you cache the result using `cache.set()`.

Run the development server and open `http://127.0.0.1:8000/` in your browser. When the view is executed, the cache key is not found and the QuerySet is executed. Open `http://127.0.0.1:8000/admin/` in your browser and click on the Memcached section to expand the statistics. You should see usage data for the cache that is similar to the following screen:

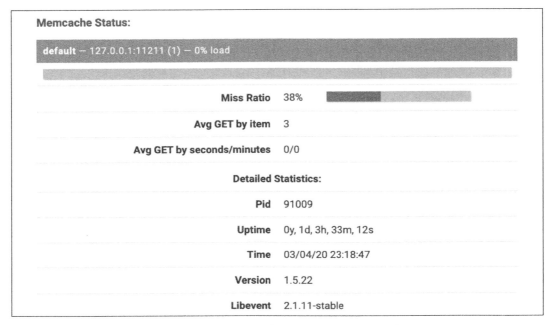

Figure 11.7: The Memcached status and usage details

Take a look at **Curr Items**, which should be **1**. This shows that there is one item currently stored in the cache. **Get Hits** shows how many get commands were successful and **Get Misses** shows the get requests for keys that are missing. The **Miss Ratio** is calculated using both of them.

Next, navigate back to `http://127.0.0.1:8000/` using your browser and reload the page several times. If you take a look at the cache statistics now, you will see several more reads (**Get Hits** and **Cmd Get** will increase).

Caching based on dynamic data

Often, you will want to cache something that is based on dynamic data. In these cases, you have to build dynamic keys that contain all the information required to uniquely identify the cached data.

Edit the `views.py` file of the `courses` application and modify the `CourseListView` view to make it look like this:

```python
class CourseListView(TemplateResponseMixin, View):
    model = Course
    template_name = 'courses/course/list.html'

    def get(self, request, subject=None):
        subjects = cache.get('all_subjects')
        if not subjects:
            subjects = Subject.objects.annotate(
                           total_courses=Count('courses'))
            cache.set('all_subjects', subjects)
        all_courses = Course.objects.annotate(
                          total_modules=Count('modules'))
        if subject:
            subject = get_object_or_404(Subject, slug=subject)
            key = f'subject_{subject.id}_courses'
            courses = cache.get(key)
            if not courses:
                courses = all_courses.filter(subject=subject)
                cache.set(key, courses)
        else:
            courses = cache.get('all_courses')
            if not courses:
                courses = all_courses
                cache.set('all_courses', courses)
        return self.render_to_response({'subjects': subjects,
                                        'subject': subject,
                                        'courses': courses})
```

In this case, you also cache both all courses and courses filtered by subject. You use the `all_courses` cache key for storing all courses if no subject is given. If there is a subject, you build the key dynamically with `f'subject_{subject.id}_courses'`.

It is important to note that you can't use a cached QuerySet to build other QuerySets, since what you cached are actually the results of the QuerySet. So you can't do the following:

```python
courses = cache.get('all_courses')
courses.filter(subject=subject)
```

Instead, you have to create the base QuerySet `Course.objects.annotate(total_modules=Count('modules'))`, which is not going to be executed until it is forced, and use it to further restrict the QuerySet with `all_courses.filter(subject=subject)` in case the data was not found in the cache.

Caching template fragments

Caching template fragments is a higher-level approach. You need to load the cache template tags in your template using `{% load cache %}`. Then, you will be able to use the `{% cache %}` template tag to cache specific template fragments. You will usually use the template tag as follows:

```
{% cache 300 fragment_name %}
    ...
{% endcache %}
```

The `{% cache %}` template tag has two required arguments: the timeout in seconds and a name for the fragment. If you need to cache content depending on dynamic data, you can do so by passing additional arguments to the `{% cache %}` template tag to uniquely identify the fragment.

Edit the `/students/course/detail.html` of the `students` application. Add the following code at the top of it, just after the `{% extends %}` tag:

```
{% load cache %}
```

Then, find the following lines:

```
{% for content in module.contents.all %}
  {% with item=content.item %}
    <h2>{{ item.title }}</h2>
    {{ item.render }}
  {% endwith %}
{% endfor %}
```

Replace them with the following ones:

```
{% cache 600 module_contents module %}
  {% for content in module.contents.all %}
    {% with item=content.item %}
      <h2>{{ item.title }}</h2>
      {{ item.render }}
    {% endwith %}
  {% endfor %}
{% endcache %}
```

You cache this template fragment using the name `module_contents` and passing the current `Module` object to it. Thus, you uniquely identify the fragment. This is important to avoid caching a module's contents and serving the wrong content when a different module is requested.

If the USE_I18N setting is set to True, the per-site middleware cache will respect the active language. If you use the {% cache %} template tag, you have to use one of the translation-specific variables available in templates to achieve the same result, such as {% cache 600 name request.LANGUAGE_CODE %}.

Caching views

You can cache the output of individual views using the cache_page decorator located at django.views.decorators.cache. The decorator requires a timeout argument (in seconds).

Let's use it in your views. Edit the urls.py file of the students application and add the following import:

```
from django.views.decorators.cache import cache_page
```

Then, apply the cache_page decorator to the student_course_detail and student_course_detail_module URL patterns, as follows:

```
path('course/<pk>/',
    cache_page(60 * 15)(views.StudentCourseDetailView.as_view()),
    name='student_course_detail'),

path('course/<pk>/<module_id>/',
    cache_page(60 * 15)(views.StudentCourseDetailView.as_view()),
    name='student_course_detail_module'),
```

Now, the result for the StudentCourseDetailView is cached for 15 minutes.

The per-view cache uses the URL to build the cache key. Multiple URLs pointing to the same view will be cached separately.

Using the per-site cache

This is the highest-level cache. It allows you to cache your entire site. To allow the per-site cache, edit the settings.py file of your project and add the UpdateCacheMiddleware and FetchFromCacheMiddleware classes to the MIDDLEWARE setting, as follows:

```
MIDDLEWARE = [
    'django.middleware.security.SecurityMiddleware',
    'django.contrib.sessions.middleware.SessionMiddleware',
```

```
    'django.middleware.cache.UpdateCacheMiddleware',
    'django.middleware.common.CommonMiddleware',
    'django.middleware.cache.FetchFromCacheMiddleware',
    # ...
]
```

Remember that middleware are executed in the given order during the request phase, and in reverse order during the response phase. UpdateCacheMiddleware is placed before CommonMiddleware because it runs during response time, when middleware are executed in reverse order. FetchFromCacheMiddleware is placed after CommonMiddleware intentionally because it needs to access request data set by the latter.

Next, add the following settings to the settings.py file:

```
CACHE_MIDDLEWARE_ALIAS = 'default'
CACHE_MIDDLEWARE_SECONDS = 60 * 15   # 15 minutes
CACHE_MIDDLEWARE_KEY_PREFIX = 'educa'
```

In these settings, you use the default cache for your cache middleware and set the global cache timeout to 15 minutes. You also specify a prefix for all cache keys to avoid collisions in case you use the same Memcached backend for multiple projects. Your site will now cache and return cached content for all GET requests.

You have done this to test the per-site cache functionality. However, the per-site cache is not suitable for you, since the course management views need to show updated data to instantly reflect any changes. The best approach to follow in your project is to cache the templates or views that are used to display course contents to students.

You have seen an overview of the methods provided by Django to cache data. You should define your cache strategy wisely and prioritize the most expensive QuerySets or calculations.

Summary

In this chapter, you implemented the public views for the course catalog. You built a system for students to register and enroll on courses. You also created the functionality to render different types of content for the course modules. Finally, you learned how to use the Django cache framework and you installed and monitored the Memcached cache backend.

In the next chapter, you will build a RESTful API for your project using Django REST framework.

12
Building an API

In the previous chapter, you built a system for student registration and enrollment on courses. You created views to display course contents and learned how to use Django's cache framework.

In this chapter, you will create a RESTful API for your e-learning platform. An API allows you to build a common core that can be used on multiple platforms like websites, mobile applications, plugins, and so on. For example, you can create an API to be consumed by a mobile application for your e-learning platform. If you provide an API to third parties, they will be able to consume information and operate with your application programmatically. An API allows developers to automate actions on your platform and integrate your service with other applications or online services. You will build a fully featured API for your e-learning platform.

In this chapter, you will:

- Install Django REST framework
- Create serializers for your models
- Build a RESTful API
- Create nested serializers
- Build custom API views
- Handle API authentication
- Add permissions to API views
- Create a custom permission
- Implement viewsets and routers
- Use the Requests library to consume the API

Let's start with the setup of your API.

Building a RESTful API

When building an API, there are several ways you can structure its endpoints and actions, but following REST principles is encouraged. The **REST** architecture comes from **Representational State Transfer**. RESTful APIs are resource-based; your models represent resources and HTTP methods such as GET, POST, PUT, or DELETE are used to retrieve, create, update, or delete objects. HTTP response codes are also used in this context. Different HTTP response codes are returned to indicate the result of the HTTP request, for example, 2XX response codes for success, 4XX for errors, and so on.

The most common formats to exchange data in RESTful APIs are JSON and XML. You will build a RESTful API with JSON serialization for your project. Your API will provide the following functionality:

* Retrieve subjects

* Retrieve available courses

* Retrieve course contents

* Enroll on a course

You can build an API from scratch with Django by creating custom views. However, there are several third-party modules that simplify creating an API for your project; the most popular among them is Django REST framework.

Installing Django REST framework

Django REST framework allows you to easily build RESTful APIs for your project. You can find all the information about REST framework at https://www.django-rest-framework.org/.

Open the shell and install the framework with the following command:

```
pip install djangorestframework==3.11.0
```

Edit the settings.py file of the educa project and add rest_framework to the INSTALLED_APPS setting to activate the application, as follows:

```
INSTALLED_APPS = [
    # ...
    'rest_framework',
]
```

Then, add the following code to the `settings.py` file:

```
REST_FRAMEWORK = {
    'DEFAULT_PERMISSION_CLASSES': [
        'rest_framework.permissions.DjangoModelPermissionsOrAnonReadOnly'
    ]
}
```

You can provide a specific configuration for your API using the `REST_FRAMEWORK` setting. REST framework offers a wide range of settings to configure default behaviors. The `DEFAULT_PERMISSION_CLASSES` setting specifies the default permissions to read, create, update, or delete objects. You set `DjangoModelPermissionsOrAnonReadOnly` as the only default permission class. This class relies on Django's permissions system to allow users to create, update, or delete objects, while providing read-only access for anonymous users. You will learn more about permissions later in the *Adding permissions to views* section.

For a complete list of available settings for REST framework, you can visit `https://www.django-rest-framework.org/api-guide/settings/`.

Defining serializers

After setting up REST framework, you need to specify how your data will be serialized. Output data has to be serialized in a specific format, and input data will be deserialized for processing. The framework provides the following classes to build serializers for single objects:

- `Serializer`: Provides serialization for normal Python class instances
- `ModelSerializer`: Provides serialization for model instances
- `HyperlinkedModelSerializer`: The same as `ModelSerializer`, but it represents object relationships with links rather than primary keys

Let's build your first serializer. Create the following file structure inside the `courses` application directory:

```
api/
    __init__.py
    serializers.py
```

You will build all the API functionality inside the `api` directory to keep everything well organized. Edit the `serializers.py` file and add the following code:

```
from rest_framework import serializers
from ..models import Subject
```

```
class SubjectSerializer(serializers.ModelSerializer):
    class Meta:
        model = Subject
        fields = ['id', 'title', 'slug']
```

This is the serializer for the `Subject` model. Serializers are defined in a similar fashion to Django's `Form` and `ModelForm` classes. The `Meta` class allows you to specify the model to serialize and the fields to be included for serialization. All model fields will be included if you don't set a `fields` attribute.

Let's try your serializer. Open the command line and start the Django shell with the following command:

python manage.py shell

Run the following code:

```
>>> from courses.models import Subject
>>> from courses.api.serializers import SubjectSerializer
>>> subject = Subject.objects.latest('id')
>>> serializer = SubjectSerializer(subject)
>>> serializer.data
{'id': 4, 'title': 'Programming', 'slug': 'programming'}
```

In this example, you get a `Subject` object, create an instance of `SubjectSerializer`, and access the serialized data. You can see that the model data is translated into Python native data types.

Understanding parsers and renderers

The serialized data has to be rendered in a specific format before you return it in an HTTP response. Likewise, when you get an HTTP request, you have to parse the incoming data and deserialize it before you can operate with it. REST framework includes renderers and parsers to handle that.

Let's see how to parse incoming data. Execute the following code in the Python shell:

```
>>> from io import BytesIO
>>> from rest_framework.parsers import JSONParser
>>> data = b'{"id":4,"title":"Programming","slug":"programming"}'
>>> JSONParser().parse(BytesIO(data))
{'id': 4, 'title': 'Programming', 'slug': 'programming'}
```

Given a JSON string input, you can use the `JSONParser` class provided by REST framework to convert it to a Python object.

REST framework also includes `Renderer` classes that allow you to format API responses. The framework determines which renderer to use through content negotiation by inspecting the request's `Accept` header to determine the expected content type for the response. Optionally, the renderer is determined by the format suffix of the URL. For example, the URL `http://127.0.0.1:8000/api/data.json` might be an endpoint that triggers the `JSONRenderer` in order to return a JSON response.

Go back to the shell and execute the following code to render the `serializer` object from the previous serializer example:

```
>>> from rest_framework.renderers import JSONRenderer
>>> JSONRenderer().render(serializer.data)
```

You will see the following output:

```
b'{"id":4,"title":"Programming","slug":"programming"}'
```

You use the `JSONRenderer` to render the serialized data into JSON. By default, REST framework uses two different renderers: `JSONRenderer` and `BrowsableAPIRenderer`. The latter provides a web interface to easily browse your API. You can change the default renderer classes with the `DEFAULT_RENDERER_CLASSES` option of the `REST_FRAMEWORK` setting.

You can find more information about renderers and parsers at `https://www.django-rest-framework.org/api-guide/renderers/` and `https://www.django-rest-framework.org/api-guide/parsers/`, respectively.

Building list and detail views

REST framework comes with a set of generic views and mixins that you can use to build your API views. They provide the functionality to retrieve, create, update, or delete model objects. You can see all the generic mixins and views provided by REST framework at `https://www.django-rest-framework.org/api-guide/generic-views/`.

Let's create list and detail views to retrieve `Subject` objects. Create a new file inside the `courses/api/` directory and name it `views.py`. Add the following code to it:

```
from rest_framework import generics
from ..models import Subject
from .serializers import SubjectSerializer
```

```
class SubjectListView(generics.ListAPIView):
    queryset = Subject.objects.all()
    serializer_class = SubjectSerializer

class SubjectDetailView(generics.RetrieveAPIView):
    queryset = Subject.objects.all()
    serializer_class = SubjectSerializer
```

In this code, you are using the generic `ListAPIView` and `RetrieveAPIView` views of REST framework. You include a `pk` URL parameter for the detail view to retrieve the object for the given primary key. Both views have the following attributes:

- `queryset`: The base `QuerySet` to use to retrieve objects
- `serializer_class`: The class to serialize objects

Let's add URL patterns for your views. Create a new file inside the `courses/api/` directory, name it `urls.py`, and make it look as follows:

```
from django.urls import path
from . import views

app_name = 'courses'

urlpatterns = [
    path('subjects/',
        views.SubjectListView.as_view(),
        name='subject_list'),

    path('subjects/<pk>/',
        views.SubjectDetailView.as_view(),
        name='subject_detail'),
]
```

Edit the main `urls.py` file of the `educa` project and include the API patterns, as follows:

```
urlpatterns = [
    # ...
    path('api/', include('courses.api.urls', namespace='api')),
]
```

You use the `api` namespace for your API URLs. Ensure that your server is running with the command `python manage.py runserver`. Open the shell and retrieve the URL `http://127.0.0.1:8000/api/subjects/` with `curl`, as follows:

```
curl http://127.0.0.1:8000/api/subjects/
```

You will get a response similar to the following one:

```
[
    {
        "id":1,
        "title":"Mathematics",
        "slug":"mathematics"
    },
    {
        "id":2,
        "title":"Music",
        "slug":"music"
    },
    {
        "id":3,
        "title":"Physics",
        "slug":"physics"
    },
    {
        "id":4,
        "title":"Programming",
        "slug":"programming"
    }
]
```

To obtain a more readable, well-indented JSON response, you can use `curl` with the `json_pp` utility, as follows:

```
curl http://127.0.0.1:8000/api/subjects/ | json_pp
```

The HTTP response contains a list of `Subject` objects in JSON format. If your operating system doesn't come with `curl` installed, you can download it from `https://curl.haxx.se/dlwiz/`. Instead of `curl`, you can also use any other tool to send custom HTTP requests, including a browser extension such as Postman, which you can get at `https://www.getpostman.com/`.

Open `http://127.0.0.1:8000/api/subjects/` in your browser. You will see REST framework's browsable API, as follows:

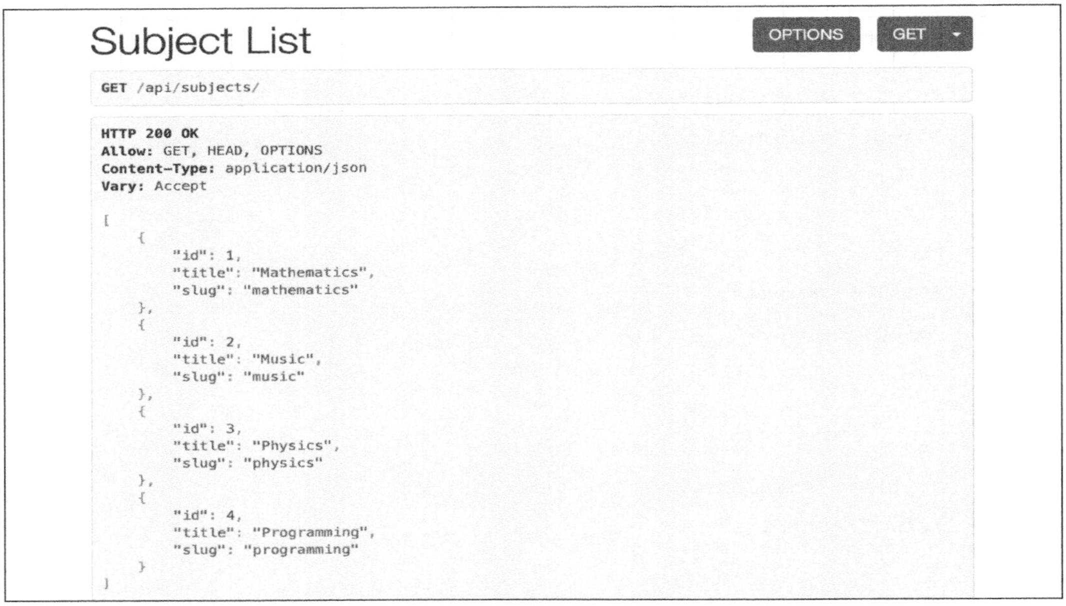

Figure 12.1: The subject list page in the REST framework browsable API

This HTML interface is provided by the `BrowsableAPIRenderer` renderer. It displays the result headers and content, and it allows you to perform requests. You can also access the API detail view for a `Subject` object by including its ID in the URL.

Open `http://127.0.0.1:8000/api/subjects/1/` in your browser. You will see a single `Subject` object rendered in JSON format.

Creating nested serializers

You are going to create a serializer for the `Course` model. Edit the `api/serializers.py` file of the `courses` application and add the following code to it:

```
from ..models import Course

class CourseSerializer(serializers.ModelSerializer):
    class Meta:
        model = Course
        fields = ['id', 'subject', 'title', 'slug', 'overview',
                  'created', 'owner', 'modules']
```

Let's take a look at how a `Course` object is serialized. Open the shell, run `python manage.py shell`, and run the following code:

```
>>> from rest_framework.renderers import JSONRenderer
>>> from courses.models import Course
>>> from courses.api.serializers import CourseSerializer
>>> course = Course.objects.latest('id')
>>> serializer = CourseSerializer(course)
>>> JSONRenderer().render(serializer.data)
```

You will get a JSON object with the fields that you included in `CourseSerializer`. You can see that the related objects of the `modules` manager are serialized as a list of primary keys, as follows:

```
"modules": [6, 7, 9, 10]
```

You want to include more information about each module, so you need to serialize `Module` objects and nest them. Modify the previous code of the `api/serializers.py` file of the `courses` application to make it look as follows:

```
from rest_framework import serializers
from ..models import Course, Module


class ModuleSerializer(serializers.ModelSerializer):
    class Meta:
        model = Module
        fields = ['order', 'title', 'description']


class CourseSerializer(serializers.ModelSerializer):
    modules = ModuleSerializer(many=True, read_only=True)

    class Meta:
        model = Course
        fields = ['id', 'subject', 'title', 'slug', 'overview',
                  'created', 'owner', 'modules']
```

You define `ModuleSerializer` to provide serialization for the `Module` model. Then, you add a `modules` attribute to `CourseSerializer` to nest the `ModuleSerializer` serializer. You set `many=True` to indicate that you are serializing multiple objects. The `read_only` parameter indicates that this field is read-only and should not be included in any input to create or update objects.

Open the shell and create an instance of `CourseSerializer` again. Render the serializer's `data` attribute with `JSONRenderer`. This time, the listed modules are being serialized with the nested `ModuleSerializer` serializer, as follows:

```
"modules": [
    {

        "order": 0,
        "title": "Introduction to overview",
        "description": "A brief overview about the Web Framework."
    },
    {
        "order": 1,
        "title": "Configuring Django",
        "description": "How to install Django."
    },
    ...
]
```

You can read more about serializers at `https://www.django-rest-framework.org/api-guide/serializers/`.

Building custom API views

REST framework provides an `APIView` class that builds API functionality on top of Django's `View` class. The `APIView` class differs from `View` by using REST framework's custom `Request` and `Response` objects, and handling `APIException` exceptions to return the appropriate HTTP responses. It also has a built-in authentication and authorization system to manage access to views.

You are going to create a view for users to enroll on courses. Edit the `api/views.py` file of the `courses` application and add the following code to it:

```
from django.shortcuts import get_object_or_404
from rest_framework.views import APIView
from rest_framework.response import Response
from ..models import Course

class CourseEnrollView(APIView):
    def post(self, request, pk, format=None):
        course = get_object_or_404(Course, pk=pk)
        course.students.add(request.user)
        return Response({'enrolled': True})
```

The `CourseEnrollView` view handles user enrollment on courses. The preceding code is as follows:

1. You create a custom view that subclasses `APIView`.

2. You define a `post()` method for `POST` actions. No other HTTP method will be allowed for this view.

3. You expect a `pk` URL parameter containing the ID of a course. You retrieve the course by the given `pk` parameter and raise a `404` exception if it's not found.

4. You add the current user to the `students` many-to-many relationship of the `Course` object and return a successful response.

Edit the `api/urls.py` file and add the following URL pattern for the `CourseEnrollView` view:

```
path('courses/<pk>/enroll/',
    views.CourseEnrollView.as_view(),
    name='course_enroll'),
```

Theoretically, you could now perform a `POST` request to enroll the current user on a course. However, you need to be able to identify the user and prevent unauthenticated users from accessing this view. Let's see how API authentication and permissions work.

Handling authentication

REST framework provides authentication classes to identify the user performing the request. If authentication is successful, the framework sets the authenticated `User` object in `request.user`. If no user is authenticated, an instance of Django's `AnonymousUser` is set instead.

REST framework provides the following authentication backends:

- `BasicAuthentication`: This is HTTP basic authentication. The user and password are sent by the client in the `Authorization` HTTP header encoded with Base64. You can learn more about it at https://en.wikipedia.org/wiki/Basic_access_authentication.

- `TokenAuthentication`: This is token-based authentication. A `Token` model is used to store user tokens. Users include the token in the `Authorization` HTTP header for authentication.

- `SessionAuthentication`: This uses Django's session backend for authentication. This backend is useful for performing authenticated AJAX requests to the API from your website's frontend.

- `RemoteUserAuthentication`: This allows you to delegate authentication to your web server, which sets a `REMOTE_USER` environment variable.

You can build a custom authentication backend by subclassing the `BaseAuthentication` class provided by REST framework and overriding the `authenticate()` method.

You can set authentication on a per-view basis, or set it globally with the `DEFAULT_AUTHENTICATION_CLASSES` setting.

 Authentication only identifies the user performing the request. It won't allow or deny access to views. You have to use permissions to restrict access to views.

You can find all the information about authentication at `https://www.django-rest-framework.org/api-guide/authentication/`.

Let's add `BasicAuthentication` to your view. Edit the `api/views.py` file of the `courses` application and add an `authentication_classes` attribute to `CourseEnrollView`, as follows:

```python
from rest_framework.authentication import BasicAuthentication

class CourseEnrollView(APIView):
    authentication_classes = (BasicAuthentication,)
    # ...
```

Users will be identified by the credentials set in the `Authorization` header of the HTTP request.

Adding permissions to views

REST framework includes a permission system to restrict access to views. Some of the built-in permissions of REST framework are:

- `AllowAny`: Unrestricted access, regardless of whether a user is authenticated or not.

- `IsAuthenticated`: Allows access to authenticated users only.

- `IsAuthenticatedOrReadOnly`: Complete access to authenticated users. Anonymous users are only allowed to execute read methods such as GET, HEAD, or OPTIONS.

- `DjangoModelPermissions`: Permissions tied to `django.contrib.auth`. The view requires a `queryset` attribute. Only authenticated users with model permissions assigned are granted permission.

- `DjangoObjectPermissions`: Django permissions on a per-object basis.

If users are denied permission, they will usually get one of the following HTTP error codes:

- HTTP 401: Unauthorized
- HTTP 403: Permission denied

You can read more information about permissions at https://www.django-rest-framework.org/api-guide/permissions/.

Edit the `api/views.py` file of the `courses` application and add a `permission_classes` attribute to `CourseEnrollView`, as follows:

```
from rest_framework.authentication import BasicAuthentication
from rest_framework.permissions import IsAuthenticated

class CourseEnrollView(APIView):
    authentication_classes = (BasicAuthentication,)
    permission_classes = (IsAuthenticated,)
    # ...
```

You include the `IsAuthenticated` permission. This will prevent anonymous users from accessing the view. Now, you can perform a POST request to your new API method.

Make sure the development server is running. Open the shell and run the following command:

```
curl -i -X POST http://127.0.0.1:8000/api/courses/1/enroll/
```

You will get the following response:

```
HTTP/1.1 401 Unauthorized
...
{"detail": "Authentication credentials were not provided."}
```

You got a `401` HTTP code as expected, since you are not authenticated. Let's use basic authentication with one of your users. Run the following command, replacing `student:password` with the credentials of an existing user:

```
curl -i -X POST -u student:password http://127.0.0.1:8000/api/courses/1/
enroll/
```

You will get the following response:

```
HTTP/1.1 200 OK
...
{"enrolled": true}
```

You can access the administration site and check that the user is now enrolled on the course.

Creating viewsets and routers

`ViewSets` allow you to define the interactions of your API and let REST framework build the URLs dynamically with a `Router` object. By using viewsets, you can avoid repeating logic for multiple views. Viewsets include actions for the following standard operations:

- Create operation: `create()`
- Retrieve operation: `list()` and `retrieve()`
- Update operation: `update()` and `partial_update()`
- Delete operation: `destroy()`

Let's create a viewset for the `Course` model. Edit the `api/views.py` file and add the following code to it:

```
from rest_framework import viewsets
from .serializers import CourseSerializer

class CourseViewSet(viewsets.ReadOnlyModelViewSet):
    queryset = Course.objects.all()
    serializer_class = CourseSerializer
```

You subclass `ReadOnlyModelViewSet`, which provides the read-only actions `list()` and `retrieve()` to both list objects, or retrieves a single object.

Edit the `api/urls.py` file and create a router for your viewset, as follows:

```
from django.urls import path, include
from rest_framework import routers
```

```
from . import views

router = routers.DefaultRouter()
router.register('courses', views.CourseViewSet)

urlpatterns = [
    # ...
    path('', include(router.urls)),
]
```

You create a `DefaultRouter` object and register your viewset with the `courses` prefix. The router takes charge of generating URLs automatically for your viewset.

Open `http://127.0.0.1:8000/api/` in your browser. You will see that the router lists all viewsets in its base URL, as shown in the following screenshot:

Figure 12.2: The API root page of the REST framework browsable API

You can access `http://127.0.0.1:8000/api/courses/` to retrieve the list of courses.

You can learn more about viewsets at `https://www.django-rest-framework.org/api-guide/viewsets/`. You can also find more information about routers at `https://www.django-rest-framework.org/api-guide/routers/`.

Adding additional actions to viewsets

You can add extra actions to viewsets. Let's change your previous `CourseEnrollView` view into a custom viewset action. Edit the `api/views.py` file and modify the `CourseViewSet` class to look as follows:

```
from rest_framework.decorators import action
```

```
class CourseViewSet(viewsets.ReadOnlyModelViewSet):
    queryset = Course.objects.all()
    serializer_class = CourseSerializer

    @action(detail=True,
            methods=['post'],
            authentication_classes=[BasicAuthentication],
            permission_classes=[IsAuthenticated])
    def enroll(self, request, *args, **kwargs):
        course = self.get_object()
        course.students.add(request.user)
        return Response({'enrolled': True})
```

In the preceding code, you add a custom `enroll()` method that represents an additional action for this viewset. The preceding code is as follows:

1. You use the `action` decorator of the framework with the parameter `detail=True` to specify that this is an action to be performed on a single object.

2. The decorator allows you to add custom attributes for the action. You specify that only the `post()` method is allowed for this view and set the authentication and permission classes.

3. You use `self.get_object()` to retrieve the `Course` object.

4. You add the current user to the `students` many-to-many relationship and return a custom success response.

Edit the `api/urls.py` file and remove the following URL, since you don't need it anymore:

```
path('courses/<pk>/enroll/',
     views.CourseEnrollView.as_view(),
     name='course_enroll'),
```

Then, edit the `api/views.py` file and remove the `CourseEnrollView` class.

The URL to enroll on courses is now automatically generated by the router. The URL remains the same, since it's built dynamically using your action name `enroll`.

Creating custom permissions

You want students to be able to access the contents of the courses they are enrolled on. Only students enrolled on a course should be able to access its contents. The best way to do this is with a custom permission class. Django provides a `BasePermission` class that allows you to define the following methods:

- `has_permission()`: View-level permission check
- `has_object_permission()`: Instance-level permission check

These methods should return `True` to grant access, or `False` otherwise.

Create a new file inside the `courses/api/` directory and name it `permissions.py`. Add the following code to it:

```
from rest_framework.permissions import BasePermission

class IsEnrolled(BasePermission):
    def has_object_permission(self, request, view, obj):
        return obj.students.filter(id=request.user.id).exists()
```

You subclass the `BasePermission` class and override the `has_object_permission()`. You check that the user performing the request is present in the `students` relationship of the `Course` object. You are going to use the `IsEnrolled` permission next.

Serializing course contents

You need to serialize course contents. The `Content` model includes a generic foreign key that allows you to associate objects of different content models. Yet, you added a common `render()` method for all content models in the previous chapter. You can use this method to provide rendered contents to your API.

Edit the `api/serializers.py` file of the `courses` application and add the following code to it:

```
from ..models import Content

class ItemRelatedField(serializers.RelatedField):
    def to_representation(self, value):
        return value.render()

class ContentSerializer(serializers.ModelSerializer):
    item = ItemRelatedField(read_only=True)

    class Meta:
        model = Content
        fields = ['order', 'item']
```

In this code, you define a custom field by subclassing the `RelatedField` serializer field provided by REST framework and overriding the `to_representation()` method. You define the `ContentSerializer` serializer for the `Content` model and use the custom field for the `item` generic foreign key.

You need an alternative serializer for the `Module` model that includes its contents, and an extended `Course` serializer as well. Edit the `api/serializers.py` file and add the following code to it:

```python
class ModuleWithContentsSerializer(serializers.ModelSerializer):
    contents = ContentSerializer(many=True)

    class Meta:
        model = Module
        fields = ['order', 'title', 'description', 'contents']

class CourseWithContentsSerializer(serializers.ModelSerializer):
    modules = ModuleWithContentsSerializer(many=True)

    class Meta:
        model = Course
        fields = ['id', 'subject', 'title', 'slug',
                  'overview', 'created', 'owner', 'modules']
```

Let's create a view that mimics the behavior of the `retrieve()` action, but includes the course contents. Edit the `api/views.py` file and add the following method to the `CourseViewSet` class:

```python
from .permissions import IsEnrolled
from .serializers import CourseWithContentsSerializer

class CourseViewSet(viewsets.ReadOnlyModelViewSet):
    # ...
    @action(detail=True,
            methods=['get'],
            serializer_class=CourseWithContentsSerializer,
            authentication_classes=[BasicAuthentication],
            permission_classes=[IsAuthenticated, IsEnrolled])
    def contents(self, request, *args, **kwargs):
        return self.retrieve(request, *args, **kwargs)
```

The description of this method is as follows:

- You use the `action` decorator with the parameter `detail=True` to specify an action that is performed on a single object.
- You specify that only the GET method is allowed for this action.
- You use the new `CourseWithContentsSerializer` serializer class that includes rendered course contents.

- You use both `IsAuthenticated` and your custom `IsEnrolled` permissions. By doing so, you make sure that only users enrolled on the course are able to access its contents.

- You use the existing `retrieve()` action to return the `Course` object.

Open `http://127.0.0.1:8000/api/courses/1/contents/` in your browser. If you access the view with the right credentials, you will see that each module of the course includes the rendered HTML for course contents, as follows:

```
{
    "order": 0,
    "title": "Introduction to Django",
    "description": "Brief introduction to the Django Web Framework.",
    "contents": [
        {
            "order": 0,
            "item": "<p>Meet Django. Django is a high-level
            Python Web framework
            ...</p>"
        },
        {
            "order": 1,
            "item": "\n<iframe width=\"480\" height=\"360\"
            src=\"http://www.youtube.com/embed/bgV39DlmZ2U?
            wmode=opaque\"
            frameborder=\"0\" allowfullscreen></iframe>\n"
        }
    ]
}
```

You have built a simple API that allows other services to access the course application programmatically. REST framework also allows you to handle creating and editing objects with the `ModelViewSet` viewset. We have covered the main aspects of Django REST framework, but you will find further information about its features in its extensive documentation at `https://www.django-rest-framework.org/`.

Consuming the RESTful API

Now that you have implemented an API, you can consume it in a programmatic manner from other applications. You can interact with the API using JavaScript in the frontend of your application, in a similar fashion to the AJAX functionalities you built in *Chapter 5, Sharing Content on Your Website*. You can also consume the API from applications built with Python or any other programming languages.

You are going to create a simple Python application that uses the RESTful API to retrieve all available courses and then enrolls a student on all of them. You will learn how to authenticate against the API using HTTP basic authentication, and perform GET and POST requests.

You will use the Python Requests library to consume the API. Requests is the most popular HTTP library for Python. It abstracts the complexity of dealing with HTTP requests and provides a very simple interface to consume HTTP services. You can find the documentation for the Requests library at https://requests.readthedocs.io/en/master/.

Open the shell and install the Requests library with the following command:

```
pip install requests==2.23
```

Create a new directory next to the educa project directory and name it api_examples. Create a new file inside the api_examples/ directory and name it enroll_all.py. The file structure should now look like this:

```
api_examples/
    enroll_all.py
educa/
    ...
```

Edit the enroll_all.py file and add the following code to it:

```python
import requests

base_url = 'http://127.0.0.1:8000/api/'

# retrieve all courses
r = requests.get(f'{base_url}courses/')
courses = r.json()

available_courses = ', '.join([course['title'] for course in courses])
print(f'Available courses: {available_courses}')
```

In this code, you perform the following actions:

1. You import the Requests library and define the base URL for the API.

2. You use requests.get() to retrieve data from the API by sending a GET request to the URL http://127.0.0.1:8000/api/courses/. This API endpoint is publicly accessible, so it does not require any authentication.

3. You use the `json()` method of the response object to decode the JSON data returned by the API.

4. You print the title attribute of each course.

Start the development server from the `educa` project directory with the following command:

```
python manage.py runserver
```

In another shell, run the following command from the `api_examples/` directory:

```
python enroll_all.py
```

You will see output with a list of all course titles, like this:

```
Available courses: Introduction to Django, Python for beginners, Algebra
basics
```

This is your first automated call to your API.

Edit the `enroll_all.py` file and change it to make it look like this:

```
import requests

username = ''
password = ''

base_url = 'http://127.0.0.1:8000/api/'

# retrieve all courses
r = requests.get(f'{base_url}courses/')
courses = r.json()

available_courses = ', '.join([course['title'] for course in courses])
print(f'Available courses: {available_courses}')

for course in courses:
    course_id = course['id']
    course_title = course['title']
    r = requests.post(f'{base_url}courses/{course_id}/enroll/',
                               auth=(username, password))
    if r.status_code == 200:
        # successful request
        print(f'Successfully enrolled in {course_title}')
```

Replace the values for the `username` and `password` variables with the credentials of an existing user.

With the new code, you perform the following actions:

1. You define the username and password of the student you want to enroll on courses.

2. You iterate over the available courses retrieved from the API.

3. You store the course ID attribute in the `course_id` variable and the title attribute in the `course_title` variable.

4. You use `requests.post()` to send a POST request to the URL `http://127.0.0.1:8000/api/courses/[id]/enroll/` for each course. This URL corresponds to the `CourseEnrollView` API view, which allows you to enroll a user on a course. You build the URL for each course using the `course_id` variable. The `CourseEnrollView` view requires authentication. It uses the `IsAuthenticated` permission and the `BasicAuthentication` authentication class. The Requests library supports HTTP basic authentication out of the box. You use the `auth` parameter to pass a tuple with the username and password to authenticate the user using HTTP basic authentication.

5. If the status code of the response is `200 OK`, you print a message to indicate that the user has been successfully enrolled on the course.

You can use different kinds of authentication with Requests. You can find more information on authentication with Requests at `https://requests.readthedocs.io/en/master/user/authentication/`.

Run the following command from the `api_examples/` directory:

```
python enroll_all.py
```

You will now see output like this:

```
Available courses: Introduction to Django, Python for beginners, Algebra
basics
Successfully enrolled in Introduction to Django
Successfully enrolled in Python for beginners
Successfully enrolled in Algebra basics
```

Great! You have successfully enrolled the user on all available courses using the API. You will see a `Successfully enrolled` message for each course in the platform. As you can see, it's very easy to consume the API from any other application. You can effortlessly build other functionalities based on the API and let others integrate your API into their applications.

Summary

In this chapter, you learned how to use Django REST framework to build a RESTful API for your project. You created serializers and views for models, and you built custom API views. You also added authentication to your API and you restricted access to API views using permissions. Next, you discovered how to create custom permissions, and you implemented viewsets and routers. Finally, you used the Requests library to consume the API from an external Python script.

The next chapter will teach you how to build a chat server using Django Channels. You will implement asynchronous communication using WebSockets and you will use Redis to set up a channel layer.

13

Building a Chat Server

In the previous chapter, you created a RESTful API for your project. In this chapter, you will build a chat server for students using Django Channels. Students will be able to access a different chat room for each course they are enrolled on. To create the chat server, you will learn how to serve your Django project through **Asynchronous Server Gateway Interface (ASGI)**, and you will implement asynchronous communication.

In this chapter, you will:

- Add Channels to your project
- Build a WebSocket consumer and appropriate routing
- Implement a WebSocket client
- Enable a channel layer with Redis
- Make your consumer fully asynchronous

Creating a chat application

You are going to implement a chat server to provide students with a chat room for each course. Students enrolled on a course will be able to access the course chat room and exchange messages in real time. You will use Channels to build this functionality. Channels is a Django application that extends Django to handle protocols that require long-running connections, such as WebSockets, chatbots, or MQTT (a lightweight publish/subscribe message transport commonly used in Internet of things projects).

Using Channels, you can easily implement real-time or asynchronous functionalities into your project in addition to your standard HTTP synchronous views. You will start by adding a new application to your project. The new application will contain the logic for the chat server.

Run the following command from the project `educa` directory to create the new application file structure:

```
django-admin startapp chat
```

Edit the `settings.py` file of the `educa` project and activate the `chat` application in your project by editing the `INSTALLED_APPS` setting, as follows:

```
INSTALLED_APPS = [
    # ...
    'chat',
]
```

The new `chat` application is now active in your project.

Implementing the chat room view

You will provide students with a different chat room for each course. You need to create a view for students to join the chat room of a given course. Only students who are enrolled on a course will be able to access the course chat room.

Edit the `views.py` file of the new `chat` application and add the following code to it:

```
from django.shortcuts import render, get_object_or_404
from django.http import HttpResponseForbidden
from django.contrib.auth.decorators import login_required


@login_required
def course_chat_room(request, course_id):
    try:
        # retrieve course with given id joined by the current user
        course = request.user.courses_joined.get(id=course_id)
    except:
        # user is not a student of the course or course does not exist
        return HttpResponseForbidden()
    return render(request, 'chat/room.html', {'course': course})
```

This is the `course_chat_room` view. In this view, you use the `@login_required` decorator to prevent any non-authenticated user from accessing the view. The view receives a required `course_id` parameter that is used to retrieve the course with the given `id`.

You access the courses that the user is enrolled on through the relationship `courses_joined` and you retrieve the course with the given `id` from that subset of courses. If the course with the given `id` does not exist or the user is not enrolled on it, you return an `HttpResponseForbidden` response, which translates to an HTTP response with status `403`. If the course with the given `id` exists and the user is enrolled on it, you render the `chat/room.html` template, passing the `course` object to the template context.

You need to add a URL pattern for this view. Create a new file inside the `chat` application directory and name it `urls.py`. Add the following code to it:

```
from django.urls import path
from . import views

app_name = 'chat'

urlpatterns = [
    path('room/<int:course_id>/', views.course_chat_room,
        name='course_chat_room'),
]
```

This is the initial URL patterns file for the `chat` application. You define the `course_chat_room` URL pattern, including the `course_id` parameter with the `int` prefix, as you only expect an integer value here.

Include the new URL patterns of the `chat` application in the main URL patterns of the project. Edit the main `urls.py` file of the `educa` project and add the following line to it:

```
urlpatterns = [
    # ...
    path('chat/', include('chat.urls', namespace='chat')),
]
```

URL patterns for the `chat` application are added to the project under the `chat/` path.

You need to create a template for the `course_chat_room` view. This template will contain an area to visualize the messages that are exchanged in the chat and a text input with a submit button to send text messages to the chat.

Create the following file structure within the `chat` application directory:

```
templates/
    chat/
        room.html
```

Edit the `chat/room.html` template and add the following code to it:

```
{% extends "base.html" %}

{% block title %}Chat room for "{{ course.title }}"{% endblock %}

{% block content %}
  <div id="chat">
  </div>
  <div id="chat-input">
    <input id="chat-message-input" type="text">
    <input id="chat-message-submit" type="submit" value="Send">
  </div>
{% endblock %}

{% block domready %}
{% endblock %}
```

This is the template for the course chat room. In this template, you extend the `base.html` template of your project and fill its `content` block. In the template, you define a `<div>` HTML element with the `chat` ID that you will use to display the chat messages sent by the user and by other students. You also define a second `<div>` element with a `text` input and a submit button that will allow the user to send messages. You include the `domready` block defined by the `base.html` template, which you are going to implement later using JavaScript, to establish a connection with a WebSocket and send or receive messages.

Run the development server and open `http://127.0.0.1:8000/chat/room/1/` in your browser, replacing `1` with the `id` of an existing course in the database. Access the chat room with a logged-in user who is enrolled on the course. You will see the following screen:

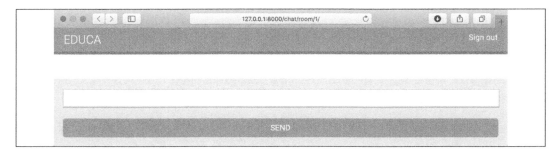

Figure 13.1: The course chat room page

This is the course chat room screen that students will use to discuss topics within a course.

Deactivating the per-site cache

In *Chapter 11*, *Rendering and Caching Content*, you added a site-wide cache to your Django project. Now, you will need to follow a more granular approach for caching to prevent the chat room pages from being cached. You will deactivate the per-site cache to avoid site-wide caching and only use caching where needed.

Edit the `settings.py` file and comment out the `UpdateCacheMiddleware` and `FetchFromCacheMiddleware` classes of the `MIDDLEWARE` setting, as follows:

```
MIDDLEWARE = [
    'django.middleware.security.SecurityMiddleware',
    'django.contrib.sessions.middleware.SessionMiddleware',
    # 'django.middleware.cache.UpdateCacheMiddleware',
    'django.middleware.common.CommonMiddleware',
    # 'django.middleware.cache.FetchFromCacheMiddleware',
    # ...
]
```

You have deactivated the per-site cache in your project to avoid the new chat room view from being cached. Next, you will learn how to add Channels to your Django project to implement a real-time chat server.

Real-time Django with Channels

You are building a chat server to provide students with a chat room for each course. Students enrolled on a course will be able to access the course chat room and exchange messages. This functionality requires real-time communication between the server and the client. The client should be able to connect to the chat and send or receive data at any time. There are several ways you could implement this feature using AJAX polling or long polling in combination with storing the messages in your database or Redis. However, there is no efficient way to implement a chat server using a standard synchronous web application. You are going to build a chat server using asynchronous communication through ASGI.

Asynchronous applications using ASGI

Django is usually deployed using **Web Server Gateway Interface** (**WSGI**), which is the standard interface for Python applications to handle HTTP requests. However, to work with asynchronous applications, you need to use another interface called ASGI, which can handle WebSocket requests as well. ASGI is the emerging Python standard for asynchronous web servers and applications.

Django 3 comes with support for running asynchronous Python through ASGI, but it does not yet support asynchronous views or middleware. However, as mentioned, Channels extends Django to handle not only HTTP, but also protocols that require long-running connections, such as WebSockets and chatbots.

WebSockets provide full-duplex communication by establishing a persistent, open, bidirectional **Transmission Control Protocol** (**TCP**) connection between servers and clients. You are going to use WebSockets to implement your chat server.

You can find more information about deploying Django with ASGI at `https://docs.djangoproject.com/en/3.0/howto/deployment/asgi/`.

The request/response cycle using Channels

It's important to understand the differences in a request cycle between a standard synchronous request cycle and a Channels implementation. The following schema shows the request cycle of a synchronous Django setup:

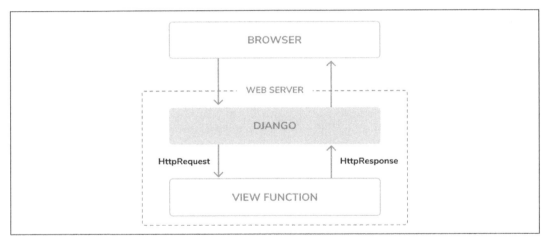

Figure 13.2: The Django request/response cycle

When an HTTP request is sent by the browser to the web server, Django handles the request and passes the `HttpRequest` object to the corresponding view. The view processes the request and returns an `HttpResponse` object that is sent back to the browser as an HTTP response. There is no mechanism to maintain an open connection or send data to the browser without an associated HTTP request.

The following schema shows the request cycle of a Django project using Channels with WebSockets:

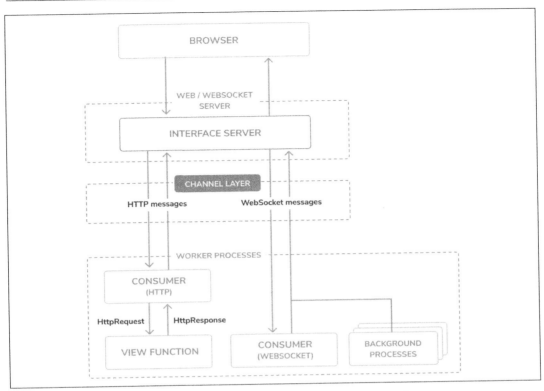

Figure 13.3: The Django Channels request/response cycle

Channels replaces Django's request/response cycle with messages that are sent across channels. HTTP requests are still routed to view functions using Django, but they get routed over channels. This allows for WebSockets message handling as well, where you have producers and consumers that exchange messages across a channel layer. Channels preserves Django's synchronous architecture, allowing you to choose between writing synchronous code and asynchronous code, or a combination of both.

Installing Channels

You are going to add Channels to your project and set up the required basic ASGI application routing for it to manage HTTP requests.

Install Channels in your virtual environment with the following command:

```
pip install channels==2.4.0
```

Edit the `settings.py` file of the `educa` project and add `channels` to the `INSTALLED_APPS` setting as follows:

```
INSTALLED_APPS = [
    # ...
    'channels',
]
```

The `channels` application is now activated in your project.

Channels expects you to define a single root application that will be executed for all requests. You can define the root application by adding the `ASGI_APPLICATION` setting to your project. This is similar to the `ROOT_URLCONF` setting that points to the base URL patterns of your project. You can place the root application anywhere in your project, but it is recommended to put it in a project-level file named `routing.py`.

Create a new file inside the `educa` project directory next to the `settings.py` file and name it `routing.py`.

Add the following code to it:

```
from channels.routing import ProtocolTypeRouter

application = ProtocolTypeRouter({
    # empty for now
})
```

Then, add the following line to the `settings.py` file of your project:

```
ASGI_APPLICATION = 'educa.routing.application'
```

In the previous code, you define the main ASGI application that will be executed when serving your Django project through ASGI. You use the `ProtocolTypeRouter` class provided by Channels as the main entry point of your routing system. `ProtocolTypeRouter` takes a dictionary that maps communication types like `http` or `websocket` to ASGI applications. You instantiate this class with an empty dictionary that later you will fill with a route for your chat application WebSocket consumer.

When Channels is added to the `INSTALLED_APPS` setting, it takes control over the `runserver` command, replacing the standard Django development server. Besides handling URL routing to Django views for synchronous requests, the Channels development server also manages routes to WebSocket consumers.

Start the development server using the following command:

```
python manage.py runserver
```

You will see output similar to the following:

```
Watching for file changes with StatReloader
Performing system checks...

System check identified no issues (0 silenced).
February 06, 2020 - 23:12:33
Django version 3.0, using settings 'educa.settings'
Starting ASGI/Channels version 2.4.0 development server at
http://127.0.0.1:8000/
Quit the server with CONTROL-C.
```

Check that the output contains the line `Starting ASGI/Channels version 2.4.0 development server`. This line confirms that you are using the Channels development server, which is capable of managing synchronous and asynchronous requests, instead of the standard Django development server. HTTP requests continue to behave the same as before, but they get routed over *channels*.

Now that Channels is installed in your project, you can build the chat server for courses. In order to implement the chat server for your project, you will need to take the following steps:

1. **Set up a consumer**: Consumers are individual pieces of code that can handle WebSockets in a very similar way to traditional HTTP views. You will build a consumer to read and write messages to a communication channel.

2. **Configure routing**: Channels provides routing classes that allow you to combine and stack your consumers. You will configure URL routing for your chat consumer.

3. **Implement a WebSocket client**: When the student accesses the chat room, you will connect to the WebSocket from the browser and send or receive messages using JavaScript.

4. **Enable a channel layer**: Channel layers allow you to talk between different instances of an application. They're a useful part of making a distributed real-time application. You will set up a channel layer using Redis.

Writing a consumer

Consumers are the equivalent of Django views for asynchronous applications. As mentioned, they handle WebSockets in a very similar way to how traditional views handle HTTP requests. Consumers are ASGI applications that can handle messages, notifications, and other things. Unlike Django views, consumers are built for long-running communication. URLs are mapped to consumers through routing classes that allow you to combine and stack consumers.

Let's implement a basic consumer that is able to accept WebSocket connections and echoes every message it receives from the WebSocket back to it. This initial functionality will allow the student to send messages to the consumer and receive back the messages it sends.

Create a new file inside the `chat` application directory and name it `consumers.py`. Add the following code to it:

```
import json
from channels.generic.websocket import WebsocketConsumer

class ChatConsumer(WebsocketConsumer):
    def connect(self):
        # accept connection
        self.accept()

    def disconnect(self, close_code):
        pass

    # receive message from WebSocket
    def receive(self, text_data):
        text_data_json = json.loads(text_data)
        message = text_data_json['message']
        # send message to WebSocket
        self.send(text_data=json.dumps({'message': message}))
```

This is the `ChatConsumer` consumer. This class inherits from the Channels `WebsocketConsumer` class to implement a basic WebSocket consumer. In this consumer, you implement the following methods:

- `connnect()`: Called when a new connection is received. You accept any connection with `self.accept()`. You can also reject a connection by calling `self.close()`.
- `disconnect()`: Called when the socket closes. You use `pass` because you don't need to implement any action when a client closes the connection.

- `receive()`: Called whenever data is received. You expect text to be received as `text_data` (this could also be `binary_data` for binary data). You treat the text data received as JSON. Therefore, you use `json.loads()` to load the received JSON data into a Python dictionary. You access the `message` key, which you expect to be present in the JSON structure received. To echo the message, you send the message back to the WebSocket with `self.send()`, transforming it in JSON format again through `json.dumps()`.

The initial version of your `ChatConsumer` consumer accepts any WebSocket connection and echoes to the WebSocket client every message it receives. Note that the consumer does not broadcast messages to other clients yet. You will build this functionality by implementing a channel layer later.

Routing

You need to define a URL to route connections to the `ChatConsumer` consumer you have implemented. Channels provides routing classes that allow you to combine and stack consumers to dispatch based on what the connection is. You can think of them as the URL routing system of Django for asynchronous applications.

Create a new file inside the `chat` application directory and name it `routing.py`. Add the following code to it:

```
from django.urls import import re_path
from . import consumers

websocket_urlpatterns = [
    re_path(r'ws/chat/room/(?P<course_id>\d+)/$', consumers.
ChatConsumer),
]
```

In this code, you map a URL pattern with the `ChatConsumer` class that you defined in the `chat/consumers.py` file. You use Django's `re_path` to define the path with regular expressions. The URL includes an integer parameter called `course_id`. This parameter will be available in the scope of the consumer and will allow you to identify the course chat room that the user is connecting to.

 It is a good practice to prepend WebSocket URLs with `/ws/` to differentiate them from URLs used for standard synchronous HTTP requests. This also simplifies the production setup when an HTTP server routes requests based on the path.

Edit the global `routing.py` file located next to the `settings.py` file so that it looks like this:

```python
from channels.auth import AuthMiddlewareStack
from channels.routing import ProtocolTypeRouter, URLRouter
import chat.routing

application = ProtocolTypeRouter({
    'websocket': AuthMiddlewareStack(
        URLRouter(
            chat.routing.websocket_urlpatterns
        )
    ),
})
```

In this code, you use `URLRouter` to map `websocket` connections to the URL patterns defined in the `websocket_urlpatterns` list of the `chat` application `routing` file. The standard `ProtocolTypeRouter` router automatically maps HTTP requests to the standard Django views if no specific `http` mapping is provided. You also use `AuthMiddlewareStack`. The `AuthMiddlewareStack` class provided by Channels supports standard Django authentication, where the user details are stored in the session. You plan to access the user instance in the scope of the consumer to identify the user who sends a message.

Implementing the WebSocket client

So far, you have created the `course_chat_room` view and its corresponding template for students to access the course chat room. You have implemented a WebSocket consumer for the chat server and tied it with URL routing. Now, you need to build a WebSocket client to establish a connection with the WebSocket in the course chat room template and be able to send/receive messages.

You are going to implement the WebSocket client with JavaScript to open and maintain a connection in the browser. You will use jQuery for interaction with Document Object Model (DOM) elements, since you already loaded it in the base template of the project.

Edit the `chat/room.html` template of the `chat` application and modify the `domready` block, as follows:

```
{% block domready %}
  var url = 'ws://' + window.location.host +
            '/ws/chat/room/' + '{{ course.id }}/';
  var chatSocket = new WebSocket(url);
{% endblock %}
```

You define a URL with the WebSocket protocol, which looks like `ws://` (or `wss://` for secure WebSockets, just like `https://`). You build the URL using the current location of the browser, which you obtain from `window.location.host`. The rest of the URL is built with the path for the chat room URL pattern that you defined in the `routing.py` file of the `chat` application.

You write the whole URL instead of building it via its name because Channels does not provide a way to reverse URLs. You use the current course `id` to generate the URL for the current course and store the URL in a new variable named `url`.

You then open a WebSocket connection to the stored URL using `new WebSocket(url)`. You assign the instantiated WebSocket client object to the new variable `chatSocket`.

You have created a WebSocket consumer, you have included routing for it, and you have implemented a basic WebSocket client. Let's try the initial version of your chat.

Start the development server using the following command:

```
python manage.py runserver
```

Open the URL `http://127.0.0.1:8000/chat/room/1/` in your browser, replacing `1` with the `id` of an existing course in the database. Take a look at the console output. Besides the HTTP GET requests for the page and its static files, you should see two lines including `WebSocket HANDSHAKING` and `WebSocket CONNECT`, like the following output:

```
HTTP GET /chat/room/1/ 200 [0.02, 127.0.0.1:57141]
HTTP GET /static/css/base.css 200 [0.01, 127.0.0.1:57141]
WebSocket HANDSHAKING /ws/chat/room/1/ [127.0.0.1:57144]
WebSocket CONNECT /ws/chat/room/1/ [127.0.0.1:57144]
```

The Channels development server listens for incoming socket connections using a standard TCP socket. The handshake is the bridge from HTTP to WebSockets. In the handshake, details of the connection are negotiated and either party can close the connection before completion. Remember that you are using `self.accept()` to accept any connection in the `connect()` method of the `ChatConsumer` class implemented in the `consumers.py` file of the `chat` application. The connection is accepted and therefore you see the `WebSocket CONNECT` message in the console.

If you use the browser developer tools to track network connections, you can also see information for the WebSocket connection that has been established.

It should look like the following screenshot:

Figure 13.4: The browser developer tools showing that the WebSocket connection has been established

Now that you are able to connect to the WebSocket, it's time to interact with it. You will implement the methods to handle common events, such as receiving a message and closing the connection. Edit the `chat/room.html` template of the chat application and modify the `domready` block, as follows:

```
{% block domready %}
  var url = 'ws://' + window.location.host +
            '/ws/chat/room/' + '{{ course.id }}/';
  var chatSocket = new WebSocket(url);

  chatSocket.onmessage = function(e) {
    var data = JSON.parse(e.data);
    var message = data.message;

    var $chat = $('#chat');
    $chat.append('<div class="message">' + message + '</div>');
    $chat.scrollTop($chat[0].scrollHeight);
  };

  chatSocket.onclose = function(e) {
    console.error('Chat socket closed unexpectedly');
  };
{% endblock %}
```

In this code, you define the following events for the WebSocket client:

- `onmessage`: Fired when data is received through the WebSocket. You parse the message, which you expect in JSON format, and access its `message` attribute. You then append a new `<div>` element with the message to the HTML element with the `chat` ID. This will add new messages to the chat log, while keeping all previous messages that have been added to the log. You scroll the chat log `<div>` to the bottom to ensure that the new message gets visibility. You achieve this by scrolling to the total scrollable height of the chat log, which can be obtained by accessing its `srollHeight` attribute.

- `onclose`: Fired when the connection with the WebSocket is closed. You don't expect to close the connection and therefore you write the error `Chat socket closed unexpectedly` to the console log if this happens.

You have implemented the action to display the message when a new message is received. You need to implement the functionality to send messages to the socket as well.

Edit the chat/room.html template of the chat application and add the following JavaScript code to the bottom of the domready block:

```
var $input = $('#chat-message-input');
var $submit = $('#chat-message-submit');

$submit.click(function() {
  var message = $input.val();
  if(message) {
    // send message in JSON format
    chatSocket.send(JSON.stringify({'message': message}));

    // clear input
    $input.val('');

    // return focus
    $input.focus();
  }
});
```

In this code, you define a function for the click event of the submit button, which you select with the ID chat-message-submit. When the button is clicked, you perform the following actions:

1. You read the message entered by the user from the value of the text input element with the ID chat-message-input

2. You check whether the message has any content with if(message)

3. If the user has entered a message, you form JSON content such as {'message': 'string entered by the user'} by using JSON.stringify()

4. You send the JSON content through the WebSocket, calling the send() method of chatSocket client

5. You clear the contents of the text input by setting its value to an empty string with $input.val('')

6. You return the focus to the text input with $input.focus() so that the user can write a new message straightaway

The user is now able to send messages using the text input and by clicking the submit button.

In order to improve the user experience, you will give focus to the text input as soon as the page loads so that the user can type directly in it. You will also capture keyboard key pressed events to identify the *Enter/Return* key and fire the `click` event on the submit button. The user will be able to either click the button or press the *Enter/Return* key to send a message.

Edit the `chat/room.html` template of the `chat` application and add the following JavaScript code to the bottom of the `domready` block:

```
$input.focus();
$input.keyup(function(e) {
  if (e.which === 13) {
    // submit with enter / return key
    $submit.click();
  }
});
```

In this code, you give the focus to the text input. You also define a function for the `keyup()` event of the input. For any key that the user presses, you check whether its key code is `13`. This is the key code that corresponds to the *Enter/Return* key. You can use the resource `https://keycode.info` to identify the key code for any key. If the *Enter/Return* key is pressed, you fire the `click` event on the submit button to send the message to the WebSocket.

The complete `domready` block of the `chat/room.html` template should now look like this:

```
{% block domready %}
  var url = 'ws://' + window.location.host +
            '/ws/chat/room/' + '{{ course.id }}/';
  var chatSocket = new WebSocket(url);

  chatSocket.onmessage = function(e) {
    var data = JSON.parse(e.data);
    var message = data.message;

    var $chat = $('#chat');
    $chat.append('<div class="message">' + message + '</div>');
    $chat.scrollTop($chat[0].scrollHeight);
  };

  chatSocket.onclose = function(e) {
    console.error('Chat socket closed unexpectedly');
  };

  var $input = $('#chat-message-input');
```

```
var $submit = $('#chat-message-submit');

$submit.click(function() {
  var message = $input.val();
  if(message) {
    // send message in JSON format
    chatSocket.send(JSON.stringify({'message': message}));

    // clear input
    $input.val('');

    // return focus
    $input.focus();
  }
});

$input.focus();
$input.keyup(function(e) {
  if (e.which === 13) {
    // submit with enter / return key
    $submit.click();
  }
});
{% endblock %}
```

Open the URL http://127.0.0.1:8000/chat/room/1/ in your browser, replacing 1 with the id of an existing course in the database. With a logged-in user who is enrolled on the course, write some text in the input field and click the send button or press the *Enter* key. You will see that your message appears in the chat log:

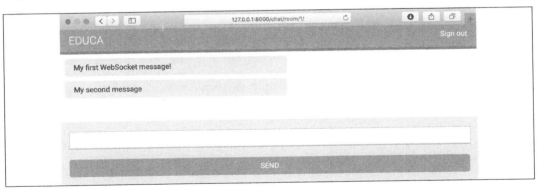

Figure 13.5: The chat room page, including messages sent through the WebSocket

Great! The message has been sent through the WebSocket and the ChatConsumer consumer has received the message and has sent it back through the WebSocket. The chatSocket client has received a message event and the onmessage function has been fired, adding the message to the chat log.

You have implemented the functionality with a WebSocket consumer and a WebSocket client to establish client/server communication and be able to send or receive events. However, the chat server is not able to broadcast messages to other clients. If you open a second browser tab and enter a message, the message will not appear on the first tab. In order to build communication between consumers, you have to enable a channel layer.

Enabling a channel layer

Channel layers allow you to communicate between different instances of an application. A channel layer is the transport mechanism that allows multiple consumer instances to communicate with each other and with other parts of Django.

In your chat server, you plan to have multiple instances of the ChatConsumer consumer for the same course chat room. Each student who joins the chat room will instantiate the WebSocket client in their browser, and that will open a connection with an instance of the WebSocket consumer. You need a common channel layer to distribute messages between consumers.

Channels and groups

Channel layers provide two abstractions to manage communications: channels and groups:

- **Channel**: You can think of a channel as an inbox where messages can be sent to or as a task queue. Each channel has a name. Messages are sent to a channel by anyone who knows the channel name and then given to consumers listening on that channel.

- **Group**: Multiple channels can be grouped into a group. Each group has a name. A channel can be added or removed from a group by anyone who knows the group name. Using the group name, you can also send a message to all channels in the group.

You will work with channel groups to implement the chat server. By creating a channel group for each course chat room, the ChatConsumer instances will be able to communicate with each other.

Setting up a channel layer with Redis

Redis is the preferred option for a channel layer, though Channels has support for other types of channel layers. Redis works as the communication store for the channel layer. Remember that you already used Redis in *Chapter 6, Tracking User Actions*, and in *Chapter 9, Extending Your Shop*.

If you haven't installed Redis yet, you can find installation instructions in *Chapter 6, Tracking User Actions*.

In order to use Redis as a channel layer, you have to install the channels-redis package. Install channels-redis in your virtual environment with the following command:

```
pip install channels-redis==2.4.2
```

Edit the `settings.py` file of the `educa` project and add the following code to it:

```
CHANNEL_LAYERS = {
    'default': {
        'BACKEND': 'channels_redis.core.RedisChannelLayer',
        'CONFIG': {
            'hosts': [('127.0.0.1', 6379)],
        },
    },
}
```

The `CHANNEL_LAYERS` setting defines the configuration for the channel layers available to the project. You define a default channel layer using the `RedisChannelLayer` backend provided by channels-redis and specify the host `127.0.0.1` and the port `6379` on which Redis is running.

Let's try the channel layer. Initialize the Redis server using the following command from the shell in your Redis directory:

```
src/redis-server
```

Open the Django shell using the following command:

```
python manage.py shell
```

To verify that the channel layer can communicate with Redis, write the following code to send a message to a test channel named `test_channel` and receive it back:

```
>>> import channels.layers
>>> from asgiref.sync import async_to_sync
>>> channel_layer = channels.layers.get_channel_layer()
>>> async_to_sync(channel_layer.send)('test_channel', {'message': 'hello'})
>>> async_to_sync(channel_layer.receive)('test_channel')
```

You should get the following output:

```
{'message': 'hello'}
```

In the previous code, you send a message to a test channel through the channel layer, and then you retrieve it from the channel layer. The channel layer is communicating successfully with Redis.

Updating the consumer to broadcast messages

You will edit the ChatConsumer consumer to use the channel layer. You will use a channel group for each course chat room. Therefore, you will use the course id to build the group name. ChatConsumer instances will know the group name and will be able to communicate with each other.

Edit the consumers.py file of the chat application, import the async_to_sync() function, and modify the connect() method of the ChatConsumer class, as follows:

```python
import json
from channels.generic.websocket import WebsocketConsumer
from asgiref.sync import async_to_sync

class ChatConsumer(WebsocketConsumer):
    def connect(self):
        self.id = self.scope['url_route']['kwargs']['course_id']
        self.room_group_name = 'chat_%s' % self.id
        # join room group
        async_to_sync(self.channel_layer.group_add)(
            self.room_group_name,
            self.channel_name
        )
        # accept connection
        self.accept()

    # ...
```

In this code, you import the async_to_sync() helper function to wrap calls to asynchronous channel layer methods. ChatConsumer is a synchronous WebsocketConsumer consumer, but it needs to call asynchronous methods of the channel layer.

In the new connect() method, you perform the following tasks:

1. You retrieve the course id from the scope to know the course that the chat room is associated with. You access self.scope['url_route']['kwargs ']['course_id'] to retrieve the course_id parameter from the URL. Every consumer has a scope with information about its connection, arguments passed by the URL, and the authenticated user, if any.

2. You build the group name with the `id` of the course that the group corresponds to. Remember that you will have a channel group for each course chat room. You store the group name in the `room_group_name` attribute of the consumer.

3. You join the group by adding the current channel to the group. You obtain the channel name from the `channel_name` attribute of the consumer. You use the `group_add` method of the channel layer to add the channel to the group. You use the `async_to_sync()` wrapper to use the channel layer asynchronous method.

4. You keep the `self.accept()` call to accept the WebSocket connection.

When the `ChatConsumer` consumer receives a new WebSocket connection, it adds the channel to the group associated with the course in its scope. The consumer is now able to receive any messages sent to the group.

In the same `consumers.py` file, modify the `disconnect()` method of the `ChatConsumer` class, as follows:

```python
class ChatConsumer(WebsocketConsumer):
    # ...

    def disconnect(self, close_code):
        # leave room group
        async_to_sync(self.channel_layer.group_discard)(
            self.room_group_name,
            self.channel_name
        )

    # ...
```

When the connection is closed, you call the `group_discard()` method of the channel layer to leave the group. You use the `async_to_sync()` wrapper to use the channel layer asynchronous method.

In the same `consumers.py` file, modify the `receive()` method of the `ChatConsumer` class, as follows:

```python
class ChatConsumer(WebsocketConsumer):
    # ...

    # receive message from WebSocket
    def receive(self, text_data):
        text_data_json = json.loads(text_data)
        message = text_data_json['message']
```

```
# send message to room group
async_to_sync(self.channel_layer.group_send)(
    self.room_group_name,
    {
        'type': 'chat_message',
        'message': message,
    }
)
```

When you receive a message from the WebSocket connection, instead of sending the message to the associated channel, you now send the message to the group. You do this by calling the `group_send()` method of the channel layer. You use the `async_to_sync()` wrapper to use the channel layer asynchronous method. You pass the following information in the event sent to the group:

- `type`: The event type. This is a special key that corresponds to the name of the method that should be invoked on consumers that receive the event. You can implement a method in the consumer named the same as the message type so that it gets executed every time a message with that specific type is received.

- `message`: The actual message you are sending.

In the same `consumers.py` file, add a new `chat_message()` method in the `ChatConsumer` class, as follows:

```
class ChatConsumer(WebsocketConsumer):
    # ...

    # receive message from room group
    def chat_message(self, event):
        # Send message to WebSocket
        self.send(text_data=json.dumps(event))
```

You name this method `chat_message()` to match the `type` key that is sent to the channel group when a message is received from the WebSocket. When a message with type `chat_message` is sent to the group, all consumers subscribed to the group will receive the message and will execute the `chat_message()` method. In the `chat_message()` method, you send the event message received to the WebSocket.

The complete `consumers.py` file should now look like this:

```
import json
from channels.generic.websocket import WebsocketConsumer
from asgiref.sync import async_to_sync
```

```python
class ChatConsumer(WebsocketConsumer):
    def connect(self):
        self.id = self.scope['url_route']['kwargs']['course_id']
        self.room_group_name = 'chat_%s' % self.id
        # join room group
        async_to_sync(self.channel_layer.group_add)(
            self.room_group_name,
            self.channel_name
        )
        # accept connection
        self.accept()

    def disconnect(self, close_code):
        # leave room group
        async_to_sync(self.channel_layer.group_discard)(
            self.room_group_name,
            self.channel_name
        )

    # receive message from WebSocket
    def receive(self, text_data):
        text_data_json = json.loads(text_data)
        message = text_data_json['message']

        # send message to room group
        async_to_sync(self.channel_layer.group_send)(
            self.room_group_name,
            {
                'type': 'chat_message',
                'message': message,
            }
        )

    # receive message from room group
    def chat_message(self, event):
        # send message to WebSocket
        self.send(text_data=json.dumps(event))
```

You have implemented a channel layer in `ChatConsumer`, allowing consumers to broadcast messages and communicate with each other.

Run the development server with the following command:

```
python manage.py runserver
```

Open the URL `http://127.0.0.1:8000/chat/room/1/` in your browser, replacing `1` with the `id` of an existing course in the database. Write a message and send it. Then, open a second browser window and access the same URL. Send a message from each browser window.

The result should look like this:

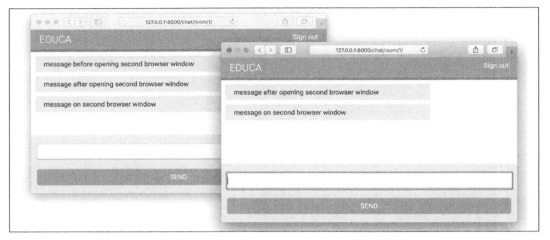

Figure 13.6: The chat room page with messages sent from different browser windows

You will see that the first message is only displayed in the first browser window. When you open a second browser window, messages sent in any of the browser windows are displayed in both of them. When you open a new browser window and access the chat room URL, a new WebSocket connection is established between the JavaScript WebSocket client in the browser and the WebSocket consumer in the server. Each channel gets added to the group associated with the course id passed through the URL to the consumer. Messages are sent to the group and received by all consumers.

Adding context to the messages

Now that messages can be exchanged between all users in a chat room, you probably want to display who sent which message and when it was sent. Let's add some context to the messages.

Edit the `consumers.py` file of the `chat` application and implement the following changes:

```
import json
from channels.generic.websocket import WebsocketConsumer
from asgiref.sync import async_to_sync
```

```python
from django.utils import timezone

class ChatConsumer(WebsocketConsumer):
    def connect(self):
        self.user = self.scope['user']
        self.id = self.scope['url_route']['kwargs']['course_id']
        self.room_group_name = 'chat_%s' % self.id
        # join room group
        async_to_sync(self.channel_layer.group_add)(
            self.room_group_name,
            self.channel_name
        )
        # accept connection
        self.accept()

    def disconnect(self, close_code):
        # leave room group
        async_to_sync(self.channel_layer.group_discard)(
            self.room_group_name,
            self.channel_name
        )

    # receive message from WebSocket
    def receive(self, text_data):
        text_data_json = json.loads(text_data)
        message = text_data_json['message']
        now = timezone.now()

        # send message to room group
        async_to_sync(self.channel_layer.group_send)(
            self.room_group_name,
            {
                'type': 'chat_message',
                'message': message,
                'user': self.user.username,
                'datetime': now.isoformat(),
            }
        )

    # receive message from room group
    def chat_message(self, event):
        # send message to WebSocket
        self.send(text_data=json.dumps(event))
```

You now import the `timezone` module provided by Django. In the `connect()` method of the consumer, you retrieve the current user from the scope with `self.scope['user']` and store them in a new `user` attribute of the consumer. When the consumer receives a message through the WebSocket, it gets the current time using `timezone.now()` and passes the current `user` and `datetime` in ISO 8601 format along with the message in the event sent to the channel group.

Edit the `chat/room.html` template of the `chat` application and find the following lines:

```
var data = JSON.parse(e.data);
var message = data.message;

var $chat = $('#chat');
$chat.append('<div class="message">' + message + '</div>');
```

Replace those lines with the following code:

```
var data = JSON.parse(e.data);
var message = data.message;

var dateOptions = {hour: 'numeric', minute: 'numeric', hour12: true};
var datetime = new Date(data['datetime']).toLocaleString('en',
dateOptions);

var isMe = data.user === '{{ request.user }}';
var source = isMe ? 'me' : 'other';
var name = isMe ? 'Me' : data.user;

var $chat = $('#chat');
$chat.append('<div class="message ' + source + '">' +
             '<strong>' + name + '</strong> ' +
             '<span class="date">' + datetime + '</span><br>' +
             message +
             '</div>');
```

In this code, you implement these changes:

1. You now convert the datetime received in the message to a JavaScript `Date` object and format it with a specific locale.

2. You retrieve the user received in the message and make a comparison with two different variables as helpers to identify the user.

3. The variable `source` gets the value `me` if the user sending the message is the current user, or `other` otherwise. You obtain the username using Django's template language with `{{ request.user }}` to check whether the message originated from the current user or another user. You then use the `source` value as a `class` of the main `<div>` element to differentiate messages sent by the current user from messages sent by others. Different CSS styles are applied based on the `class` attribute.

4. The variable `name` gets the value `Me` if the user sending the message is the current user or the name of the user sending the message otherwise. You use it to display the name of the user sending the message.

5. You use the username and the datetime in the message that you append to the chat log.

Open the URL `http://127.0.0.1:8000/chat/room/1/` in your browser, replacing `1` with the `id` of an existing course in the database. With a logged-in user who is enrolled on the course, write a message and send it.

Then, open a second browser window in incognito mode to prevent the use of the same session. Log in with a different user, also enrolled on the same course, and send a message.

You will be able to exchange messages using the two different users and see the user and time, with a clear distinction between messages sent by the user and messages sent by others. The conversation between two users should look similar to the following one:

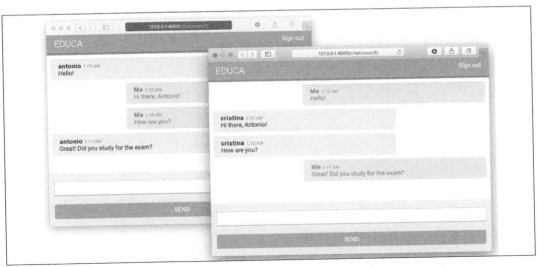

Figure 13.7: The chat room page with messages from two different user sessions

Modifying the consumer to be fully asynchronous

The ChatConsumer you have implemented inherits from the base WebsocketConsumer class, which is synchronous. Synchronous consumers are convenient for accessing Django models and calling regular synchronous I/O functions. However, asynchronous consumers present a higher performance, since they don't require additional threads when handling requests. Since you are using the asynchronous channel layer functions, you can easily rewrite the ChatConsumer class to be asynchronous.

Edit the consumers.py file of the chat application and implement the following changes:

```python
import json
from channels.generic.websocket import AsyncWebsocketConsumer
from asgiref.sync import async_to_sync
from django.utils import timezone


class ChatConsumer(AsyncWebsocketConsumer):
    async def connect(self):
        self.user = self.scope['user']
        self.id = self.scope['url_route']['kwargs']['course_id']
        self.room_group_name = 'chat_%s' % self.id
        # join room group
        await self.channel_layer.group_add(
            self.room_group_name,
            self.channel_name
        )
        # accept connection
        await self.accept()

    async def disconnect(self, close_code):
        # leave room group
        await self.channel_layer.group_discard(
            self.room_group_name,
            self.channel_name
        )

    # receive message from WebSocket
    async def receive(self, text_data):
        text_data_json = json.loads(text_data)
        message = text_data_json['message']
        now = timezone.now()
```

```
# send message to room group
await self.channel_layer.group_send(
    self.room_group_name,
    {
        'type': 'chat_message',
        'message': message,
        'user': self.user.username,
        'datetime': now.isoformat(),
    }
)

# receive message from room group
async def chat_message(self, event):
    # send message to WebSocket
    await self.send(text_data=json.dumps(event))
```

You have implemented the following changes:

- The `ChatConsumer` consumer now inherits from the `AsyncWebsocketConsumer` class to implement asynchronous calls
- You have changed the definition of all methods from `def` to `async def`
- You use `await` to call asynchronous functions that perform I/O operations
- You no longer use the `async_to_sync()` helper function when calling methods on the channel layer

Open the URL `http://127.0.0.1:8000/chat/room/1` with two different browser windows again and verify that the chat server still works. The chat server is now fully asynchronous!

Integrating the chat application with existing views

The chat server is now fully implemented and students enrolled on a course are able to communicate with each other. Let's add a link for students to join the chat room for each course.

Edit the `students/course/detail.html` template of the `students` application and add the following `<h3>` HTML element code at the bottom of the `<div class="contents">` element:

```
<div class="contents">
    ...
```

```
<h3>
  <a href="{% url "chat:course_chat_room" object.id %}">
    Course chat room
  </a>
</h3>
</div>
```

Open the browser and access any course that the student is enrolled on to view the course contents. The sidebar will now contain a **Course chat room** link that points to the course chat room view. If you click on it, you will enter the chat room.

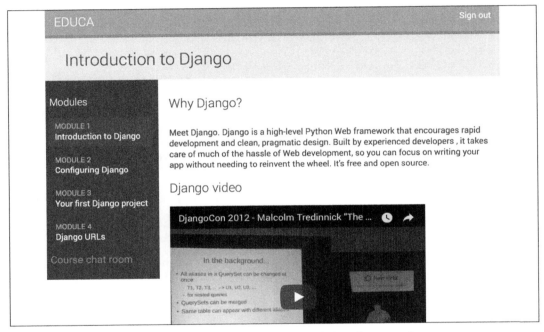

Figure 13.8: The course detail page, including a link to the course chat room

Summary

In this chapter, you learned how to create a chat server using Channels. You implemented a WebSocket consumer and client. You also enabled communication between consumers using a channel layer with Redis and modified the consumer to be fully asynchronous.

The next chapter will teach you how to build a production environment for your Django project using NGINX, uWSGI, and Daphne. You will also learn how to implement a custom middleware and create custom management commands.

14

Going Live

In the previous chapter, you built a real-time chat server for students using Django Channels. Now that you have created a fully functional e-learning platform, you need to set up a production environment on an online server so that it can be accessed over the Internet. Until now, you have been working in a development environment, using the Django development server to run your site. In this chapter, you will learn how to set up a production environment that is able to serve your Django project in a secure and efficient manner.

This chapter will cover the following topics:

- Configuring a production environment
- Creating a custom middleware
- Implementing custom management commands

Creating a production environment

It's time to deploy your Django project in a production environment. You are going to follow these steps to get your project live:

- Configure project settings for a production environment
- Use a PostgreSQL database
- Set up a web server with uWSGI and NGINX
- Serve static assets through NGINX
- Secure connections using SSL
- Use Daphne to serve Django Channels

Managing settings for multiple environments

In real-world projects, you will have to deal with multiple environments. You will have at least a local and a production environment, but you could have other environments as well, such as testing or preproduction environments. Some project settings will be common to all environments, but others will have to be overridden per environment. Let's set up project settings for multiple environments, while keeping everything neatly organized.

Create a `settings/` directory next to the `settings.py` file of the `educa` project. Rename the `settings.py` file to `base.py` and move it into the new `settings/` directory. Create the following additional files inside the `settings/` folder so that the new directory looks as follows:

```
settings/
    __init__.py
    base.py
    local.py
    pro.py
```

These files are as follows:

- `base.py`: The base settings file that contains common settings (previously `settings.py`)
- `local.py`: Custom settings for your local environment
- `pro.py`: Custom settings for the production environment

Edit the `settings/base.py` file and replace the following line:

```
BASE_DIR = os.path.dirname(os.path.dirname(os.path.abspath(__file__)))
```

with the following one:

```
BASE_DIR = os.path.dirname(os.path.dirname(os.path.abspath(
                          os.path.join(__file__, os.pardir))))
```

You have moved your settings files to a directory one level lower, so you need BASE_DIR to point to the parent directory to be correct. You achieve this by pointing to the parent directory with `os.pardir`.

Edit the `settings/local.py` file and add the following lines of code:

```
from .base import *

DEBUG = True

DATABASES = {
```

```
    'default': {
        'ENGINE': 'django.db.backends.sqlite3',
        'NAME': os.path.join(BASE_DIR, 'db.sqlite3'),
    }
}
```

This is the settings file for your local environment. You import all settings defined in the `base.py` file and you only define specific settings for this environment. You copy the DEBUG and DATABASES settings from the `base.py` file, since these will be set per environment. You can remove the DATABASES and DEBUG settings from the `base.py` settings file.

Edit the `settings/pro.py` file and make it look as follows:

```
from .base import *

DEBUG = False

ADMINS = (
    ('Antonio M', 'email@mydomain.com'),
)

ALLOWED_HOSTS = ['*']

DATABASES = {
    'default': {
    }
}
```

These are the settings for the production environment. Let's take a closer look at each of them:

- DEBUG: Setting DEBUG to False should be mandatory for any production environment. Failing to do so will result in the traceback information and sensitive configuration data being exposed to everyone.

- ADMINS: When DEBUG is False and a view raises an exception, all information will be sent by email to the people listed in the ADMINS setting. Make sure that you replace the name/email tuple with your own information.

- ALLOWED_HOSTS: Django will only allow the hosts included in this list to serve the application. This is a security measure. You include the asterisk symbol, *, to refer to all hostnames. You will limit the hostnames that can be used for serving the application later.

- DATABASES: You just keep this setting empty. We are going to cover the database setup for production later.

> When handling multiple environments, create a base settings file and a settings file for each environment. Environment settings files should inherit the common settings and override environment-specific settings.

You have placed the project settings in a different location than the default `settings.py` file. You will not be able to execute any commands with the `manage.py` tool unless you specify the settings module to use. You will need to add a `--settings` flag when you run management commands from the shell or set a `DJANGO_SETTINGS_MODULE` environment variable.

Open the shell and run the following command:

```
export DJANGO_SETTINGS_MODULE=educa.settings.pro
```

This will set the `DJANGO_SETTINGS_MODULE` environment variable for the current shell session. If you want to avoid executing this command for each new shell, add this command to your shell's configuration in the `.bashrc` or `.bash_profile` files. If you don't set this variable, you will have to run management commands, including the `--settings` flag, as follows:

```
python manage.py shell --settings=educa.settings.pro
```

You have successfully organized settings for handling multiple environments.

Using PostgreSQL

Throughout this book, you have mostly used the SQLite database. SQLite is simple and quick to set up, but for a production environment, you will need a more powerful database, such as PostgreSQL, MySQL, or Oracle. You already learned how to install PostgreSQL and set up a PostgreSQL database in *Chapter 3, Extending Your Blog Application*. If you need to install PostgreSQL, you can read the *Installing PostgreSQL* section of *Chapter 3*.

Let's create a PostgreSQL user. Open the shell and run the following commands to create a database user:

```
su postgres
createuser -dP educa
```

You will be prompted for a password and the permissions that you want to give to this user. Enter the desired password and permissions, and then create a new database with the following command:

```
createdb -E utf8 -U educa educa
```

Then, edit the `settings/pro.py` file and modify the DATABASES setting to make it look as follows:

```
DATABASES = {
    'default': {
        'ENGINE': 'django.db.backends.postgresql',
        'NAME': 'educa',
        'USER': 'educa',
        'PASSWORD': '*****',
    }
}
```

Replace the preceding data with the database name and credentials for the user you created. The new database is empty. Run the following command to apply all database migrations:

```
python manage.py migrate
```

Finally, create a superuser with the following command:

```
python manage.py createsuperuser
```

Checking your project

Django includes the `check` management command for checking your project at any time. This command inspects the applications installed in your Django project and outputs any errors or warnings. If you include the `--deploy` option, additional checks only relevant for production use will be triggered. Open the shell and run the following command to perform a check:

```
python manage.py check --deploy
```

You will see output with no errors, but several warnings. This means the check was successful, but you should go through the warnings to see if there is anything more you can do to make your project safe for production. We are not going to go deeper into this, but keep in mind that you should check your project before production use to look for any relevant issues.

Serving Django through WSGI

Django's primary deployment platform is WSGI. **WSGI** stands for **Web Server Gateway Interface** and it is the standard for serving Python applications on the web.

When you generate a new project using the `startproject` command, Django creates a `wsgi.py` file inside your project directory. This file contains a WSGI application callable, which is an access point to your application.

WSGI is used for both running your project with the Django development server and deploying your application with the server of your choice in a production environment.

You can learn more about WSGI at `https://wsgi.readthedocs.io/en/latest/`.

Installing uWSGI

Throughout this book, you have been using the Django development server to run projects in your local environment. However, you need a real web server for deploying your application in a production environment.

uWSGI is an extremely fast Python application server. It communicates with your Python application using the WSGI specification. uWSGI translates web requests into a format that your Django project can process.

Install uWSGI using the following command:

```
pip install uwsgi==2.0.18
```

In order to build uWSGI, you will need a C compiler, such as `gcc` or `clang`. In a Linux environment, you can install a C compiler with the command `apt-get install build-essential`.

If you are using macOS, you can install uWSGI with the Homebrew package manager using the command `brew install uwsgi`.

If you want to install uWSGI on Windows, you will need Cygwin: `https://www.cygwin.com`. However, it's desirable to use uWSGI in UNIX-based environments.

You can read uWSGI's documentation at `https://uwsgi-docs.readthedocs.io/en/latest/`.

Configuring uWSGI

You can run uWSGI from the command line. Open the shell and run the following command from the `educa` project directory:

```
sudo uwsgi --module=educa.wsgi:application \
--env=DJANGO_SETTINGS_MODULE=educa.settings.pro \
--master --pidfile=/tmp/project-master.pid \
--http=127.0.0.1:8000 \
--uid=1000 \
--virtualenv=/home/env/educa/
```

Replace the path in the `virtualenv` option with your actual virtual environment directory. If you are not using a virtual environment, you can skip this option.

You might have to prepend `sudo` to this command if you don't have the required permissions. You might also need to add the `--plugin=python3` option if the module is not loaded by default.

With this command, you can run uWSGI on your localhost with the following options:

- You use the `educa.wsgi:application` WSGI callable
- You load the settings for the production environment
- You tell uWSGI to use the `educa` virtual environment

If you are not running the command within the project directory, include the option `--chdir=/path/to/educa/` with the path to your project.

Open `http://127.0.0.1:8000/` in your browser. You should see a screen like the following one:

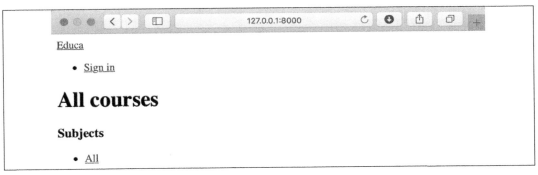

Figure 14.1: The course list page served with uWSGI

You can see the rendered HTML that corresponds to the course list view, but no CSS style sheets or images are being loaded. The reason for this is that you didn't configure uWSGI to serve static files. You will configure serving static files in the production environment later in this chapter.

uWSGI allows you to define a custom configuration in a `.ini` file. This is more convenient than passing options through the command line.

Create the following file structure inside the global `educa/` directory:

```
config/
    uwsgi.ini
logs/
```

Edit the `config/uwsgi.ini` file and add the following code to it:

```
[uwsgi]
# variables
projectname = educa
base = /home/projects/educa

# configuration
master = true
virtualenv = /home/env/%(projectname)
pythonpath = %(base)
chdir = %(base)
env = DJANGO_SETTINGS_MODULE=%(projectname).settings.pro
module = %(projectname).wsgi:application
socket = /tmp/%(projectname).sock
chmod-socket = 666
```

In the `uwsgi.ini` file, you define the following variables:

- `projectname`: The name of your Django project, which is `educa`.
- `base`: The absolute path to the `educa` project. Replace it with the absolute path to your project.

These are custom variables that you will use in the uWSGI options. You can define any other variables you like as long as the names are different to the uWSGI options.

You set the following options:

- `master`: Enable the master process.
- `virtualenv`: The path to your virtual environment. Replace this path with the appropriate path.
- `pythonpath`: The paths to add to your Python path.
- `chdir`: The path to your project directory, so that uWSGI changes to that directory before loading the application.
- `env`: Environment variables. You include the DJANGO_SETTINGS_MODULE variable, pointing to the settings for the production environment.
- `module`: The WSGI module to use. You set this to the `application` callable contained in the `wsgi` module of your project.
- `socket`: The UNIX/TCP socket to bind the server.
- `chmod-socket`: The file permissions to apply to the socket file. In this case, you use 666 so that NGINX can read/write the socket.

The `socket` option is intended for communication with some third-party router, such as NGINX, while the `http` option is for uWSGI to accept incoming HTTP requests and route them by itself. You are going to run uWSGI using a socket, since you are going to configure NGINX as your web server and communicate with uWSGI through the socket.

You can find the list of available uWSGI options at `https://uwsgi-docs.readthedocs.io/en/latest/Options.html`.

Now, you can run uWSGI with your custom configuration using this command:

```
uwsgi --ini config/uwsgi.ini
```

You will not be able to access your uWSGI instance from your browser now, since it's running through a socket. Let's complete the production environment.

Installing NGINX

When you are serving a website, you have to serve dynamic content, but you also need to serve static files, such as CSS style sheets, JavaScript files, and images. While uWSGI is capable of serving static files, it adds an unnecessary overhead to HTTP requests and therefore, it is encouraged to set up a web server, such as NGINX, in front of it.

NGINX is a web server focused on high concurrency, performance, and low memory usage. NGINX also acts as a reverse proxy, receiving HTTP requests and routing them to different backends. As mentioned, generally, you will use a web server, such as NGINX, in front of uWSGI for serving static files efficiently and quickly, and you will forward dynamic requests to uWSGI workers. By using NGINX, you can also apply rules and benefit from its reverse proxy capabilities.

Install NGINX with the following command:

```
sudo apt-get install nginx
```

If you are using macOS, you can install NGINX using the command `brew install nginx`.

You can find NGINX binaries for Windows at `https://nginx.org/en/download.html`.

Open a shell and run NGINX with the following command:

```
sudo nginx
```

Open the URL `http://127.0.0.1` in your browser. You should see the following screen:

Figure 14.2: The NGINX default page

If you see this screen, NGINX is successfully installed. `80` is the port for the default NGINX configuration.

The production environment

The following diagram shows the request/response cycle of the production environment that you are setting up:

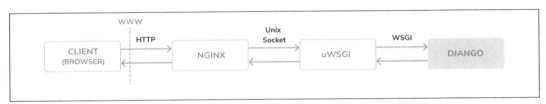

Figure 14.3: The production environment request/response cycle

The following will happen when the client browser sends an HTTP request:

1. NGINX receives the HTTP request
2. NGINX delegates the request to uWSGI through a socket
3. uWSGI passes the request to Django for processing
4. Django returns an HTTP response that is passed back to NGINX, which in turn passes it back to the client browser

Configuring NGINX

Create a new file inside the `config/` directory and name it `nginx.conf`. Add the following code to it:

```
# the upstream component nginx needs to connect to
upstream educa {
    server       unix:///tmp/educa.sock;
}

server {
    listen       80;
    server_name  www.educaproject.com educaproject.com;

    access_log   off;
    error_log    /home/projects/educa/logs/nginx_error.log;

    location / {
        include      /etc/nginx/uwsgi_params;
        uwsgi_pass   educa;
    }
}
```

This is the basic configuration for NGINX. You set up an upstream named `educa`, which points to the socket created by uWSGI. You use the `server` block and add the following configuration:

- You tell NGINX to listen on port `80`.

- You set the server name to both `www.educaproject.com` and `educaproject.com`. NGINX will serve incoming requests for both domains.

- You explicitly set `access_log` to `off`. You can use this directive to store access logs in a file.

- You use the `error_log` directive to set the path to the file where you will be storing error logs. Replace this path with the path where you would like to store NGINX error logs. Analyze this log file if you run into any issue while using NGINX.

- You include the default uWSGI configuration parameters that come with NGINX. These are located next to the default configuration file for NGINX. You can usually find them in any of these three locations: `/usr/local/nginx/conf/usgi_params`, `/etc/nginx/usgi_params`, or `/usr/local/etc/nginx/usgi_params`.

- You specify that everything under the `/` path has to be routed to the `educa` socket (uWSGI).

You can find the NGINX documentation at `https://nginx.org/en/docs/`.

The default configuration file for NGINX is named `nginx.conf` and it usually resides in any of these three directories: `/usr/local/nginx/conf`, `/etc/nginx`, or `/usr/local/etc/nginx`.

Locate your `nginx.conf` configuration file and add the following `include` directive inside the `http` block:

```
http {
    include /home/projects/educa/config/nginx.conf;
    # ...
}
```

Replace `/home/projects/educa/config/nginx.conf` with the path to the configuration file you created for the `educa` project. In this code, you include the NGINX configuration file for your project in the default NGINX configuration.

Open a shell and run uWSGI if you are not running it yet:

```
uwsgi --ini config/uwsgi.ini
```

Open a second shell and reload NGINX with the following command:

```
sudo nginx -s reload
```

Whenever you want to stop NGINX, you can gracefully do so with the following command:

```
sudo nginx -s quit
```

If you want to quickly stop NGINX, instead of `quit` use the signal `stop`. The `quit` signal waits for worker processes to finish serving current requests, while the `stop` signal stops NGINX abruptly.

Since you are using a sample domain name, you need to redirect it to your local host. Edit your `/etc/hosts` file and add the following line to it:

```
127.0.0.1 educaproject.com www.educaproject.com
```

By doing so, you are routing both hostnames to your local server. In a production server, you won't need to do this, since you will have a fixed IP address and you will point your hostname to your server in your domain's DNS configuration.

Open `http://educaproject.com/` in your browser. You should be able to see your site, still without any static assets loaded. Your production environment is almost ready.

Now you can restrict the hosts that can serve your Django project. Edit the production settings file `settings/pro.py` of your project and change the `ALLOWED_HOSTS` setting, as follows:

```
ALLOWED_HOSTS = ['educaproject.com', 'www.educaproject.com']
```

Django will now only serve your application if it's running under any of these hostnames. You can read more about the `ALLOWED_HOSTS` setting at `https://docs.djangoproject.com/en/3.0/ref/settings/#allowed-hosts`.

Serving static and media assets

uWSGI is capable of serving static files flawlessly, but it is not as fast and effective as NGINX. For the best performance, you will use NGINX to serve the static files in your production environment. You will set up NGINX to serve both the static files of your application (CSS style sheets, JavaScript files, and images) and media files uploaded by instructors for the course contents.

Edit the settings/base.py file and add the following line just below the STATIC_URL setting:

```
STATIC_ROOT = os.path.join(BASE_DIR, 'static/')
```

Each application in your Django project may contain static files in a static/ directory. Django provides a command to collect static files from all applications into a single location. This simplifies the setup for serving static files in production. The collectstatic command collects the static files from all applications of the project into the path defined in STATIC_ROOT.

Open the shell and run the following command:

python manage.py collectstatic

You will see this output:

165 static files copied to '/educa/static'.

Files located under the static/ directory of each application present in the INSTALLED_APPS setting have been copied to the global /educa/static/ project directory.

Now, edit the config/nginx.conf file and change its code, like this:

```
# the upstream component nginx needs to connect to
upstream educa {
    server      unix:///tmp/educa.sock;
}

server {
    listen      80;
    server_name www.educaproject.com educaproject.com;

    access_log  off;
    error_log   /home/projects/educa/logs/nginx_error.log;

    location / {
        include      /etc/nginx/uwsgi_params;
```

```
        uwsgi_pass    educa;
    }

    location /static/ {
        alias /home/projects/educa/static/;
    }

    location /media/ {
        alias /home/projects/educa/media/;
    }
}
```

Remember to replace the /home/projects/educa/ path with the absolute path to your project directory. These directives tell NGINX to serve static files located under the /static/ and /media/ paths directly. These paths are as follows:

- /static/: Corresponds to the path of the STATIC_URL setting. The target path corresponds to the value of the STATIC_ROOT setting. You use it to serve the static files of your application.

- /media/: Corresponds to the path of the MEDIA_URL setting, and its target path corresponds to the value of the MEDIA_ROOT setting. You use it to serve the media files uploaded to the course contents.

The schema of the production environment now looks like this:

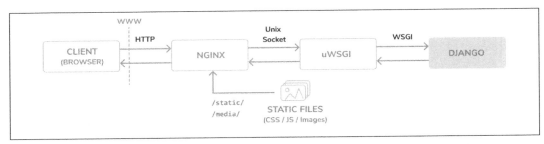

Figure 14.4: The production environment request/response cycle, including static files

Files under the /static/ and /media/ paths are now served by NGINX directly, instead of being forwarded to uWSGI. Requests to any other paths are still passed by NGINX to uWSGI through the UNIX socket.

Reload NGINX's configuration with the following command to keep track of the new paths:

```
sudo nginx -s reload
```

Open `http://educaproject.com/` in your browser. You should see the following screen:

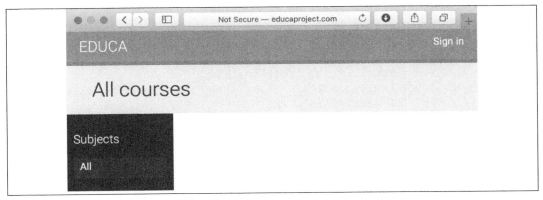

Figure 14.5: The course list page served with NGINX and uWSGI

Static resources, such as CSS style sheets and images, are now loaded correctly. HTTP requests for static files are now being served by NGINX directly, instead of being forwarded to uWSGI.

Great! You have successfully configured NGINX for serving static files.

Securing connections with SSL/TLS

The **Transport Layer Security (TLS)** protocol is the standard for serving websites through a secure connection. The TLS predecessor is **Secure Sockets Layer (SSL)**. Although SSL is now deprecated, in multiple libraries and online documentation you will find references to both the terms TLS and SSL. It's strongly encouraged that you serve your websites under HTTPS. You are going to configure an SSL/TLS certificate in NGINX to serve your site securely.

Creating an SSL/TLS certificate

Create a new directory inside the `educa` project directory and name it `ssl`. Then, generate an SSL/TLS certificate from the command line with the following command:

```
sudo openssl req -x509 -nodes -days 365 -newkey rsa:2048 -keyout ssl/
educa.key -out ssl/educa.crt
```

You are generating a private key and a 2048-bit SSL/TLS certificate that is valid for one year. You will be asked to enter data, as follows:

```
Country Name (2 letter code) []:
State or Province Name (full name) []:
Locality Name (eg, city) []:
Organization Name (eg, company) []:
Organizational Unit Name (eg, section) []:
Common Name (eg, fully qualified host name) []: educaproject.com
Email Address []: email@domain.com
```

You can fill in the requested data with your own information. The most important field is the Common Name. You have to specify the domain name for the certificate. You use educaproject.com. This will generate, inside the ssl/ directory, an educa.key private key file and an educa.crt file, which is the actual certificate.

Configuring NGINX to use SSL/TLS

Edit the nginx.conf file of the educa project and edit the server block to include SSL/TLS, as follows:

```
server {
    listen              80;
    listen              443 ssl;
    ssl_certificate     /home/projects/educa/ssl/educa.crt;
    ssl_certificate_key /home/projects/educa/ssl/educa.key;
    server_name         www.educaproject.com educaproject.com;

    # ...
}
```

With the preceding code, your server now listens both to HTTP through port 80 and HTTPS through port 443. You indicate the path to the SSL/TLS certificate with ssl_certificate and the certificate key with ssl_certificate_key.

Reload NGINX with the following command:

```
sudo nginx -s reload
```

NGINX will load the new configuration. Open https://educaproject.com/ with your browser. You should see a warning message similar to the following one:

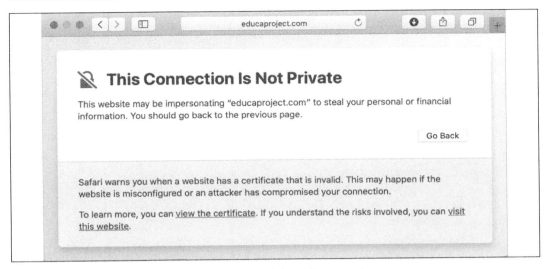

Figure 14.6: An invalid certificate warning

This screen might vary depending on your browser. It alerts you that your site is not using a trusted or valid certificate; the browser can't verify the identity of your site. This is because you signed your own certificate instead of obtaining one from a trusted **certification authority (CA)**. When you own a real domain, you can apply for a trusted CA to issue an SSL/TLS certificate for it, so that browsers can verify its identity. If you want to obtain a trusted certificate for a real domain, you can refer to the *Let's Encrypt* project created by the Linux Foundation. It is a nonprofit CA that simplifies obtaining and renewing trusted SSL/TLS certificates for free. You can find more information at `https://letsencrypt.org`.

Click on the link or button that provides additional information and choose to visit the website, ignoring warnings. The browser might ask you to add an exception for this certificate or verify that you trust it. If you are using Chrome, you might not see any option to proceed to the website. If this is the case, type `thisisunsafe` or `badidea` directly in Chrome on the same warning page. Chrome will then load the website. Note that you do this with your own issued certificate; don't trust any unknown certificate or bypass the browser SSL/TLS certificate checks for other domains.

When you access the site, you will see that the browser displays a lock icon next to the URL, as follows:

Figure 14.7: The browser address bar, including a secure connection padlock icon

If you click the lock icon, SSL/TLS certificate details will be displayed as follows:

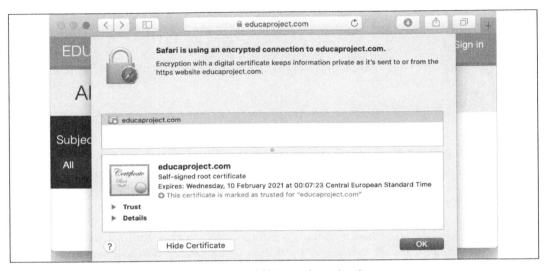

Figure 14.8: TLS/SSL certificate details

In the certificate details, you can see it is a self-signed certificate and you can see its expiration date. You are now serving your site securely.

Configuring your Django project for SSL/TLS

Django comes with specific settings for SSL/TLS support. Edit the `settings/pro.py` settings file and add the following settings to it:

```
SECURE_SSL_REDIRECT = True
CSRF_COOKIE_SECURE = True
```

These settings are as follows:

- `SECURE_SSL_REDIRECT`: Whether HTTP requests have to be redirected to HTTPS

- `CSRF_COOKIE_SECURE`: Has to be set for establishing a secure cookie for **cross-site request forgery (CSRF)** protection

Django will now redirect HTTP requests to HTTPS, and cookies for CSRF protection will now be secure.

Redirecting HTTP traffic over to HTTPS

You are redirecting HTTP requests to HTTPS using Django. However, this can be handled in a more efficient way using NGINX.

Edit the `nginx.conf` file of the `educa` project and change it as follows:

```
# the upstream component nginx needs to connect to
upstream educa {
    server        unix:///tmp/educa.sock;
}

server {
    listen 80;
    server_name www.educaproject.com educaproject.com;
    return 301 https://educaproject.com$request_uri;
}

server {
    listen                443 ssl;
    ssl_certificate        /home/projects/educa/ssl/educa.crt;
    ssl_certificate_key    /home/projects/educa/ssl/educa.key;
    server_name    www.educaproject.com educaproject.com;

    access_log    off;
    error_log     /home/projects/educa/logs/nginx_error.log;

    location / {
        include       /etc/nginx/uwsgi_params;
        uwsgi_pass    educa;
    }

    location /static/ {
        alias /home/projects/educa/static/;
    }

    location /media/ {
        alias /home/projects/educa/media/;
    }
}
```

In this code, you remove the directive `listen 80;` from the original `server` block, so that the platform is only available through SSL/TLS (port 443). On top of the original `server` block, you add an additional `server` block that only listens on port 80 and redirects all HTTP requests to HTTPS. To achieve this, you return an HTTP response code 301 (permanent redirect) that redirects to the `https://` version of the requested URL.

Reload NGINX with the following command:

```
sudo nginx -s reload
```

You are now redirecting all HTTP traffic to HTTPS using NGINX.

Using Daphne for Django Channels

In *Chapter 13*, *Building a Chat Server*, you used Django Channels to build a chat server using WebSockets. uWSGI is suitable for running Django or any other WSGI application, but it doesn't support asynchronous communication using **Asynchronous Server Gateway Interface (ASGI)** or WebSockets. In order to run Channels in production, you need an ASGI web server that is capable of managing WebSockets.

Daphne is a HTTP, HTTP2, and WebSocket server for ASGI developed to serve Channels. You can run Daphne alongside uWSGI to serve both ASGI and WSGI applications efficiently.

Daphne is installed automatically as a dependency of Channels. If you went through the steps to install Channels in *Chapter 13*, *Building a Chat Server*, Daphne is already installed in your Python environment. You can also install Daphne with the following command:

```
pip install daphne==2.4.1
```

You can find more information about Daphne at `https://github.com/django/daphne`.

Django 3 supports WSGI and ASGI, but it doesn't support WebSockets yet. Therefore, you are going to edit the `asgi.py` file of the `educa` project to use Channels.

Edit the `educa/asgi.py` file of your project and make it look like this:

```
import os
import django
from channels.routing import get_default_application
```

```
os.environ.setdefault('DJANGO_SETTINGS_MODULE', 'educa.settings')
django.setup()
application = get_default_application()
```

You are loading the default ASGI application using Channels instead of the standard Django ASGI module. You can find more information about deploying Daphne with protocol servers at https://channels.readthedocs.io/en/latest/deploying.html#run-protocol-servers.

Open a new shell and set the DJANGO_SETTINGS_MODULE environment variable with the production environment using the following command:

```
export DJANGO_SETTINGS_MODULE=educa.settings.pro
```

In the same shell, from the educa project directory run the following command:

```
daphne -u /tmp/daphne.sock educa.asgi:application
```

You will see the following output:

```
2020-02-11 00:49:44,223 INFO      Starting server at unix:/tmp/daphne.sock
2020-02-11 00:49:44,223 INFO      HTTP/2 support not enabled (install the
http2 and tls Twisted extras)
2020-02-11 00:49:44,223 INFO      Configuring endpoint unix:/tmp/daphne.
sock
```

The output shows that Daphne is successfully running on a UNIX socket.

Using secure connections for WebSockets

You have configured NGINX to use secure connections through SSL/TLS. You need to change ws (WebSocket) connections to use the wss (WebSocket Secure) protocol now, in the same way that HTTP connections are now being served through HTTPS.

Edit the chat/room.html template of the chat application and find the following line in the domready block:

```
var url = 'ws://' + window.location.host +
```

Replace that line with the following one:

```
var url = 'wss://' + window.location.host +
```

Now you will be explicitly connecting to a secure WebSocket.

Including Daphne in the NGINX configuration

In your production setup, you will be running Daphne on a UNIX socket and using NGINX in front of it. NGINX will pass requests to Daphne based on the requested path. You will expose Daphne to NGINX through a UNIX socket interface, just like the uWSGI setup.

Edit the `config/nginx.conf` file of the `educa` project and make it look as follows:

```
# the upstream components nginx needs to connect to
upstream educa {
    server unix:/tmp/educa.sock;
}

upstream daphne {
    server unix:/tmp/daphne.sock;
}

server {
    listen 80;
    server_name www.educaproject.com educaproject.com;
    return 301 https://educaproject.com$request_uri;
}

server {
    listen              443 ssl;
    ssl_certificate     /home/projects/educa/ssl/educa.crt;
    ssl_certificate_key /home/projects/educa/ssl/educa.key;

    server_name www.educaproject.com educaproject.com;

    access_log  off;
    error_log   /home/projects/educa/logs/nginx_error.log;

    location / {
        include     /etc/nginx/uwsgi_params;
        uwsgi_pass  educa;
    }

    location /ws/ {
        proxy_http_version 1.1;
        proxy_set_header    Upgrade $http_upgrade;
        proxy_set_header    Connection "upgrade";
        proxy_redirect      off;

        proxy_pass          http://daphne;
```

```
    }

    location /static/ {
        alias /home/projects/educa/static/;
    }

    location /media/ {
        alias /home/projects/educa/media/;
    }
}
```

In this configuration, you set up a new upstream named `daphne`, which points to a socket created by Daphne. In the `server` block, you configure the `/ws/` location to forward requests to Daphne. You use the `proxy_pass` directive to pass requests to Daphne and you include some additional proxy directives.

With this configuration, NGINX will pass any URL request that starts with the `/ws/` prefix to Daphne and the rest to uWSGI, except for files under the `/static/` or `/media/` paths, which will be served directly by NGINX.

The production setup including Daphne now looks like this:

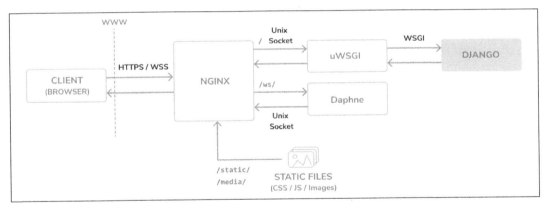

Figure 14.9: The production environment request/response cycle, including Daphne

NGINX runs in front of uWSGI and Daphne as a reverse proxy server. NGINX faces the Web and passes requests to the application server (uWSGI or Daphne) based on their path prefix. Besides this, NGINX also serves static files and redirects non-secure requests to secure ones. This setup reduces downtime, consumes less server resources, and provides greater performance and security.

Stop and start uWSGI and Daphne, and then reload NGINX with the following command to keep track of the latest configuration:

```
sudo nginx -s reload
```

Use your browser to create a sample course with an instructor user, log in with a user who is enrolled on the course, and open `https://educaproject.com/chat/room/1/` with your browser. You should be able to send and receive messages like the following example:

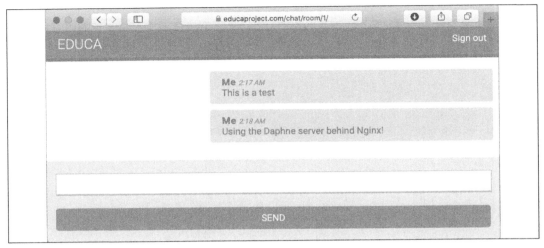

Figure 14.10: Course chat room messages served with NGINX and Daphne

Daphne is working correctly and NGINX is passing requests to it. All connections are secured through SSL/TLS.

Congratulations! You have built a custom production-ready stack using NGINX, uWSGI, and Daphne. You could do further optimization for additional performance and enhanced security through configuration settings in NGINX, uWSGI and Daphne. However, this production setup is a great start!

Creating a custom middleware

You already know the MIDDLEWARE setting, which contains the middleware for your project. You can think of it as a low-level plugin system, allowing you to implement hooks that get executed in the request/response process. Each middleware is responsible for some specific action that will be executed for all HTTP requests or responses.

> Avoid adding expensive processing to middleware, since they are executed in every single request.

When an HTTP request is received, middleware are executed in order of appearance in the MIDDLEWARE setting. When an HTTP response has been generated by Django, the response passes through all middleware back in reverse order.

A middleware can be written as a function, as follows:

```
def my_middleware(get_response):

    def middleware(request):
        # Code executed for each request before
        # the view (and later middleware) are called.

        response = get_response(request)

        # Code executed for each request/response after
        # the view is called.

        return response

    return middleware
```

A middleware factory is a callable that takes a get_response callable and returns a middleware. A middleware is a callable that takes a request and returns a response, just like a view. The get_response callable might be the next middleware in the chain or the actual view in the case of the last listed middleware.

If any middleware returns a response without calling its get_response callable, it short circuits the process; no further middleware get executed (also not the view), and the response returns through the same layers that the request passed in through.

The order of middleware in the MIDDLEWARE setting is very important because a middleware can depend on data set in the request by other middleware that have been executed previously.

When adding a new middleware to the MIDDLEWARE setting, make sure to place it in the right position. Middleware are executed in order of appearance in the setting during the request phase, and in reverse order for responses.

You can find more information about middleware at https://docs.djangoproject.com/en/3.0/topics/http/middleware/.

Creating a subdomain middleware

You are going to create a custom middleware to allow courses to be accessible through a custom subdomain. Each course detail URL, which looks like https:// educaproject.com/course/django/, will also be accessible through the subdomain that makes use of the course slug, such as https://django.educaproject.com/. Users will be able to use the subdomain as a shortcut to access the course details. Any requests to subdomains will be redirected to each corresponding course detail URL.

Middleware can reside anywhere within your project. However, it's recommended to create a middleware.py file in your application directory.

Create a new file inside the courses application directory and name it middleware. py. Add the following code to it:

```python
from django.urls import reverse
from django.shortcuts import get_object_or_404, redirect
from .models import Course

def subdomain_course_middleware(get_response):
    """
    Subdomains for courses
    """
    def middleware(request):
        host_parts = request.get_host().split('.')
        if len(host_parts) > 2 and host_parts[0] != 'www':
            # get course for the given subdomain
            course = get_object_or_404(Course, slug=host_parts[0])
            course_url = reverse('course_detail',
                                 args=[course.slug])
            # redirect current request to the course_detail view
            url = '{}://{}{}'.format(request.scheme,
                                     '.'.join(host_parts[1:]),
                                     course_url)
            return redirect(url)

        response = get_response(request)
        return response

    return middleware
```

When an HTTP request is received, you perform the following tasks:

1. You get the hostname that is being used in the request and divide it into parts. For example, if the user is accessing `mycourse.educaproject.com`, you generate the list `['mycourse', 'educaproject', 'com']`.

2. You check whether the hostname includes a subdomain by checking whether the split generated more than two elements. If the hostname includes a subdomain, and this is not www, you try to get the course with the slug provided in the subdomain.

3. If a course is not found, you raise an HTTP 404 exception. Otherwise, you redirect the browser to the course detail URL.

Edit the `settings/base.py` file of the project and add `'courses.middleware.SubdomainCourseMiddleware'` at the bottom of the `MIDDLEWARE` list, as follows:

```
MIDDLEWARE = [
    # ...
    'courses.middleware.subdomain_course_middleware',
]
```

The middleware will now be executed in every request.

Remember that the hostnames allowed to serve your Django project are specified in the `ALLOWED_HOSTS` setting. Let's change this setting so that any possible subdomain of `educaproject.com` is allowed to serve your application.

Edit the `settings/pro.py` file and modify the `ALLOWED_HOSTS` setting, as follows:

```
ALLOWED_HOSTS = ['.educaproject.com']
```

A value that begins with a period is used as a subdomain wildcard; `'.educaproject.com'` will match `educaproject.com` and any subdomain for this domain, for example `course.educaproject.com` and `django.educaproject.com`.

Serving multiple subdomains with NGINX

You need NGINX to be able to serve your site with any possible subdomain. Edit the `config/nginx.conf` file of the `educa` project and replace the two occurrences of the following line:

```
server_name  www.educaproject.com educaproject.com;
```

with the following one:

```
server_name  *.educaproject.com educaproject.com;
```

By using the asterisk, this rule applies to all subdomains of `educaproject.com`. In order to test your middleware locally, you need to add any subdomains you want to test to `/etc/hosts`. For testing the middleware with a `Course` object with the slug `django`, add the following line to your `/etc/hosts` file:

```
127.0.0.1  django.educaproject.com
```

Stop and start uWSGI again, and reload NGINX with the following command to keep track of the latest configuration:

```
sudo nginx -s reload
```

Then, open `https://django.educaproject.com/` in your browser. The middleware will find the course by the subdomain and redirect your browser to `https://educaproject.com/course/django/`.

Implementing custom management commands

Django allows your applications to register custom management commands for the `manage.py` utility. For example, you used the management commands `makemessages` and `compilemessages` in *Chapter 9, Extending Your Shop*, to create and compile translation files.

A management command consists of a Python module containing a `Command` class that inherits from `django.core.management.base.BaseCommand` or one of its subclasses. You can create simple commands or make them take positional and optional arguments as input.

Django looks for management commands in the `management/commands/` directory for each active application in the `INSTALLED_APPS` setting. Each module found is registered as a management command named after it.

You can learn more about custom management commands at `https://docs.djangoproject.com/en/3.0/howto/custom-management-commands/`.

You are going to create a custom management command to remind students to enroll at least on one course. The command will send an email reminder to users who have been registered for longer than a specified period who aren't enrolled on any course yet.

Create the following file structure inside the `students` application directory:

```
management/
    __init__.py
    commands/
        __init__.py
        enroll_reminder.py
```

Edit the `enroll_reminder.py` file and add the following code to it:

```python
import datetime
from django.conf import settings
from django.core.management.base import BaseCommand
from django.core.mail import send_mass_mail
from django.contrib.auth.models import User
from django.db.models import Count
from django.utils import timezone


class Command(BaseCommand):
    help = 'Sends an e-mail reminder to users registered more \
            than N days that are not enrolled into any courses yet'

    def add_arguments(self, parser):
        parser.add_argument('--days', dest='days', type=int)

    def handle(self, *args, **options):
        emails = []
        subject = 'Enroll in a course'
        date_joined = timezone.now().today() - \
                    datetime.timedelta(days=options['days'])
        users = User.objects.annotate(course_count=Count('courses_
joined'))\
                .filter(course_count=0,
                    date_joined__date__lte=date_joined)
        for user in users:
            message = """Dear {},
            We noticed that you didn't enroll in any courses yet.
            What are you waiting for?""".format(user.first_name)
            emails.append((subject,
                            message,
                            settings.DEFAULT_FROM_EMAIL,
                            [user.email]))
        send_mass_mail(emails)
        self.stdout.write('Sent {} reminders'.format(len(emails)))
```

This is your `enroll_reminder` command. The preceding code is as follows:

- The `Command` class inherits from `BaseCommand`.

- You include a `help` attribute. This attribute provides a short description of the command that is printed if you run the command `python manage.py help enroll_reminder`.

- You use the `add_arguments()` method to add the `--days` named argument. This argument is used to specify the minimum number of days a user has to be registered, without having enrolled on any course, in order to receive the reminder.

- The `handle()` command contains the actual command. You get the `days` attribute parsed from the command line. You use the `timezone` utility provided by Django to retrieve the current timezone-aware date with `timezone.now().date()`. (You can set the timezone for your project with the `TIME_ZONE` setting.) You retrieve the users who have been registered for more than the specified days and are not enrolled on any courses yet. You achieve this by annotating the QuerySet with the total number of courses each user is enrolled on. You generate the reminder email for each user and append it to the `emails` list. Finally, you send the emails using the `send_mass_mail()` function, which is optimized to open a single SMTP connection for sending all emails, instead of opening one connection per email sent.

You have created your first management command. Open the shell and run your command:

```
python manage.py enroll_reminder --days=20
```

If you don't have a local SMTP server running, you can take a look at *Chapter 2, Enhancing Your Blog with Advanced Features*, where you configured SMTP settings for your first Django project. Alternatively, you can add the following setting to the `settings.py` file to make Django output emails to the standard output during development:

```
EMAIL_BACKEND = 'django.core.mail.backends.console.EmailBackend'
```

Let's schedule your management command so that the server runs it every day at 8 a.m. If you are using a UNIX-based system such as Linux or macOS, open the shell and run `crontab -e` to edit your `crontab`. Add the following line to it:

```
0 8 * * * python /path/to/educa/manage.py enroll_reminder --days=20
--settings=educa.settings.pro
```

If you are not familiar with **cron**, you can find an introduction to cron at `http://www.unixgeeks.org/security/newbie/unix/cron-1.html`.

If you are using Windows, you can schedule tasks using the Task Scheduler. You can find more information about it at `https://docs.microsoft.com/en-us/windows/win32/taskschd/task-scheduler-start-page`.

Another option for executing actions periodically is to create tasks and schedule them with Celery. Remember that you used Celery in *Chapter 7, Building an Online Shop,* to execute asynchronous tasks. Instead of creating management commands and scheduling them with cron, you can create asynchronous tasks and execute them with the Celery beat scheduler. You can learn more about scheduling periodic tasks with Celery at `https://celery.readthedocs.io/en/latest/userguide/periodic-tasks.html`.

 Use management commands for standalone scripts that you want to schedule with cron or the Windows scheduler control panel.

Django also includes a utility to call management commands using Python. You can run management commands from your code as follows:

```
from django.core import management
management.call_command('enroll_reminder', days=20)
```

Congratulations! You can now create custom management commands for your applications and schedule them when needed.

Summary

In this chapter, you configured a production environment using NGINX, uWSGI, and Daphne. You secured your environment through SSL/TLS. You also implemented a custom middleware and you learned how to create custom management commands.

You have reached the end of this book. Congratulations! You have learned the skills required to build successful web applications with Django. This book has guided you through the process of developing real-life projects and integrating Django with other technologies. Now you are ready to create your own Django project, whether it is a simple prototype or a large-scale web application.

Good luck with your next Django adventure!

Other Books
You May Enjoy

If you enjoyed this book, you may be interested in these other books by Packt:

Pandas 1.x Cookbook - Second Edition

Matt Harrison, Theodore Petrou

ISBN: 978-1-83921-310-6

- Master data exploration in pandas through dozens of practice problems
- Group, aggregate, transform, reshape, and filter data
- Merge data from different sources through pandas SQL-like operations
- Create visualizations via pandas hooks to matplotlib and seaborn
- Use pandas, time series functionality to perform powerful analyses
- Create workflows for processing big data that doesn't fit in memory

Advanced Deep Learning with TensorFlow 2 and Keras - Second Edition

Rowel Atienza

ISBN: 978-1-83882-165-4

- Use mutual information maximization techniques to perform unsupervised learning
- Use segmentation to identify the pixel-wise class of each object in an image
- Identify both the bounding box and class of objects in an image using object detection
- Learn the building blocks for advanced techniques - MLPss, CNN, and RNNs
- Understand deep neural networks - including ResNet and DenseNet
- Understand and build autoregressive models – autoencoders, VAEs, and GANs
- Discover and implement deep reinforcement learning methods

Leave a review - let other readers know what you think

Please share your thoughts on this book with others by leaving a review on the site that you bought it from. If you purchased the book from Amazon, please leave us an honest review on this book's Amazon page. This is vital so that other potential readers can see and use your unbiased opinion to make purchasing decisions, we can understand what our customers think about our products, and our authors can see your feedback on the title that they have worked with Packt to create. It will only take a few minutes of your time, but is valuable to other potential customers, our authors, and Packt. Thank you!

Index

Symbols

A

B

P

pagination
  adding 34, 35
  working 34
parsers
  reference link 447
path converters
  reference link 28
payment authorization
  reference link 283
Payment Card Industry (PCI) 270
payment gateway
  Braintree, integrating with Hosted
      Fields 274-280
  Braintree Python module, installing 271, 272
  Braintree sandbox account,
      creating 270, 271
  integrating 269-274
payments
  testing 280-283
PDF files
  rendering 294-297
  sending, by email 297-300
PDF invoices
  generating 292
PDFs, outputting with Django
  reference link 292
PDF template
  creating 292, 293
permissions
  reference link 455
per-site cache
  deactivating 471
  using 441, 442
pip installation
  reference link 3
pip package
  used, for installing Django 3, 4
Poedit
  download link 323
post detail template
  comments, adding 54-57
PostgreSQL
  download link 83
  installing 83, 84
PostgreSQL full-text search

reference link 82
Postman
  reference link 449
post() method 399
posts by similarity
  retrieving 64-66
posts, via email
  emails, sending with Django 43-45
  forms, creating with Django 40, 41
  forms, handling in views 41, 42
  forms, rendering in templates 45-49
  sharing 40
prefetch_related()
  using 208
product catalog models
  creating 227-229
  registering, on administration site 229
product catalog views
  building 230-232
product detail page 347
product recommendation 347-356
project 9
proxy model 366
Python
  Redis, using 217, 218
Python 3.8.0
  download link 2
Python code
  code translation 320-324
  lazy translation 319
  plural forms translation 319, 320
  standard translation 319
  translating 318
  variable translation 319
Python environment
  creating 3
Python installer
  download link 2
Python Social Auth
  reference link 131

Q

QuerySet
  about 21
  evaluating 25
  exclude(), using 24

language prefix, adding 332, 333
reference link 115
translating 333, 334
URL patterns, with regular expressions
reference link 29
URLs utility functions
reference link 30
user actions
adding, to activity stream 205, 206
user model
extending 119-125
user profiles
about 115
detail view, creating 191-195
list view, creating 191-195
user registration 115-119
users
access, to switch language 334, 335
uWSGI options
reference link 505
uWSGI's documentation
reference link 502

V

views
adapting, for translations 341-344
caching 441
forms, handling 41, 42
templates, creating 30-33
viewsets
reference link 457
virtual environment (venv)
reference link 3

W

WeasyPrint
installing 292
reference link 292
Web Server Gateway Interface (WSGI)
about 5,471
about 501
reference link 502
WebSocket client
implementing 478-484
weighting queries 89
Windows Subsystem for Linux (WSL) 216

Printed in Great Britain
by Amazon

41516739R00323